Depression
SOURCEBOOK

FIFTH EDITION

Health Reference Series

Depression
SOURCEBOOK

FIFTH EDITION

Basic Consumer Health Information about the Prevalence, Symptoms, Diagnosis, Causes, Treatment, and Types of Depression, Including Major Depression, Atypical Depression, Bipolar Disorder, Depression during and after Pregnancy, Premenstrual Dysphoric Disorder, and Seasonal Affective Disorder, as well as the Impact of Depression and Strategies for Managing Depression

Along with Facts about Depression and Chronic Illness, Treatment-Resistant Depression and Suicide, Mental-Health Medications, Therapies, and Treatments, Tips for Improving Self-Esteem, Resilience, and Quality of Life While Living with Depression, a Glossary of Related Terms, and Resources for Additional Help and Information

OMNIGRAPHICS

615 Griswold St., Ste. 520, Detroit, MI 48226

Bibliographic Note
Because this page cannot legibly accommodate all the copyright notices, the Bibliographic
Note portion of the Preface constitutes an extension of the copyright notice.

* * *

OMNIGRAPHICS
Angela L. Williams, *Managing Editor*
* * *

ISBN 978-0-7808-1735-7
E-ISBN 978-0-7808-1736-4

Library of Congress Cataloging-in-Publication Data

Names: Williams, Angela, 1963- editor.

Title: Depression sourcebook: basic consumer health information about the
symptoms, causes, and types of depression, including major depression, dysthymia,
atypical depression, bipolar disorder, depression during and after pregnancy,
premenstrual dysphoric disorder, schizoaffective disorder, and seasonal affective
disorder; along with facts about depression and chronic illness, treatment-resistant
depression and suicide, mental health medications, therapies, and treatments, tips
for improving self-esteem, resilience, and quality of life while living with depression,
a glossary of related terms, and resources for additional help and information /
[edited by] Angela L. Williams.

Description: Fifth edition. | Detroit, MI: Omnigraphics, [2019] | Series: Health
reference series | Includes bibliographical references and index. | Summary:
"Provides basic consumer health information about the causes, symptoms, diagnosis,
and treatment of various forms of depression, along with coping tips and strategies
for building resilience and self-esteem. Includes index, glossary of related terms, and
other resources"--Provided by publisher"-- Provided by publisher.

Identifiers: LCCN 2019033087 (print) | LCCN 2019033088 (ebook) | ISBN
9780780817357 (library binding) | ISBN 9780780817364 (ebook)

Subjects: LCSH: Depression, Mental--Popular works.

Classification: LCC RC537 .D4455 2019 (print) | LCC RC537 (ebook) | DDC
616.85/27--dc23

LC record available at https://lccn.loc.gov/2019033087

LC ebook record available at https://lccn.loc.gov/2019033088

∞

Table of Contents

Part III: Who Develops Depression

Part IV: Causes and Risk Factors of Depression

Part VII: Strategies for Managing Depression

Preface

About This Book

Depression is one of the most common disabling mental-health problems in the world. Depressive disorder is characterized by persistent sadness, hopelessness, trouble concentrating, excessive fatigue, and drastic changes in appetite and sleep habits. According to the 2017 National Institute of Mental Health statistics, an estimated 17.3 million adults in the United States have experienced at least one major depressive episode, accounting for 7.1 percent of all American adults. It is found that the prevalence of a major depressive episode is higher in adult females (8.7%) than in adult males (5.3%). Research indicates that a variety of genetic, biologic, and environmental factors contribute to the development of this chronic illness. Research also indicates that timely diagnosis and treatment help the affected manage their symptoms effectively and develop strategies for better living.

Depression Sourcebook, Fifth Edition offers basic information about the prevalence, symptoms, diagnosis, and treatment of depression. It talks about atypical depression, bipolar disorder, depression during and after pregnancy, depression with psychosis, and seasonal affective disorder. It examines the impact of depression on children, adolescents, college students, men, women, and older adults. It describes strategies for managing depression, along with information about the warning signs and prevalence of suicide. It also provides insight into alternative and complementary therapies used to improve depression symptoms.

The book concludes with a glossary of related terms and a directory of resources for additional help and information.

How to Use This Book

This book is divided into parts and chapters. Parts focus on broad areas of interest. Chapters are devoted to single topics within a part.

Part I: Introduction to Mental-Health Disorders and Depression defines depression and discusses how the function of the brain plays a vital role in the development and severity of mental-health disorders. It discusses various myths and facts about mental-health disorders and provides information on potential reasons for depression. The part concludes with statistical reports on depression and other related mental-health disorders.

Part II: Types of Depression gives an overview of the most common types of depression and related mental-health disorders, including major depression, atypical depression, bipolar disorder, premenstrual syndrome, disruptive mood dysregulation disorder, psychotic depression, and seasonal affective disorder.

Part III: Who Develops Depression provides information about gender, age, and racial disparities in the diagnosis of depression. Facts about depression in men, women, children, adolescents, college students, pregnant women, and seniors are discussed, including reproductive health in women and postpartum depression. Information about the prevalence of depression in minority populations, such as lesbian, gay, bisexual, and transgender (LGBT) adults, prison inmates, and caregivers, is also provided.

Part IV: Causes and Risk Factors of Depression highlights genetic and environmental factors that can predispose a person to developing depression. It discusses the impact of trauma, unemployment, substance use, and addiction on depression, including parental stress, isolation, and climate change.

Part V: Chronic Illness and Depression discusses chronic diseases that are often linked to depression, such as autoimmune diseases, brain injury, cancer, diabetes, heart disease, human immunodeficiency virus (HIV), multiple sclerosis, and stroke.

Part VI: Diagnosis and Treatment of Depression describes the process of receiving a depression diagnosis, paying for mental-healthcare, and finding and choosing a therapist. It also identifies mental-health medications used to treat depression, including psychotherapy (talk therapy) and cognitive-behavioral therapy. Other forms of treatment, such as light therapy for seasonal affective disorder, brain stimulation therapies, and strategies for treating severe or relapsed forms of depression, are discussed.

Part VII: Strategies for Managing Depression discusses how to maintain emotional wellness in people who have depression, including stress in disaster responders and recovery workers. Information on developing resilience, avoiding depression triggers, improving self-esteem, as well as dealing with trauma and coping with grief, bereavement, and loss, is included.

Part VIII: Suicide offers information about the prevalence of suicide among those who are affected with depression. It describes the warning signs of suicide and provides information on how to recover from a suicide attempt. It also suggests steps to overcome trauma when a family member attempts suicide.

Part IX: Additional Help and Information provides a glossary of important terms related to depression and a directory of organizations that help people with depression and suicidal thoughts.

Bibliographic Note

This volume contains documents and excerpts from publications issued by the following U.S. government agencies: Agency for Healthcare Research and Quality (AHRQ); Centers for Disease Control and Prevention (CDC); Centers for Medicare & Medicaid Services (CMS); Child Welfare Information Gateway; Early Childhood Learning and Knowledge Center (ECLKC); Genetics Home Reference (GHR); National Cancer Institute (NCI); National Center for Complementary and Integrative Health (NCCIH); National Center for Posttraumatic Stress Disorder (NCPTSD); National Council on Disability (NCD);National Heart, Lung, and Blood Institute (NHLBI); National Human Genome Research Institute (NHGRI); National Institute of Arthritis and Musculoskeletal and Skin Diseases (NIAMS); National Institute of Mental Health (NIMH); National Institute of Neurological Disorders and Stroke (NINDS); National Institute on Aging (NIA); National Institute on Alcohol Abuse and Alcoholism (NIAAA); National Institute on Drug Abuse (NIDA); National Institutes of Health (NIH); *NIH News in Health*; Office of Disease Prevention and Health Promotion (ODPHP); Office of Minority Health (OMH); Office of the Assistant

Secretary for Planning and Evaluation (ASPE); Office of the Assistant Secretary for Preparedness and Response (ASPR); Office on Women's Health (OWH); Substance Abuse and Mental Health Services Administration (SAMHSA); U.S. Department of Education (ED); U.S. Department of Health and Human Services (HHS); U.S. Department of Veterans Affairs (VA); U.S. Food and Drug Administration (FDA); U.S. Global Change Research Program (USGCRP); and Youth.gov.

It may also contain original material produced by Omnigraphics and reviewed by medical consultants.

About the Health Reference Series

The *Health Reference Series* is designed to provide basic medical information for patients, families, caregivers, and the general public. Each volume takes a particular topic and provides comprehensive coverage. This is especially important for people who may be dealing with a newly diagnosed disease or a chronic disorder in themselves or in a family member. People looking for preventive guidance, information about disease warning signs, medical statistics, and risk factors for health problems will also find answers to their questions in the *Health Reference Series*. The *Series*, however, is not intended to serve as a tool for diagnosing illness, in prescribing treatments, or as a substitute for the physician/patient relationship. All people concerned about medical symptoms or the possibility of disease are encouraged to seek professional care from an appropriate healthcare provider.

A Note about Spelling and Style

Health Reference Series editors use *Stedman's Medical Dictionary* as an authority for questions related to the spelling of medical terms and *The Chicago Manual of Style* for questions related to grammatical structures, punctuation, and other editorial concerns. Consistent adherence is not always possible, however, because the individual volumes within the *Series* include many documents from a wide variety of different producers, and the editor's primary goal is to present material from each source as accurately as is possible. This sometimes means that information in different chapters or sections may follow other guidelines and alternate spelling authorities. For example, occasionally a copyright holder may require that eponymous terms be shown in possessive forms (Crohn's disease vs. Crohn disease) or that British spelling norms be retained (leukaemia vs. leukemia).

Medical Review

Omnigraphics contracts with a team of qualified, senior medical professionals who serve as medical consultants for the *Health Reference Series*. As necessary, medical consultants review reprinted and originally written material for currency and accuracy. Citations including the phrase "Reviewed (month, year)" indicate material reviewed by this team. Medical consultation services are provided to the *Health Reference Series* editors by:

Dr. Vijayalakshmi, MBBS, DGO, MD
Dr. Senthil Selvan, MBBS, DCH, MD
Dr. K. Sivanandham, MBBS, DCH, MS (Research), PhD

Our Advisory Board

We would like to thank the following board members for providing initial guidance on the development of this series:

- Dr. Lynda Baker, Associate Professor of Library and Information Science, Wayne State University, Detroit, MI

- Nancy Bulgarelli, William Beaumont Hospital Library, Royal Oak, MI

- Karen Imarisio, Bloomfield Township Public Library, Bloomfield Township, MI

- Karen Morgan, Mardigian Library, University of Michigan-Dearborn, Dearborn, MI

- Rosemary Orlando, St. Clair Shores Public Library, St. Clair Shores, MI

Health Reference Series *Update Policy*

The inaugural book in the *Health Reference Series* was the first edition of *Cancer Sourcebook* published in 1989. Since then, the *Series* has been enthusiastically received by librarians and in the medical community. In order to maintain the standard of providing high-quality health information for the layperson the editorial staff at Omnigraphics felt it was necessary to implement a policy of updating volumes when warranted.

Medical researchers have been making tremendous strides, and it is the purpose of the *Health Reference Series* to stay current with the most recent advances. Each decision to update a volume is made on an individual basis. Some of the considerations include how much new information is available and the feedback we receive from people who use the books. If there is a topic you would like to see added to the update list, or an area of medical concern you feel has not been adequately addressed, please write to:

Managing Editor
Health Reference Series
Omnigraphics
615 Griswold St., Ste. 520
Detroit, MI 48226

Part One

Introduction to Mental-Health Disorders and Depression

Chapter 1

What Are Mental-Health Disorders?

What Is Mental Illness?

Mental illnesses are conditions that affect a person's thinking, feeling, mood or behavior. These conditions, which include depression, anxiety, bipolar disorder, or schizophrenia, may be occasional or long-lasting (chronic) and affect someone's ability to relate to others and function each day.

What Is Mental Health?

Mental health includes emotional, psychological, and social well-being. It affects how we think, feel, and act. It also helps determine how we handle stress, relate to others, and make healthy choices. Mental health is important at every stage of life, from childhood and adolescence through adulthood.

Although the terms are often used interchangeably, poor mental health and mental illness are not the same things. A person can experience poor mental health and not be diagnosed with a mental illness. Likewise, a person diagnosed with a mental illness can experience periods of physical, mental, and social well-being.

This chapter includes text excerpted from "Learn about Mental Health," Centers for Disease Control and Prevention (CDC), January 26, 2018.

How Common Are Mental Illnesses?

Mental illnesses are among the most common health conditions in the United States:

- More than 50 percent will be diagnosed with a mental illness or disorder at some point in their lifetime.

- 1 in 5 Americans will experience a mental illness in a given year.

- 1 in 5 children, either currently or at some point during their life, have had a seriously debilitating mental illness.

- 1 in 25 Americans lives with a serious mental illness, such as schizophrenia, bipolar disorder, or major depression.

What Causes Mental Illness

There is no single cause for mental illness. A number of factors can contribute to risk for mental illness, such as:

- Early adverse life experiences, such as trauma or a history of abuse (for example, child abuse, sexual assault, witnessing violence, etc.)

- Experiences related to other ongoing (chronic) medical conditions, such as cancer or diabetes

- Biological factors, such as genes or chemical imbalances in the brain

- Use of alcohol or recreational drugs

- Having a few friends

- Having a feeling of loneliness or isolation

Types of Mental Illness

People can experience different types of mental illnesses or disorders, and they can often occur at the same time. Mental illnesses can occur over a short period of time or be episodic. This means that the mental illness comes and goes with discrete beginnings and ends. Mental illness can also be ongoing or long-lasting.

There are more than 200 classified types of mental illness. Some of the main types of mental illness and disorders are listed below:

Anxiety Disorders

People with anxiety disorders respond to certain objects or situations with fear and dread or terror. Anxiety disorders include generalized anxiety disorder, social anxiety, panic disorders, and phobias.

Attention Deficit Hyperactivity Disorder

Attention deficit hyperactivity disorder (ADHD) is one of the most common childhood mental disorders. It can continue through adolescence and adulthood. People diagnosed with ADHD may have trouble paying attention, controlling impulsive behaviors (may act without thinking about what the result will be), or be overly active.

Disruptive Behavioral Disorders

Behavioral disorders involve a pattern of disruptive behaviors in children that last for at least six months and cause problems in school, at home, and in social situations. Behavioral symptoms can also continue into adulthood.

Depression and Other Mood Disorders

While bad moods are common, and usually pass in a short period, people suffering from mood disorders live with more constant and severe symptoms. People living with this mental illness find that their mood impacts both mental and psychological well-being, nearly every day, and often for much of the day.

It is estimated that 1 in 10 adults suffer from some type of mood disorder, with the most common conditions being depression and bipolar disorder. With proper diagnosis and treatment, most of those living with mood disorders lead to healthy, normal and productive lives. If left untreated, this illness can affect role functioning, quality of life and many long-lasting physical health problems such as diabetes and heart disease.

Eating Disorders

Eating disorders involve obsessive and sometimes distressing thoughts and behaviors, including:

- Reduction of food intake
- Overeating

- Feelings of depression or distress

- Concern about weight, body shape, poor self-image

Common types of eating disorders include anorexia, bulimia, and binge eating.

Personality Disorders

People with personality disorders have extreme and inflexible personality traits that cause problems in work, school, or social relationships. Personality disorders include antisocial personality disorder and borderline personality disorder (BPD).

Posttraumatic Stress Disorder

A person can get posttraumatic stress disorder (PTSD) after living through or seeing a traumatic event such as war, a hurricane, physical abuse, or a serious accident. PTSD can make someone feel stressed and afraid after the danger is over. People with PTSD may experience symptoms like reliving the event over and over, sleep problems, become very upset if something causes memories of the event, constantly looking for possible threats, and changes in emotions such as irritability, outbursts, helplessness, or feelings of numbness.

Schizophrenia Spectrum and Other Psychotic Disorders

People with psychotic disorders hear, see, and believe things that are not real or true. They may also show signs of disorganized thinking, confused speech, and muddled or abnormal motor behavior. An example of a psychotic disorder is schizophrenia. People with schizophrenia may also have low motivation and blunted emotions.

Substance-Use Disorders

Substance-use disorders (SUD) occur when frequent or repeated use of alcohol and/or drugs causes significant impairment, such as health problems, disability, and failure to meet major responsibilities at work, school, or home. Substance-use problems can be fatal to the user or others. Examples include drunk driving fatalities and drug overdoses.

Mental illnesses and substance use disorders often occur together. Sometimes one disorder can be a contributing factor to or can make the other worse. Sometimes they simply occur at the same time.

Chapter 2

Brain Function and Mental Health

The brain is the most complex part of the human body. This three-pound organ is the seat of intelligence, interpreter of the senses, initiator of body movement, and controller of behavior. Lying in its bony shell and washed by protective fluid, the brain is the source of all the qualities that define our humanity. The brain is the crown jewel of the human body.

For centuries, scientists and philosophers have been fascinated by the brain, they viewed the brain as nearly incomprehensible. Now, however, the brain is beginning to relinquish its secrets. Scientists have learned more about the brain in the last 10 years than in all previous centuries because of the accelerating pace of research in neurological and behavioral science and the development of the research techniques. As a result, Congress named the 1990s the Decade of the Brain. At the forefront of research on the brain and other elements of the nervous system is the National Institute of Neurological Disorders

This chapter contains text excerpted from the following sources: Text in this chapter begins with excerpts from "Brain Basics: Know Your Brain," National Institute of Neurological Disorders and Stroke (NINDS), August 13, 2019; Text under the heading "Mental Illness Defined as Disruption in Neural Circuits" is excerpted from "Post by Former NIMH Director Thomas Insel: Mental Illness Defined as Disruption in Neural Circuits," National Institute of Mental Health (NIMH), August 12, 2011. Reviewed October 2019.

and Stroke (NINDS), which conducts and supports scientific studies in the United States and around the world.

This chapter is a basic introduction to the human brain. It may help you understand how the healthy brain works, how to keep it healthy, and what happens when the brain is diseased or dysfunctional.

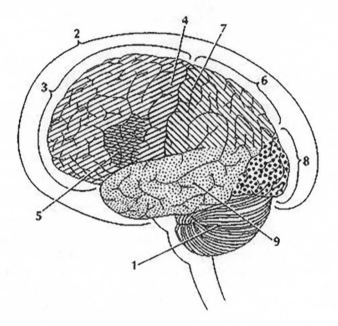

Figure 2.1. *Human Brain*

The Architecture of the Brain

The brain is like a committee of experts. All the parts of the brain work together, but each part has its own special properties. The brain can be divided into three basic units: the forebrain, the midbrain, and the hindbrain.

The hindbrain includes the upper part of the spinal cord, the brain stem, and a wrinkled ball of tissue called the "cerebellum" **(1)**. The hindbrain controls the body's vital functions such as respiration and heart rate. The cerebellum coordinates movement and is involved in learned rote movements. When you play the piano or hit a tennis ball you are activating the cerebellum. The uppermost part of the brainstem is the "midbrain," which controls some reflex actions and is part of the circuit involved in the control of eye movements and other voluntary movements. The forebrain is the largest and most highly developed part of the human brain: it consists primarily of the cerebrum **(2)** and the structures hidden beneath it.

When people see the brain it is usually the cerebrum that they notice. The cerebrum sits at the topmost part of the brain and is the source of intellectual activities. It holds your memories, allows you to plan, enables you to imagine and think. It allows you to recognize friends, read books, and play games.

The cerebrum is split into two halves (hemispheres) by a deep fissure. Despite the split, the two cerebral hemispheres communicate with each other through a thick tract of nerve fibers that lies at the base of this fissure. Although the two hemispheres seem to be mirror images of each other, they are different. For instance, the ability to form words seems to lie primarily in the left hemisphere, while the right hemisphere seems to control many abstract reasoning skills.

For some as-yet-unknown reason, nearly all of the signals from the brain to the body and vice-versa cross over on their way to and from the brain. This means that the right cerebral hemisphere primarily controls the left side of the body and the left hemisphere primarily controls the right side. When one side of the brain is damaged, the opposite side of the body is affected. For example, a stroke in the right hemisphere of the brain can leave the left arm and leg paralyzed.

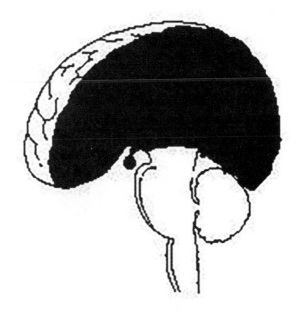

Figure 2.2. *The Forebrain*

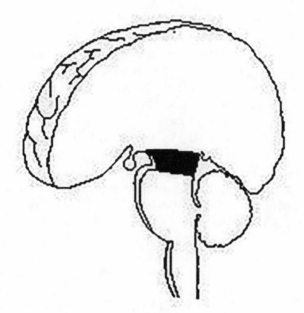

Figure 2.3. *The Midbrain*

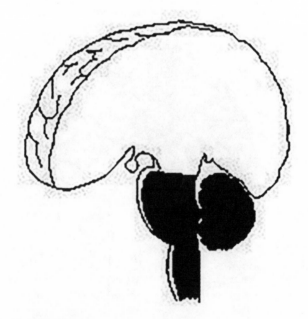

Figure 2.4. *The Hindbrain*

The Geography of Thought

Each cerebral hemisphere can be divided into sections, or lobes, each of which specializes in different functions. To understand each lobe and its specialty we will take a tour of the cerebral hemispheres, starting with the two frontal lobes **(3)**, which lie directly behind the forehead. When you plan a schedule, imagine the future, or use reasoned arguments, these two lobes do much of the work. One of the ways the frontal lobes seem to do these things is by acting as short-term storage sites, allowing one idea to be kept in mind while other ideas are considered. In the rearmost portion of each frontal lobe is a motor area **(4)**, which helps control voluntary movement. A nearby place on the left frontal lobe called "Broca's area" **(5)** allows thoughts to be transformed into words.

When you enjoy a good meal—the taste, aroma, and texture of the food—two sections behind the frontal lobes called the "parietal lobes" **(6)** are at work. The forward parts of these lobes, just behind the motor areas, are the "primary sensory areas" **(7)**. These areas receive information about temperature, taste, touch, and movement from the rest of the body. Reading and arithmetic are also functions in the repertoire of each parietal lobe.

As you look at the words and pictures on this page, two areas at the back of the brain are at work. These lobes, called the "occipital lobes" **(8)**, process images from the eyes and link that information with images stored in memory. Damage to the occipital lobes can cause blindness.

The last lobes on our tour of the cerebral hemispheres are the "temporal lobes" **(9)**, which lie in front of the visual areas and nest under the parietal and frontal lobes. Whether you appreciate symphonies or rock music, your brain responds through the activity of these lobes. At the top of each temporal lobe is an area responsible for receiving information from the ears. The underside of each temporal lobe plays a crucial role in forming and retrieving memories, including those associated with music. Other parts of this lobe seem to integrate memories and sensations of taste, sound, sight, and touch.

The Cerebral Cortex

Coating the surface of the cerebrum and the cerebellum is a vital layer of tissue the thickness of a stack of two or three dimes. It is called the "cortex," from the Latin word for bark. Most of the actual information processing in the brain takes place in the cerebral cortex.

When people talk about "gray matter" in the brain they are talking about this thin rind. The cortex is gray because nerves in this area lack the insulation that makes most other parts of the brain appear to be white. The folds in the brain add to its surface area and, therefore, increase the amount of gray matter and the quantity of information that can be processed.

The Inner Brain

Deep within the brain, hidden from view, lie structures that are the gatekeepers between the spinal cord and the cerebral hemispheres. These structures not only determine our emotional state, they also modify our perceptions and responses depending on that state, and allow us to initiate movements that you make without thinking about them. Like the lobes in the cerebral hemispheres, the structures described below come in pairs: each is duplicated in the opposite half of the brain.

The hypothalamus (**10**), about the size of a pearl, directs a multitude of important functions. It wakes you up in the morning, and gets the adrenaline flowing during a test or job interview. The hypothalamus is also an important emotional center, controlling the molecules that make you feel exhilarated, angry, or unhappy. Near the hypothalamus lies the thalamus (**11**), a major clearinghouse for information going to and from the spinal cord and the cerebrum.

An arching tract of nerve cells leads from the hypothalamus and the thalamus to the hippocampus (**12**). This tiny nub acts as a memory indexer—sending memories out to the appropriate part of the cerebral hemisphere for long-term storage and retrieving them when necessary. The basal ganglia (not shown) are clusters of nerve cells surrounding the thalamus. They are responsible for initiating and integrating movements. Parkinson disease, which results in tremors, rigidity, and a stiff, shuffling walk, is a disease of nerve cells that lead into the basal ganglia.

Making Connections

The brain and the rest of the nervous system are composed of many different types of cells, but the primary functional unit is a cell called the "neuron." All sensations, movements, thoughts, memories, and feelings are the result of signals that pass through neurons. Neurons consist of three parts. The cell body (**13**) contains the nucleus, where most of the molecules that the neuron needs to survive and function are manufactured. Dendrites **(14)** extend out from the cell body like the branches of a tree and receive messages from other nerve cells. Signals then pass from the dendrites through the cell body and may travel away from the cell body down an axon **(15)** to another neuron, a muscle cell, or cells in some other organ. The neuron is usually surrounded by many support cells. Some types of cells wrap around the axon to form an insulating sheath **(16)**. This sheath can include a fatty molecule called "myelin," which provides insulation for the axon and helps nerve signals travel faster and farther. Axons may be very short, such as those that carry signals from one cell in the cortex to another cell less than a hair's width away. Or axons may be very long, such as those that carry messages from the brain all the way down the spinal cord.

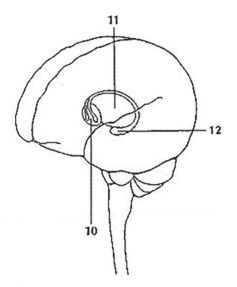

Figure 2.5. *The Inner Brain*

Scientists have learned a great deal about neurons by studying the synapse—the place where a signal passes from the neuron to another cell. When the signal reaches the end of the axon it stimulates the release of tiny sacs **(17)**. These sacs release chemicals known as "neurotransmitters" **(18)** into the synapse **(19)**. The neurotransmitters cross the synapse and attach to receptors **(20)** on the neighboring cell. These receptors can change the properties of the receiving cell. If the receiving cell is also a neuron, the signal can continue the transmission to the next cell.

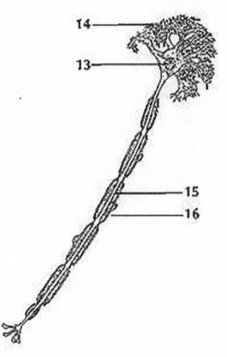

Figure 2.6. *Neurons*

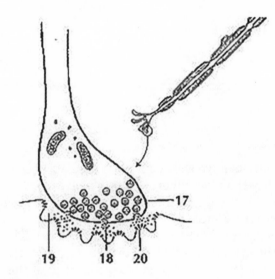

Figure 2.7. *Neurons Cell Passes*

Some Key Neurotransmitters at Work

Acetylcholine is called an "excitatory neurotransmitter" because it generally makes cells more excitable. It governs muscle contractions and causes glands to secrete hormones. Alzheimer disease, which initially affects memory formation, is associated with a shortage of acetylcholine.

Gamma-aminobutyric acid (GABA) is called an "inhibitory neurotransmitter" because it tends to make cells less excitable. It helps control muscle activity and is an important part of the visual system. Drugs that increase GABA levels in the brain are used to treat epileptic seizures and tremors in patients with Huntington disease (HD).

Serotonin is a neurotransmitter that constricts blood vessels and brings on sleep. It is also involved in temperature regulation. Dopamine is an inhibitory neurotransmitter involved in mood and the control of complex movements. The loss of dopamine activity in some portions of the brain leads to the muscular rigidity of Parkinson disease. Many medications used to treat behavioral disorders work by modifying the action of dopamine in the brain.

Mental Illness Defined as Disruption in Neural Circuits

The National Institute of Mental Health (NIMH) mantra to describe mental disorders as brain disorders. What does this mean? Is it accurate to group schizophrenia, depression, and attention deficit hyperactivity disorder (ADHD) together with Alzheimer disease (AD), Parkinson disease (PD), and HD? Is a neurologic approach to mental disorders helpful or does this focus on the brain lead to less attention to the mind?

First, mental disorders appear to be disorders of brain circuits, in contrast to classical neurological disorders in which focal lesions are apparent. By analogy, heart disease can involve arrhythmias or infarction (death) of the heart muscle. Both can be fatal, but the arrhythmia may not have a demonstrable lesion. In past decades, there was little hope of finding abnormal brain circuitry beyond the coarse approach of an electroencephalogram (EEG), which revealed little detail about regional cortical function. With the advent of imaging techniques such as positron emission tomography (PET), functional magnetic resonance imaging (fMRI), magnetoencephalography (MEG), and high-resolution EEG, we can map the broad range of cortical function with high spatial and temporal resolution. For the first time, we can study the mind via the brain. Mapping patterns of cortical activity reveals mechanisms of mental function that are just not apparent by observing behavior.

Has brain imaging been useful for understanding mental disorders? While we are still in the early days of using these powerful technologies, a survey of the literature reveals some excellent examples of how studying the brain forces us to "rethink" mental disorders. For instance, studies of brain development demonstrate delays in cortical maturation in children with attention deficit hyperactivity disorder. How curious that this disorder, which is defined by cognitive (attention) and behavioral (hyperactivity) symptoms, increasingly appears to be a disorder of cortical development. Viewing ADHD as a brain disorder raises, important questions: What causes delayed maturation? What treatments might accelerate cortical development?

A brain disorder approach also may transform the way we diagnose mental disorders. The NIMH Research Domain Criteria (R-DoC) project is involved in rethinking diagnosis based on understanding the underlying brain changes. As an example, what we now call "major depressive disorder" (MDD) probably represents many unique syndromes, responding to different interventions. Neuroimaging is beginning to yield biomarkers, that is, patterns that predict response to treatment or possibly reflect changes in physiology prior to changes in behavior or mood. And studies with deep brain stimulation addressing depression as a "brain arrhythmia" are demonstrating how changing the activity of specific circuits leads to remission of otherwise treatment-refractory depressive episodes.

An important implication of this approach is that abnormal behavior and cognition (e.g., mood, attention) may be late and convergent outcomes of altered brain development. This is a familiar lesson from neurodegenerative disorders: the symptoms of Alzheimer, Parkinson, and Huntington diseases emerge years after changes in the brain. Could the same be true of these circuit disorders that appear early in life? If so, could imaging allow earlier detection and preemption of the behavioral and cognitive changes from the social isolation of autism to the psychosis of schizophrenia? This preemptive approach, which has transformed outcomes in heart disease and cancer, could also transform psychiatry, by focusing on prevention for those at risk rather than the partial amelioration of symptoms late in the process.

But we need to recognize the range of unknowns that remain. In truth, we still do not know how to define a circuit. Where does a circuit begin or end? How do the patterns of "activity" on imaging scans actually translate to what is happening in the brain? What is the direction of information flow? In fact, the metaphor of a circuit in the sense of the flow of electricity may be woefully inadequate for describing how mental activity emerges from neuronal activity in the brain. Hence the need for continuing research into fundamental neuroscience. The advent of the tools, such as optogenetics, which uses light for precise manipulation of cells in awake, behaving animals will take us a long way towards understanding the characteristics of a neuronal circuit.

While the neuroscience discoveries are coming fast and furious, one thing we can say already is that earlier notion of mental disorders as chemical imbalances or as social constructs are beginning to look antiquated. Much of what we are learning about the neural basis of mental illness is not yet ready for the clinic, but there can be little doubt that clinical neuroscience will soon be helping people with mental disorders to recover.

Chapter 3

Myths and Facts about Mental-Health Disorders

Mental-Health Problems Affect Everyone

Myth: Mental-health problems do not affect me.

Fact: Mental-health problems are very common. In 2014, about:

- One in five American adults experienced a mental-health issue

- One in 10 young people experienced a period of major depression

- One in 25 Americans lived with a serious mental illness, such as schizophrenia, bipolar disorder, or major depression

Suicide is the 10th leading cause of death in the United States. It accounts for the loss of more than 41,000 American lives each year, more than double the number of lives lost to homicide.

Myth: Children do not experience mental-health problems.

Fact: Even very young children may show early warning signs of mental-health concerns. These mental-health problems are often clinically diagnosable and can be a product of the interaction of biological, psychological, and social factors.

This chapter includes text excerpted from "Mental Health Myths and Facts," MentalHealth.gov, U.S. Department of Health and Human Services (HHS), August 29, 2017.

Half of all mental-health disorders show first signs before a person turns 14 years old, and three-quarters of mental-health disorders begin before age 24.

Unfortunately, less than 20 percent of children and adolescents with diagnosable mental-health problems receive the treatment they need. Early mental-health support can help a child before problems interfere with other developmental needs.

Myth: People with mental-health problems are violent and unpredictable.

Fact: The vast majority of people with mental-health problems are no more likely to be violent than anyone else. Most people with mental illness are not violent and only 3 to 5 percent of violent acts can be attributed to individuals living with a serious mental illness. In fact, people with severe mental illnesses are over 10 times more likely to be victims of violent crime than the general population. You probably know someone with a mental-health problem and do not even realize it, because many people with mental-health problems are highly active and productive members of our communities.

Myth: People with mental-health needs, even those who are managing their mental illness, cannot tolerate the stress of holding down a job.

Fact: People with mental-health problems are just as productive as other employees. Employers who hire people with mental-health problems report good attendance and punctuality as well as motivation, good work, and job tenure on par with or greater than other employees. When employees with mental-health problems receive effective treatment, it can result in:

- Lower total medical costs
- Increased productivity
- Lower absenteeism
- Decreased disability costs

Myth: Personality weakness or character flaws cause mental-health problems. People with mental-health problems can snap out of it if they try hard enough.

Fact: Mental-health problems have nothing to do with being lazy or weak and many people need help to get better. Many factors contribute to mental-health problems, including:

- Biological factors, such as genes, physical illness, injury, or brain chemistry

- Life experiences, such as trauma or a history of abuse

- Family history of mental-health problems

People with mental-health problems can get better and many recover completely.

Helping Individuals with Mental-Health Problems

Myth: There is no hope for people with mental-health problems. Once a friend or family member develop mental-health problems, she or he will never recover.

Fact: Studies show that people with mental-health problems get better and many recover completely. Recovery refers to the process in which people are able to live, work, learn, and participate fully in their communities. There are more treatments, services, and community support systems than ever before, and they work.

Myth: Therapy and self-help are a waste of time. Why bother when you can just take a pill?

Fact: Treatment for mental-health problems varies depending on the individual and could include medication, therapy, or both. Many individuals work with a support system during the healing and recovery process.

Myth: I cannot do anything for a person with a mental-health problem.

Fact: Friends and loved ones can make a big difference. Only 44 percent of adults with diagnosable mental-health problems and less than 20 percent of children and adolescents receive needed treatment. Friends and family can be important influences to help someone get the treatment and services they need by:

- Reaching out and letting them know you are available to help

- Helping them access mental-health services

- Learning and sharing the facts about mental-health, especially if you hear something that is not true

- Treating them with respect, just as you would anyone else

- Refusing to define them by their diagnosis or using labels such as "crazy"

Myth: Prevention does not work. It is impossible to prevent mental illnesses.

Fact: Prevention of mental, emotional, and behavioral disorders focuses on addressing known risk factors such as exposure to trauma that can affect the chances that children, youth, and young adults will develop mental-health problems. Promoting the social-emotional well-being of children and youth leads to:

- Higher overall productivity
- Better educational outcomes
- Lower crime rates
- Stronger economies
- Lower healthcare costs
- Improved quality of life (QOL)
- Increased lifespan
- Improved family life

Chapter 4

Depression: What You Need to Know

Do you feel sad, empty, and hopeless most of the day, nearly every day? Have you lost interest or pleasure in your hobbies or being with friends and family? Are you having trouble sleeping, eating, and functioning? If you have felt this way for at least two weeks, you may have depression, a serious but treatable mood disorder.

What Is Depression?

Everyone feels sad or low sometimes, but these feelings usually pass with a little time. Depression—also called "clinical depression" or a "depressive disorder"—is a mood disorder that causes distressing symptoms that affect how you feel, think, and handle daily activities, such as sleeping, eating, or working. To be diagnosed with depression, symptoms must be present most of the day, nearly every day for at least two weeks.

What Are the Different Types of Depression?

Two of the most common forms of depression are:

- **Major depression**—having symptoms of depression most of the day, nearly every day for at least two weeks that interfere with

This chapter includes text excerpted from "Depression Basics," National Institute of Mental Health (NIMH), May 2016. Reviewed October 2019.

your ability to work, sleep, study, eat and enjoy life. An episode can occur only once in a person's lifetime, but more often, a person has several episodes.

- **Persistent depressive disorder (PDD)** (dysthymia)—having symptoms of depression that last for at least two years. A person diagnosed with this form of depression may have episodes of major depression along with periods of less severe symptoms.

Some forms of depression are slightly different, or they may develop under unique circumstances, such as:

- **Perinatal depression:** Women with perinatal depression experience full-blown major depression during pregnancy or after delivery (postpartum depression).

- **Seasonal affective disorder (SAD):** SAD is a type of depression that comes and goes with the seasons, typically starting in the late fall and early winter and going away during the spring and summer.

- **Psychotic depression:** This type of depression occurs when a person has severe depression plus some form of psychosis, such as having disturbing false fixed beliefs (delusions) or hearing or seeing upsetting things that others cannot hear or see (hallucinations).

Other examples of depressive disorders include disruptive mood dysregulation disorder (diagnosed in children and adolescents) and premenstrual dysphoric disorder (PMDD). Depression can also be one phase of bipolar disorder (formerly called "manic-depression"). But a person with bipolar disorder also experiences extreme high—euphoric or irritable—moods called "mania" or a less severe form called "hypomania."

What Causes Depression

Scientists at the National Institute of Mental Health (NIMH) and across the country are studying the causes of depression. Research suggests that a combination of genetic, biological, environmental, and psychological factors play a role in depression.

Depression can occur along with other serious illnesses, such as diabetes, cancer, heart disease, and Parkinson disease (PD). Depression can make these conditions worse and vice versa. Sometimes medications taken for these illnesses may cause side effects that contribute to depression symptoms.

What Are the Signs and Symptoms of Depression?

Sadness is only one small part of depression and some people with depression may not feel sadness at all. Different people have different symptoms. Some symptoms of depression include:

- Persistent sad, anxious, or "empty" mood
- Feelings of hopelessness or pessimism
- Feelings of guilt, worthlessness, or helplessness
- Loss of interest or pleasure in hobbies or activities
- Decreased energy, fatigue, or being "slowed down"
- Difficulty concentrating, remembering, or making decisions
- Difficulty sleeping, early-morning awakening, or oversleeping
- Appetite and/or weight changes
- Thoughts of death or suicide or suicide attempts
- Restlessness or irritability
- Aches or pains, headaches, cramps, or digestive problems without a clear physical cause and/or that do not ease even with treatment

Does Depression Look the Same in Everyone?

No. Depression affects different people in different ways. For example:

- **Women** have depression more often than men. Biological, lifecycle and hormonal factors that are unique to women may be linked to their higher depression rate. Women with depression typically have symptoms of sadness, worthlessness, and guilt.

- **Men** with depression are more likely to be very tired, irritable, and sometimes angry. They may lose interest in work or activities they once enjoyed, have sleep problems, and behave recklessly, including the misuse of drugs or alcohol. Many men do not recognize their depression and fail to seek help.

- **Older adults** with depression may have less obvious symptoms, or they may be less likely to admit to feelings of sadness or grief. They are also more likely to have medical conditions, such as heart disease, which may cause or contribute to depression.

- **Younger children** with depression may pretend to be sick, refuse to go to school, cling to a parent, or worry that a parent may die.

- **Older children and teens** with depression may get into trouble at school, sulk, and be irritable. Teens with depression may have symptoms of other disorders, such as anxiety, eating disorders, or substance abuse.

How Is Depression Treated?

The first step in getting the right treatment is to visit a healthcare provider or mental-health professionals, such as a psychiatrist or psychologist. Your healthcare provider can do an exam, interview, and lab tests to rule out other health conditions that may have the same symptoms as depression. Once diagnosed, depression can be treated with medications, psychotherapy, or a combination of the two. If these treatments do not reduce symptoms, brain stimulation therapy may be another treatment option to explore.

Medications

Medications called "antidepressants" can work well to treat depression. They can take two to four weeks to work. Antidepressants can have side effects, but many side effects may lessen over time. Talk to your healthcare provider about any side effects that you have. Do not stop taking your antidepressant without first talking to your healthcare provider.

Psychotherapy

Psychotherapy helps by teaching ways of thinking and behaving and changing habits that may be contributing to depression. Therapy can help you understand and work through difficult relationships or situations that may be causing your depression or making it worse.

Brain Stimulation Therapies

Electroconvulsive therapy (ECT) and other brain stimulation therapies may be an option for people with severe depression who do not respond to antidepressant medications. ECT is the best-studied brain stimulation therapy and has the longest history of use. Other stimulation therapies discussed here are newer, and in some cases still experimental methods.

How Can I Help Myself If I Am Depressed?

As you continue treatment, you may start to feel better gradually. Remember that if you are taking an antidepressant, it may take two to four weeks to start working. Try to do things that you used to enjoy. Go easy on yourself. Other things that may help include:

- Trying to be active and exercise
- Breaking up large tasks into small ones, set priorities, and do what you can as you can
- Spending time with other people and confide in a trusted friend or relative
- Postponing important life decisions until you feel better. Discuss decisions with others who know you well
- Avoiding self-medication with alcohol or with drugs not prescribed for you

How Can I Help a Loved One Who Is Depressed?

If you know someone who has depression, first help her or him see a healthcare provider or mental-health professional. You can also:

- Offer support, understanding, patience, and encouragement
- Never ignore comments about suicide, and report them to your loved one's healthcare provider or therapist
- Invite her or him out for walks, outings, and other activities
- Help her or him adhere to the treatment plan, such as setting reminders to take prescribed medications
- Help her or him by ensuring that she or he has transportation to therapy appointments
- Remind her or him that, with time and treatment, the depression will lift

Chapter 5

Why Do People Get Depressed?

Depression Is Widespread

Depression is one of the most common disorders that affect people irrespective of age, race, or economic background. It is a pressing and widespread mental-health condition that requires treatment just like any other disease or illness. Factors such as genes, brain chemistry, and medical conditions often contribute to whether a person gets depressed. In addition to these physical causes of depression, other causes include adverse life events, available daylight hours during the seasons of the year, and cultural backgrounds.

Depression is caused when the neurotransmitters of the brain, which control mood, fail to function properly. A person's viewpoint may intensify depression as well. You might have heard of the glass half-full or glass-half-empty test—that is, a person may get upset quickly and see the glass as half-empty while others let setbacks slide off easily and see the glass as half-full. The ways in which a person thinks, responds, and reacts to given situations may contribute to depression.

"Why Do People Get Depressed?" © 2020 Omnigraphics. Reviewed October 2019.

Genes Could Be a Reason for Depression

Studies show that depression may run in families and that some people inherit genes that put them at greater risk of becoming depressed. However, not all who acquire these genes get depressed (whereas all people whose ancestors suffer from diabetes are affected). Also, studies indicate that people who do not have any family history of depression can still get depressed. Hence, although genes may be one of the causes of depression, they are not a stand-alone factor to the disorder.

Brain Chemistry Could Be a Leading Cause of Depression

Depression primarily affects the brain's fragile chemistry involving neurotransmitter signaling. Neurotransmitters send communications between the nerve cells in the brain. They help control the mood of a person. However, when a person is depressed, these neurotransmitters are low in secretion or are imbalanced. Genes and brain chemistry can be interrelated since people who are genetically susceptible to depression are more prone to developing the neurotransmitter activity imbalance, which leads to depression. It's a vicious circle.

Various factors can affect the secretion and stability of the neurotransmitters, including stress and exposure to daylight. The use of alcohol and drugs can also cause chemical alterations in the brain that influence the mood. However, an imbalance of the neurotransmitters can be completely restored with appropriate medications prescribed by a doctor.

Seasons and Daylight Could Affect Neurotransmitters in the Brain

Exposure to daylight can affect the secretion and stability of the neurotransmitters melatonin and serotonin. The brain tends to produce more melatonin when there is less daylight. Similarly, when there is more daylight, the brain tends to secrete more serotonin.

Melatonin and serotonin play a vital role in balancing a person's sleep and wake patterns, stamina, and mood. Longer hours of darkness and the shorter days in winter and fall may cause an increase in the secretion of melatonin and a simultaneous decrease in the level of serotonin. Such chemical imbalances can result in one type of depression, which is known as "seasonal affective disorder" (SAD). Light therapy, also called "phototherapy," along with medications and talk therapy, can help improve the mood of people affected by SAD.

Adverse Life Events Could Trigger Depression

The death of a family member, friend, or peer results in grief that can lead to depression. Other adverse life experiences such as a marriage separation, divorce, or a remarriage can trigger depression. Even situations such as a change in school or a move can be so emotionally difficult that they can trigger depression in a person. However, many people are resilient and can endure adverse life experiences without being affected by depression.

Dismal Family and Social Environments Could Breed Mental Stress

For some people, a harmful, demanding, or troublesome family environment can affect their self-esteem and lead to depression. Various other stressful conditions, such as poverty, homelessness, or exposure to violence can play a part in this, too. Facing peer pressure, bullying, or harassment can often leave a person feeling upset, withdrawn, and victimized. And unhealthy or weak relationships could cause depression. Adverse circumstances, left unattended, can lead to depression.

Hormonal Changes Could Affect the Brain

Hormonal imbalances in the body could cause certain changes in health and thus affect a person's mood. Certain disorders, such as hyperthyroidism, etc., are understood to cause depression in some people. However, when sound medical guidance is followed, hormones can remain balanced and the brain can function optimally. Hormonal imbalances that occur during puberty could also affect the mood of a person and trigger depression.

Poor Sleeping Habits Are a Sign of Depression

When a person is deprived of sleep, an associated increase in the level of anxiety the person experiences can lead to depression. Overworked people are more likely to compromise on their sleep. This could eventually lead to excessive fatigue, affect the brain, and result in the loss of mental health. Sleep is necessary to replenish brain cells. Hence, compromising on sleep may lead to depression.

Depression is a mental disorder that can be treated. Staying positive and receiving appropriate medical care could help people who suffer from depression cope well and lead a normal life.

References

1. "Brain and Nervous System, Why Do People Get Depressed?" Rady Children's Hospital-San Diego, July 2014.

2. "Why Do People Get Depressed?" National Sleep Foundation (NSF), January 11, 2013.

Chapter 6

Statistics on Depression and Related Mental-Health Disorders

Chapter Contents

Section 6.1

Statistics on Depression

This section includes text excerpted from "Major Depression,"
National Institute of Mental Health (NIMH), February 2019.

Major depression is one of the most common mental disorders in
the United States. For some individuals, major depression can result
in severe impairments that interfere with or limit one's ability to carry
out major life activities.

The past year prevalence data presented here for the major depressive episode are from the 2017 National Survey on Drug Use and
Health (NSDUH). The NSDUH study definition of a major depressive
episode is based mainly on the *Diagnostic and Statistical Manual of
Mental Disorders (DSM-5)*:

- A period of at least two weeks when a person experienced a
  depressed mood or loss of interest or pleasure in daily activities
  and had a majority of specified symptoms, such as problems with
  sleep, eating, energy, concentration, or self-worth

- No exclusions were made for major depressive episode
  symptoms caused by medical illness, substance use disorders, or
  medication

Prevalence of Major Depressive Episode among Adults

- Figure 6.1 shows the past year prevalence of major depressive
  episode among U.S. adults aged 18 or older in 2017.

  - An estimated 17.3 million adults in the United States had at
    least one major depressive episode. This number represented
    7.1 percent of all U.S. adults.

  - The prevalence of major depressive episodes was higher
    among adult females (8.7%) compared to males (5.3%).

  - The prevalence of adults with a major depressive episode was
    highest among individuals aged 18 to 25 (13.1%).

  - The prevalence of major depressive episodes was highest
    among adults reporting two or more races (11.3%).

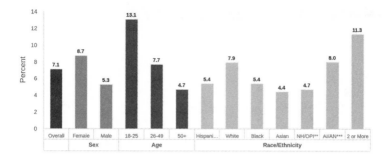

Figure 6.1. *Prevalence of Major Depressive Episode among U.S. Adults (2017)* (Source: Substance Abuse and Mental Health Services Administration (SAMHSA).)

*All other groups are non-Hispanic or Latino
**NH/OPI=Native Hawaiian/Other Pacific Islander
***AI/AN=American Indian/Alaskan Native

Major Depressive Episode with Impairment among Adults

- In 2017, an estimated 11 million U.S. adults aged 18 or older had at least one major depressive episode with severe impairment. This number represented 4.5 percent of all U.S. adults.

- Figure 6.2 shows the overall past-year prevalence of major depressive episodes with and without severe impairment. Of adults with a major depressive episode, 63.8 percent had severe impairment.

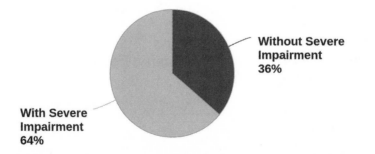

Figure 6.2. *Major Depressive Episode with Impairment among U.S. Adults (2017)* (Source: Substance Abuse and Mental Health Services Administration (SAMHSA).)

Treatment of Major Depressive Episode among Adults

- Figure 6.3 shows data on treatment received within the past year by U.S. adults aged 18 or older with a major depressive episode. Treatment types include health professionals only, medication only, and health professionals and medication combined.

  - An estimated 65 percent received combined care by a health professional and medication treatment.

  - Treatment with medication alone was the least common (6%).

  - Approximately 35 percent of adults with a major depressive episode did not receive treatment.

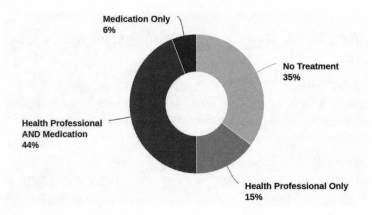

Figure 6.3. *Treatment of Major Depressive Episode among U.S. Adults (2017)* (Source: Substance Abuse and Mental Health Services Administration (SAMHSA).)

Prevalence of Major Depressive Episode among Adolescents

- Figure 6.4 shows the past year prevalence of major depressive episode among U.S. adolescents in 2017.

  - An estimated 3.2 million adolescents aged 12 to 17 in the United States had at least one major depressive episode. This number represented 13.3 percent of the U.S. population aged 12 to 17.

- The prevalence of major depressive episodes was higher among adolescent females (20.0%) compared to males (6.8%).

- The prevalence of major depressive episode was highest among adolescents reporting two or more races (16.9%).

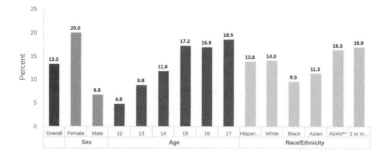

Figure 6.4. *Prevalence of Major Depressive Episode among U.S. Adolescents (2017)* (Source: Substance Abuse and Mental Health Services Administration (SAMHSA).)

*All other groups are non-Hispanic or Latino
**AI/AN= American Indian/Alaska Native

Major Depressive Episode with Impairment among Adolescents

- In 2017, an estimated 2.3 million adolescents aged 12 to 17 in the United States had at least one major depressive episode with severe impairment. This number represented 9.4 percent of the U.S. population aged 12 to 17.

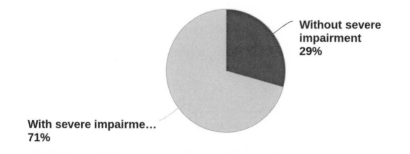

Figure 6.5. *Major Depressive Episode with Impairment among Adolescents (2017)* (Source: Substance Abuse and Mental Health Services Administration (SAMHSA).)

- Figure 6.5 shows the overall past-year prevalence of major depressive episodes with and without severe impairment among U.S. adolescents. Of adolescents with major depressive episodes, approximately 70.77 percent had severe impairment.

Section 6.2

Statistics on Other Common Mental Illnesses

This section contains text excerpted from the following sources: Text beginning with the heading "Prevalence of Any Mental Illness" is excerpted from "Statistics—Mental Illness," National Institute of Mental Health (NIMH), February 2019; Text under the heading "Prevalence of Any Anxiety Disorder among Adults" is excerpted from "Statistics—Any Anxiety Disorder," National Institute of Mental Health (NIMH), November 2017; Text under the heading "Prevalence of Bipolar Disorder among Adults" is excerpted from "Statistics—Bipolar Disorder," National Institute of Mental Health (NIMH), November 2017.

Prevalence of Any Mental Illness

- Figure 6.6 shows the past year prevalence of any mental illness (AMI) among U.S. adults.

- In 2017, there were an estimated 46.6 million adults aged 18 or older in the United States with AMI. This number represented 18.9 percent of all U.S. adults.

- The prevalence of AMI was higher among women (22.3%) than men (15.1%).

- Young adults aged 18 to 25 years had the highest prevalence of AMI (25.8%) compared to adults aged 26 to 49 years (22.2%) and aged 50 and older (13.8%).

- The prevalence of AMI was highest among the adults reporting two or more races (28.6%), followed by White adults (20.4%). The prevalence of AMI was lowest among Asian adults (14.5%).

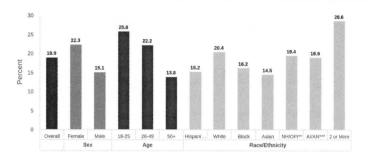

Figure 6.6. *Prevalence of Any Mental Illness (2017)* (Source: Substance Abuse and Mental Health Services Administration (SAMHSA).)

*All other groups are non-Hispanic or Latino
**NH/OPI = Native Hawaiian/Other Pacific Islander
***AI/AN = American Indian/Alaska Native

Prevalence of Serious Mental Illness

- Figure 6.7 shows the past year prevalence of serious mental illness (SMI) among U.S. adults.

- In 2017, there were an estimated 11.2 million adults aged 18 or older in the United States with SMI. This number represented 4.5 percent of all U.S. adults.

- The prevalence of SMI was higher among women (5.7%) than men (3.3%).

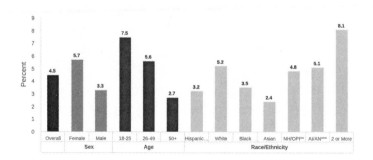

Figure 6.7. *Prevalence of Serious Mental Illness among U.S. Adults (2017)* (Source: Substance Abuse and Mental Health Services Administration (SAMHSA).)

*All other groups are non-Hispanic or Latino
**NH/OPI = Native Hawaiian/Other Pacific Islander
***AI/AN = American Indian/Alaskan Native

- Young adults aged 18 to 25 years had the highest prevalence of SMI (7.5%) compared to adults aged 26 to 49 years (5.6%) and aged 50 and older (2.7%).

- The prevalence of SMI was highest among the adults reporting two or more races (8.1%), followed by White adults (5.2%). The prevalence of SMI was lowest among Asian adults (2.4%).

Prevalence of Any Anxiety Disorder among Adults

- Based on diagnostic interview data from the National Comorbidity Study Replication (NCS-R), Figure 6.8 shows the past-year prevalence of any anxiety disorder among U.S. adults aged 18 or older.

  - An estimated 19.1 percent of U.S. adults had any anxiety disorder in the past year.

  - The past year prevalence of any anxiety disorder was higher for females (23.4%) than for males (14.3%).

- An estimated 31.1 percent of U.S. adults experience any anxiety disorder at some time in their lives.

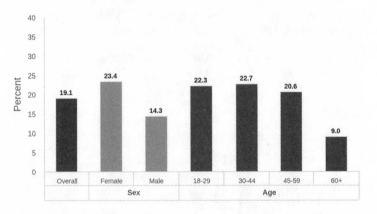

Figure 6.8. *Prevalence of Any Anxiety Disorder among U.S. Adults (2001 to 2003)* (Source: National Comorbidity Survey Replication (NCS-R).)

Prevalence of Bipolar Disorder among Adults

- Based on diagnostic interview data from National Comorbidity Survey Replication (NCS-R), Figure 6.9 shows the past-year prevalence of bipolar disorder among U.S. adults aged 18 or older.

- An estimated 2.8 percent of U.S. adults had bipolar disorder in the past year.

- The past year's prevalence of bipolar disorder among adults was similar for males (2.9%) and females (2.8%).

- An estimated 4.4 percent of U.S. adults experience bipolar disorder at some time in their lives.

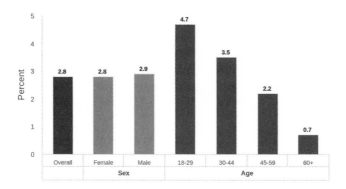

Figure 6.9. *Prevalence of Bipolar Disorder among Adults (2001 to 2003)* (Source: National Comorbidity Survey Replication (NCS-R).)

Part Two

Types of Depression

Chapter 7

Major Depression

What Is Major Depression?

Major depression is a medical condition distinguished by one or more major depressive episodes. A major depressive episode is characterized by at least two weeks of depressed mood or loss of interest (pleasure) and accompanied by at least four more symptoms of depression. Such symptoms can include changes in appetite, weight, difficulty in thinking and concentrating, and recurrent thoughts of death or suicide. Depression differs from feeling "blue" in that it causes severe enough problems to interfere with a person's day-to-day functioning.

People's experience with major depression varies. some people describe it as a total loss of energy or enthusiasm to do anything. Others may describe it as constantly living with a feeling of impending doom. There are treatments that help improve functioning and relieve many symptoms of depression. Recovery is possible!

How Common Is Major Depression?

Major depression is a common psychiatric disorder. It is more common in adolescent and adult women than in adolescent and adult men. Between 15 to 20 out of every 100 people (15–20%) experience

This chapter includes text excerpted from "What Is Major Depression?" Mental Illness Research, Education and Clinical Centers (MIRECC), U.S. Department of Veterans Affairs (VA), 2015. Reviewed October 2019.

an episode of major depression during their lifetime. Prevalence has not been found to be related to ethnicity, income, education, or marital status.

How Is Major Depression Diagnosed?

Major depression cannot be diagnosed with a blood test, computerized axial tomography (CAT) scan, or any other laboratory test. The only way to diagnose major depression is with a clinical interview. The interviewer checks to see if the person has experienced severe symptoms for at least two weeks. If the symptoms are less severe, but last over long periods of time, the person may be diagnosed with persistent depressive disorder. The clinician must also check to be sure there are no physical problems that could cause symptoms like those of major depression, such as a brain tumor or a thyroid problem.

Course of Illness

The average age of onset is in the mid-20s, however, major depression can begin at any age in life. The frequency of episodes varies from person to person. Some people have isolated episodes over many years, while others suffer from frequent episodes clustered together. The number of episodes generally increases as the person grows older. The severity of the initial episode of major depression seems to indicate persistence. episodes also seem to follow major stressors, such as the death of a loved one or a divorce. Chronic medical conditions and substance abuse may further exacerbate depressive episodes.

Causes of Major Depression

There is no simple answer to what causes depression because several factors play a part in the onset of the disorder. These include a genetic or family history of depression, environmental stressors, life events, biological factors, and psychological vulnerability to depression.

Research shows that the risk for depression results from the influence of multiple genes acting together with environmental factors. This is called the "stress-vulnerability model." A family history of depression does not necessarily mean children or other relatives will develop major depression. However, those with a family history of depression have a slightly higher chance of becoming depressed at some stage in their lives. Although genetic research suggests that depression can run in families, genetics alone are unlikely to cause depression. environmental factors, such as a traumatic childhood or adult life events, may act as triggers. Studies show that early childhood trauma and losses, such as the death or separation of parents, or adult life events, such as the death of a loved one, divorce, loss of a job, retirement, serious financial problems, and family conflict, can lead to the onset of depression. Subsequent episodes are usually caused by more mild stressors or even none at all.

Many scientists believe the cause is biological, such as an imbalance in brain chemicals, specifically serotonin and norepinephrine. There are also theories that physical changes to the body may play a role in depression. Such physical changes can include viral and other infections, heart attack, cancer, or hormonal disorders. Personality style may also contribute to the onset of depression. People are at a greater risk of becoming depressed if they have low self-esteem, tend to worry a lot, are overly dependent on others, are perfectionists, or expect too much from themselves and others.

Symptoms of Depression

To meet the criteria for major depressive disorder (MDD), a person must meet at least five symptoms of depression for at least a two week period. social, occupational, and other areas of functioning must be significantly impaired, or at least require increased effort. Depressed mood caused by substances (such as drugs, alcohol, or medications) or related to another medical condition is not considered to be a MDD. MDD also cannot be diagnosed if a person has a history of manic, hypomanic, or mixed episodes (e.g., bipolar disorder) or if the depressed mood is better accounted for by schizoaffective disorder.

Not all symptoms must be present for a person to be diagnosed with depression. Five (or more) of the following symptoms have to be present during the same two week period and represent a change from previous functioning. At least one of the symptoms must be either depressed mood or loss of interest or pleasure.

- Depressed mood most of the day, nearly every day, as indicated by either subjective report (e.g., feels sad or empty) or observation made by others (e.g., appears tearful). in children and adolescents, this may be characterized as an irritable mood rather than a sad mood.

- Markedly diminished interest or pleasure in all, or almost all, activities most of the day, nearly every day. This includes activities that were previously found enjoyable.

- Significant weight loss when not dieting or weight gain (e.g., a change of more than 5 percent of body weight in a month), or a decrease or increase in appetite nearly every day.

- Insomnia or hypersomnia nearly every day. The person may have difficulty falling asleep, staying asleep, or waking early in the morning and not being able to get back to sleep. Alternatively, the person may sleep excessively (such as over 12 hours per night) and spend much of the day in bed.

- Psychomotor agitation (e.g., inability to sit still or pacing) or psychomotor retardation (e.g., slowed speech, thinking, and body movements) nearly every day. Changes in activity levels are common in depression. The person may feel agitated, "on edge," and restless. Alternatively, they may experience decreased activity levels reflected by slowness and lethargy, both in terms of the person's behavior and thought processes.

- Fatigue or loss of energy nearly every day.

- Feelings of worthlessness or excessive or inappropriate guilt nearly every day. Depressed people may feel they are worthless or that there is no hope for improving their lives. Feelings of guilt may be present about events with which the person had no involvement, such as a catastrophe, a crime, or an illness.

- Diminished ability to think or concentrate, or indecisiveness, nearly every day. A significant decrease in the ability to concentrate makes it difficult to pay attention to others or contemplate simple tasks. The person may be quite indecisive about even minor things.

- Recurrent thoughts of death (not just fear of dying), recurrent suicidal ideation without a specific plan, a specific plan for committing suicide, or a suicide attempt.

There are other psychiatric symptoms that depressed people often experience. They might complain of bodily aches and pains rather than feelings of sadness. They might report or exhibit persistent anger, angry outbursts, and an exaggerated sense of frustration over seemingly minor events. Symptoms of anxiety are also very common among people with depression. Other symptoms include hallucinations (false perceptions, such as hearing voices) and delusions (false beliefs, such as paranoid delusions). These symptoms usually disappear when the symptoms of depression have been controlled.

Similar Psychiatric Disorders

Major depression shares symptoms with some of the other psychiatric disorders. If the person experiences very high or euphoric moods called "mania," they would be given a diagnosis of bipolar disorder. If the person exhibits psychotic symptoms while not depressed, they might be diagnosed with schizoaffective disorder. Major depression must also be distinguished from a depressive disorder due to another medical condition. In this case, the mood disturbances are caused by physiological changes due to a medical condition.

Treatments of Depression

There are a variety of antidepressant medications and therapies available to those suffering from depression. Antidepressant medications help to stabilize mood. People can also learn to manage their symptoms with psychotherapy. People with a milder form of depression may benefit from psychotherapy alone, while those with more severe symptoms and episodes may benefit from antidepressants. A combination of both types of treatment is often most helpful to people. The treatments listed here are ones which research has shown to be effective for people with depression. They are considered to be evidence-based practices.

Medication

There are five different classes of antidepressant medications.

- Antidepressant class number 1: Serotonin reuptake inhibitors (SSRIs)

- Antidepressant class number 2: Serotonin and norepinephrine reuptake inhibitors (SNRIs)

- Antidepressant class number 3: Atypical antidepressants

- Antidepressant class number 4: Tricyclics and tetracyclics (TCA and TECA)

- Antidepressant class number 5: Monoamine oxidase inhibitors (MAOI)

Cognitive-Behavioral Therapy

Cognitive-behavioral therapy (CBT) is a well-established treatment for people with depression. CBT is a blend of two therapies: cognitive therapy and behavioral therapy. Cognitive therapy focuses on a person's thoughts and beliefs, and how they influence a person's mood and actions, and aims to change a person's thinking to be more adaptive and healthy. Behavioral therapy focuses on a person's actions and aims to change unhealthy behavior patterns.

Cognitive-behavioral therapy helps a person focus on her or his current problems and how to solve them. Both patient and therapist need to be actively involved in this process. The therapist helps the patient learn how to identify and correct distorted thoughts or negative self-talk often associated with depressed feelings, recognize and change inaccurate beliefs, engage in more enjoyable activities, relate to self and others in more positive ways, learn problem-solving skills, and change behaviors. another focus of CBT is behavioral activation (i.e., increasing activity levels and helping the patient take part in rewarding activities which can improve mood). CBT is a structured, weekly intervention. Weekly homework assignments help the individual apply the learned techniques.

Family Psychoeducation

Mental illness affects the whole family. Family treatment can play an important role to help both the person with depression and her or his relatives. Family psychoeducation is one way, families can work together towards recovery. The family and clinician will meet together to discuss the problems they are experiencing. Families will then attend educational sessions where they will learn basic facts about mental illness, coping skills, communication skills, problem-solving skills, and ways to work together toward recovery.

Assertive Community Treatment

Assertive community treatment (ACT) is an approach that is most effective with individuals with the greatest service needs, such as those with a history of multiple hospitalizations. In ACT, the person receives treatment from an interdisciplinary team of usually 10 to 12 professionals, including case managers, a psychiatrist, several nurses and social workers, vocational specialists, substance-abuse treatment specialists, and peer specialists. The team provides coverage 24 hours a day, 7 days a week, and utilizes small caseloads, usually one staff for every 10 clients. services provided include case management, comprehensive treatment planning, crisis intervention, medication management, individual supportive therapy, substance-abuse treatment, rehabilitation services (i.e., supported employment), and peer support.

Electroconvulsive Therapy

Electroconvulsive therapy (ECT) is a procedure used to treat severe or life-threatening depression. it is used when other treatments such as psychotherapy and antidepressant medications have not worked. Electrical currents are briefly sent to the brain through electrodes placed on the head. The electrical current can last up to 8 seconds, producing a short seizure. It is believed this brain stimulation helps relieve symptoms of depression by altering brain chemicals, including neurotransmitters such as serotonin and natural pain relievers called "endorphins." ECT treatments are usually done two to three times a week for two to three weeks. Maintenance treatments may be done one time each week, tapering down to one time each month. They may continue for several months to a year, to reduce the risk of relapse. ECT is usually given in combination with medication, psychotherapy, family therapy, and behavioral therapy.

Chapter 8

Persistent Depressive Disorder

What Is Persistent Depressive Disorder?

Persistent depressive disorder (PDD), also called "dysthymic disorder" or "dysthymia," is a chronic depression that typically influences a person's mood for at least a two-year period. Compared to other types of depression, such as atypical depression, the symptoms of PDD are less extreme. Dysthymic disorder is one of the most common types of depression that affects a person. It is estimated that almost four percent of people have this disorder, which can begin to affect a person at any time, including during childhood.

Causes of Persistent Depressive Disorder

The exact causes of PDD are still unknown. A person with dysthymic disorder can have physical alterations in the brain. The neurotransmitters in the brain play a major role in a person being depressed. Studies show that any change in the functioning or effect of these neurotransmitters and how they communicate can affect the stability of a person's mood.

Also, it appears that PDD is more common in people with blood relatives who have the same condition. PDD is present more often in

---

"Persistent Depressive Disorder," © 2020 Omnigraphics. Reviewed October 2019.

women than in men. Other medical conditions and exposure to continuous stress can also play a role in PDD.

Symptoms of Persistent Depressive Disorder

The symptoms of PDD generally come and go for years and their intensity may change with time. The major symptom of PDD is a deep, dull, or sad mood on most days for a minimum of two years. However, the symptoms may not appear for more than two months at some points. Major depression experiences also may happen before or during PDD; these co-occurring conditions are referred to as "double depression." In the cases of children and teens, the mood may be sensitive rather than depressed and may last for at least one year.

Two or more of the following symptoms present in nearly all cases of depression:

- Loss of engagement in regular activities
- Feeling empty, sad, or downcast
- Getting too much or too little sleep
- Feelings of hopelessness
- Experiencing fatigue or a lack of energy
- Exhibiting a decrease in activity, efficiency, and productivity
- Experiencing low self-esteem, or feeling ineffective
- Experiencing difficulty in concentrating and making decisions
- Overeating or experiencing a loss of appetite
- Exhibiting impatience or extreme anger
- Avoiding social engagement
- Feeling guilty or worrying about the past

Diagnosis of Persistent Depressive Disorder

To diagnose PDD, the following tests may be done.

Physical Exam

This includes a physical examination. The doctor will ask questions about the patient's medical history and health to determine the root cause of the depression. In some cases, depression may be caused by underlying physical health conditions that the doctor will need to identify or rule out.

Lab Tests

Lab tests are recommended by the doctor to ensure that other medical conditions, such as an underactive thyroid (hypothyroidism), are not the major cause of depression. This is usually done through blood tests.

Psychological Evaluations

Psychological evaluations include discussing a patient's behavior, thoughts, and feelings. They may include a questionnaire that the patient fills out to help the doctor pinpoint a diagnosis. These tests help to determine whether the patient has PDD or another disorder that affects a persons' mood, such as seasonal affective disorder, major depression, or bipolar disorder.

Treatment of Persistent Depressive Disorder

The most effective treatment for PDD is medication and talk therapy (psychotherapy).

The treatment selected by the doctor may depend upon any of the following factors:

- The severity of the symptoms

- Personal preferences

- A person's desire to address an emotional or circumstantial issue that is adversely affecting their life

- Previous treatment history

- A person's tolerance of medication

Medications Used

Some of the commonly used antidepressants used to treat PDD are listed below.

- Selective serotonin reuptake inhibitors (SSRIs)

- Tricyclic antidepressants (TCAs)

- Serotonin and norepinephrine reuptake inhibitors (SNRIs)

A patient may have to try several medications or a combination of one or more medications before the symptoms of PDD are effectively controlled.

Living with Persistent Depressive Disorder

Persistent depressive disorder is a chronic condition that requires constant care. Following the guidelines below, when combined with medication and therapy, will help people deal with PDD.

- Follow a healthy and nutritious diet.
- Improve the sleep schedule so that one gets enough sleep.
- Take medications on time and discuss the side effects with your doctor, if you experience any.
- Exercise regularly.
- Discuss your symptoms and experiences with a trustworthy friend or family member.
- Avoid drugs and alcohol.
- Do not stop any medications without discussing this with your physician first.

When to Contact a Medical Professional

When the feelings and symptoms associated with PDD have prevailed for a long time, patients often assume that they are a permanent part of one's life. However, any symptom of PDD requires medication attention. Make an appointment with the doctor:

- If a person continuously feels depressed or dejected
- If the symptoms of PDD are getting worse

Also, get help immediately if anyone you know exhibits these signs of suicide risk:

- Giving away personal belongings, talking about getting things in order since they are going away
- Inflicting self-harm, such as cutting or otherwise injuring themselves
- Speaking about death or suicide either directly or indirectly
- Retreating from friends or showing a reluctance to go out anywhere

Getting the right help at the right time can and will improve the symptoms of PDD.

References

1. "Persistent Depressive Disorder," MedlinePlus, National Institutes of Health (NIH), July 31, 2019.

2. "Persistent Depressive Disorder (Dysthymia)," Mayo Clinic, December 8, 2018.

3. "Persistent Depressive Disorder (PDD)," American Academy of Family Physicians (AAFP), August 29, 2017.

Chapter 9

Atypical Depression

What Is Atypical Depression?

Atypical depression is a subtype of major depressive disorder. Although the name suggests otherwise, it is actually quite common. According to the Diagnostic and Statistical Manual of Mental Disorders, the main symptoms of atypical depression include moods that react strongly to environmental circumstances, overeating, oversleeping, and a sensation of heavy limbs or being weighed down. These symptoms contrast with—or are atypical of—the symptoms of another subtype, melancholic depression. Melancholic depression is usually characterized by a lack of mood reactivity, loss of appetite, insomnia, and a diminished ability to experience pleasure.

Causes and Symptoms of Atypical Depression

Researchers believe that depression, or dysthymic/persistent depressive disorder, is caused by differences in brain circuits that transmit signal-carrying chemicals called "neurotransmitters." These chemicals—such as dopamine, norepinephrine, and serotonin—help regulate mood. When the brain circuits are impaired or the chemical signals are abnormal, mood disorders can result. Although the exact cause of depression remains unknown, some of the known risk factors include a family history, a significant loss or traumatic life event, interpersonal conflicts, social isolation, or serious illness.

"Atypical Depression," © 2017 Omnigraphics. Reviewed October 2019.

People with common depression often feel sad, hopeless, dejected, and unable to enjoy themselves. In people with melancholic depression, these feelings are persistent and do not change in response to environmental circumstances. People with atypical depression, on the other hand, usually experience significant changes in mood in response to pleasurable experiences or positive events. In addition to mood reactivity, the diagnostic criteria for atypical depression requires patients to present at least two of the following symptoms:

- Increased appetite, overeating (hyperphagia), or significant weight gain

- Excessive fatigue, sleepiness, or hypersomnia (sleeping more than ten hours per day)

- A sensation of weakness, heaviness, or being weighed down (leaden paralysis)

- Extreme sensitivity to interpersonal rejection that affects the workplace and social relationships

The risk of atypical depression is two times higher in women than in men. People with bipolar disorder and seasonal affective disorder are also more likely to experience atypical depression symptoms. On average, it tends to have an earlier onset than melancholic depression, and it is also associated with an increased risk of anxiety disorders and suicidal ideation.

Diagnosis and Treatment of Atypical Depression

The first step in diagnosing atypical depression involves a complete medical examination to determine whether the patient's symptoms may have a physical cause. Hypothyroidism, for instance, may cause symptoms such as mood changes, fatigue, and weight gain due to low levels of thyroid hormones. If a physical examination and blood tests fail to reveal an underlying health condition, the doctor may recommend a psychological evaluation. A mental health professional will typically ask questions about the patient's symptoms, recent experiences, feelings, and behavior patterns and compare that information to the diagnostic criteria for atypical depression.

The treatment for atypical depression usually involves a combination of psychotherapy (talk therapy) and medications. Both treatment methods have proven to be effective, depending on the patient's condition and symptoms. Psychotherapy involves meeting with a mental health professional to identify unhealthy thoughts or behaviors, explore problematic relationships and experiences, and develop new coping and problem-solving methods.

A number of prescription medications have also proven effective in treating atypical depression. These antidepressant medications work by improving the function of brain circuits and neurotransmitters that help regulate mood. Research suggests that many patients with atypical depression respond well to monoamine oxidase inhibitors (MAOIs), whereas fewer patients experience good results with tricyclic antidepressants. All patients are different, however, so it may be necessary to try several different types or combinations of medications to find the option that works best.

References

1. "Atypical Depression," WebMD, 2016.

2. Lieber, Arnold. "Atypical Depression: An Overview of Depression with Atypical Symptoms," PsyCom, n.d.

3. Moran, Mark. "Atypical Depression: What's in a Name?" Psychiatric News, October 17, 2003.

Chapter 10

Bipolar Disorder (Manic-Depressive Illness)

What Is Bipolar Disorder?

Bipolar disorder, also known as "manic-depressive illness," is a brain disorder that causes unusual shifts in mood, energy, activity levels, and the ability to carry out day-to-day tasks.

Types of Bipolar Disorder

There are four basic types of bipolar disorder; all of them involve clear changes in mood, energy, and activity levels. These moods range from periods of extremely "up," elated, and energized behavior (known as "manic episodes") to very sad, "down," or hopeless periods (known as "depressive episodes"). Less severe manic periods are known as "hypomanic episodes."

Bipolar I Disorder

Bipolar I Disorder defined by manic episodes that last at least seven days, or by manic symptoms that are so severe that the person needs immediate hospital care. Usually, depressive episodes occur as well, typically lasting at least two weeks. Episodes of depression with mixed

This chapter includes text excerpted from "Bipolar Disorder," National Institute of Mental Health (NIMH), April 2016. Reviewed October 2019.

features (having depression and manic symptoms at the same time) are also possible.

Bipolar II Disorder

Bipolar II Disorder defined by a pattern of depressive episodes and hypomanic episodes, but not the full-blown manic episodes described above.

Cyclothymic Disorder

Cyclothymic Disorder (also called "cyclothymia") defined by numerous periods of hypomanic symptoms as well as numerous periods of depressive symptoms lasting for at least two years (1 year in children and adolescents). However, the symptoms do not meet the diagnostic requirements for a hypomanic episode and a depressive episode.

Signs and Symptoms of Bipolar Disorder

People with bipolar disorder experience periods of unusually intense emotion, changes in sleep patterns and activity levels, and unusual behaviors. These distinct periods are called "mood episodes." Mood episodes are drastically different from the moods and behaviors that are typical for the person. Extreme changes in energy, activity, and sleep go along with mood episodes.

People Having a Manic Episode May

- Feel very "up," "high," or "elated"
- Have a lot of energy
- Have increased activity levels
- Feel "jumpy" or "wired"
- Have trouble sleeping
- Become more active than usual
- Talk really fast about a lot of different things
- Be agitated, irritable, or "touchy"
- Feel like their thoughts are going very fast
- Think they can do a lot of things at once

- Do risky things, such as spend a lot of money or have reckless sex

People Having a Depressive Episode May

- Feel very sad, down, empty, or hopeless

- Have very little energy

- Have decreased activity levels

- Have trouble sleeping, they may sleep too little or too much

- Feel like they cannot enjoy anything

- Feel worried and empty

- Have trouble concentrating

- Forget things a lot

- Eat too much or too little

- Feel tired or "slowed down"

- Think about death or suicide

Sometimes a mood episode includes symptoms of both manic and depressive symptoms. This is called an "episode with mixed features." People experiencing an episode with mixed features may feel very sad, empty, or hopeless, while at the same time feeling extremely energized.

Bipolar disorder can be present even when mood swings are less extreme. For example, some people with bipolar disorder experience hypomania, a less severe form of mania. During a hypomanic episode, an individual may feel very good, be highly productive, and function well. The person may not feel that anything is wrong, but family and friends may recognize the mood swings and/or changes in activity levels as possible bipolar disorder. Without proper treatment, people with hypomania may develop severe mania or depression.

How Is Bipolar Disorder Diagnosed?

Proper diagnosis and treatment help people with bipolar disorder lead healthy and productive lives. Talking with a doctor or other licensed mental health professional is the first step for anyone who thinks she or he may have bipolar disorder. The doctor can complete a physical exam to rule out other conditions. If the problems are not caused by other illnesses, the doctor may conduct a mental health evaluation or provide a referral to a trained mental health professional, such as a psychiatrist, who is experienced in diagnosing and treating bipolar disorder.

Bipolar Disorder and Other Illnesses

Some bipolar disorder symptoms are similar to other illnesses, which can make it hard for a doctor to make a diagnosis. Many people have bipolar disorder along with another illness such as anxiety disorder, substance abuse, or an eating disorder. People with bipolar disorder are also at a higher risk for thyroid disease, migraine headaches, heart disease, diabetes, obesity, and other physical illnesses.

Psychosis

Sometimes, a person with severe episodes of mania or depression has psychotic symptoms, such as hallucinations or delusions. The psychotic symptoms tend to match the person's extreme mood. For example:

- Someone having psychotic symptoms during a manic episode may believe she is famous, has a lot of money, or has special powers.

- Someone having psychotic symptoms during a depressive episode may believe he is ruined and penniless, or that he has committed a crime.

As a result, people with bipolar disorder who also have psychotic symptoms are sometimes misdiagnosed with schizophrenia.

Anxiety and Attention Deficit Hyperactivity Disorder

Anxiety disorders and attention deficit hyperactivity disorder (ADHD) are often diagnosed among people with bipolar disorder.

Substance Abuse

People with bipolar disorder may also misuse alcohol or drugs, have relationship problems, or perform poorly in school or at work. Family, friends, and people experiencing symptoms may not recognize these problems as signs of a major mental illness such as bipolar disorder.

Risk Factors of Bipolar Disorder

Scientists are studying the possible causes of bipolar disorder. Most agree that there is no single cause. Instead, it is likely that many factors contribute to the illness or increase risk.

Brain Structure and Functioning

Some studies show how the brains of people with bipolar disorder may differ from the brains of healthy people or people with other mental disorders. Learning more about these differences, along with information from genetic studies, helps scientists better understand bipolar disorder and predict which types of treatment will work most effectively.

Genetics

Some research suggests that people with certain genes are more likely to develop bipolar disorder than others. But genes are not the only risk factor for bipolar disorder. Studies of identical twins have shown that even if one twin develops bipolar disorder, the other twin does not always develop the disorder, despite the fact that identical twins share all of the same genes.

Family History

Bipolar disorder tends to run in families. Children with a parent or sibling who has bipolar disorder are much more likely to develop the illness, compared with children who do not have a family history of the disorder. However, it is important to note that most people with a family history of bipolar disorder will not develop the illness.

Treatments and Therapies of Bipolar Disorder

Treatment helps many people—even those with the most severe forms of bipolar disorder—gain better control of their mood swings and other bipolar symptoms. An effective treatment plan usually includes a combination of medication and psychotherapy (also called "talk therapy"). Bipolar disorder is a lifelong illness. Episodes of mania and depression typically come back over time. Between episodes, many people with bipolar disorder are free of mood changes, but some people may have lingering symptoms. Long-term, continuous treatment helps to control these symptoms.

Medications

Different types of medications can help control symptoms of bipolar disorder. An individual may need to try several different medications before finding ones that work best.

Medications generally used to treat bipolar disorder include:

• Mood stabilizers

• Atypical antipsychotics

• Antidepressants

Anyone taking a medication should:

• Talk with a doctor or pharmacist to understand the risks and benefits of the medication

• Report any concerns about side effects to a doctor right away. The doctor may need to change the dose or try a different medication.

• Avoid stopping a medication without talking to a doctor first. Suddenly stopping a medication may lead to a "rebound" or worsening of bipolar disorder symptoms. Other uncomfortable or potentially dangerous withdrawal effects are also possible.

• Report serious side effects to the U.S. Food and Drug Administration (FDA) MedWatch Adverse Event Reporting program online at www.fda.gov/Safety/MedWatch or by phone at 800-332-1088. Clients and doctors may send reports.

Psychotherapy

When done in combination with medication, psychotherapy (also called "talk therapy") can be an effective treatment for bipolar disorder. It can provide support, education, and guidance to people with bipolar disorder and their families. Some psychotherapy treatments used to treat bipolar disorder include:

• Cognitive-behavioral therapy (CBT)

• Family-focused therapy (FFT)

• Interpersonal and social rhythm therapy (IPSRT)

• Psychoeducation

Other Treatment Options of Bipolar Disorder
Electroconvulsive Therapy

Electroconvulsive Therapy (ECT) can provide relief for people with severe bipolar disorder who have not been able to recover with other treatments. Sometimes ECT is used for bipolar symptoms when other medical conditions, including pregnancy, make taking medications too risky. ECT may cause some short-term side effects, including confusion, disorientation, and memory loss. People with bipolar disorder should discuss possible benefits and risks of ECT with a qualified health professional.

Sleep Medications

People with bipolar disorder who have trouble sleeping usually find that treatment is helpful. However, if sleeplessness does not improve, a doctor may suggest a change in medications. If the problem continues, the doctor may prescribe sedatives or other sleep medications.

Supplements

Not much research has been conducted on herbal or natural supplements and how they may affect bipolar disorder.

It is important for a doctor to know about all prescription drugs, over-the-counter (OTC) medications, and supplements a client is taking. Certain medications and supplements taken together may cause unwanted or dangerous effects.

Keeping a Life Chart

Even with proper treatment, mood changes can occur. Treatment is more effective when a client and doctor work closely together and talk openly about concerns and choices. Keeping a life chart that records daily mood symptoms, treatments, sleep patterns, and life events can help clients and doctors track and treat bipolar disorder most effectively.

Chapter 11

Disruptive Mood Dysregulation Disorder

What Is Disruptive Mood Dysregulation Disorder?

Disruptive mood dysregulation disorder (DMDD) is a childhood condition of extreme irritability, anger, and frequent, intense temper outbursts. DMDD symptoms go beyond a being a "moody" child—children with DMDD experience severe impairment that requires clinical attention.

Sign and Symptoms of Disruptive Mood Dysregulation Disorder

Disruptive mood dysregulation disorder symptoms typically begin before the age of 10, but the diagnosis is not given to children under 6 or adolescents over 18. A child with DMDD experiences:

- Irritable or angry mood most of the day, nearly every day

- Severe temper outbursts (verbal or behavioral) at an average of three or more times per week that are out of keeping with the situation and the child's developmental level

---

This chapter includes text excerpted from "Disruptive Mood Dysregulation Disorder," National Institute of Mental Health (NIMH), January 15, 2017.

- Trouble functioning due to irritability in more than one place (e.g., home, school, with peers)

To be diagnosed with DMDD, a child must have these symptoms steadily for 12 or more months.

Risk Factors of Disruptive Mood Dysregulation Disorder

It is not clear how widespread DMDD is in the general population, but it is common among children who visit pediatric mental-health clinics. Researchers are exploring risk factors and brain mechanisms of this disorder.

Treatment and Therapies of Disruptive Mood Dysregulation Disorder

Disruptive mood dysregulation disorder is a new diagnosis. Therefore, treatment is often based on what has been helpful for other disorders that share the symptoms of irritability and temper tantrums. These disorders include attention deficit hyperactivity disorder (ADHD), anxiety disorders, oppositional defiant disorder (ODD), and major depressive disorder (MDD).

If you think your child has DMDD, it is important to seek treatment. DMDD can impair a child's quality of life (QOL) and school performance and disrupt relationships with her or his family and peers. Children with DMDD may find it hard to participate in activities or make friends. Having DMDD also increases the risk of developing depression or anxiety disorders in adulthood.

While researchers are still determining which treatments work best, two major types of treatment are currently used to treat DMDD symptoms:

- Medication
- Psychological treatments
  - Psychotherapy
  - Parent training
  - Computer-based training

Psychological treatments should be considered first, with medication added later if necessary, or psychological treatments can be provided along with medication from the beginning.

It is important for parents or caregivers to work closely with the doctor to make a treatment decision that is best for their child.

Medication

Many medications used to treat children and adolescents with mental illness are effective in relieving symptoms. However, some of these medications have not been studied in depth and/or do not have U.S. Food and Drug Administration (FDA) approval for use with children or adolescents. All medications have side effects and the need for continuing them should be reviewed frequently with your child's doctor.

Stimulants

Stimulants are medications that are commonly used to treat ADHD. There is evidence that, in children with irritability and ADHD, stimulant medications also decrease irritability.

Stimulants should not be used in individuals with serious heart problems. According to the FDA, people on stimulant medications should be periodically monitored for a change in heart rate and blood pressure.

Antidepressants

Antidepressant medication is sometimes used to treat the irritability and mood problems associated with DMDD. Ongoing studies are testing whether these medicines are effective for this problem. It is important to note that, although antidepressants are safe and effective for many people, they carry a risk of suicidal thoughts and behavior in children and teens. A "black box" warning—the most serious type of warning that a prescription can carry—has been added to the labels of these medications to alert parents and patients to this risk. For this reason, a child taking an antidepressant should be monitored closely, especially when they first start taking the medication.

Atypical Antipsychotic

An atypical antipsychotic medication may be prescribed for children with very severe temper outbursts that involve physical aggression toward people or property. Risperidone and aripiprazole are FDA-approved for the treatment of irritability associated with autism and are sometimes used to treat DMDD. Atypical antipsychotic medications are associated with many significant side-effects, including suicidal ideation/behaviors, weight gain, metabolic abnormalities, sedation, movement disorders, hormone changes, and others.

Psychological Treatments
Psychotherapy

Cognitive-behavioral therapy (CBT), a type of psychotherapy, is commonly used to teach children and teens how to deal with thoughts and feelings that contribute to their feeling depressed or anxious. Clinicians can use similar techniques to teach children to more effectively regulate their mood and to increase their tolerance for frustration. The therapy also teaches coping skills for regulating anger and ways to identify and relabel the distorted perceptions that contribute to outbursts.

Parent Training

Parent training aims to help parents interact with a child in a way that will reduce aggression and irritable behavior and improve the parent-child relationship. Multiple studies show that such interventions can be effective. Specifically, parent training teaches parents more effective ways to respond to irritable behavior, such as anticipating events that might lead a child to have a temper outburst and working ahead to avert the outburst. Training also focuses on the importance of predictability, being consistent with children, and rewarding positive behavior.

Computer-Based Training

Evidence suggests that irritable youth with DMDD may be prone to misperceiving ambiguous facial expressions as angry. There is preliminary evidence that computer-based training designed to correct this problem may help youth with DMDD or severe irritability.

Chapter 12

Premenstrual Syndrome and Dysphoric Disorder

Facts about Premenstrual Syndrome
What Is Premenstrual Syndrome?

Premenstrual syndrome (PMS) is a combination of physical and emotional symptoms that many women get after ovulation and before the start of their menstrual period. Researchers think that PMS happens in the days after ovulation because estrogen and progesterone levels begin falling dramatically if you are not pregnant. PMS symptoms go away within a few days after a woman's period starts as hormone levels begin rising again.

Some women get their periods without any signs of PMS or only very mild symptoms. For others, PMS symptoms may be so severe that it makes it hard to do everyday activities such as going to work or school. Severe PMS symptoms may be a sign of premenstrual dysphoric disorder (PMDD). PMS goes away when you no longer get a period,

This chapter contains text excerpted from the following sources: Text under the heading "Facts about Premenstrual Syndrome" is excerpted from "Premenstrual Syndrome (PMS)," Office on Women's Health (OWH), U.S.Department of Health and Human Services (HHS), March 16, 2018; Text under the heading "Facts about Premenstrual Dysphoric Disorder" is excerpted from "Premenstrual Dysphoric Disorder (PMDD)," Office on Women's Health (OWH), U.S.Department of Health and Human Services (HHS), March 16, 2018.

such as after menopause. After pregnancy, PMS might come back, but you might have different PMS symptoms.

Who Gets Premenstrual Syndrome

As many as three in four women say they get PMS symptoms at some point in their lifetime. For most women PMS symptoms are mild.

Less than five percent of women of childbearing age get a more severe form of PMS, called "premenstrual dysphoric disorder" (PMDD).

Premenstrual syndrome may happen more often in women who:

- Have high levels of stress

- Have a family history of depression

- Have a personal history of either postpartum depression or depression

Does Premenstrual Syndrome Change with Age?

Yes. PMS symptoms may get worse as you reach your late 30s or 40s and approach menopause and are in the transition to menopause, called "perimenopause."

This is especially true for women whose moods are sensitive to changing hormone levels during the menstrual cycle. In the years leading up to menopause, your hormone levels also go up and down in an unpredictable way as your body slowly transitions to menopause. You may get the same mood changes, or they may get worse.

Premenstrual syndrome stops after menopause when you no longer get a period.

What Are the Symptoms of Premenstrual Syndrome?

Premenstrual syndrome symptoms are different for every woman. You may get physical symptoms, such as bloating or gassiness, or emotional symptoms, such as sadness, or both. Your symptoms may also change throughout your life.

Physical Symptoms

- Swollen or tender breasts

- Constipation or diarrhea

- Bloating or a gassy feeling

- Cramping
- Headache or backache
- Clumsiness
- Lower tolerance for noise or light

Emotional or Mental Symptoms

- Irritability or hostile behavior
- Feeling tired
- Sleep problems (sleeping too much or too little)
- Appetite changes or food cravings
- Trouble with concentration or memory
- Tension or anxiety
- Depression, feelings of sadness, or crying spells
- Mood swings
- Less interest in sex

Talk to your doctor or nurse if your symptoms bother you or affect your daily life.

What Causes Premenstrual Syndrome

Researchers do not know exactly what causes PMS. Changes in hormone levels during the menstrual cycle may play a role. These changing hormone levels may affect some women more than others.

How Is Premenstrual Syndrome Diagnosed?

There is no single test for PMS. Your doctor will talk with you about your symptoms, including when they happen and how much they affect your life.

You probably have PMS if you have symptoms that:

- Happen in the five days before your period for at least three menstrual cycles in a row
- End within four days after your period starts
- Keep you from enjoying or doing some of your normal activities

Keep track of which PMS symptoms you have and how severe they are for a few months. Write down your symptoms each day on a calendar or with an app on your phone. Take this information with you when you see your doctor.

How Does Premenstrual Syndrome Affect Other Health Problems?

About half of women who need relief from PMS also have another health problem, which may get worse in the time before their menstrual period. These health problems share many symptoms with PMS and include:

Depression and Anxiety Disorders

These are the most common conditions that overlap with PMS. Depression and anxiety symptoms are similar to PMS and may get worse before or during your period.

Myalgic Encephalomyelitis / Chronic Fatigue Syndrome

Some women report that their symptoms often get worse right before their period. Research shows that women with myalgic encephalomyelitis/chronic fatigue syndrome (ME/CFS) may also be more likely to have heavy menstrual bleeding and early or premature menopause.

Irritable Bowel Syndrome

Irritable bowel syndrome (IBS) causes cramping, bloating, and gas. Your IBS symptoms may get worse right before your period.

Bladder Pain Syndrome

Women with bladder pain syndrome (BPS) are more likely to have painful cramps during PMS.

Premenstrual syndrome may also worsen some health problems, such as asthma, allergies, and migraines.

What Can I Do at Home to Relieve Premenstrual Syndrome Symptoms?

These tips will help you be healthier in general and may relieve some of your PMS symptoms.

- **Get regular aerobic physical activity throughout the Month.** Exercise can help with symptoms such as depression, difficulty concentrating, and fatigue.

- **Choose healthy foods most of the time.** Avoiding foods and drinks with caffeine, salt, and sugar in the two weeks before your period may lessen many PMS symptoms.

- **Get enough sleep.** Try to get about eight hours of sleep each night. Lack of sleep is linked to depression and anxiety and can make PMS symptoms such as moodiness worse.

- **Find healthy ways to cope with stress.** Talk to your friends or write in a journal. Some women also find yoga, massage, or meditation helpful.

- **Do not smoke.** In one large study, women who smoked reported more PMS symptoms and worse PMS symptoms than women who did not smoke.

What Medicines Can Treat Premenstrual Syndrome Symptoms?

Over-the-counter (OTC) and prescription medicines can help treat some PMS symptoms.

You can buy OTC pain relievers in most stores that may help lessen physical symptoms, such as cramps, headaches, backaches, and breast tenderness. These include:

- Ibuprofen

- Naproxen

- Aspirin

Some women find that taking an OTC pain reliever right before their period starts reduces the amount of pain and bleeding they have during their period.

Prescription medicines may help if OTC pain medicines do not work:

- **Hormonal birth control** may help with the physical symptoms of PMS, but it may make other symptoms worse. You may need to try several different types of birth control before you find one that helps your symptoms.

- **Antidepressants** can help relieve the emotional symptoms of PMS for some women when other medicines do not help.

Selective serotonin reuptake inhibitors, or SSRIs, are the most common type of antidepressant used to treat PMS.

- **Diuretics** (water pills) may reduce symptoms of bloating and breast tenderness.

- **Antianxiety** medicine may help reduce feelings of anxiousness.

All medicines have risks. Talk to your doctor or nurse about the benefits and risks.

Should I Take Vitamins or Minerals to Treat Premenstrual Syndrome Symptoms?

Maybe. Studies show that certain vitamins and minerals may help relieve some PMS symptoms. The U.S. Food and Drug Administration (FDA) does not regulate vitamins or minerals and herbal supplements in the same way they regulate medicines. Talk to your doctor before taking any supplements.

Studies have found benefits for:

- **Calcium.** Studies show that calcium can help reduce some PMS symptoms, such as fatigue, cravings, and depression. Calcium is found in foods such as milk, cheese, and yogurt. Some foods, such as orange juice, cereal, and bread, have calcium added (fortified). You can also take a calcium supplement.

- **Vitamin B_6.** Vitamin B_6 may help with PMS symptoms, including moodiness, irritability, forgetfulness, bloating, and anxiety. Vitamin B_6 can be found in foods such as fish, poultry, potatoes, fruit (except for citrus fruits), and fortified cereals. You can also take it as a dietary supplement.

Studies have found mixed results for:

- **Magnesium.** Magnesium may help relieve some PMS symptoms, including migraines. If you get menstrual migraines, talk to your doctor about whether you need more magnesium. Magnesium is found in green, leafy vegetables such as spinach, as well as in nuts, whole grains, and fortified cereals. You can also take a supplement.

- **Polyunsaturated fatty acids.** Studies show that taking a supplement with one to two grams of polyunsaturated fatty acids (omega-3 and omega-6) may help reduce cramps and other PMS symptoms. Good sources of polyunsaturated fatty acids include flaxseed, nuts, fish, and green leafy vegetables.

What Complementary or Alternative Medicines May Help Relieve Premenstrual Syndrome Symptoms?

Some women report relief from their PMS symptoms with yoga or meditation. Others say herbal supplements help relieve symptoms. Talk with your doctor or nurse before taking any of these supplements. They may interact with other medicines you take, making your other medicine not work or cause dangerous side effects. The U.S. Food and Drug Administration (FDA) does not regulate herbal supplements at the same level that it regulates medicines.

Some research studies show relief from PMS symptoms with these herbal supplements, but other studies do not. Many herbal supplements should not be used with other medicines. Some herbal supplements women use to ease PMS symptoms include:

- **Black cohosh.** The underground stems and root of black cohosh are used fresh or dried to make tea, capsules, pills, or liquid extracts. Black cohosh is most often used to help treat menopausal symptoms, and some women use it to help relieve PMS symptoms.

- **Chasteberry.** Dried ripe chasteberry is used to prepare liquid extracts or pills that some women take to relieve PMS symptoms. Women taking hormonal birth control or hormone therapy for menopausal symptoms should not take chasteberry.

- **Evening primrose oil.** The oil is taken from the plant's seeds and put into capsules. Some women report that the pill helps relieve PMS symptoms, but the research results are mixed.

Facts about Premenstrual Dysphoric Disorder
What Is Premenstrual Dysphoric Disorder?

Premenstrual dysphoric disorder (PMDD) is a condition similar to PMS that also happens in a week or two before your period starts as hormone levels begin to fall after ovulation. PMDD causes more severe symptoms than PMS, including severe depression, irritability, and tension.

Who Gets Premenstrual Dysphoric Disorder

Premenstrual dysphoric disorder affects up to five percent of women of childbearing age. Many women with PMDD may also have anxiety or depression.

What Are the Symptoms of Premenstrual Dysphoric Disorder?

Symptoms of PMDD include:

- Lasting irritability or anger that may affect other people
- Feelings of sadness or despair, or even thoughts of suicide
- Feelings of tension or anxiety
- Panic attacks
- Mood swings or crying often
- Lack of interest in daily activities and relationships
- Trouble thinking or focusing
- Tiredness or low energy
- Food cravings or binge eating
- Trouble sleeping
- Feeling out of control
- Physical symptoms, such as cramps, bloating, breast tenderness, headaches, and joint or muscle pain

What Causes Premenstrual Dysphoric Disorder

Researchers do not know for sure what causes PMDD. Hormonal changes throughout the menstrual cycle may play a role. A brain chemical called "serotonin" may also play a role in PMDD. Serotonin levels change throughout the menstrual cycle. Some women may be more sensitive to these changes.

How Is Premenstrual Dysphoric Disorder Diagnosed?

Your doctor will talk to you about your health history and do a physical examination. You will need to keep a calendar or diary of your symptoms to help your doctor diagnose PMDD.

You must have five or more PMDD symptoms, including one mood-related symptom, to be diagnosed with PMDD.

How Is Premenstrual Dysphoric Disorder Treated?

Treatments for PMDD include:

- **Antidepressants** called "selective serotonin reuptake inhibitors" (SSRIs). SSRIs change serotonin levels in the brain. The U.S. Food and Drug Administration (FDA) approved three SSRIs to treat PMDD

  - Sertraline

  - Fluoxetine

  - Paroxetine HCI

- **Birth control pills.** The FDA has approved a birth control pill containing drospirenone and ethinyl estradiol to treat PMDD.

- **Over-the-counter (OTC) pain relievers** may help relieve physical symptoms, such as cramps, joint pain, headaches, backaches, and breast tenderness. These include:

  - Ibuprofen

  - Naproxen

  - Aspirin

- **Stress management,** such as relaxation techniques and spending time on activities you enjoy.

Making healthy changes, such as eating a healthy combination of foods across the food groups, cutting back on salty and sugary foods, and getting more physical activity, may also help relieve some PMDD symptoms. But PMDD can be serious enough that some women should go to a doctor or nurse to discuss treatment options. And, if you are thinking of hurting yourself or others, call 911 immediately.

Chapter 13

Psychotic Depression

Chapter Contents

Section 13.1

Psychosis

This section includes text excerpted from "RAISE Questions and Answers," National Institute of Mental Health (NIMH), October 7, 2015. Reviewed October 2019.

What Is Psychosis?

The word "psychosis" is used to describe conditions that affect the mind, where there has been some loss of contact with reality. When someone becomes ill in this way it is called a "psychotic episode." During a period of psychosis, a person's thoughts and perceptions are disturbed and the individual may have difficulty understanding what is real and what is not. Symptoms of psychosis include delusions (false beliefs) and hallucinations (seeing or hearing things that others do not see or hear). Other symptoms include incoherent speech and behavior that is inappropriate for the situation. A person in a psychotic episode may also experience depression, anxiety, sleep problems, social withdrawal, lack of motivation and difficulty functioning overall.

How Common Is Psychosis?

Approximately 3 percent of the people in the United States (3 out of 100 people) will experience psychosis at some time in their lives. About 100,000 adolescents and young adults in the United States experience the first episode psychosis each year.

What Causes Psychosis

There is no specific cause of psychosis. Psychosis may be a symptom of mental illness, such as schizophrenia or bipolar disorder, but there are other causes, as well. Sleep deprivation, some general medical conditions, certain prescription medications, and the abuse of alcohol or other drugs, such as marijuana, can cause psychotic symptoms. Because there are many different causes of psychosis, it is important to see a qualified healthcare professional (e.g., psychologist, psychiatrist, or trained social worker) in order to receive a thorough assessment and accurate diagnosis. A mental illness, such as schizophrenia, is typically diagnosed by excluding all of these other causes of psychosis.

What Is the Connection between Psychosis and Schizophrenia?

"Schizophrenia" is a mental illness characterized by periods of psychosis. An individual must experience psychotic symptoms for at least six months in order to be diagnosed with schizophrenia. However, a person may experience psychosis and never be diagnosed with schizophrenia or any other mental health condition. This is because there are many different causes of psychosis, such as sleep deprivation, general medical conditions, the use of certain prescription medications, and the abuse of alcohol or other drugs.

What Are the Early Warning Signs of Psychosis?

Typically, a person will show changes in their behavior before psychosis develops. The list below includes behavioral warning signs for psychosis.

- Worrisome drop in grades or job performance
- New trouble thinking clearly or concentrating
- Suspiciousness, paranoid ideas or uneasiness with others
- Withdrawing socially, spending a lot more time alone than usual
- Unusual, overly intense new ideas, strange feelings or having no feelings at all
- Decline in self-care or personal hygiene
- Difficulty telling reality from fantasy
- Confused speech or trouble communicating

Any one of these items by itself may not be significant, but someone with several of the items on the list should consult a mental health professional. A qualified psychologist, psychiatrist or trained social worker will be able to make a diagnosis and help develop a treatment plan. Early treatment of psychosis increases the chance of a successful recovery. If you notice these changes in behavior and they begin to intensify or do not go away, it is important to seek help.

What Does "Duration of Untreated Psychosis" Mean?

The length of time between the start of psychotic symptoms and the beginning of treatment is called the "duration of untreated psychosis"

(DUP). In general, research has shown that treatments for psychosis work better when they are delivered closer to the time when symptoms first appear.

Do People Recover from Psychosis?

With early diagnosis and appropriate treatment, it is possible to recover from psychosis. Many people who receive early treatment never have another psychotic episode. For other people, recovery means the ability to live a fulfilling and productive life, even if psychotic symptoms return sometimes.

What Should I Do If I Think Someone Is Having a Psychotic Episode?

If you think someone you know is experiencing psychosis, encourage the person to seek treatment as early as possible. Psychosis can be treated effectively, and early intervention increases the chance of a successful outcome. To find a qualified treatment program, contact your healthcare professional. If someone is having a psychotic episode or is in distress or you are concerned about their safety, consider taking them to the nearest emergency room, or call 911.

Why Is Early Treatment Important?

Left untreated, psychotic symptoms can lead to disruptions in school and work, strained family relations, and separation from friends. The longer the symptoms go untreated, the greater the risk of additional problems. These problems can include substance abuse, going to the emergency department, being admitted to the hospital, having legal trouble, or becoming homeless.

People experiencing first episode psychosis in the United States typically have symptoms for more than a year before receiving treatment. It is important to reduce this duration of untreated psychosis because people tend to do better when they receive effective treatment as early as possible.

What Is Coordinated Speciality Care?

"Coordinated specialty care (CSC)" is a recovery-oriented treatment program for people with first episode psychosis (FEP). CSC uses a team of specialists who work with the client to create a personal treatment plan. The specialists offer psychotherapy, medication management geared to individuals with FEP, case management, family education, and support, and work or education support, depending on the individual's needs and preferences. The client and the team work together to make treatment decisions, involving family members as much as possible. The goal is to link the individual with a CSC team as soon as possible after psychotic symptoms begin.

What Is Shared Decision Making and How Does It Work in Early Treatment?

Shared decision making means individuals and their healthcare providers work together to find the best treatment options based on the individual's unique needs and preferences. Clients, treatment-team members, and (when appropriate) relatives are active participants in the process.

What Is the Role of Medication in Treatment?

Antipsychotic medications help reduce psychotic symptoms. Like medications for any illness, antipsychotic drugs have benefits and risks. Individuals should talk with their healthcare providers about the benefits of taking antipsychotic medication as well as potential side effects, dosage, and preferences like taking a daily pill or a monthly injection.

What Is Supported Employment and Education and Why Is It Important?

For young adults, psychosis can hurt school attendance and academic performance or make it difficult to find or keep a job. Supported Employment and Education (SEE) is one way to help individuals return to work or school. A SEE specialist helps clients develop the skills they need to achieve school and work goals. In addition, the specialist can be a bridge between clients and educators or employers. SEE services are an important part of coordinated specialty care and are valued by many clients.

Section 13.2

Schizophrenia

This section includes text excerpted from "Schizophrenia," National
Institute of Mental Health (NIMH), January 17, 2018.

What Is Schizophrenia?

Schizophrenia is a serious and lifelong neurodevelopmental disorder that affects how a person thinks, feels, and behaves. People with
schizophrenia may experience delusions, hallucinations, disorganized
speech or behavior, and impaired cognitive ability. They may hear
voices or see things that are not there. They may believe other people
are reading their minds, controlling their thoughts, or plotting to harm
them. These behaviors can be scary and upsetting to people with the
illness and make them withdrawn or extremely agitated. It can also
be scary and upsetting to the people around them.

People with schizophrenia may sometimes talk about strange or
unusual ideas, which can make it difficult to carry on a conversation.
They may sit for hours without moving or talking. Sometimes people
with schizophrenia seem perfectly fine until they talk about what they
are thinking. People with schizophrenia may cope with symptoms
throughout their lives, but treatment helps many to recover sufficiently
and pursue their life goals.

What Causes Schizophrenia

Many factors may cause schizophrenia, including:

- **Genetics.** Schizophrenia sometimes runs in families. However,
  it is important to know that just because someone in a family
  has schizophrenia, it does not mean that other members of the
  family will have it as well.

- **Environment.** Many environmental factors may be involved,
  such as living in poverty, stressful surroundings, and exposure
  to viruses or nutritional problems before birth.

- **Disruptions in brain structures, brain function, and brain
  chemistry.** These disruptions could be the result of genetic or
  environmental factors and, in turn, may cause schizophrenia.

Researchers have learned a lot about schizophrenia, but more
research is needed to help explain its causes.

What Are the Signs of Schizophrenia?

It is important to know the signs and symptoms of schizophrenia and seek help early. The signs usually appear between ages 16 and 30. In rare cases, children can have schizophrenia too. Schizophrenia symptoms fall into three categories: positive, negative, and cognitive.

Positive Symptoms

"Positive" symptoms are referred to as positive because the symptoms are additional behaviors not generally seen in healthy people. For some people, these symptoms come and go. For others, the symptoms become stable over time. These symptoms can be severe, but at other times unnoticeable. Positive symptoms include:

- **Hallucinations.** When a person sees, hears, smells, tastes, or feels things that are not real. Hearing voices is common for people with schizophrenia. People who hear voices may hear them for a long time before family or friends notice a problem.

- **Delusions.** When a person believes things that are not true. For example, a person may believe that people on the radio and television are talking directly to her or him. Sometimes people who have delusions may believe that they are in danger or that others are trying to hurt them.

- **Thought disorders.** When a person has ways of thinking that are odd or illogical. People with thought disorders may have trouble organizing their thoughts. Sometimes a person will stop talking in the middle of a thought or make up words that have no meaning.

- **Movement disorders.** When a person exhibits abnormal body movements. A person may repeat certain motions over and over. This is called "stereotypies." At the other extreme, a person may stop moving or talking for a while, which is a rare condition called "catatonia."

Negative Symptoms

"Negative" symptoms refer to social withdrawal, difficulty showing emotions, or difficulty functioning normally. People with negative symptoms may need help with everyday tasks. Negative symptoms include:

91

- Talking in a dull voice
- Showing no facial expression, such as a smile or frown
- Having trouble experiencing happiness
- Having trouble planning and sticking with an activity, such as grocery shopping
- Talking very little to other people, even when it is important

These symptoms are harder to recognize as part of schizophrenia and can be mistaken for depression or other conditions.

Cognitive Symptoms

Cognitive symptoms are not easy to see, but they can make it hard for people to have a job or take care of themselves. The level of cognitive function is one of the best predictors of a person's ability to improve how they function overall. Often, these symptoms are detected only when specific tests are performed. Cognitive symptoms include:

- Difficulty processing information to make decisions
- Problems using the information immediately after learning it
- Trouble paying attention

Risk of Violence

Most people with schizophrenia are not violent. If a person has symptoms of schizophrenia, it is important to help her or him get treatment as quickly as possible. The risk of violence is greatest when schizophrenia is untreated since the illness may get worse over time. People with schizophrenia are much more likely than those without the illness, to be harmed by others as well as harm themselves.

Drugs and Alcohol

It is common for people with schizophrenia to have problems with illicit drugs and alcohol. A treatment program that includes treatment for both illnesses is critical for recovery because the misuse of drugs and alcohol can interfere with treatment for schizophrenia. Drug abuse can increase the risk of suicide, trauma, and homelessness in people with schizophrenia as well as increase the risk of developing other mental illnesses.

How Is Schizophrenia Treated?

Two main types of treatment can help with symptoms: antipsychotic medications and psychosocial treatments.

Antipsychotic Medications

Antipsychotic medications help patients with psychotic symptoms of schizophrenia. Some people have side effects when they start taking medications, but most side effects go away after a few days. People respond to antipsychotic medications differently, so it is important to report any of these side effects to a doctor. Sometimes a person needs to try several medications before finding the right one.

A patient should not stop taking a medication without first talking to a doctor. Suddenly stopping medication can be dangerous, and it can make schizophrenia symptoms worse. Choosing the right medication, medication dose, and treatment plan should be done under an expert's care and based on an individual's needs and medical situation. Only an expert clinician can help a patient decide whether the medication's ability to help is worth the risk of a side effect.

Psychosocial Treatments

Psychosocial treatments help patients deal with everyday challenges of schizophrenia. These treatments are often most helpful after patients find a medication that works. Examples of treatment include:

- **Family education.** Teaches the whole family how to cope with the illness and help their loved ones.

- **Illness management skills.** Helps the patient learn about schizophrenia and manage it from day-to-day.

- **Cognitive-behavioral therapy (CBT).** Helps the patient identify current problems and how to solve them. A CBT therapist focuses on changing unhelpful patterns of thinking and behavior.

- **Rehabilitation.** Helps with getting and keeping a job or going to school and everyday living skills.

- **Peer counseling.** Encourages individuals to receive help from other people who are further along in their recovery from schizophrenia.

- **Self-help groups.** Provides support from other people with the illness and their families.

- **Treatment for drug and alcohol misuse.** Is often combined with other treatments for schizophrenia.

Coordinated Speciality Care

This treatment model integrates medication, psychosocial therapies, case management, family involvement, and supported education and employment services, all aimed at reducing symptoms and improving quality of life (QOL). Coordinated Speciality Care (CSC) is most effective when the patient receives coordinated specialty care treatment in the earliest stages of the disorder.

Chapter 14

Seasonal Affective Disorder

Seasonal affective disorder (SAD) is a type of depression that comes and goes with the seasons, typically starting in the late fall and early winter and going away during the spring and summer. Depressive episodes linked to the summer can occur but are much less common than winter episodes of SAD.

Signs and Symptoms of Seasonal Affective Disorder

Seasonal affective disorder is not considered as a separate disorder. It is a type of depression displaying a recurring seasonal pattern. To be diagnosed with SAD, people must meet full criteria for major depression coinciding with specific seasons (appearing in the winter or summer months) for at least two years. Seasonal depressions must be much more frequent than any nonseasonal depressions.

Symptoms of Major Depression

- Feeling depressed most of the day, nearly every day
- Feeling hopeless or worthless
- Having low energy

This chapter includes text excerpted from "Seasonal Affective Disorder," National Institute of Mental Health (NIMH), March 2016. Reviewed October 2019.

- Losing interest in activities you once enjoyed

- Having problems with sleep

- Experiencing changes in your appetite or weight

- Feeling sluggish or agitated

- Having difficulty concentrating

- Having frequent thoughts of death or suicide

Symptoms of the Winter Pattern of Seasonal Affective Disorder

- Having low energy

- Hypersomnia

- Overeating

- Weight gain

- Craving for carbohydrates

- Social withdrawal (feel like "hibernating")

Symptoms of the Less Frequently Occurring Summer Seasonal Affective Disorder

- Poor appetite with associated weight loss

- Insomnia

- Agitation

- Restlessness

- Anxiety

- Episodes of violent behavior

Risk Factors of Seasonal Affective Disorder

Attributes that may increase your risk of SAD include:

- **Being female.** SAD is diagnosed four times more often in women than in men.

- **Living far from the equator.** SAD is more frequent in people who live far north or south of the equator. For example, one percent of those who live in Florida and nine percent of those who live in New England or Alaska suffer from SAD.

- **Family history.** People with a family history of other types of depression are more likely to develop SAD than people who do not have a family history of depression.

- **Having depression or bipolar disorder.** The symptoms of depression may worsen with the seasons if you have one of these conditions (but SAD is diagnosed only if seasonal depressions are the most common).

- **Younger age.** Younger adults have a higher risk of SAD than older adults. SAD has been reported even in children and teens.

The causes of SAD are unknown, but research has found some biological clues:

- **People with SAD may have trouble regulating one of the key neurotransmitters involved in mood, serotonin.** One study found that people with SAD have five percent more serotonin transporter protein in winter months than summer months. Higher serotonin transporter protein leaves less serotonin available at the synapse because the function of the transporter is to recycle neurotransmitters back into the presynaptic neuron.

- **People with SAD may overproduce the hormone melatonin.** Darkness increases the production of melatonin, which regulates sleep. As winter days become shorter, melatonin production increases, leaving people with SAD to feel sleepier and more lethargic, often with delayed circadian rhythms.

- **People with SAD also may produce less Vitamin D.** Vitamin D is believed to play a role in serotonin activity. Vitamin D insufficiency may be associated with clinically significant depression symptoms.

Treatments and Therapies of Seasonal Affective Disorder

There are four major types of treatment for SAD:

- Medication
- Light therapy

- Psychotherapy

- Vitamin D

These may be used alone or in combination.

Medication

Selective serotonin reuptake inhibitors (SSRIs) are used to treat SAD. The U.S. Food and Drug Administration (FDA) has also approved the use of bupropion, another type of antidepressant, for treating SAD. As with other medications, there are side effects to SSRIs. Talk to your doctor about the possible risks of using this medication for your condition. You may need to try several different antidepressant medications before finding the one that improves your symptoms without causing problematic side effects.

Light Therapy

Light therapy has been a mainstay of treatment for SAD since the 1980s. The idea behind light therapy is to replace the diminished sunshine of the fall and winter months using daily exposure to bright, artificial light. Symptoms of SAD may be relieved by sitting in front of a lightbox first thing in the morning, on a daily basis from the early fall until spring. Most typically, light boxes filter out the ultraviolet rays and require 20 to 60 minutes of exposure to 10,000 lux of cool-white fluorescent light, an amount that is about 20 times greater than ordinary indoor lighting.

Psychotherapy

Cognitive-behavioral therapy (CBT) is a type of psychotherapy that is effective for SAD. Traditional cognitive behavioral therapy has been adapted for use with SAD (CBT-SAD). CBT-SAD relies on basic techniques of CBT such as identifying negative thoughts and replacing them with more positive thoughts along with a technique called "behavioral activation." Behavioral activation seeks to help the person identify activities that are engaging and pleasurable, whether indoors or outdoors, to improve coping with winter.

Vitamin D

At present, vitamin D supplementation by itself is not regarded as an effective SAD treatment. The reason behind its use is that low blood levels of vitamin D were found in people with SAD. The low levels are usually due to insufficient dietary intake or insufficient exposure to sunshine. However, the evidence for its use has been mixed. While some studies suggest vitamin D supplementation may be as effective as light therapy, others found vitamin D had no effect.

Part Three

Who Develops Depression

Chapter 15

People and Depression

Not everyone who is depressed experiences every symptom. Some people experience only a few symptoms. Some people have many. The severity and frequency of symptoms, and how long they last, will vary depending on the individual and her or his particular illness. Symptoms may also vary depending on the stage of the illness.

Women and Depression

Women with depression do not all experience the same symptoms. However, women with depression typically have symptoms of sadness, worthlessness, and guilt.

Depression is more common among women than among men. Biological, life cycle, hormonal, and psychosocial factors that are unique to women may be linked to their higher depression rate. For example, women are especially vulnerable to developing postpartum depression after giving birth, when hormonal and physical changes and the new responsibility of caring for a newborn can be overwhelming.

Children and Depression

Before puberty, girls and boys are equally likely to develop depression. A child with depression may pretend to be sick, refuse to go to school, cling to a parent, or worry that a parent may die. Because

This chapter includes text excerpted from "Depression: What You Need to Know," National Institute of Mental Health (NIMH), December 13, 2015. Reviewed October 2019.

normal behaviors vary from one childhood stage to another, it can be difficult to tell whether a child is just going through a temporary "phase" or is suffering from depression. Sometimes the parents become worried about how the child's behavior has changed, or a teacher mentions that "your child does not seem to be himself." In such a case, if a visit to the child's pediatrician rules out physical symptoms, the doctor will probably suggest that the child be evaluated, preferably by a mental health professional who specializes in the treatment of children. Most chronic mood disorders, such as depression, begin as high levels of anxiety in children.

Teens and Depression

The teen years can be tough. Teens are forming an identity apart from their parents, grappling with gender issues and emerging sexuality, and making independent decisions for the first time in their lives. Occasional bad moods are to be expected, but depression is different.

Older children and teens with depression may sulk, get into trouble at school, be negative and irritable, and feel misunderstood. If you are unsure if an adolescent in your life is depressed or just "being a teenager," consider how long the symptoms have been present, how severe they are, and how different the teen is acting from her or his usual self. Teens with depression may also have other disorders such as anxiety, eating disorders, or substance abuse. They may also be at higher risk for suicide.

Children and teenagers usually rely on parents, teachers, or other caregivers to recognize their suffering and get them the treatment they need. Many teens do not know where to go for mental-health treatment or believe that treatment will not help. Others do not get help because they think depression symptoms may be just part of the typical stress of school or being a teen. Some teens worry what other people will think if they seek mental-healthcare.

Depression often persists, recurs, and continues into adulthood, especially if left untreated. If you suspect a child or teenager in your life is suffering from depression, speak up right away.

Men and Depression

Men often experience depression differently than women. While women with depression are more likely to have feelings of sadness, worthlessness, and excessive guilt, men are more likely to be very tired, irritable, lose interest in once pleasurable activities, and have difficulty sleeping.

Men may turn to alcohol or drugs when they are depressed. They also may become frustrated, discouraged, irritable, angry, and sometimes abusive. Some men may throw themselves into their work to avoid talking about their depression with family or friends, or behave recklessly. And although more women attempt suicide, many more men die by suicide in the United States.

Older Adults and Depression

Having depression for a long period of time is not a normal part of growing older. Most older adults feel satisfied with their lives, despite having more illnesses or physical problems. But depression in older adults may be difficult to recognize because they may show different, less obvious symptoms.

Sometimes older people who are depressed appear to feel tired, have trouble sleeping, or seem grumpy and irritable. Confusion or attention problems caused by depression can sometimes look like Alzheimer disease or other brain disorders. Older adults also may have more medical conditions such as heart disease, stroke, or cancer, which may cause depressive symptoms. Or they may be taking medications with side effects that contribute to depression.

Some older adults may experience what doctors call vascular depression, also called "arteriosclerotic depression" or "subcortical ischemic depression." Vascular depression may result when blood vessels become less flexible and harden over time, becoming constricted. The hardening of vessels prevents normal blood flow to the body's organs, including the brain. Those with vascular depression may have or be at risk for heart disease or stroke.

Sometimes it can be difficult to distinguish grief from major depression. Grief after loss of a loved one is a normal reaction and generally does not require professional mental-health treatment. However, grief that is complicated and lasts for a very long time following a loss may require treatment.

Older adults who had depression when they were younger are more at risk for developing depression in late life than those who did not have the illness earlier in life.

Chapter 16

Women and Depression

Depression Is a Real Medical Condition

Depression is a common but serious mood disorder. Depression symptoms can interfere with your ability to work, sleep, study, eat, and enjoy your life. Although the causes of depression are still being studied, research suggests that depression is caused by a combination of genetic, biological, environmental, and psychological factors. Most people with depression need treatment to feel better.

You Cannot Just 'Snap Out' of Depression

Well-meaning friends or family members may try to tell someone with depression to "snap out of it," "just be positive," or "you can be happier if you just try harder." But depression is not a sign of a person's weakness or a character flaw. The truth is that most people who experience depression need treatment to get better.

If you are a friend or family member of a woman with depression, you can offer emotional support, understanding, patience, and encouragement. But never dismiss her feelings. Encourage her to talk to her doctor and remind her that with time and treatment, she can feel better.

This chapter includes text excerpted from "Depression in Women: 5 Things You Should Know," National Institute of Mental Health (NIMH), February 12 2009. Reviewed October 2019.

Most People with Depression Need Treatment to Feel Better

If you think you may have depression, start by making an appointment to see your doctor or healthcare provider. This could be your primary doctor or a health provider who specializes in diagnosing and treating mental-health conditions (for example, a psychologist or psychiatrist). Certain medications, and some medical conditions, such as viruses or a thyroid disorder, can cause the same symptoms as depression. A doctor can rule out these possibilities by doing a physical exam, interview, and lab tests. Your doctor or healthcare provider will examine you and talk to you about treatment options and next steps.

Depression Can Hurt

Sadness is only a small part of depression. In fact, some people with depression do not feel sadness at all. A person with depression may also experience many physical symptoms, such as aches or pains, headaches, cramps, or digestive problems. Someone with depression may also have trouble with sleeping, waking up in the morning, and feeling tired.

If you have been experiencing any of the following signs and symptoms for at least two weeks, you may be suffering from depression:

- Persistent sad, anxious, or "empty" mood
- Feelings of hopelessness or pessimism
- Irritability
- Feelings of guilt, worthlessness, or helplessness
- Decreased energy or fatigue
- Difficulty sleeping, early-morning awakening, or oversleeping
- Loss of interest or pleasure in hobbies and activities
- Moving or talking more slowly
- Feeling restless or having trouble sitting still
- Difficulty concentrating, remembering, or making decisions
- Appetite and/or weight changes
- Thoughts of death or suicide, or suicide attempts
- Aches or pains, headaches, cramps, or digestive problems without a clear physical cause and/or that do not ease even with treatment

Talk to your doctor about these symptoms. Be honest, clear, and concise—the doctor needs to know how you feel. Your doctor may ask when your symptoms started, what time of day they happen, how long they last, how often they occur, if they seem to be getting worse or better, and if they keep you from going out or doing your usual activities. It may help to take the time to make some notes about your symptoms before your doctor's visit.

Certain Types of Depression Are Unique to Women

Pregnancy, the postpartum period, perimenopause, and the menstrual cycle are all associated with dramatic physical and hormonal changes. Certain types of depression that occur at different stages of a woman's life include:

Premenstrual Dysphoric Disorder

Most people are familiar with the term "PMS" or premenstrual syndrome. Moodiness and irritability in the weeks before menstruation are quite common and the symptoms are usually mild. But there is a less common, more severe form of PMS called "premenstrual dysphoric disorder" (PMDD). PMDD is a serious condition with disabling symptoms such as irritability, anger, depressed mood, sadness, suicidal thoughts, appetite changes, bloating, breast tenderness, and joint or muscle pain.

Perinatal Depression

Being pregnant is not easy. Pregnant women commonly deal with morning sickness, weight gain, and mood swings. Caring for a newborn is challenging too. Many new moms experience the "baby blues"—a term used to describe feelings of worry, unhappiness, mood swings, and fatigue. These feelings are usually somewhat mild, last a week or two, and then go away as a new mom adjusts to having a newborn.

Perinatal depression is depression during or after (postpartum) pregnancy. Perinatal depression is much more serious than the "baby blues." The feelings of extreme sadness, anxiety, and exhaustion that accompany perinatal depression may make it difficult to complete daily care activities for a new mom and/or her baby. If you think you have perinatal depression, you should talk to your doctor or a trained mental-healthcare professional. If you see any signs of depression in a loved one during her pregnancy or after the child is born, encourage her to see a healthcare provider or visit a clinic.

Perimenopausal Depression

Perimenopause (the transition into menopause) is a normal phase in a woman's life that can sometimes be challenging. If you are going through perimenopause, you might be experiencing abnormal periods, problems sleeping, mood swings, and hot flashes. But it is a myth that it is "normal" to feel depressed. If you are struggling with irritability, anxiety, sadness, or loss of enjoyment at the time of the menopause transition, you may be experiencing perimenopausal depression.

Depression Affects Each Woman Differently

Not every woman who is depressed experiences every symptom. Some women experience only a few symptoms. Others have many. The severity and frequency of symptoms, and how long they last, will vary depending on the individual and her particular illness. Symptoms may also vary depending on the stage of the illness.

Depression Can Be Treated

Even the most severe cases of depression can be treated. Depression is commonly treated with medication, psychotherapy (where a person talks with a trained professional about her or his thoughts and feelings; sometimes called "talk therapy"), or a combination of the two. If these treatments do not reduce symptoms, electroconvulsive therapy (ECT) and other brain stimulation therapies may be options to explore.

Remember depression affects each individual differently. There is no "one-size-fits-all" for treatment. It may take some trial and error to find the treatment that works best.

Chapter 17

Depression in Children and Adolescents

Chapter Contents

Section 17.1

Understanding Depression in Children

This section includes text excerpted from "Anxiety and Depression in Children," Centers for Disease Control and Prevention (CDC), September 5, 2019.

Many children have fears and worries, and may feel sad and hopeless from time to time. Strong fears may appear at different times during development. For example, toddlers are often very distressed about being away from their parents, even if they are safe and cared for. Although fears and worries are typical in children, persistent or extreme forms of fear and sadness could be due to anxiety or depression. Because the symptoms primarily involve thoughts and feelings, they are called "internalizing disorders."

Anxiety

When children do not outgrow the fears and worries that are typical in young children, or when there are so many fears and worries that they interfere with school, home, or play activities, the child may be diagnosed with an anxiety disorder.

Examples of different types of anxiety disorders include:

- Being very afraid when away from parents (separation anxiety)

- Having extreme fear of a specific thing or situation, such as dogs, insects, or going to the doctor (phobias)

- Being very afraid of school and other places where there are people (social anxiety)

- Being very worried about the future and about bad things happening (general anxiety)

- Having repeated episodes of sudden, unexpected, intense fear that come with symptoms like heart pounding, having trouble breathing, or feeling dizzy, shaky, or sweaty (panic disorder)

Anxiety may present as fear or worry, but can also make children irritable and angry. Anxiety symptoms can also include trouble sleeping, as well as physical symptoms like fatigue, headaches, or stomachaches. Some anxious children keep their worries to themselves and, thus, the symptoms can be missed.

Depression

Occasionally being sad or feeling hopeless is a part of every child's life. However, some children feel sad or uninterested in things that they used to enjoy, or feel helpless or hopeless in situations they are able to change. When children feel persistent sadness and hopelessness, they may be diagnosed with depression.

Examples of behaviors often seen in children with depression include:

- Feeling sad, hopeless, or irritable a lot of the time

- Not wanting to do or enjoy doing fun things

- Showing changes in eating patterns—eating a lot more or a lot less than usual

- Showing changes in sleep patterns—sleeping a lot more or a lot less than normal

- Showing changes in energy—being tired and sluggish or tense and restless a lot of the time

- Having a hard time paying attention

- Feeling worthless, useless, or guilty

- Showing self-injury and self-destructive behavior

Extreme depression can lead a child to think about suicide or plan for suicide. For youth ages 10 to 24 years, suicide is among the leading causes of death.

Some children may not talk about their helpless and hopeless thoughts, and may not appear sad. Depression might also cause a child to make trouble or act unmotivated, causing others not to notice that the child is depressed or to incorrectly label the child as a trouble-maker or lazy.

Section 17.2

Depression among Teens

This chapter includes text excerpted from "Teen Depression,"
National Institute of Mental Health (NIMH), 2018.

Being a teenager can be tough. There are changes taking place in your body and brain that can affect how you learn, think, and behave. And if you are facing tough or stressful situations, it is normal to have emotional ups and downs.

But if you have been overwhelmingly sad for a long time (a few weeks to months) and you are not able to concentrate or do the things you usually enjoy, you may want to talk to a trusted adult about depression.

What Are the Signs and Symptoms of Depression?

Sadness is something we all experience. It is a normal reaction to a loss or a setback, but it usually passes with a little time. Depression is different.

If you are wondering if you may have depression, ask yourself these questions:

- Do you constantly feel sad, anxious, or even "empty," like you feel nothing?

- Do you feel hopeless or like everything is going wrong?

- Do you feel like you are worthless or helpless? Do you feel guilty about things?

- Do you feel irritable much of the time?

- Do you find yourself spending more time alone and withdrawing from friends and family?

- Are your grades dropping?

- Have you lost interest or pleasure in activities and hobbies that you used to enjoy?

- Have your eating or sleeping habits changed (eating or sleeping more than usual or less than usual)?

- Do you always feel tired? Like you have less energy than normal or no energy at all?

- Do you feel restless or have trouble sitting still?

- Do you feel like you have trouble concentrating, remembering information, or making decisions?

- Do you have aches or pains, headaches, cramps, or stomach problems without a clear cause?

- Do you ever think about dying or suicide? Have you ever tried to harm yourself?

What Should I Do If I Am Considering Suicide or Harming Myself?

If you are in crisis and need help, call this toll-free number for the National Suicide Prevention Lifeline (NSPL), available 24 hours a day, every day: 800-273-8255. The service is available to everyone. The deaf and hard of hearing can contact the Lifeline via Toll-Free TTY at 800-799-4889. All calls are confidential.

The Crisis Text Line is another free, confidential resource available 24 hours a day, 7 days a week. Text "HOME" to 741741 and a trained crisis counselor will respond to you with support and information over a text message.

Not everyone with depression experiences every symptom. Some people experience only a few symptoms. Others may have many. The symptoms and how long they last will vary from person to person.

How Do I Get Help?

If you think you might have depression, you are not alone. Depression is common, but it is also treatable. Ask for help! Here are a few steps you can take:

- **Step 1**: Try talking to a trusted adult, such as your parent or guardian, your teacher, or a school counselor. If you do not feel comfortable speaking to an adult, try talking to a friend. If you are not sure where to turn, you can use TXT 4 HELP Interactive, which allows you to text live with a mental-health professional.

- **Step 2**: If you are under the age of 18, ask your parent or guardian to make an appointment with your doctor for an evaluation. Your doctor can make sure you do not have a physical illness that may be affecting your mental health. Your doctor may also talk to you about the possibility of seeing a mental-health professional, such as a psychiatrist, counselor, psychologist, or therapist. These practitioners can diagnose and treat depression and other mental disorders.

How Is Depression Treated?

Depression is usually treated with psychotherapy, medication, or a combination of the two.

What Is Psychotherapy?

Psychotherapy (sometimes called "talk therapy") is a term for treatment techniques that can help you identify and manage troubling emotions, thoughts, and behavior. Psychotherapy can take place in a one-on-one meeting with you and a licensed mental-health professional. Sometimes you might be part of a group guided by a mental-health professional.

What Medications Treat Depression

If your doctor thinks you need medicine to treat your depression, she or he might prescribe an antidepressant.

When you are taking an antidepressant, it is important to carefully follow your doctor's directions for taking your medicine. The medication could take up to six weeks to work and you should not stop taking it without the help of a doctor. You should also avoid using alcohol or drugs that have not been prescribed to you so that your medications can work.

When it is time to stop the medication, the doctor will help you slowly and safely decrease the dose so that your body can adjust. If you stop taking the medication too soon, your depression symptoms may return. Another reason to stop medication gradually is that stopping suddenly can cause withdrawal symptoms such as anxiety and irritability.

Antidepressants can have side effects. These side effects are usually mild (possible stomach upsets or headaches) and may go away on their own. But talk to your doctor about any side effects that you experience because your doctor might adjust the dose or change the medicine.

Although antidepressants can be effective, they may present serious risks to some, especially children and teens. Anyone taking antidepressants should be monitored closely, especially when they first start taking them. Severe anxiety or agitation early in treatment can be especially distressing and should be reported to the doctor immediately.

What Else Can I Do to Help Manage My Depression?

Be patient and know that treatment takes time to work. In the meantime, you can:

- Stay active and exercise, even if it is just going for a walk.

- Try to keep a regular sleep schedule.

- Spend time with friends and family.

- Break down school or work tasks into smaller ones and organize them in order of what needs to get done first. Then, do what you can.

Chapter 18

Depression in College Students

What Is Depression?

Depression is a common but serious mental illness typically marked by sad or anxious feelings. Most college students occasionally feel sad or anxious, but these emotions usually pass quickly, within a couple of days. Untreated depression lasts for a long time, interferes with day-to-day activities, and is much more than just being "a little down" or "feeling blue."

How Does Depression Affect College Students?

Many people experience the first symptoms of depression during their college years. Unfortunately, many college students who have depression are not getting the help they need. They may not know where to go for help, or they may believe that treatment will not help. Others do not get help because they think their symptoms are just

This chapter contains text excerpted from the following sources: Text beginning with the heading "What Is depression?" is excerpted from "Depression and College Students," National Institute of Mental Health (NIMH), 2012. Reviewed October 2019; Text under the heading "Benefits of Providing Mental Health Services and Supports to Students," is excerpted from "Mental Health on College Campuses," National Council on Disability (NCD), July 21, 2017.

part of the typical stress of college, or they worry about being judged if they seek mental-healthcare.

In reality,

- Most colleges offer free or low-cost mental-health services to students.

- Depression is a medical illness and treatments can be very effective.

- Early diagnosis and treatment of depression can relieve depression symptoms, prevent depression from returning, help students succeed in college and after graduation.

In a nationwide survey of college students at 2 and 4 year institutions, it was found that about 30 percent of college students reported feeling "so depressed that it was difficult to function" at some time in the past year. Depression can affect your academic performance in college. Studies suggest that college students who have depression are more likely to smoke. Research suggests that students with depression do not necessarily drink alcohol more heavily than other college students. But, students with depression, especially women, are more likely to get drunk and experience problems related to alcohol abuse, such as engaging in unsafe sex. Depression and other mental disorders often co-occur with substance abuse, which can complicate treatment. Depression is also a major risk factor for suicide. Better diagnosis and treatment of depression can help reduce suicide rates among college students. Suicide is the third leading cause of death for teens and young adults ages 15 to 24. Students should also be aware that warning signs can be different in women versus men.

Are There Different Types of Depression?

The most common depressive disorders are:

- **Major depressive disorder** is also called "major depression." The symptoms of major depression are disabling and interfere with everyday activities such as studying, eating, and sleeping. People with this disorder may have only one episode of major depression in their lifetimes. But, more often, depression comes back repeatedly.

- **Dysthymic disorder** is also called "dysthymia." Dysthymia is mild, chronic depression. The symptoms of dysthymia last for a long time up to two years or more. Dysthymia is less severe than major depression, but it can still interfere with everyday activities. People with dysthymia may also experience one or more episodes of major depression during their lifetimes.

- **Minor depression** is similar to major depression and dysthymia. Symptoms of minor depression are less severe and/ or are usually shorter-term. Without treatment, however, people with minor depression are at high risk for developing a major depressive disorder.

Other types of depression include:

- **Psychotic depression** which is severe depression accompanied by some form of psychosis, such as hallucinations and delusions.
- **Seasonal affective disorder (SAD)** is a depression that begins during the winter months and lifts during spring and summer.

Bipolar disorder, also called "manic-depressive illness," is not as common as major depression or dysthymia but often develops in a person's late teens or early adult years. At least half of all cases start before age 25. People with bipolar disorder may show symptoms of depression and are more likely to seek help when they are depressed than when experiencing mania or hypomania. Bipolar disorder requires different treatment than major depression, so a careful and complete medical exam is needed to assure a person receives the right diagnosis.

What Are the Signs and Symptoms of Depression?

The symptoms of depression vary. If you are depressed, you may feel:

- Sad
- Anxious
- Empty
- Hopeless
- Guilty
- Worthless
- Helpless
- Irritable
- Restless

You may also experience one or more of the following:

- Loss of interest in activities you used to enjoy

- Lack of energy

- Problems concentrating, remembering information, or making decisions

- Problems falling asleep, staying asleep, or sleeping too much

- Loss of appetite or eating too much

- Thoughts of suicide or suicide attempts

- Aches, pains, headaches, cramps, or digestive problems that do not go away

What Causes Depression

Depression does not have a single cause. Several factors can lead to depression. Some people carry genes that increase their risk of depression. But, not all people with depression have these genes, and not all people with these genes have depression. Environment, your surroundings and life experiences, such as stress, also affects your risk for depression.

Stresses of college may include:

- Living away from family for the first time

- Missing family or friends

- Feeling alone or isolated

- Experiencing conflict in relationships

- Facing difficult school work

- Worrying about finances

How Can I Find Out If I Have Depression?

The first step is to talk with a doctor or mental-healthcare provider. Your family doctor, campus health center staff, or other trusted adult may be able to help you find appropriate care. She or he can perform an exam to help determine if you have depression or if you have another health or mental-health problem. Some medical conditions or medications can produce symptoms similar to depression.

A doctor or mental-healthcare provider will ask you about:

- Your symptoms
- Your history of depression
- Your family's history of depression
- Your medical history
- Alcohol or drug use
- Any thoughts of death or suicide

How Is Depression Treated?

A number of very effective treatments for depression are available. The most common treatments are **antidepressants** and **psychotherapy**. Some people find that a combination of antidepressants and psychotherapy works best. A doctor or mental-healthcare provider can help you find a treatment that is right for you.

What Are Antidepressants?

Antidepressants work on brain chemicals called "neurotransmitters" especially serotonin and norepinephrine. Other antidepressants work on the neurotransmitter dopamine. Scientists have found that these particular chemicals are involved in regulating mood, but they are unsure of the exact ways that they work.

If a Doctor Prescribes an Antidepressant, How Long Will I Have to Take It?

Always follow the directions of the doctor or healthcare provider when taking medication. You will need to take regular doses of antidepressants and the full effect of these medications may not take effect for several weeks or months. Some people need to take antidepressants for a short time. If your depression is long-lasting or comes back repeatedly, you may need to take antidepressants longer.

What Is Psychotherapy?

Psychotherapy involves talking with a mental-healthcare professional to treat mental illness. Types of psychotherapy that have been shown to be effective in treating depression include:

- **Cognitive-behavioral therapy (CBT),** which helps people change negative styles of thinking and behavior that may contribute to depression.

- **Interpersonal therapy (IPT),** which helps people understand and work through troubled personal relationships that may cause or worsen depression.

Depending on the type and severity of your depression, a mental-health professional may recommend short-term therapy, lasting 10 to 20 weeks, or longer-term therapy.

If I Think I May Have Depression, Where Can I Get Help?

Most colleges provide mental-health services through counseling centers, student health centers, or both.

- **Counseling centers** offer students free or very low-cost mental-health services. Some counseling centers provide short-term or long-term counseling or psychotherapy, also called "talk therapy." These centers may also refer you to mental-healthcare providers in the community for additional services.

- **Student health centers** provide basic healthcare services to students at little or no cost. A doctor or healthcare provider may be able to diagnose and treat depression or refer you to other mental-health services.

If your college does not provide all of the mental-healthcare you need, your insurance may cover additional mental-health services. Many college students have insurance through their colleges, parents, or employers. If you are insured, contact your insurance company to find out about your mental-healthcare coverage.

How Can I Help Myself If I Am Depressed?

If you have depression, you may feel exhausted, helpless, and hopeless. But, it is important to realize that these feelings are part of the illness. Treatment can help you feel better.

To help yourself feel better:

- Try to see a professional as soon as possible. Research shows that getting treatment sooner rather than later can relieve symptoms quicker and reduce the length of time treatment is needed.

- Give treatment a fair chance. Attend sessions and follow your doctor's or therapist's advice, including advice about specific exercises or "homework" to try between appointments.

- Break up large tasks into small ones, and do what you can as you can; try not to do too many things at once.

- Spend time with other people and talk to a friend or relative about your feelings.

- Do not make important decisions until you feel better; talk about decisions with others whom you trust and who know you well.

- Engage in mild physical activity or exercise. Participate in activities that you used to enjoy.

- Expect your mood to improve gradually with treatment.

- Remember that positive thinking will replace negative thoughts as your depression responds to treatment.

How Can I Help a Friend Who Is Depressed?

If you suspect a friend may have depression, you can help her or him get diagnosed and treated. You may need to help your friend find a doctor, mental-healthcare provider, or mental-health services on your college campus. If your friend seems unable or unwilling to seek help, offer to go with her or him, tell your friend that her or his health and safety are important to you.

You can also:

- Offer support, understanding, patience, and encouragement.

- Talk to your friend and listen carefully.

- Never ignore comments about suicide, and report them to your friend's therapist or doctor.

- Invite your friend out for walks, outings, and other activities. If they refuse your invite keep on trying, but do not push.

- Ensure that your friend gets to doctor's appointments and encourage her or him to report any concerns about medications to their healthcare professional.

- Remind your friend that with time and professional treatment, the depression will lift.

What If I or Someone I Know Is in Crisis?

If you are thinking about harming yourself or having thoughts of suicide, or if you know someone who is, seek help right away:

- Call your doctor or mental-healthcare provider.

- Call 911 or go to a hospital emergency room to get immediate help, or ask a friend or family member to help you do these things.

- Call your campus suicide or crisis hotline.

- Call the National Suicide Prevention Lifeline's toll-free, 24-hour hotline at 800-273-TALK (800-273-8255) or toll-free TTY: 800-799-4TTY (800-799-4889) to talk to a trained counselor.

- Call your college counseling center or student health services.

- If you are in crisis, make sure you are not left alone.

- If someone else is in crisis, make sure she or he is not left alone.

Benefits of Providing Mental-Health Services and Supports to Students

Strong mental and behavioral health services and supports can improve the academic performance of students and increase their resilience and ability to handle stress, with reduced suicide rates, substance abuse, and eating disorders. Additionally, colleges face less liability by addressing student mental-health issues and benefit financially by retaining and graduating more students. Colleges have a unique opportunity through which they can make a positive impact on the mental health of their students. College represents the only time in many people's lives when a single setting encompasses its main activities as well as health services.

Improved Academic Performance

Mental-health problems can have a negative impact on the academic performance, retention, and graduation rates of students who do not receive support. The American College Health Association (ACHA) finds strong evidence that mental health needs are related to measures of academic success. Their survey found that students who reported psychological distress also reported the following:

- They received lower grades on exams or important projects.

- They received lower grades in courses.

- They received incompletes or dropped courses.

- They experienced significant disruptions in thesis, dissertation, research, or practicum work.

Students who experience mild or moderate symptoms of depression or anxiety also demonstrate more academic difficulties and lower grades than nondepressed students. Not surprisingly, students who receive treatment for mental-health disabilities report gains in academic performance. For example, 31 percent of students at one university receiving treatment for depression reported an increase in satisfaction with their ability to study or work, and 34 percent reported an increased sense of satisfaction with how much schoolwork they could do.

Increased Resilience and Reduced Stress

Resilience is a personality characteristic that moderates the negative effects of stress, promotes adaptation, and has been associated with increased psychological well-being. University students with low levels of resilience reported significantly lower levels of perceived social support or campus connectedness and higher levels of psychological distress in comparison to those with high levels of resilience. According to the American Council on Education's (ACEs) strategic primer on college student mental health, "the best way for colleges and universities to nurture resilience among students is to promote health and well-being, especially mental and behavioral health, at both individual and community levels." Resilient students learn more and graduate more prepared; less resilient students take fewer intellectual and creative risks.

Reduced Substance Abuse

Excessive alcohol and drug use during college is linked to negative academic performance. Students who use substances are more likely to have disruptions in their enrollment in college and fail to graduate. Students with poor mental health or depression were less likely to report never drinking; as likely to report frequent, heavy, and heavy episodic drinking; and more likely to report drinking to get drunk than other students. Further, the former group of students were more likely to report drinking-related harms and alcohol abuse.

127

Reduced Suicide Rates

Suicide is the second leading cause of death among college students. The suicide rate among people 15 to 24 years of age has tripled since the 1950s. In any year, 6 percent of undergraduate students and 4 percent of graduate students will have seriously considered suicide. Community colleges serve a high proportion of students, including older students and commuter students, who are at greater risk of suicide than traditional students. Also at high risk are international students and lesbian, gay, bisexual, transgender, and queer or questioning (LGBTQ) students.

Economic Benefits for Colleges

Students who receive support for mental-health disabilities such as depression are more likely to stay in school and to graduate. Increased student retention leads to higher tuition revenue, a strong financial benefit to the institution.

Chapter 19

Men and Depression

What Is Depression?

Everyone feels sad or irritable and has trouble sleeping once in a while. But these feelings and troubles usually pass after a couple of days. Depression is a common but serious mood disorder that may cause severe symptoms. Depression affects the ability to feel, think, and handle daily activities. Also known as "major depressive disorder" (MDD) or "clinical depression," a man must have symptoms for at least two weeks to be diagnosed with depression.

Both men and women get depression but their willingness to talk about their feelings may be very different. This is one of the reasons that depression symptoms for men and women may be very different as well.

For example, some men with depression hide their emotions and may seem to be angry, irritable, or aggressive while many women seem sad or express sadness. Men with depression may feel very tired and lose interest in work, family, or hobbies. They may be more likely to have difficulty sleeping than women who have depression. Sometimes mental-health symptoms appear to be physical issues. For example, a racing heart, tightening chest, ongoing headaches, or digestive issues can be signs of a mental-health problem. Many men are more likely to see their doctor about physical symptoms than emotional symptoms.

This chapter includes text excerpted from "Men and Depression," National Institute of Mental Health (NIMH), January 2017.

Some men may turn to drugs or alcohol to try to cope with their emotional symptoms. Also, while women with depression are more likely to attempt suicide, men are more likely to die by suicide because they tend to use more lethal methods. Depression can affect any man at any age. With the right treatment, most men with depression can get better and gain back their interest in work, family, and hobbies.

What Are the Signs and Symptoms of Depression in Men?

Different men have different symptoms, but some common depression symptoms include:

- Anger, irritability, or aggressiveness
- Feeling anxious, restless, or "on the edge"
- Loss of interest in work, family, or once pleasurable activities
- Problems with sexual desire and performance
- Feeling sad, "empty," flat, or hopeless
- Not being able to concentrate or remember details
- Feeling very tired, not being able to sleep, or sleeping too much
- Overeating or not wanting to eat at all
- Thoughts of suicide or suicide attempts
- Physical aches or pains, headaches, cramps, or digestive problems
- Inability to meet the responsibilities of work, caring for family, or other important activities
- Engaging in high-risk activities
- A need for alcohol or drugs
- Withdrawing from family and friends or becoming isolated

Not every man who is depressed experiences every symptom. Some men experience only a few symptoms while others may experience many.

What Are the Different Types of Depression?

The most common types of depression are,

Major Depression

Depressive symptoms that interfere with a man's ability to work, sleep, study, eat, and enjoy most aspects of life. An episode of major depression may occur only once in a person's lifetime. But it is common for a person to have several episodes. Special forms (subtypes) of major depression include,

Psychotic Depression

Psychotic depression is a severe depression associated with delusions (false, fixed beliefs) or hallucinations (hearing or seeing things that are not really there). These psychotic symptoms are depression-themed. For example, a man may believe he is sick or poor when he is not, or he may hear voices that are not real that say that he is worthless.

Seasonal Affective Disorder

Seasonal affective disorder (SAD) is characterized by depression symptoms that appear every year during the winter months when there is less natural sunlight.

Persistent Depressive Disorder

Persistent depressive disorder (PDD) is also called "dysthymia" is characterized by depressive symptoms that last a long time (2 years or longer) but are less severe than those of major depression.

Minor Depression

Minor depression is similar to major depression and persistent depressive disorder, but symptoms are less severe and may not last as long.

Bipolar Disorder

Bipolar disorder is different from depression. It is included in this list because a person with bipolar disorder experiences episodes of extreme low moods (depression). But a person with this disorder also experiences extreme high moods (called "mania").

What Causes Depression in Men

Depression is one of the most common mental disorders in the U.S. research suggests that depression is caused by a combination of risk factors including:

Genetic factors

Men with a family history of depression may be more likely to develop it than those whose family members do not have the illness.

Environmental Stress

Financial problems, loss of a loved one, a difficult relationship, major life changes, work problems, or any stressful situation may trigger depression in some men.

Illness

Depression can occur with other serious medical illnesses, such as diabetes, cancer, heart disease, or Parkinson disease (PD). Depression can make these conditions worse and vice versa. Sometimes, medications taken for these illnesses may cause side effects that trigger or worsen depression.

How Is Depression Treated?

Men often avoid addressing their feelings and, in many cases, friends and family members are the first to recognize that their loved one is depressed. It is important that friends and family support their loved one and encourage him to visit a doctor or mental-health professional for an evaluation. A health professional can do an exam or lab tests to rule out other conditions that may have symptoms that are like those of depression. She or he also can tell if certain medications are affecting the depression.

The doctor needs to get a complete history of symptoms, such as when they started, how long they have lasted, how bad they are, whether they have occurred before, and if so, how they were treated. It is important that the man seeking help be open and honest about any efforts at "self-medication" with alcohol, nonprescribed drugs, gambling, or high-risk activities. A complete history should include information about a family history of depression or other mental disorders.

After a diagnosis, depression is usually treated with medications or psychotherapy, or a combination of the two. The increasingly-popular "collaborative care" approach combines physical and behavioral healthcare. Collaborative care involves a team of healthcare providers and managers, including a primary care doctor and specialists.

Medication

Medications called "antidepressants" can work well to treat depression, but they can take several weeks to be effective. Often with medication, symptoms such as sleep, appetite, and concentration problems improve before mood lifts, so it is important to give medication a chance before deciding whether it is effective or not.

Antidepressants can have side effects including,

- Headache

- Nausea or feeling sick to your stomach

- Difficulty sleeping and nervousness

- Agitation or restlessness

- Sexual problems

Most side effects lessen over time but it is important to talk with your doctor about any side effects that you may have. Starting antidepressant medication at a low dose and gradually increasing to a full therapeutic dose may help minimize adverse effects.

It is important to know that although antidepressants can be safe and effective for many people, they may present serious risks to some, especially children, teens, and young adults. A "black box" warning—the most serious type of warning that a prescription drug can have—has been added to the labels of antidepressant medications to warn people that antidepressants may cause some young people to have suicidal thoughts or may increase the risk for suicide attempts. This is especially true for those who become agitated when they first start taking the medication and before it begins to work. Anyone taking antidepressants should be monitored closely, especially when they first start taking them.

For most people, though, the risks of untreated depression far outweigh those of taking antidepressant medications under a doctor's supervision. Careful monitoring by a health professional will also minimize any potential risks.

For reasons that are not well-understood, many people respond better to some antidepressants than to others. If one does not respond to one medication, her or his doctor may suggest trying another. Sometimes, a medication may be only partially effective. In that case, another medication might be added to help make the antidepressant more effective.

If you begin taking antidepressants, do not stop taking them without the help of a doctor. Sometimes people taking antidepressants to feel better and then stop taking the medication on their own, and the depression returns. When it is time to stop the medication, usually after a course of 6 to 12 months, the doctor will help you slowly and safely decrease your dose. Stopping them abruptly can cause withdrawal symptoms.

Some people who relapse back into depression after stopping an antidepressant benefit from staying on medication for additional months or years.

Psychotherapy

Several types of psychotherapy or "talk therapy" can help treat depression. Some therapies are just as effective as medications for certain types of depression. Therapy helps by teaching new ways of thinking and behaving, and changing habits that may be contributing to the depression. Therapy can also help men understand and work through difficult situations or relationships that may be causing their depression or making it worse. Cognitive-behavioral therapy (CBT), interpersonal therapy (IPT), and problem-solving therapy are examples of evidence-based talk therapy treatments for depression. Treatment for depression should be personalized. Some men, might try therapy first and add antidepressant medication later if it is needed. Others might start treatment with both medication and psychotherapy.

How Can I Help a Loved One Who Is Depressed?

It is important to remember that a person with depression cannot simply "snap out of it." It is also important to know that she or he may not recognize the symptoms and may not want to get professional treatment.

If you think someone has depression, you can support her or him by finding a doctor or mental-health professional and then helping him make an appointment. Even men who have trouble recognizing that they are depressed may agree to seek help for physical symptoms, such as feeling tired or run down. They may be willing to talk with their regular health professional about a new difficulty they are having at work or losing interest in doing things they usually enjoy. Talking with a primary care provider may be a good first step toward learning about and treating possible depression.

Other ways to help include,

- Offering him support, understanding, patience, and encouragement

- Listening carefully and talking with him

- Never ignoring comments about suicide, and alerting his therapist or doctor

- Helping him increase his level of physical and social activity by inviting him out for hikes, games, and other events. If he says, "no," keep trying, but do not push him to take on too much too soon.

- Encouraging him to report any concerns about medications to his healthcare provider

- Ensuring that he gets to his doctor's appointments

- Reminding him that with time and treatment, the depression will lift

How Can I Help Myself If I Am Depressed?

As you continue treatment, gradually you will start to feel better. Remember that if you are taking an antidepressant, it may take several weeks for it to start working. Try to do things that you used to enjoy before you had depression. Go easy on yourself.

Other things that may help include,

- Spending time with other people and talking with a friend or relative about your feelings

- Increasing your level of physical activity. Regular exercise can help people with mild to moderate depression and maybe one part of a treatment plan for those with severe depression. Talk with your healthcare professional about what kind of exercise is right for you.

- Breaking up large tasks into small ones, and tackling what you can as you can. Do not try to do too many things at once

- Delaying important decisions until you feel better. Discuss decisions with others who know you well.

- Keeping stable daily routines. For example, eating and going to bed at the same time every day.

- Avoiding alcohol

Where Can I Go for Help?

If you are unsure of where to go for help, ask your family doctor or healthcare provider. You can also find resources online including the National Institute of Mental Health (NIMH) website at www.nimh.nih.gov/FindHelp, or check with your insurance carrier to find someone who participates in your plan. Hospital doctors can help in an emergency. If you are unsure of where to go for help, ask your family doctor or healthcare provider. You can also find resources online including the NIMH website at www.nimh.nih.gov/FindHelp, or check with your insurance carrier to find someone who participates in your plan. Hospital doctors can help in an emergency.

Chapter 20

Depression in Older Adults

Depression Is Not a Normal Part of Aging

Depression is a common problem among older adults, but it is not a normal part of aging. In fact, studies show that most older adults feel satisfied with their lives, despite having more illnesses or physical problems. However, important life changes that happen as they get older may cause feelings of uneasiness, stress, and sadness.

For instance, the death of a loved one, moving from work into retirement, or dealing with a serious illness can leave people feeling sad or anxious. After a period of adjustment, many older adults can regain their emotional balance, but others do not and may develop depression.

Recognizing Symptoms of Depression in Older Adults

Depression in older adults may be difficult to recognize because they may show different symptoms than younger people. For some older adults with depression, sadness is not their main symptom. They may have other, less obvious symptoms of depression, or they may not be willing to talk about their feelings. Therefore, doctors may be less likely to recognize that their patient has depression.

This chapter includes text excerpted from "Depression and Older Adults," National Institute on Aging (NIA), National Institutes of Health (NIH), May 1, 2017.

Sometimes older people who are depressed appear to feel tired, have trouble sleeping, or seem grumpy and irritable. Confusion or attention problems caused by depression can sometimes look such as Alzheimer disease or other brain disorders. Older adults also may have more medical conditions, such as heart disease, stroke, or cancer, which may cause depressive symptoms. Or they may be taking medications with side effects that contribute to depression.

Types of Depression

There are several types of depressive disorders.

Major depression involves severe symptoms that interfere with the ability to work, sleep, study, eat, and enjoy life. An episode can occur only once in a person's lifetime, but more often, a person has several episodes.

Persistent depressive disorder is a depressed mood that lasts for at least two years. A person diagnosed with persistent depressive disorder may have episodes of major depression along with periods of less severe symptoms, but symptoms must last for two years to be considered persistent depressive disorder.

Other forms of depression include psychotic depression, postpartum depression, and seasonal affective disorder.

Causes and Risk Factors of Depression

Several factors, or a combination of factors, may contribute to depression.

- **Genes**—People with a family history of depression may be more likely to develop it than those whose families do not have the illness.

- **Personal history**—Older adults who had depression when they were younger are more at risk for developing depression in late life than those who did not have the illness earlier in life.

- **Brain chemistry**—People with depression may have different brain chemistry than those without the illness.

- **Stress**—Loss of a loved one, a difficult relationship, or any stressful situation may trigger depression.

Vascular Depression

For older adults who experience depression for the first time later in life, the depression may be related to changes that occur in the brain and body as a person ages. For example, older adults may suffer from restricted blood flow, a condition called "ischemia." Over time, blood vessels may stiffen and prevent blood from flowing normally to the body's organs, including the brain.

If this happens, an older adult with no family history of depression may develop what is sometimes called "vascular depression." Those with vascular depression also may be at risk for heart disease, stroke, or other vascular illness.

Depression Can Co-Occur with Other Illnesses

Depression, especially in middle-aged or older adults, can co-occur with other serious medical illnesses such as diabetes, cancer, heart disease, and Parkinson's disease. Depression can make these conditions worse and vice versa. Sometimes medications taken for these physical illnesses may cause side effects that contribute to depression. A doctor with experience in treating these complicated illnesses can help work out the best treatment strategy.

All these factors can cause depression to go undiagnosed or untreated in older people. Yet, treating the depression will help an older adult better manage other conditions she or he may have.

Common Symptoms of Depression

There are many symptoms associated with depression, and some will vary depending on the individual. However, some of the most common symptoms are listed below. If you have several of these symptoms for more than two weeks, you may have depression:

- Persistent sad, anxious, or "empty" mood

- Feelings of hopelessness, guilt, worthlessness, or helplessness

- Irritability, restlessness, or having trouble sitting still

- Loss of interest in once pleasurable activities, including sex

- Decreased energy or fatigue

- Moving or talking more slowly

- Difficulty concentrating, remembering, making decisions

- Difficulty sleeping, early-morning awakening, or oversleeping

- Eating more or less than usual, usually with unplanned weight gain or loss

- Thoughts of death or suicide, or suicide attempts

- Aches or pains, headaches, cramps, or digestive problems without a clear physical cause and/or that do not ease with treatment

- Frequent crying

Treatments of Depression

Depression, even severe depression, can be treated. If you think you may have depression, start by making an appointment to see your doctor or healthcare provider. This could be your primary doctor or a provider who specializes in diagnosing and treating mental-health conditions (a psychologist or psychiatrist). Certain medications and some medical conditions can cause the same symptoms as depression. A doctor can rule out these possibilities by doing a physical exam, interview, and lab tests. If the doctor can find no medical condition that may be causing the depression, the next step is a psychological evaluation.

Treatment choices differ for each person, and sometimes multiple treatments must be tried to find one that works. It is important to keep trying until you find something that works for you.

The most common forms of treatment for depression are therapies and medications.

Therapies for Depression

Psychotherapy, also called "talk therapy," can help people with depression. Some treatments are short-term, lasting 10 to 20 weeks; others are longer, depending on the person's needs.

Cognitive-behavioral therapy is one type of talk therapy used to treat depression. It focuses on helping people change negative thinking and any behaviors that may be making depression worse. Interpersonal therapy can help an individual understand and work through troubled relationships that may cause depression or make it worse. Other types of talk therapy, such as problem-solving therapy, can be helpful for people with depression.

Medications for Depression

Antidepressants are medicines that treat depression. There are many different types of antidepressants. They may help improve the way your brain uses certain chemicals that control mood or stress. You may need to try several different antidepressant medicines before finding one that improves your symptoms and has manageable side effects.

Antidepressants take time, usually two to four weeks, to work. Often symptoms such as sleep, appetite, and concentration problems improve before mood lifts, so it is important to give the medication a chance to work before deciding whether it works for you.

If you begin taking antidepressants, do not stop taking them without the help of a doctor. Sometimes people taking antidepressants feel better and then stop taking the medication on their own, but then the depression returns. When you and your doctor have decided it is time to stop the medication, usually after 6 to 12 months, the doctor will help you slowly and safely decrease your dose. Stopping antidepressants abruptly can cause withdrawal symptoms.

Most antidepressants are generally safe, but the U.S. Food and Drug Administration (FDA) requires that all antidepressants carry black box warnings, the strictest warnings for prescriptions. The warning says that patients of all ages taking antidepressants should be watched closely, especially during the first few weeks of treatment. Talk to your doctor about any side effects of your medication that you should watch for.

For older adults who are already taking several medications for other conditions, it is important to talk with a doctor about any adverse drug interactions that may occur while taking antidepressants.

Do not use herbal medicines such as St. John's wort before talking with your healthcare provider. It should never be combined with a prescription antidepressant, and you should not use it to replace conventional care or to postpone seeing a healthcare provider.

Preventing Depression

What can be done to lower the risk of depression? How can people cope? There are a few steps you can take. Try to prepare for major changes in life, such as retirement or moving from your home for many years. Stay in touch with family. Let them know when you feel sad.

Regular exercise may also help prevent depression or lift your mood if you are depressed. Pick something you like to do. Being physically fit and eating a balanced diet may help avoid illnesses that can bring on disability or depression.

Chapter 21

Depression in Minority Populations

Mental Health and African Americans

- Poverty level affects mental-health status. African Americans living below the poverty level, as compared to those over twice the poverty level, are twice as likely to report psychological distress.

- In 2017, suicide was the second leading cause of death for African Americans, ages 15 to 24.

- The death rate from suicide for African American men was more than four times greater than for African American women, in 2017.

- However, the overall suicide rate for African Americans is 60 percent lower than that of the non-Hispanic White population.

This chapter contains text excerpted from the following sources: Text under the heading "Mental Health and African Americans" is excerpted from "Mental and Behavioral Health—African Americans," Office of Minority Health (OMH), U.S. Department of Health and Human Services (HHS), September 25, 2019; Text under the heading "Mental Health and American Indians/Alaska Natives" is excerpted from "Mental and Behavioral Health—American Indians/Alaska Natives," Office of Minority Health (OMH), U.S. Department of Health and Human Services (HHS), September 25, 2019; Text under the heading "Mental Health and Asian Americans" is excerpted from "Mental and Behavioral Health—Asian Americans," Office of Minority Health (OMH), U.S. Department of Health and Human Services (HHS), September 25, 2019; Text under the heading "Mental Health and Hispanics" is excerpted from "Mental and Behavioral Health—Hispanics," Office of Minority Health (OMH), U.S. Department of Health and Human Services (HHS), September 25, 2019.

- African American females, grades 9 to 12, were 70 percent more likely to attempt suicide in 2017, as compared to non-Hispanic white females of the same age.

- A report from the U.S. Surgeon General found that from 1980 to 1995, the suicide rate among African Americans ages 10 to 14 increased 233 percent, as compared to 120 percent of non-Hispanic Whites.

Table 21.1. Serious Psychological Distress among Adults 18 Years of Age and Over, Percent, 2015–2016.

Non-Hispanic Black	Non-Hispanic White	Non-Hispanic Black/ Non-Hispanic White Ratio
3.6	3.7	1.0

(Source: Centers for Disease Control and Prevention (CDC), 2018. Health United States, 2017.)

Mental Health and American Indians/Alaska Natives

- In 2017, suicide was the second leading cause of death for American Indian/Alaska Natives between the ages of 10 and 34.

- American Indian/Alaska Natives are twice as likely to experience the feeling that everything is an effort, all or most of the time, as compared to non-Hispanic Whites.

- Violent deaths, unintentional injuries, homicide, and suicide, account for 75 percent of all mortality in the second decade of life for American Indian/Alaska Natives.

- The overall death rate from suicide for American Indian/Alaska Native adults is about 20 percent higher as compared to the non-Hispanic White population.

- Adolescent American Indian/Alaska Native females, ages 15 to 19, have a death rate that is three times higher than for non-Hispanic White females in the same age groups.

Table 21.2. Serious Psychological Distress among Adults 18 Years of Age and Over, Percent, 2015–2016.

American Indian/ Alaska Native*	Non-Hispanic White	American Indian/Alaska Native/ Non-Hispanic White Ratio
9.2	3.7	2.5

(Source: Centers for Disease Control and Prevention (CDC), 2018. Health United States, 2017.)
All data in the above survey relate to non-Hispanic Asian Americans.

Mental Health and Asian Americans

- Suicide was the leading cause of death for Asian Americans, ages 15 to 24, in 2017.

- Asian American females, in grades 9-12, were 20 percent more likely to attempt suicide as compared to non-Hispanic White female students, in 2017.

- Southeast Asian refugees are at risk for posttraumatic stress disorder (PTSD) associated with trauma experienced before and after immigration to the U.S. One study found that 70 percent of Southeast Asian refugees receiving mental-health care were diagnosed with PTSD.

- The overall suicide rate for Asians Americans is half that of the non-Hispanic White population.

Table 21.3. Serious Psychological Distress among Adults 18 Years of Age and Over, Percent, 2015–2016.

Asian American*	Non-Hispanic White	Asian American/ Non-Hispanic White Ratio
2.1	3.7	0.6

(Source: Centers for Disease Control and Prevention (CDC), 2018. Health United States, 2017.)
All data in the above survey relate to non-Hispanic Asian Americans.

Mental Health and Hispanics

- Poverty level affects mental-health status. Hispanics living below the poverty level, as compared to Hispanics over twice the poverty level, are over twice as likely to report psychological distress.

- The death rate from suicide for Hispanic men was four times the rate for Hispanic women, in 2017.

- However, the suicide rate for Hispanics is less than half that of the non-Hispanic White population.

- In 2017, suicide was the second leading cause of death for Hispanics, ages 15 to 34.1

- Suicide attempts for Hispanic girls, grades 9 to 12, were 40 percent higher than for non-Hispanic White girls in the same age group, in 2017.

- Non-Hispanic Whites received mental-health treatment twice as often as Hispanics, in 2018.

Table 21.4. Serious Psychological Distress among Adults 18 Years of Age and Over, Percent, 2015–2016.

Hispanic	Non-Hispanic White	Hispanic/Non-Hispanic White Ratio
3.7	3.7	1

(Source: Centers for Disease Control and Prevention (CDC), 2018. Health United States, 2017.)

Chapter 22

Depression and Violence in LGBT Population

Experiences with Violence

When compared with other students, negative attitudes toward lesbian, gay, and bisexual (LGB) persons may put these youth at increased risk for experiences with violence. "Violence" can include behaviors such as bullying, teasing, harassment, and physical assault.

According to data from the 2015 national Youth Risk Behavior Survey (YRBS), of surveyed LGB students:

- 10 percent were threatened or injured with a weapon on school property

- 34 percent were bullied on school property

- 28 percent were bullied electronically

- 23 percent of LGB students who had dated or went out with someone during the 12 months before the survey had experienced sexual dating violence in the prior year

- 18 percent of LGB students had experienced physical dating violence

This chapter includes text excerpted from "LGBT Youth," Centers for Disease Control and Prevention (CDC), June 21, 2017.

- 18 percent of LGB students had been forced to have sexual intercourse at some point in their lives.

Effects on Education and Mental Health

Exposure to violence can have negative effects on the education and health of any young person and may account for some of the health-related disparities between LGB and heterosexual youth. LGB students are more likely to not go to school at least one day during the 30 days prior to the survey because of safety concerns, compared with heterosexual students. While not a direct measure of school performance, absenteeism has been linked to low graduation rates, which can have lifelong consequences.

A complex combination of factors can impact youth health outcomes. LGB youth are at greater risk for depression, suicide, substance use, and sexual behaviors that can place them at increased risk for human immunodeficiency virus (HIV) and other sexually transmitted diseases (STDs). Nearly one-third (29%) of LGB youth had attempted suicide at least once in the prior year compared to 6 percent of heterosexual youth.

What Parents Can Do

Positive parenting practices, such as having honest and open conversations, can help reduce teen health risk behaviors. How parents engage with their LGB teen can have a tremendous impact on their adolescent's current and future mental and physical health. Supportive and accepting parents can help youth cope with the challenges of being an LGB teen. On the other hand, unsupportive parents who react negatively to learning that their daughter or son is LGB can make it harder for their teen to thrive. Parental rejection has been linked to depression, use of drugs and alcohol, and risky sexual behavior among teens.

To be supportive, parents should talk openly and supportively with their teen about any problems or concerns. It is also important for parents to watch for behaviors that might indicate their teen is a victim of bullying or violence, or that their teen may be victimizing others. If bullying, violence, or depression is suspected, parents should take immediate action, working with school personnel and other adults in the community.

The following are research-based steps parents can take to support the health and well-being of their LGB teen:

- **Talk and listen.** Parents who talk with and listen to their teens in a way that invites an open discussion about sexual orientation can help their teen feel loved and supported. Parents should have honest conversations with their teens about sex and how to avoid risky behaviors and unsafe situations.

- **Provide support.** Parents who take time to come to terms with how they feel about their teen's sexual orientation will be more able to respond calmly and use respectful language. Parents should develop common goals with their teen, including being healthy and doing well in school.

- **Stay involved.** Parents who make an effort to know their teen's friends and know what their teen is doing can help their teens stay safe and feel cared about.

- **Be proactive.** Parents can access many organizations and online information resources to learn more about how they can support their LGB teen, other family members, and their teen's friends.

Chapter 23

Depression Related to Occupation

Among the leading physical and mental-health conditions in terms of direct medical costs and lost productivity to U.S. employers are several chronic disease (e.g., heart disease), depression, and musculoskeletal disorders (e.g., back pain). With workers in America today spending more than one-third of their day on the job, employers are in a unique position to promote the health and safety of their employees. The use of effective workplace health programs and policies can reduce health risks and improve the quality of life for 138 million workers in the United States.

The workplace provides many opportunities for promoting health and preventing disease and injury. Workplace health programs can:

- Influence social norms.

- Establish health-promoting policies.

This chapter contains text excerpted from the following sources: Text in this chapter begins with excerpts from "Workplace Health Strategies," Centers for Disease Control and Prevention (CDC), February 1, 2018; Text under the heading "Depression Evaluation Measures" is excerpted from "Depression Evaluation Measures," Centers for Disease Control and Prevention (CDC), April 1, 2016. Reviewed October 2019; Text under the heading "Severe Depressive Symptoms and Work, Home, and Social Activities" is excerpted from "Depression in the U.S. Household Population, 2009–2012," Centers for Disease Control and Prevention (CDC), November 6, 2015. Reviewed October 2019.

- Increase healthy behaviors such as dietary and physical activity changes.

- Improve employees' health knowledge and skills.

- Help employees get necessary health screenings, immunizations, and follow-up care.

- Reduce employees' on-the-job exposure to substances and hazards that can cause diseases and injury.

Depression Evaluation Measures

The mental health of workers is an area of increasing concern for organizations. Depression is a major cause of disability, absenteeism, presenteeism, and productivity loss among working-age adults. The ability to identify major depression in the workplace is complicated by a number of issues such as employees' concerns about confidentiality or the impact it may have on their job that causes some people to avoid screening.

- 80 percent of persons with depression reported some level of functional impairment because of their depression, and 27 percent reported serious difficulties in work and home life.

- In a 3 month period, patients with depression miss an average of 4.8 workdays and suffer 11.5 days of reduced productivity.

- Depression is estimated to cause 200 million lost workdays each year at a cost to employers of $17 to 44 billion.

- The rates of depression vary by occupation and industry type. Among full-time workers aged 18 to 64 years, the highest rates of workers experiencing a major depressive episode were found in the personal care and service occupations (10.8%) and the food preparation and serving related occupations (10.3%).

- Occupations with the lowest rates of workers experiencing a major depressive episode in the past year were engineering, architecture, and surveying (4.3%); life, physical, and social science (4.4%); and installation, maintenance, and repair (4.4%).

Evidence linking work organization with depression and other mental health problems, and with increased productivity losses, is beginning to accumulate. A number of studies of a diverse group of occupations have identified several job stressors (e.g., high job demands; low job control; lack of social support in the workplace) that may be associated with depression. There is not enough evidence of effective interventions to prevent depression in the workplace.

There are a number of strategies employers can pursue to support employees' mental health such as holding depression recognition screenings; placing confidential self-rating sheets in cafeterias, break rooms, or bulletin boards; promoting greater awareness through employee assistance programs (EAP); training supervisors in depression recognition; and ensuring workers' access to needed psychiatric services through health insurance benefits and benefit structures.

In addition to its direct medical and workplace costs, depression also increases healthcare costs and lost productivity indirectly by contributing to the severity of other costly conditions such as heart disease, diabetes, and stroke. However, routine, systematic clinical screening can successfully identify patients who are depressed, allowing them to access care earlier in the course of their illnesses. Research suggests that 80 percent of patients with depression will improve with treatment.

Severe Depressive Symptoms and Work, Home, and Social Activities

Nearly 90 percent of persons with severe depressive symptoms reported difficulty with work, home, or social activities related to their symptoms; rates of any difficulty with work, home, or social activities related to depressive symptoms increased as the severity of those symptoms increased, from 45.7 percent among persons with mild depressive symptoms to 88.0 percent among those with severe depressive symptoms.

Chapter 24

Reproductive Health and Mental Health in Women

Hormones can affect a woman's emotions and moods in different ways throughout her lifetime. Sometimes the impact on mood can affect a woman's quality of life. This is true for most women. But, women with a mental-health condition may have other symptoms related to their menstrual cycles or menopause. Throughout all these stages, you can learn ways to help your mental and reproductive health.

How Does My Mental-Health Condition Affect My Menstrual Cycle?

Throughout your monthly menstrual cycle, levels of certain hormones rise and fall. These hormone levels can affect how you think and feel mentally and physically.

Mental-health conditions can cause period problems or make some period problems worse:

- **Premenstrual syndrome (PMS).** Most women have some symptoms of PMS in the week or two before their period. PMS can cause bloating, headaches, and moodiness. Women with depression or anxiety disorders may experience worse symptoms

This chapter includes text excerpted from "Reproductive Health and Mental Health," Office on Women's Health (OWH), U.S. Department of Health and Human Services (HHS), August 28, 2018.

of PMS. Also, many women seeking treatment for PMS have depression or anxiety. Symptoms of these mental-health conditions are similar to symptoms of PMS and may get worse before or during your period. Talk to your doctor or nurse about ways to relieve PMS symptoms.

- **Premenstrual dysphoric disorder (PMDD).** PMDD is a condition similar to PMS but with more severe symptoms, including severe depression, irritability, and tension. Symptoms of PMDD can be so difficult to manage that your daily life is disrupted. PMDD is more common in women with anxiety or depression. Talk to your doctor about ways to help if you experience worse symptoms of depression or anxiety around your period.

- **Irregular periods.** Studies show that women with anxiety disorder or substance use disorder are more likely to have shorter menstrual cycles (shorter than 24 days). Irregular cycles are also linked to eating disorders and depression. Women with bipolar disorder are also twice as likely to have irregular periods.

How Do Mental-Health Conditions Affect Pregnancy?

Changing hormones during pregnancy can cause mental-health conditions that have been treated in the past to come back (this is called a "relapse"). Women with mental-health conditions are also at higher risk of problems during pregnancy.

- **Depression.** Depression is the most common mental-health condition during pregnancy. How long symptoms last and how often they happen are different for each woman. Women who are depressed during pregnancy have a greater risk of depression after giving birth, called "postpartum depression." If you take medicine for depression, stopping your medicine when you become pregnant can cause your depression to come back.

- **Eating disorders.** Women with eating disorders may experience relapses during pregnancy, which can cause miscarriage, premature birth (birth before 37 weeks of pregnancy), and low birth weight.

- **Bipolar disorder.** Women may experience relief from symptoms of bipolar disorder during pregnancy. But, they are at a very high risk of a relapse of symptoms in the weeks after pregnancy.

Women with anxiety disorders and obsessive-compulsive disorder (OCD) are more likely to have a relapse during and after pregnancy.

Talk to your doctor or nurse about your mental-health condition and your symptoms. Do not stop any prescribed medicines without first talking to your doctor or nurse. Not using medicine that you need may hurt you or your baby.

Will My Mental-Health Condition Affect My Chances of Getting Pregnant?

Maybe. Certain mental-health conditions can make it harder to get pregnant:

* Eating disorders can affect your menstrual cycle. The extreme weight loss that happens with anorexia can cause you to miss your menstrual periods. If you have bulimia, your menstrual cycle may be irregular, or your period may stop for several months. Both of these period problems can affect whether you ovulate. Not ovulating regularly can make it harder to get pregnant. Also, the longer you have an eating disorder, the higher the risk that you will face some type of problem getting pregnant.

* Depression, anxiety, and stress can also affect the hormones that control ovulation. This could make it difficult for a woman to become pregnant.

If you are having problems getting pregnant, the stress, worry, or sadness can make your mental-health condition worse. Talk to your doctor or nurse about your feelings. Treatment for your mental-health condition helps both you and your chances of having a baby. During pregnancy, it can also lower your baby's chances of developing depression or other mental-health conditions later in life.

Can I Continue to Take My Medicine If I Am Trying to Get Pregnant?

Maybe. Some medicines, such as antidepressants, may make it more difficult for you to get pregnant. Also, some medicines may not be safe to take during pregnancy or when trying to get pregnant. Talk to your doctor or nurse about other treatments for mental-health conditions, such as depression, that do not involve medicine.

Women who are already taking an antidepressant and who are trying to get pregnant should talk to their doctor or nurse about the benefits and risks of stopping the medicine. Some women who have been diagnosed with severe depression may need to keep taking their prescribed medicine during pregnancy. If you are unsure whether to take your medicine, talk to your doctor or nurse.

Talk therapy is one way to help women with depression. This type of therapy has no risks for women who are trying to get pregnant. During talk therapy, you work with a mental-health professional to explore why you are depressed and train yourself to replace negative thoughts with positive ones. Certain mental-healthcare professionals specialize in depression related to infertility.

Regular physical activity is another safe and healthy option for most women who are trying to get pregnant. Exercise can help with symptoms such as depression, difficulty concentrating, and fatigue.

Is My Medicine Safe to Take during Pregnancy or Breastfeeding?

It depends on the medicine. Some medicines can be taken safely during pregnancy or while you are breastfeeding, but others are not safe. Your doctor or nurse can help you decide. It is best to discuss these medicines with your doctor or nurse before you ever become pregnant.

How Does the Time before Menopause (Perimenopause) Affect My Mental Health?

As you approach menopause, certain levels of hormones in your body begin to change. This initial transition to menopause when you still get a period is called "perimenopause." During perimenopause, some women begin to feel symptoms such as intense heat and sweating ("hot flashes"), trouble sleeping, and changing moods.

As you get closer to menopause, you may notice other symptoms, such as pain during sex, urinary problems, and irregular periods. These changes can be stressful on you and your relationships and cause you to feel more extreme emotions.

- Women with mental-health conditions may experience more symptoms of menopause or go through perimenopause differently than women who do not have mental-health conditions.

- Women with depression are more likely to go through perimenopause earlier than other women. Studies show that women with depression have lower levels of estrogen.

- Bipolar disorder symptoms may get worse during perimenopause

- Insomnia affects up to half of women going through menopause. Insomnia may be more common in women with anxiety or depression.

- Menopause can cause a relapse of obsessive-compulsive disorder (OCD) or a change in symptoms.

What Steps Can I Take to Stay Mentally Healthy throughout Life?

Steps you can take to support good mental health include the following:

- **Get enough sleep.** Good sleep helps you stay in good mental health. If pregnancy or your menopause symptoms, such as hot flashes, are keeping you awake at night, talk to a doctor or nurse about treatments that can help.

- **Get enough physical activity.** Exercise may help prevent or treat some mental-health conditions. Researchers know that physical activity or exercise can help many people with mental-health conditions, including depression, anxiety, schizophrenia, bipolar disorder, posttraumatic stress disorder (PTSD), eating disorders, and substance abuse. Exercise alone does not usually treat or cure mental-health conditions, but combined with other treatments such as therapy or medicine, it can make your symptoms less severe.

- **Choose healthy foods most of the time.** Getting the right nutrients, including enough fiber, and staying hydrated can help you feel better physically and can boost your mood.

- **Take your medicines.** If you take medicines for a mental-health condition, do not stop without first talking to your doctor or nurse. Once you go through menopause, medicines may work differently for you. They may not be as effective or may have different or worse side effects. Talk to your doctor or nurse about whether you need to switch medicines.

- **Keep a support network.** Whether you talk to friends, family, or a therapist, stay in good communication with people who know you well. Ask for help if you need it.

- **Stay involved as you get older.** Retirement can be a positive opportunity for change, but it can also be stressful. You may miss going to work each day. Having a chronic disease such as diabetes or heart disease may change how much you see friends and family. Find opportunities for volunteering, social activities such as golf or community gardening, or even part-time work to stay connected to others and your community.

Chapter 25

Postpartum Depression

What Is Postpartum Depression?

Your body and mind go through many changes during and after pregnancy. If you feel empty, emotionless, or sad all or most of the time for longer than two weeks during or after pregnancy, reach out for help. If you feel like you do not love or care for your baby, you might have postpartum depression. Treatment for depression, such as therapy or medicine, works and will help you and your baby to be as healthy as possible in the future.

"Postpartum" means the time after childbirth. Most women get the "baby blues," or feel sad or empty, within a few days of giving birth. For many women, the baby blues go away in three to five days. If your baby blues do not go away or you feel sad, hopeless, or empty for longer than two weeks, you may have postpartum depression. Feeling hopeless or empty after childbirth is not a regular or expected part of being a mother.

Postpartum depression is a serious mental illness that involves the brain and affects your behavior and physical health. If you have depression, then sad, flat, or empty feelings do not go away and can interfere with your day-to-day life. You might feel unconnected to your baby, as if you are not the baby's mother, or you might not love or care for the baby. These feelings can be mild to severe.

This chapter includes text excerpted from "Postpartum Depression," Office on Women's Health (OWH), U.S. Department of Health and Human Services (HHS), May 14, 2019.

How Do I Know If I Have Postpartum Depression?

Depression is a common problem after pregnancy. One in nine new mothers has postpartum depression. Some normal changes after pregnancy can cause symptoms similar to those of depression. Many mothers feel overwhelmed when a new baby comes home. But if you have any of the following symptoms of depression for more than two weeks, call your doctor, nurse, or midwife:

- Feeling restless or moody

- Feeling sad, hopeless, or overwhelmed

- Crying a lot

- Having thoughts of hurting the baby

- Having thoughts of hurting yourself

- Not having any interest in the baby, not feeling connected to the baby, or feeling as if your baby is someone else's baby

- Having no energy or motivation

- Eating too little or too much

- Sleeping too little or too much

- Having trouble focusing or making decisions

- Having memory problems

- Feeling worthless, guilty, or like a bad mother

- Losing interest or pleasure in activities you used to enjoy

- Withdrawing from friends and family

- Having headaches, aches, and pains, or stomach problems that do not go away

Some women do not tell anyone about their symptoms. New mothers may feel embarrassed, ashamed, or guilty about feeling depressed when they are supposed to be happy. They may also worry they will be seen as bad mothers. Any woman can become depressed during pregnancy or after having a baby. It does not mean you are a bad mom. You and your baby do not have to suffer. Your doctor can help you figure out whether your symptoms are caused by depression or something else.

What Causes Postpartum Depression

Hormonal changes may trigger symptoms of postpartum depression. When you are pregnant, levels of the female hormones estrogen and progesterone are the highest they will ever be. In the first 24 hours after childbirth, hormone levels quickly drop back to normal, prepregnancy levels. Researchers think this sudden change in hormone levels may lead to depression. This is similar to hormone changes before a woman's period but involves much more extreme swings in hormone levels.

Levels of thyroid hormones may also drop after giving birth. The thyroid is a small gland in the neck that helps regulate how your body uses and stores energy from food. Low levels of thyroid hormones can cause symptoms of depression. A simple blood test can tell whether this condition is causing your symptoms. If so, your doctor can prescribe thyroid medicine.

Other feelings may contribute to postpartum depression. Many new mothers say they feel:

- Tired after labor and delivery
- Tired from a lack of sleep or broken sleep
- Overwhelmed with a new baby
- Doubts about their ability to be a good mother
- Stress from changes in work and home routines
- An unrealistic need to be a perfect mom
- Grief about the loss of who they were before having the baby
- Less attractive
- A lack of free time

These feelings are common among new mothers. But postpartum depression is a serious health condition and can be treated. Postpartum depression is not a regular or expected part of being a new mother.

Are Some Women More at Risk of Postpartum Depression?

Yes. You may be more at risk of postpartum depression if you:

- Have a personal history of depression or bipolar disorder
- Have a family history of depression or bipolar disorder

- Do not have support from family and friends
- Were depressed during pregnancy
- Had problems with a previous pregnancy or birth
- Have relationship or money problems
- Are younger than 20
- Have alcoholism, use illegal drugs, or have some other problem with drugs
- Have a baby with special needs
- Have difficulty breastfeeding
- Had an unplanned or unwanted pregnancy

The U.S. Preventive Services Task Force (USPSTF) recommends that doctors look for and ask about symptoms of depression during and after pregnancy, regardless of a woman's risk of depression.

What Is the Difference between "Baby Blues" and Postpartum Depression?

Many women have the baby blues in the days after childbirth. If you have the baby blues, you may:

- Have mood swings
- Feel sad, anxious, or overwhelmed
- Have crying spells
- Lose your appetite
- Have trouble sleeping

The baby blues usually go away in three to five days after they start. The symptoms of postpartum depression last longer and are more severe. Postpartum depression usually begins within the first month after childbirth, but it can begin during pregnancy or for up to a year after birth.

What Is Postpartum Psychosis?

Postpartum psychosis is rare. It happens in up to four new mothers out of every 1,000 births. It usually begins in the first two weeks after childbirth. It is a medical emergency. Women who have bipolar disorder or another mental-health condition called "schizoaffective disorder" have a higher risk of postpartum psychosis. Symptoms may include:

- Seeing or hearing things that are not there
- Feeling confused most of the time
- Having rapid mood swings within several minutes (for example, crying hysterically, then laughing a lot, followed by extreme sadness)
- Trying to hurt yourself or your baby
- Paranoia (thinking that others are focused on harming you)
- Restlessness or agitation
- Behaving recklessly or in a way that is not normal for you

What Should I Do If I Have Symptoms of Postpartum Depression?

Call your doctor, nurse, midwife, or pediatrician if:

- Your baby blues do not go away after two weeks
- Symptoms of depression get more and more intense
- Symptoms of depression begin within one year of delivery and last more than two weeks
- It is difficult to work or get things done at home
- You cannot care for yourself or your baby (e.g., eating, sleeping, bathing)
- You have thoughts about hurting yourself or your baby

Ask your partner or a loved one to call for you if necessary. Your doctor, nurse, or midwife can ask you questions to test for depression. They can also refer you to a mental-health professional for help and treatment.

What Can I Do at Home to Feel Better while Seeing a Doctor for Postpartum Depression?

Here are some ways to begin feeling better or getting more rest, in addition to talking to a healthcare professional:

- Rest as much as you can. Sleep when the baby is sleeping.

- do not try to do too much or to do everything by yourself. Ask your partner, family, and friends for help.

- Make time to go out, visit friends, or spend time alone with your partner.

- Talk about your feelings with your partner, supportive family members, and friends.

- Talk with other mothers so that you can learn from their experiences.

- Join a support group. Ask your doctor or nurse about groups in your area.

- do not make any major life changes right after giving birth. More major life changes in addition to a new baby can cause unneeded stress. Sometimes big changes cannot be avoided.

When that happens, try to arrange support and help in your new situation ahead of time.

It can also help to have a partner, a friend, or another caregiver who can help take care of the baby while you are depressed. If you are feeling depressed during pregnancy or after having a baby, do not suffer alone. Tell a loved one and call your doctor right away.

How Is Postpartum Depression Treated?

The common types of treatment for postpartum depression are:

- **Therapy.** During therapy, you talk to a therapist, psychologist, or social worker to learn strategies to change how depression makes you think, feel, and act.

- **Medicine.** There are different types of medicines for postpartum depression. All of them must be prescribed by your doctor or nurse. The most common type is antidepressants. Antidepressants can help relieve symptoms of depression and some can be taken while you are breastfeeding. Antidepressants may take several weeks to start working.

The Food and Drug Administration (FDA) has also approved a medicine called "brexanolone" to treat postpartum depression in adult women. Brexanolone is given by a doctor or nurse through an IV for 2½ days (60 hours). Because of the risk of side effects, this medicine can only be given in a clinic or office while you are under the care of a doctor or nurse. Brexanolone may not be safe to take while pregnant or breastfeeding.

Another type of medicine called "esketamine" can treat depression and is given as a nasal (nose) spray in a doctor's office or clinic. Esketamine can hurt an unborn baby. You should not take esketamine if you are pregnant or breastfeeding.

- **Electroconvulsive therapy (ECT).** This can be used in extreme cases to treat postpartum depression.

These treatments can be used alone or together. Talk with your doctor or nurse about the benefits and risks of taking medicine to treat depression when you are pregnant or breastfeeding.

Having depression can affect your baby. Getting treatment is important for you and your baby. Taking medicines for depression or going to therapy does not make you a bad mother or a failure. Getting help is a sign of strength.

What Can Happen If Postpartum Depression Is Not Treated?

Untreated postpartum depression can affect your ability to parent. You may:

- Not have enough energy
- Have trouble focusing on the baby's needs and your own needs
- Feel moody
- Not be able to care for your baby
- Have a higher risk of attempting suicide
- Feeling like a bad mother can make depression worse. It is important to reach out for help if you feel depressed

Researchers believe postpartum depression in a mother can affect her child throughout childhood, causing:

- Delays in language development and problems learning
- Problems with mother-child bonding
- Behavior problems
- More crying or agitation

- Shorter height and higher risk of obesity in preschoolers
- Problems dealing with stress and adjusting to school and other social situations

Chapter 26

Caregivers and Depression

What Is a Caregiver?

A caregiver is anyone who provides care for another person in need, such as a child, an aging parent, a husband or wife, a relative, friend, or neighbor. A caregiver also may be a paid professional who provides care in the home or at a place that is not the person's home.

People who are not paid to give care are called "informal caregivers" or " family caregivers." This chapter focuses on family caregivers who provide care on a regular basis for a loved one with an injury, an illness such as dementia, or a disability. The family caregiver often has to manage the person's daily life. This can include helping with daily tasks such as bathing, eating, or taking medicine. It can also include arranging activities and making health and financial decisions.

Who Are Caregivers?

Most Americans will be informal caregivers at some point during their lives. A survey found that 36 percent of Americans provided unpaid care to another adult with an illness or disability in the past year. That percentage is expected to go up as the proportion of people in the United States who are elderly increases. Also, changes in healthcare mean family caregivers now provide more home-based

This chapter includes text excerpted from "Caregiver Stress," Office on Women's Health (OWH), U.S. Department of Health and Human Services (HHS), June 3, 2019.

medical care. Nearly half of family caregivers give injections or manage medicines daily. Most caregivers are women. And nearly three in five family caregivers have paid jobs in addition to their caregiving.

Who Gets Caregiver Stress

Anyone can get caregiver stress, but more women caregivers say they have stress and other health problems than men caregivers. And some women have a higher risk for health problems from caregiver stress, including those who:

- **Care for a loved one who needs constant medical care and supervision.** Caregivers of people with Alzheimer disease or dementia are more likely to have health problems and to be depressed than caregivers of people with conditions that do not require constant care.

- **Care for a spouse.** Women who are caregivers of spouses are more likely to have high blood pressure, diabetes, and high cholesterol and are twice as likely to have heart disease as women who provide care for others, such as parents or children.

Women caregivers also may be less likely to get regular screenings, and they may not get enough sleep or regular physical activity.

What Are the Signs and Symptoms of Caregiver Stress?

Caregiver stress can take many forms. For instance, you may feel frustrated and angry one minute and helpless the next. You may make mistakes when giving medicines. Or you may turn to unhealthy behaviors such as smoking or drinking too much alcohol.

Other signs and symptoms include:

- Feeling overwhelmed
- Feeling alone, isolated, or deserted by others
- Sleeping too much or too little
- Gaining or losing a lot of weight
- Feeling tired most of the time
- Losing interest in activities you used to enjoy
- Becoming easily irritated or angered

- Feeling worried or sad often

- Having headaches or body aches often

Talk to your doctor about your symptoms and ways to relieve stress. Also, let others give you a break. Reach out to family, friends, or a local resource.

How Does Caregiver Stress Affect My Health?

Some stress can be good for you, as it helps you cope and respond to a change or challenge. But long-term stress of any kind, including caregiver stress, can lead to serious health problems.

Some of the ways stress affects caregivers include:

- **Depression and anxiety.** Women who are caregivers are more likely than men to develop symptoms of anxiety and depression. Anxiety and depression also raise your risk for other health problems, such as heart disease and stroke.

- **Weak immune system.** Stressed caregivers may have weaker immune systems than noncaregivers and spend more days sick with the cold or flu. A weak immune system can also make vaccines such as flu shots less effective. Also, it may take longer to recover from surgery.

- **Obesity.** Stress causes weight gain in more women than men. Obesity raises your risk for other health problems, including heart disease, stroke, and diabetes.

- **Higher risk for chronic diseases.** High levels of stress, especially when combined with depression, can raise your risk for health problems, such as heart disease, cancer, diabetes, or arthritis.

- **Problems with short-term memory or paying attention.** Caregivers of spouses with Alzheimer disease are at higher risk for problems with short-term memory and focusing.

Caregivers also report symptoms of stress more often than people who are not caregivers.

What Can I Do to Prevent or Relieve Caregiver Stress?

Taking steps to relieve caregiver stress helps prevent health problems. Also, taking care of yourself helps you take better care of your loved one and enjoy the rewards of caregiving.

Here are some tips to help you prevent or manage caregiver stress:

- **Learn ways to better help your loved one.** Some hospitals offer classes that can teach you how to care for someone with an injury or illness. To find these classes, ask your doctor or call your local Area Agency on Aging (AAA).

- **Find caregiving resources in your community to help you.** Many communities have adult day care services or respite services to give primary caregivers a break from their caregiving duties.

- **Ask for and accept help.** Make a list of ways others can help you. Let helpers choose what they would like to do. For instance, someone might sit with the person you care for while you do an errand. Someone else might pick up groceries for you.

- **Join a support group for caregivers.** You can find a general caregiver support group or a group with caregivers who care for someone with the same illness or disability as your loved one. You can share stories, pick up caregiving tips, and get support from others who face the same challenges as you do.

- **Get organized.** Make to-do lists, and set a daily routine.

- **Take time for yourself.** Stay in touch with family and friends, and do things you enjoy with your loved ones.

- **Take care of your health.** Find time to be physically active on most days of the week, choose healthy foods, and get enough sleep.

- **See your doctor for regular checkups.** Make sure to tell your doctor or nurse you are a caregiver. Also, tell them about any symptoms of depression or sickness you may have.

If you work outside the home and are feeling overwhelmed, consider taking a break from your job. Under the federal Family and Medical Leave Act (FMLA), eligible employees can take up to 12 weeks of unpaid leave per year to care for relatives. Ask your human resources office about your options

What Caregiving Services Can I Find in My Community?

Caregiving services include:

- Meal delivery

- Home healthcare services, such as nursing or physical therapy

- Nonmedical home care services, such as housekeeping, cooking, or companionship

- Making changes to your home, such as installing ramps or modified bathtubs

- Legal and financial counseling

- Respite care, which is a substitute caregiving (someone comes to your home, or you may take your loved one to an adult day care center or day hospital)

- The National Eldercare Locator, a service of the U.S. Administration on Aging (AOA), can help you find caregiving services in your area. You can also contact your local Area Agency on Aging.

How Can I Pay for Home Healthcare and Other Caregiving Services?

Medicare, Medicaid, and private insurance companies will cover some costs of home healthcare. Other costs you will have to pay for yourself.

- If the person who needs care has insurance, check with the person's insurance provider to find out what is included in the plan.

- If the person who needs care has Medicare, find out what home health services are covered.

- If the person who needs care has Medicaid, coverage of home health services vary between states. Check with your state's Medicaid program to learn what the benefits are.

If you or the person who needs caregiving also needs health insurance, learn about the services covered under Marketplace plans at Healthcare.gov.

Chapter 27

Depression in Prison Inmates

The State of the Prisons

Prisoners in the United States have confronted a unique set of contingencies and pressures to which they were required to react and adapt in order to survive the prison experience. The challenges prisoners face in order to both survive the prison experience and, eventually, reintegrate into the free world upon release have changed and intensified. Changes in the nature of imprisonment have included a series of interrelated, negative trends in American corrections. The most dramatic changes have come about as a result of the unprecedented increases in the rate of incarceration, the size of the U.S. prison population, and the widespread overcrowding that has occurred as a result. Over the past 25 years, penologists repeatedly have described U.S. prisons as "in crisis" and have characterized each new level of overcrowding as "unprecedented." It has been documented that the U.S. rates of incarceration have consistently been between 4 and 8 times those for other nations.

The combination of overcrowding and the rapid expansion of prison systems across the country adversely affected living conditions in

This chapter includes text excerpted from "The Psychological Impact of Incarceration: Implications for Post-Prison Adjustment," Office of the Assistant Secretary for Planning and Evaluation (ASPE), December 2001, Reviewed October 2019.

many prisons, jeopardized prisoner safety, compromised prison management, and greatly limited prisoner access to meaningful programming. Federal courts have found that the prison system had failed to provide adequate treatment services for those prisoners who suffered the most extreme psychological effects of confinement in deteriorated and overcrowded conditions.

The rapid influx of new prisoners, serious shortages in staffing and other resources, and the embrace of an openly punitive approach to corrections led to the "deskilling" of many correctional staff members who often resorted to extreme forms of prison discipline (such as punitive isolation or "supermax" confinement) that had especially destructive effects on prisoners and repressed conflict rather than resolving it. Increased tensions and higher levels of fear and danger resulted.

Increased sentence length and a greatly expanded scope of incarceration resulted in prisoners experiencing the psychological strains of imprisonment for longer periods of time.

Thus, in the first decade of the 21st century, more people have been subjected to the pains of imprisonment, for longer periods of time, under conditions that threaten greater psychological distress and potential long-term dysfunction, and they will be returned to communities that have already been disadvantaged by a lack of social services and resources.

The Psychological Effects of Incarceration on the Nature of Institutionalization

Prison is painful, and incarcerated persons often suffer long-term consequences from having been subjected to pain, deprivation, and extremely atypical patterns and norms of living and interacting with others. The more extreme, harsh, dangerous, or otherwise psychologically taxing the nature of the confinement, the greater the number of people who will suffer and the deeper the damage that they will incur.

The process of prisonization involves the incorporation of the norms of prison life into one's habits of thinking, feeling, and acting.

Natural and normal adaptations are made by prisoners in response to the unnatural and abnormal conditions of prisoner life. The longer someone is incarcerated the more significant the nature of the institutional transformation. When most people first enter prison, they find that being forced to adapt to an often harsh and rigid institutional routine, deprived of privacy and liberty, and subjected to a diminished, stigmatized status and extremely sparse material conditions is stressful, unpleasant, and difficult.

In the course of becoming institutionalized, a transformation begins. Persons gradually become more accustomed to the restrictions that institutional life imposes. The various psychological mechanisms that must be employed to adjust (and, in some harsh and dangerous correctional environments, to survive) become increasingly "natural," second nature, and, to a degree, internalized. The longer someone remains in an institution, the greater the likelihood that the process will transform them.

Among other things, the process of institutionalization (or "prisonization") includes some or all of the following psychological adaptations:

Dependence on Institutional Structure and Contingencies

Inmates need to relinquish the freedom and autonomy to make their own choices and decisions and this process requires a painful adjustment for most people. Some people never adjust to it. Over time, prisoners may adjust to the muting of self-initiative and independence and become increasingly dependent on institutional contingencies that they once resisted. In the final stages of the process, some inmates may come to depend heavily on institutional decision makers to make choices for them and to rely on the structure and schedule of the institution to organize their daily routine. Rarely, some people do lose the capacity to initiate behavior on their own and the judgment to make decisions for themselves. In extreme cases, profoundly institutionalized persons may become extremely uncomfortable when and if their previous freedom and autonomy is returned.

Thus, institutionalization or prisonization renders some people so dependent on external constraints that they gradually lose the capacity to rely on internal organization and self-imposed personal limits to guide their actions and restrain their conduct. When this external structure is taken away, severely institutionalized persons may find that they no longer know how to do things on their own, or how to refrain from doing those things that are ultimately harmful or self-destructive.

Hypervigilance, Interpersonal Distrust, and Suspicion

Many prisons are clearly dangerous places from which there is no exit or escape, prisoners learn quickly to become hypervigilant and ever-alert for signs of threat or personal risk. Because the stakes are high, and because there are people in their immediate environment poised to take advantage of weakness or exploit carelessness or inattention, interpersonal distrust and suspicion often result. Some prisoners learn to project a tough convict veneer that keeps all others at a distance.

Emotional Over-Control, Alienation, and Psychological Distancing

Prisoners struggle to control and suppress their own internal emotional reactions to events around them. Emotional over-control and a generalized lack of spontaneity may occur as a result. Admissions of vulnerability to persons inside the immediate prison environment are potentially dangerous because they invite exploitation.

Prisoners who labor at both an emotional and behavioral level to develop a "prison mask" that is unrevealing and impenetrable risk alienation from themselves and others, may develop emotional flatness that becomes chronic and debilitating in social interaction and relationships, and find that they have created a permanent and unbridgeable distance between themselves and other people. Many for whom the mask becomes especially thick and effective in prison find that the disincentive against engaging in open communication with others that prevails there has led them to withdrawal from authentic social interactions altogether.

Social Withdrawal and Isolation

Some prisoners learn to find safety in social invisibility by becoming as inconspicuous and disconnected from others as possible. The self-imposed social withdrawal and isolation may mean that they retreat deeply into themselves, trust virtually no one, and adjust to prison stress by leading isolated lives of quiet desperation. In extreme cases, especially when combined with prisoner apathy and loss of the capacity to initiate behavior on one's own, the pattern closely resembles that of clinical depression. Long-term prisoners are particularly vulnerable to this form of psychological adaptation.

Incorporation of Exploitative Norms of Prison Culture

In addition to obeying the formal rules of the institution, there are also informal rules and norms that are part of the unwritten but essential institutional and inmate culture and code that, at some level, must be abided. For some prisoners this means defending against the dangers and deprivations of the surrounding environment by embracing all of its informal norms, including some of the most exploitative and extreme values of prison life. Prisoners typically are given no alternative culture to which to ascribe or in which to participate. In many institutions, the lack of meaningful programming has deprived them of prosocial or positive activities in which to engage while incarcerated. Few prisoners are given access to gainful employment where they can obtain meaningful job skills and earn adequate compensation; those who do work are assigned to menial tasks that they perform for only a few hours a day.

Diminished Sense of Self-Worth and Personal Value

Prisoners typically are denied their basic privacy rights, and lose control over mundane aspects of their existence that most citizens have long taken for granted. They live in small, sometimes extremely cramped and deteriorating spaces (a 60 square foot cell is roughly the size of king-size bed), have little or no control over the identify of the person with whom they must share that space (and the intimate contact it requires), often have no choice over when they must get up or go to bed, and when or what they may eat. The degraded conditions under which they live serve to repeatedly remind them of their compromised social status and stigmatized social role as prisoners. A diminished sense of self-worth and personal value may result. Prisoners may come to think of themselves as "the kind of person" who deserves only the degradation and stigma to which they have been subjected while incarcerated.

Posttraumatic Stress Reactions to the Pains of Imprisonment

For some prisoners, incarceration is so stark and psychologically painful that it represents a form of traumatic stress severe enough to produce posttraumatic stress reactions once released. Moreover, there are certain basic commonalities that characterize the lives of many of the persons who have been convicted of crime in our society. events (like poverty, abusive and neglectful mistreatment, and other forms of victimization) in the social histories of many criminal offenders. A high percentage of persons presently incarcerated have experienced childhood trauma, which means that the harsh, punitive, and uncaring nature of prison life may represent a kind of "retraumatization" experience for many of them. Time spent in prison may rekindle not only memories but the disabling psychological reactions and consequences of these earlier damaging experiences.

The most negative consequences of institutionalization may first occur in the form of internal chaos, disorganization, stress, and fear. Yet, institutionalization has taught most people to cover their internal states, and not to openly or easily reveal intimate feelings or reactions. So, the outward appearance of normality and adjustment may mask a range of serious problems in adapting to the free world.

This is true of persons who return to the free world lacking a network of close, personal contacts with people who know them well enough to sense that something may be wrong. Eventually, however, when severely institutionalized persons confront complicated problems or conflicts, especially in the form of unexpected events that cannot be planned for in advance, the myriad of challenges may become overwhelming. The facade of normality begins to deteriorate, and persons may behave in dysfunctional or even destructive ways because all of the external structure and supports upon which they relied to keep themselves controlled, directed, and balanced have been removed.

Implications for the Transition from Prison to Home

The psychological consequences of incarceration may represent significant impediments to postprison adjustment. They may interfere with the transition from prison to home, impede an ex-convict's successful reintegration into a social network and employment setting, and may compromise an incarcerated parent's ability to resume her or his role with family and children.

The implications of these psychological effects for parenting and family life can be profound. Parents who return from periods of incarceration cannot be expected to effectively organize the lives of their children or exercise the initiative and autonomous decision making that parenting requires. They will find it difficult to promote trust and authenticity within their children. Those who remain emotionally over-controlled and alienated from others will experience problems being psychologically available and nurturant. Tendencies to socially withdraw, remain aloof or seek social invisibility is high. The residual effects of the posttraumatic stress of imprisonment and the retraumatization experiences can jeopardize the mental health of persons attempting to reintegrate back into the free world communities from which they came.

Policy and Programmatic Responses to the Adverse Effects of Incarceration

It is important to provide psychological resources and social services for persons who have been adversely affected by incarceration for a successful transition from prison to home is to occur on a consistent and effective basis.

There are three areas in which policy interventions must be concentrated in order to address these two levels of concern:

- Prison conditions, policies, and procedures

- Transitional services to prepare prisoners for community release

- Community-based services to facilitate and maintain reintegration

Part Four

Causes and Risk Factors of Depression

Chapter 28

What Causes Depression

Chapter Contents

Section 28.1

Overview of the Causes of Depression

This section includes text excerpted from the following sources:
Text in this section begins with excerpts from "Depression,"
Genetics Home Reference (GHR), National Institutes of Health
(NIH), September 3, 2019; Text under the heading "Other Causes
of Depression" is excerpted from "Depression," Office on Women's
Health (OWH), U.S. Department of Health and Human
Services (HHS), May 21, 2018.

Depression is known to run in families, suggesting that genetic factors contribute to the risk of developing this disease. However, research into the genetics of depression is in its early stages, and very little is known for certain about the genetic basis of the disease. Studies suggest that variations in many genes, each with a small effect, combine to increase the risk of developing depression.

Genetic Factors

Determining the genetic risk factors for depression is challenging for several reasons. It is possible that what is currently considered to be a single disease called "depression" is actually multiple disorders with similar signs and symptoms; these disorders could have different genetic risk factors. The genetic variations related to depression may also be somewhat different between men and women. Researchers suspect that studies with many more people will be required to pinpoint the genetic variations that influence the risk of depression.

The genes thought to be associated with depression have diverse functions in the brain. Some of these genes may control the production (synthesis), transport, and activity of chemicals called "neurotransmitters," which relay chemical signals that allow nerve cells (neurons) to communicate with one another. Other genes that may influence the risk of depression are involved in the growth, maturation, and maintenance of neurons, as well as the ability of the connections between neurons (synapses) to change and adapt over time in response to experience, a characteristic known as "synaptic plasticity."

Nongenetic Factors

Nongenetic (environmental) factors also play critical roles in a person's risk of developing depression. The disorder can be triggered by substance abuse, certain medications, or stressful life events (such as divorce or the death of a loved one). Other risk factors include difficulties in relationships or social isolation, unemployment, financial problems, and childhood abuse or neglect. Some physical illnesses, such as cancer, thyroid disease, and chronic pain, are also associated with an increased risk of developing depression. It is likely that environmental conditions interact with genetic factors to determine the overall risk of developing this disease.

Other Causes of Depression

There are many reasons why a person may have depression:

- **Family history.** People with a family history of depression may be more at risk. But depression can also happen in women who do not have a family history of depression.

- **Brain changes.** The brains of people with depression look and function differently from those of people who do not have depression.

- **Chemistry.** In someone who has depression, parts of the brain that manage mood, thoughts, sleep, appetite, and behavior may not have the right balance of chemicals.

- **Hormone levels.** Changes in levels of the female hormones estrogen and progesterone during the menstrual cycle, pregnancy, postpartum period, perimenopause, or menopause may raise a woman's risk for depression. Having a miscarriage can also put a woman at higher risk for depression.

- **Stress.** Serious and stressful life events, or the combination of several stressful events, such as trauma, loss of a loved one, a bad relationship, work responsibilities, caring for children and aging parents, abuse, and poverty, may trigger depression in some people.

- **Medical problems.** Dealing with a serious health problem, such as stroke, heart attack, or cancer, can lead to depression. Research shows that people who have a serious illness and depression are more likely to have more serious types of both conditions. Some medical illnesses, like Parkinson disease (PD), hypothyroidism, and stroke, can cause changes in the brain that can trigger depression.

- **Pain.** Those who feel emotional or physical pain for long periods are much more likely to develop depression. The pain can come from a chronic (long-term) health problem, accident, or trauma such as sexual assault or abuse.

Section 28.2

Probing the Depression–Rumination Cycle

"Probing the Depression-Rumination Cycle,"
© 2017 Omnigraphics. Reviewed October 2019.

Rumination is a thought process in which people obsessively focus on negative experiences and replay them over and over in their minds. The word is derived from the Latin term for ruminant animals, which are species with digestive systems that require them to regurgitate and rechew food. People who ruminate tend to chew over unpleasant situations repeatedly or brood about troubling issues constantly. Although self-reflection and analysis of past experiences can be helpful in problem solving, rumination rarely offers new insights or leads to a better understanding of a situation. Instead, people who ruminate focus so intensely on negative feelings that they lose perspective and become unable to experience positive feelings, which can cause anxiety and depression.

Rumination and Depression

Research has found links between rumination and several mental-health conditions, including depression, anxiety, posttraumatic stress disorder (PTSD), substance abuse, and eating disorders. For instance, studies indicate that people who ruminate are four times more likely than other people to develop major depression. Rumination intensifies the negative feelings associated with depression, such as hopelessness, inadequacy, and worthlessness. In addition, rumination destroys self-confidence and creates uncertainty that makes people doubt their own judgment and avoid taking positive steps toward finding solutions to problems.

Rumination also reduces the level of social support available to help with personal problems. Research has shown that ruminators seek help more often than other people. Yet their persistently negative outlook and tendency to dwell on unpleasantness can create social friction and drive friends and relatives away. After a while, people being asked for support become frustrated and respond less compassionately, perhaps telling the ruminator to just forget about whatever they are obsessing over and move on with their life. The ruminator may interpret this response as rejection or abandonment, which then provides another negative experience for them to ruminate about. In this way, rumination and depression can become locked in a self-reinforcing cycle.

Rumination Triggers

Many of the triggers for rumination are similar to those for depression. In women, grief, sadness, and regret often serve as triggers for depressive rumination. In men, anger and resentment are the most common emotions that trigger rumination. Rumination is often associated with traumatic or stressful life events, such as losing a job, experiencing the death of a loved one, or having an illness or accident.

People who are prone to rumination often share some basic personality characteristics. Many ruminators are perfectionists who struggle to cope with less-than-perfect results. Many ruminators also tend to exhibit neuroticism and place an excessive value on interpersonal relationships. Finally, ruminators are likely to feel as if they face constant sources of pressure or stress that are beyond their control. Most do not view their rumination as part of the problem, but rather as a means of gaining necessary insight to deal with their problems.

Breaking the Rumination Cycle

Since rumination and depression can become linked in a self-perpetuating cycle, finding ways to stop ruminating can also help lighten symptoms of depression. Although depression is a medical condition that cannot be simply willed away, some people experience improvements in mood when they utilize techniques to avoid ruminating on negative thoughts and feelings. Some suggested methods of stopping or preventing rumination include the following:

Healthy Distraction

With practice, many ruminators can learn to recognize when they become focused on negative thoughts and experiences and employ various methods to distract themselves. Possible distraction techniques include doing chores such as vacuuming or mowing the lawn; watching a movie; taking a nap, or engaging in meditation or prayer. It may also be helpful to imagine a soothing image, such as a slowly rotating fan, a babbling brook, or the details of a childhood bedroom or yard. Practicing mindfulness is another valuable distraction tool. When negative thoughts about past events intrude upon enjoyment of the present, it may be helpful to redirect thoughts toward the immediate moment by carefully recognizing and considering what each sense is experiencing. Research has shown that distraction techniques can help reduce the time ruminators spend dwelling on and discussing negative events, which can also help improve the quality of their relationships.

Positive Thinking

The rumination-depression cycle works by activating neural networks in the brain that are attuned to negative thoughts and emotions. One bad memory of a negative outcome triggers additional memories of negative experiences, which leads to anxiety, self-doubt, and depression. With practice, however, many people can develop the skill of deliberately shifting their focus away from these neural networks and instead of activating memories of positive experiences. Interrupting rumination and shifting to a network of positive thoughts can be difficult for people with depression. Some tips for accessing positive memories include asking family and friends for help and encouragement in remembering good times; listening to music associated with happy times and good moods; looking at photographs or videos of joyful experiences and trying to remember the sounds, smells, and other sensations; and physically going to a place connected with positive outcomes and states of mind. Accessing a positive neural network can provide a change of perspective and reveal new approaches to dealing with problems.

Planning

Depressive ruminators tend to become immobilized by negative thoughts and feel incapable of moving forward. They envision terrible outcomes and become afraid to try because they might fail. Breaking the cycle requires letting go of unattainable goals and things that are beyond one's control or ability to change. It may be helpful to break down a seemingly big problem into smaller, actionable pieces. Then, instead of focusing on the big problem, it may be possible to plan a series of small steps toward solving each part of the problem. Making a plan of action and achieving small goals can help increase self-confidence and decrease feelings of inadequacy and hopelessness. To avoid becoming paralyzed by inaction, it is important to view inevitable mistakes and failures as opportunities for learning and personal growth.

Containment

Of course, it is not possible to keep negative thoughts at bay all of the time. But there are proven techniques for containing those thoughts, reducing their power, and preventing them from turning into harmful rumination. One way to eliminate the power of negative thoughts and insecurities is to identify and confront them directly. Keeping a journal of emotions and triggers can help to clarify the source of negative thoughts. Once the underlying fear has been identified, the next step is to envision the worst-case scenario. Someone who panics at the thought of speaking in front of an audience, for instance, could picture forgetting a speech and looking foolish. In most cases, confronting the worst-case scenario helps people realize that they are resilient enough to handle it. To avoid ruminating, it may be helpful to contain negative thoughts by scheduling 15 to 30 minutes of worry time per day to dwell upon them. This method makes it easier to dismiss negative thoughts when they intrude at other times.

Therapy

Seeing a professional counselor may be helpful for people whose rumination interferes with their enjoyment of life. Mental-health professionals can offer support, encouragement, and additional techniques and guidance to help people break out of the rumination-depression cycle and improve their mood, confidence, and self-esteem.

References

1.   Chand, Suma. "Uplift Your Mood: Stop Ruminating," Anxiety and Depression Association of America (ADAA), 2016.

2. Feiner, Lauren. "Eight Tips to Help Stop Ruminating," Psych Central, February 16, 2014.

3. Law, Bridget Murray. "Probing the Depression-Rumination Cycle," APA Monitor, November 2005.

4. Wehrenberg, Margaret. "Rumination: A Problem in Anxiety and Depression," Psychology Today, April 20, 2016.

Chapter 29

Stress, Resilience, and the Risk of Depression

Chapter Contents

Section 29.1

Stress and Your Health

This section includes text excerpted from "Manage Stress,"
Office of Disease Prevention and Health Promotion (ODPHP),
U.S. Department of Health and Human Services (HHS),
September 26, 2018.

The Basics

Not all stress is bad. But, chronic (ongoing) stress can lead to health problems.

Preventing and managing chronic stress can lower your risk for serious conditions, such as heart disease, obesity, high blood pressure, and depression.

You can prevent or reduce stress by:

- Planning ahead
- Deciding which tasks need to be done first
- Preparing for stressful events

Some stress is hard to avoid. You can find ways to manage stress by:

- Noticing when you feel stressed
- Taking time to relax
- Getting active and eating healthy
- Talking to friends and family

What Are the Signs of Stress?

When people are under stress, they may feel:

- Worried
- Angry
- Irritable
- Depressed
- Unable to focus

Stress also affects your body. Physical signs of stress include:

- Headaches

- Back pain
- Problems sleeping
- Upset stomach
- Weight gain or loss
- Tense muscles
- Frequent or more serious colds

What Are the Benefits of Managing Stress?

Over time, chronic stress can lead to health problems. Managing stress can help you:

- Sleep better
- Control your weight
- Get sick less often
- Feel better faster when you do get sick
- Have less neck and back pain
- Be in a better mood
- Get along better with family and friends

Take Action

You cannot always avoid stress, but you can take steps to deal with your stress in a positive way. Follow these tips for preventing and managing stress.

Being prepared and feeling in control of your situation might help lower your stress.

Plan Your Time

Think ahead about how you are going to use your time. Write a to-do list and figure out what is most important, then do that thing first. Be realistic about how long each task will take.

Prepare Yourself

Prepare ahead of time for stressful events such as a job interview or a hard conversation with a loved one.

- Stay positive

- Picture what the room will look like and what you will say.

- Have a back-up plan.

Relax with Deep Breathing or Meditation

Deep breathing and meditation are two ways to relax your muscles and clear your mind. Try meditating for a few minutes.

Relax Your Muscles

Stress causes tension in your muscles. Try stretching or taking a hot shower to help you relax.

Get Active

Regular physical activity can help prevent and manage stress. It can also help relax your muscles and improve your mood.

- Aim for two hours and 30 minutes a week of physical activity. Try going for a bike ride or taking a walk.

- Be sure to exercise for at least ten minutes at a time.

- Do strengthening activities such as crunches or lifting weights at least two days a week.

Eat Healthy

Give your body plenty of energy by eating healthy, including vegetables, fruits, and lean sources of protein.

Drink Alcohol Only in Moderation

Avoid using alcohol or other drugs to manage stress. If you choose to drink, drink only in moderation. This means no more than one drink a day for women and no more than two drinks a day for men.

Talk to Friends and Family

Tell your friends and family if you are feeling stressed. They may be able to help.

Get Help If You Need It

Stress is a normal part of life. But, if your stress does not go away or keeps getting worse, you may need help. Over time, stress can lead to serious problems, such as depression or anxiety.

- If you are feeling down or hopeless, talk to a doctor about depression.

- If you are feeling anxious, get help for anxiety.

- If you have lived through an unsafe event, get treated for posttraumatic stress disorder (PTSD).

A mental-health professional (such as a psychologist or social worker) can help treat these conditions with talk therapy (called "psychotherapy") or medicine.

Lots of people need help dealing with stress, it is nothing to be ashamed of.

Section 29.2

Resilience Factors and the Risk of Developing Mental-Health Problems

This section includes text excerpted from "Effects of Disasters: Risk and Resilience Factors," National Center for Posttraumatic Stress Disorder (NCPTSD), U.S. Department of Veterans Affairs (VA), September 30, 2018.

Stress reactions after a disaster look very much like the common reactions seen after any type of trauma. Disasters can cause a full range of mental and physical reactions. You may also react to problems that occur after the event, as well as to triggers or reminders of the trauma.

Risk Factors

A number of factors make it more likely that someone will have more severe or longer-lasting stress reactions after disasters:

Severity of Exposure

The amount of exposure to the disaster is highly related to the risk of future mental problems. At highest risk are those that go through the disaster themselves. Next, are those in close contact with victims. At the lower risk of lasting impact are those who only had indirect exposure, such as news of the severe damage. Injury and life threats are the factors that lead most often to mental-health problems. Studies have looked at severe natural disasters, such as the Armenian earthquake, mudslides in Mexico, and Hurricane Andrew in the United States. The findings show that at least half of these survivors suffer from distress or mental-health problems that need clinical care.

Gender and Family

Almost always, women or girls suffer more negative effects than men or boys. Disaster recovery is more stressful when children are present in the home. Women with spouses also experience more distress during recovery. Having a family member in the home who is extremely distressed is related to more stress for everyone. Marital stress has been found to increase after disasters. Also, conflicts between family members or lack of support in the home make it harder to recover from disasters.

Age

Adults who are in the age range of 40 to 60 are likely to be more distressed after disasters. The thinking is that if you are in that age range, you have more demands from job and family. Research on how children react to natural disasters is limited. In general, children show more severe distress after disasters than do adults. Higher stress in the parents is related to worse recovery in children.

Other Factors Specific to the Survivor

Several factors related to a survivor's background and resources are important for recovery from disaster. Recovery is worse if you:

- Were not functioning well before the disaster

- Have had no experience dealing with disasters

- Must deal with other stressors after the disaster

- Have poor self-esteem

- Think you are uncared for by others
- Think you have little control over what happens to you
- Lack the capacity to manage stress

Other factors have also been found to predict worse outcomes:

- Bereavement (death of someone close)
- Injury to self or another family member
- Life threat
- Panic, horror, or similar feelings during the disaster
- Being separated from family (especially among youth)
- Great loss of property
- Displacement (being forced to leave home)

Developing Countries

These risk factors can be made worse if a disaster occurs in a developing country. Disasters in developing countries have more severe mental-health impact than do disasters in developed countries. This is true even with less serious disasters. For example, natural disasters are generally thought to be less serious than human-caused. In developing countries, though, natural disasters have more severe effects than do human-caused disasters in developed countries.

Low or Negative Social Support

The support of others can be both a risk and a resilience factor. Social support can weaken after disasters. This may be due to stress and the need for members of the support network to get on with their own lives. Sometimes the responses from others you rely on for support are negative. For example, someone may play down your problems, needs, or pain, or expect you to recover more quickly than is realistic. This is strongly linked to long-term distress in trauma survivors.

After a mass trauma, social conflicts, even those that have been resolved, may again be seen. Racial, religious, ethnic, social, and tribal divisions may recur as people try to gain access to much-needed resources. In families, conflicts may arise if family members went through different things in the disaster. This sets up different courses of recovery that often are not well understood among family members.

Family members may also serve as distressing reminders to each other of the disaster.

Keep in mind that while millions of people have been directly affected by disasters, most of them do recover. Human nature is resilient, and most people have the ability to come back from a disaster. Plus, people sometimes report positive changes after the disaster. They may rethink what is truly important and come to appreciate what they value most in life.

Resilience Factors

Human resilience dictates that a large number of survivors naturally recover from disasters over time. They will move on without having severe, long-lasting mental-health issues. Certain factors increase resilience after disasters:

Social Support

Social support is one of the keys to recovery after any trauma, including disaster. Social support increases well-being and limits distress after mass trauma. Being connected to others makes it easier to obtain the knowledge needed for disaster recovery. Through social support, you can also find:

- Practical help solving problems.

- A sense of being understood and accepted.

- Sharing of trauma experiences.

- Some comfort that what you went through and how you responded is not "abnormal."

- Shared tips about coping.

Coping Confidence

Over and over, research has found that coping self-efficacy, "believing that you can do it" is related to better mental-health outcomes for disaster survivors. When you think that you can cope no matter what happens to you, you tend to do better after a disaster. It is not so much feeling like you can handle things in general. Rather, it is believing you can cope with the results of a disaster that has been found to help survivors to recover.

Hope

Better outcomes after disasters or mass trauma are likely if you have one or more of the following:

- Optimism (because you can hope for the future)
- Expecting the positive
- Confidence that you can predict your life and yourself
- Belief that it is very likely that things will work out as well as can reasonably be expected
- Belief that outside sources, such as the government, are acting on your behalf with your welfare at heart
- Belief in God
- Positive superstitious belief, such as "I am always lucky"
- Practical resources, including housing, job, money

Summing It Up

Disasters can cause both mental and physical reactions. Being closer to the disaster and having weak social support can lead to worse recovery. On the other hand, being connected to others and being confident that you can handle the results of the disaster make mental-health problems less likely. Overall, human beings are resilient, and most survivors will recover from the disaster. For those with higher risk factors, self-care and seeking help are recommended.

Chapter 30

Trauma as a Risk Factor for Depression

Chapter Contents

Section 30.1

Depression, Trauma, and Posttraumatic Stress Disorder

This section includes text excerpted from "Depression, Trauma, and PTSD," National Center for Posttraumatic Stress Disorder (NCPTSD), U.S. Department of Veterans Affairs (VA), August 13, 2015. Reviewed October 2019.

Depression is a common problem that can occur following trauma. It involves feelings of sadness or low mood that lasts more than just a few days. Unlike a blue mood that comes and goes, depression is longer lasting. Depression can get in the way of daily life and make it hard to function. It can affect your eating and sleeping, how you think, and how you feel about yourself.

How Common Is Depression Following Trauma?

Depression is more than just feeling sad. Most people with depression feel down or sad more days than not for at least two weeks. Or they find they no longer enjoy or have an interest in things anymore. If you have depression, you may notice that you are sleeping and eating a lot more or less than you used to. You may find it hard to stay focused. You may feel down on yourself or hopeless. With more severe depression, you may think about hurting or killing yourself.

How Are Depression and Trauma Related?

Depression can sometimes seem to come from out of the blue. It can also be caused by a stressful event such as a divorce or a trauma. Trouble coping with painful experiences or losses often leads to depression. For example, Veterans returning from a war zone may have painful memories and feelings of guilt or regret about their war experiences. They may have been injured or lost friends. Disaster survivors may have lost a loved one, a home, or have been injured. Survivors of violence or abuse may feel like they can no longer trust other people. These kinds of experiences can lead to both depression and PTSD.

Many symptoms of depression overlap with the symptoms of PTSD. For example, with both depression and PTSD, you may have trouble sleeping or keeping your mind focused. You may not feel pleasure or interest in things you used to enjoy. You may not want to be with other people as much. Both PTSD and depression may involve greater irritability. It is quite possible to have both depression and PTSD at the same time.

How Is Depression Treated?

There are many treatment options for depression. You should be assessed by a healthcare professional who can decide which type of treatment is best for you. In many cases, milder forms of depression are treated by counseling or therapy. More severe depression is treated with medicines or with both therapy and medicine.

Research has shown that certain types of therapy and medicine are effective for both depression and PTSD. Since the symptoms of PTSD and depression can overlap, treatment that helps with PTSD may also result in improvement of depression. Cognitive-behavioral therapy (CBT) is a type of therapy that is proven effective for both problems. CBT can help patients change negative styles of thinking and acting that can lead to both depression and PTSD. A type of medicine that is effective for both depression and PTSD is a selective serotonin reuptake inhibitor (SSRI).

What Can I Do about Feelings of Depression?

Depression can make you feel worn out, worthless, helpless, hopeless, and sad. These feelings can make you feel as though you are never going to feel better. You may even think that you should just give up. Some symptoms of depression, such as being tired or not having the desire to do anything, can also get in the way of your seeking treatment.

It is very important for you to know that these negative thoughts and feelings are part of depression. If you think you might be depressed, you should seek help in spite of these feelings. You can expect them to change as treatment begins working. In the meantime, here is a list of things you can do that may improve your mood:

- Talk with your doctor or healthcare provider.

- Talk with family and friends.

- Spend more time with others and get support from them. Do not close yourself off.

- Take part in activities that might make you feel better. Do the things you used to enjoy before you began feeling depressed. Even if you do not feel like it, try doing some of these things. Chances are you will feel better after you do.

- Engage in mild exercise.

- Set realistic goals for yourself.

- Break up goals and tasks into smaller ones that you can manage.

Conclusions

Depression is common in those who have PTSD. The symptoms of depression can make it hard to function, and may also get in the way of your getting treatment. Be aware that there are effective treatments for both depression and PTSD. If you think you may be depressed, talk to your doctor.

Section 30.2

Adverse Childhood Experiences

This section includes text excerpted from "Adverse Childhood Experiences (ACEs)," Centers for Disease Control and Prevention (CDC), April 9, 2019.

About Adverse Childhood Experiences

Adverse childhood experiences (ACEs) is the term used to describe all types of abuse, neglect, and other potentially traumatic experiences that occur to people under the age of 18.

Adverse childhood experiences have been linked to:

- Risky health behaviors,

- Chronic health conditions,

- Low life potential, and

- Early death

Adverse childhood experiences have a tremendous impact on future violence victimization and perpetration, and lifelong health and opportunity.

As the number of ACEs increases, so does the risk for these outcomes.

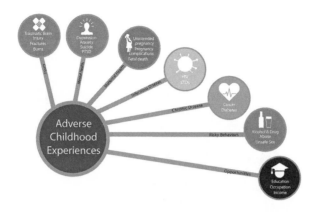

Figure 30.1. *Early Adversity Has Lasting Impacts*

The presence of ACEs does not mean that a child will experience poor outcomes. However, children's positive experiences or protective factors can prevent children from experiencing adversity and can protect against many of the negative health and life outcomes even after adversity has occurred.

It is important to address the conditions that put children and families at risk of ACEs so that can prevent ACEs before they happen.

About the Centers for Disease Control and Prevention-Kaiser Adverse Childhood Experiences Study

The Centers for Disease Control and Prevention (CDC)-Kaiser Permanente ACE Study is one of the largest investigations of childhood abuse and neglect and household challenges and later-life health and well-being.

The original ACE Study was conducted at Kaiser Permanente from 1995 to 1997 with two waves of data collection. Over 17,000 Health Maintenance Organization (HMO) members from Southern California receiving physical exams completed confidential surveys regarding their childhood experiences health status and behaviors.

The Adverse Childhood Experiences Pyramid

The ACE Pyramid represents the conceptual framework for the ACE Study. The ACE Study has uncovered how ACEs are strongly related to development of risk factors for disease, and well-being throughout the life course.

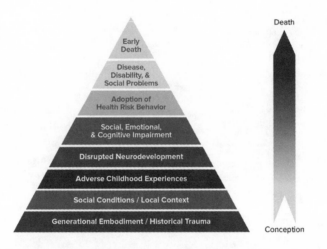

Figure 30.2. *Mechanism by Which Adverse Childhood Experiences Influence Health and Well-Being throughout the Lifespan*

Section 30.3

Child Abuse Leaves Epigenetic Marks

This section includes text excerpted from "Child Abuse Leaves Epigenetic Marks," National Human Genome Research Institute (NHGRI), July 3, 2013. Reviewed October 2019.

Child abuse is a serious national and global problem that cuts across economic, racial and cultural lines. Each year, more than 1.25 million children are abused or neglected in the United States, with that number expanding to at least 40 million per year worldwide.

In addition to harming the immediate wellbeing of the child, maltreatment and extreme stress during childhood can impair early brain development and metabolic and immune system function, leading to chronic health problems. As a consequence, abused children are at increased risk for a wide range of physical health conditions including obesity, heart disease, and cancer, as well as psychiatric conditions such as depression, suicide, drug, and alcohol abuse, high-risk behaviors, and violence.

They are also more susceptible to developing posttraumatic stress disorder (PTSD)—a severe and debilitating stress-related psychiatric disorder—after experiencing other types of trauma in life.

Part of the explanation is that child abuse can leave marks, not only physically and emotionally, but also in the form of epigenetic marks on a child's genes. Although these epigenetic marks do not cause mutations in the deoxyribonucleic acid (DNA) itself, the chemical modifications-including DNA methylation-change gene expression by silencing (or activating) genes. This can alter fundamental biological processes and adversely affect health outcomes throughout life.

New research, published in the May 14, 2013, issue of the Proceedings for the National Academy of Sciences, shows that PTSD patients who were abused as children have different patterns of DNA methylation and gene expression compared to those who were not.

Researchers from the Max Planck Institute in Germany and Emory University in the United States investigated whether the timing of trauma, specifically childhood abuse early in life, had an effect on the underlying biology of PTSD at the genome-wide level. To address this question, the authors examined a subset of 169 participants from the Grady Trauma Project-a survey of more than 5,000 individuals in Atlanta with a high lifetime exposure to multiple types of trauma, violence, and abuse.

Among the 169 participants in the current study, most were African Americans in their late thirties and forties, and all had suffered from at least two types of trauma other than child abuse and seven types of trauma on average. In spite of multiple trauma exposure, the majority (108 people) did not develop PTSD. Of the 61 that did, however, 32 reported a history of childhood abuse and 29 did not.

To focus on the effect of childhood abuse in PTSD, the researchers examined genetic changes in peripheral blood cells from PTSD patients with and without previous exposure to childhood maltreatment. These were then compared to the trauma-exposed group that did not develop PTSD to rule out changes associated with trauma exposure alone.

Despite sharing a few common biological pathways, 98 percent of the changes in gene expression patterns in PTSD patients with childhood abuse did not overlap with those found in PTSD patients without childhood abuse. Interestingly, PTSD patients who experienced significant abuse as children exhibited more changes in genes associated with central nervous system development and immune system regulation, whereas those without a history of childhood abuse displayed more changes in genes associated with cell death and growth rate regulation.

Furthermore, the researchers found that epigenetic marks associated with gene expression changes were up to 12-fold higher in PTSD patients with a history of childhood abuse. This suggests that although all patients with PTSD may show similar symptoms, abused children who subsequently develop PTSD may experience a systematically and biologically different form of the disorder compared to those without childhood abuse.

What this means is that we may need to rethink our classification of PTSD and the notion of providing the same treatment for all PTSD patients, said Dr. Divya Mehta, corresponding author at the Max Planck Institute of Psychiatry.

"At the biological level, these individuals may be very distinct, as we see with the epigenetics," Dr. Mehta explained. "As we move forward with more personalized medicine, we will need to delve a bit further into the environment and history of each individual to understand the biology of their PTSD and to determine the best treatment for their disorder."

Although, it is currently unclear whether the epigenetic marks left by child abuse can be removed or the damage reversed, this discovery is important in the search for biomarkers with clinical indications that can be used to identify different forms of PTSD. This will help to direct more precise avenues for therapy and guide treatments tailored specifically to the biological process of individual patients.

By starting to distinguish subtypes of PTSD, this study highlights the multifactorial nature of psychiatric disorders triggered by a combination of environmental and genetic factors. As the next step, Dr. Mehta and her team plan to study whether the age at which abuse occurs or the type of abuse affects the biology of PTSD.

Since even small changes in DNA methylation signatures in child abuse can have long-term implications for fundamental biological processes and health, Dr. Mehta hopes their research will also increase public awareness and strengthen efforts to protect children from the consequences of childhood abuse and neglect.

Chapter 31

Unemployment, Poverty, and Depression

Depressive disorders are among the most common mental-health problems. As a leading cause of disability, depression is related to reduced quality of life (QOL) and increased risk for physical health problems. Although depression has substantial consequences throughout the lifespan, depression during emerging adulthood, the period of transition from adolescence to adulthood, influences long-term consequences through recurrent depressive episodes and worse socioeconomic outcomes. Annually, 8.3 percent of adults aged 18 to 25 report having had at least one major depressive episode.

Although many factors contribute to depression, unemployment is consistently associated with high rates of depression among adults. Unemployment may contribute to depression because of losses in social contact and status or stress related to income loss. For emerging adults, long experiences of unemployment increase the likelihood of experiencing depression throughout the transition.

This chapter includes text excerpted from "Unemployment and Depression Among Emerging Adults in 12 States, Behavioral Risk Factor Surveillance System, 2010," Centers for Disease Control and Prevention (CDC), March 19, 2015. Reviewed October 2019.

Unemployment and Depression among Emerging Adults

The high unemployment rate among emerging adults, around 20 percent in 2010, is a substantial public health problem. The potential situational stressor of being unemployed and the developmental stressor of transitioning to young adulthood may combine to increase experiences of depression.

Unemployment among emerging adults may contribute to depression, which is consistent with research focusing on unemployed adults. Developmental factors, such as uncertainty related to the transition to adulthood and changes in social relationships and support structures, may contribute to different experiences of unemployment among emerging adults compared with older adults. Depression among unemployed emerging adults may be associated with stress because of delays in achieving development goals related to the transition to adulthood, including identity formation through exploring work opportunities. Alternatively, some may experience stressors similar to those of older adults, including stigma related to unemployment or material deprivation. Furthermore, other social factors will contribute to mental-health outcomes, such as socioeconomic status.

Those who experience depression during this transitional period are more likely to have recurrent depressive episodes during adulthood. Additionally, depressive symptoms during emerging adulthood may contribute to the erosion of personal and social resources and affect socioeconomic outcomes. Depression during the transition to adulthood may interfere with establishing romantic relationships and identifying suitable career development and employment opportunities as well as contribute to health risk behaviors. Early interventions within the population may not only ameliorate the negative effects of unemployment and depression among this group but also portend better mental-health futures for them.

Methods and Analysis of Data

Data were analyzed from the 2010 Behavioral Risk Factor Surveillance System (BRFSS). The BRFSS is a national survey that assesses health risk behaviors among the noninstitutionalized U.S. adult population (aged ≥18 years). State health departments work with the Centers for Disease Control and Prevention (CDC) to collect BRFSS data. A core set of questions is asked in all 50 states as well as the District of Columbia, Puerto Rico, and the U.S. Virgin Islands. In addition, state health departments may choose to include supplemental modules that ask questions on specific topics, such as depression. In 2010, 12 states (Arizona, Georgia, Hawaii, Indiana, Louisiana, Mississippi, Missouri, Nevada, South Carolina, Vermont, Wisconsin, and Wyoming) included an optional module assessing the prevalence of anxiety and depression. The overall response rates for these states ranged from 25.6 to 49.2 percent.

The dependent variable was depression. A score for depression was calculated based on responses to eight questions from the Patient Health Questionnaire (PHQ-8). The questions ask about depressive symptoms over the previous two weeks. For example, "Over the last two weeks, how many days have you had little interest or pleasure in doing things?" For each question, individuals received a score between 0 and 3, depending on the number of days they reported having the specific depressive symptoms. Those who responded that they had had depressive symptoms for zero days or one day received a score of zero. Those who responded that they had had a depressive symptom for 2 to 6, 7 to 11, or 12 to 14 days, inclusive, received scores of one, two, or three, respectively. The scores for each question were summed. By using criteria from other BRFSS studies of the PHQ-8, we classified those who had a total score greater than or equal to 10 as depressed.

The main independent variable of interest was the unemployment status. Those who responded that they had been out of work for less than one year or more than one year were classified as unemployed. Respondents who indicated they were "employed for wages" or "self-employed" were classified as employed.

In addition, potentially confounding variables were included in the analyses because of their association with both depression and employment status. These variables were disability status, smoking status, and body mass index (BMI), and health insurance status as well as sociodemographic variables. These variables were selected based on previous work by Brown et al examining the relationship between unemployment and mental distress among adults.

Disability status was measured by creating three categories of respondents using two questions in the 2010 BRFSS. The questions ask "Are you limited in any way in any activities because of physical, mental, or emotional problems?" and "Do you now have any health problems that require you to use special equipment, such as a cane, a wheelchair, a special bed, or a special telephone? (Include occasional use or use in certain circumstances)." Respondents who indicated that yes, they were limited in activities but that they did not require any special equipment were one group (no equipment needed). Respondents who indicated that yes, they were limited in activities and they needed special equipment were another group (equipment needed). The reference group responded no to both questions about disability.

Smoking status was assessed by categorizing responses to the question "Do you now smoke cigarettes every day, some days, or not at all?" Individuals who responded every day or some days were classified as smokers. Individuals who responded not at all were classified as nonsmokers.

Respondents were classified into three BMI categories based on a calculated variable that divided respondents' weight in kilograms (kg) by their height in meters squared (m2). Those with BMIs less than 25.0 were categorized as normal weight or underweight, those with BMIs between 25.0 and 29.9 were categorized as overweight, and those with BMIs greater than or equal to 30.0 were categorized as obese.

Health insurance status was assessed by categorizing responses to the question "Do you have any kind of healthcare coverage, including health insurance, prepaid plans, or government plans such as Medicare?" Response options were yes, no, or not sure. Those who responded yes were classified as individuals with health insurance and those who responded no were classified as individuals without health insurance. A do not know/not sure response was considered a nonresponse.

Almost 12 percent of emerging adults were depressed (PHQ-8 ≥10), and about 23 percent were unemployed. Most of the weighted population was male (58.6%) and white (64.5%). Most had received a high school degree or higher (87.3%).

Population Affected

Being unemployed was associated with other independent variables. Blacks or African Americans (37.0%) were significantly more likely to report being unemployed compared with Hispanics or Latinos (22.5%), members of other races/ethnicities (19.5%), and whites (19.7%). Those without a high school degree (38.7%) were significantly more likely to report being unemployed compared with those with a high school degree or higher (20.7%). Emerging adults who were not married (24.6%) were more likely to report being unemployed compared with those who were married (12.8%). Emerging adults without health insurance (32.9%) were more likely to report being unemployed compared with those with health insurance (17.2%). Additionally, 31.9 percent of smokers reported being unemployed compared with 19.6 percent of nonsmokers.

The high rate of unemployment among emerging adults is a public health problem. In light of this elevated prevalence, the association between poor health outcomes, including mental health, and unemployment warrants attention from individuals, families, and policymakers. The above findings suggest that unemployed emerging adults have three times greater odds of reporting depression compared with employed emerging adults, even when controlling for potentially confounding variables such as disability status.

These results suggest that unemployment among emerging adults may contribute to depression, which is consistent with research focusing on unemployed adults. Developmental factors, such as uncertainty related to the transition to adulthood and changes in social relationships and support structures, may contribute to different experiences of unemployment among emerging adults compared with older adults. Depression among unemployed emerging adults may be associated with stress because of delays in achieving development goals related to the transition to adulthood, including identity formation through exploring work opportunities. Alternatively, some may experience stressors similar to those of older adults, including stigma related to unemployment or material deprivation. Examining mediators between unemployment and depression could inform whether the factors that contribute to depression are similar for emerging adults and older adults. Furthermore, other social factors that contribute to mental-health outcomes, such as socioeconomic status, could moderate this relationship. Additional research examining the factors that contribute to depression among unemployed emerging adults is warranted.

Reducing the prevalence of depression during the transitional period of early adulthood may contribute to improved outcomes throughout the lifespan. Those who experience depression during this transitional period are more likely to have recurrent depressive episodes during adulthood. Additionally, depressive symptoms during emerging adulthood may contribute to the erosion of personal and social resources and affect socioeconomic outcomes. Depression during the transition to adulthood may interfere with establishing romantic relationships and identifying suitable career development and employment opportunities as well as contribute to health risk behaviors. In light of the consequences related to experiencing depression and unemployment during this transitional period, it is important to develop interventions targeted to these young people. Early interventions within the population may not only ameliorate the negative effects of unemployment and depression among this group but also portend better mental-health futures for them.

Chapter 32

Depression, Substance Use, and Addiction

Chapter Contents

Section 32.1

Addiction Can Lead to Depression and Other Mental Disorders

This section includes text excerpted from "The Connection between Substance Use Disorders and Mental Illness," National Institute on Drug Abuse (NIDA), February 2018.

The Connection between Substance-Use Disorders and Mental Illness

Many individuals who develop substance-use disorders (SUD) are also diagnosed with mental disorders, and vice versa. Multiple national population surveys have found that about half of those who experience a mental illness during their lives will also experience a substance-use disorder and vice versa. Although there are fewer studies on comorbidity among youth, research suggests that adolescents with substance-use disorders also have high rates of co-occurring mental illness; over 60 percent of adolescents in community-based substance-use disorder treatment programs also meet diagnostic criteria for another mental illness.

Data show high rates of comorbid substance-use disorders and anxiety disorders—which include generalized anxiety disorder, panic disorder, and posttraumatic stress disorder (PTSD). Substance-use disorders also co-occur at high prevalence with mental disorders, such as depression and bipolar disorder, attention deficit hyperactivity disorder (ADHD), psychotic illness, borderline personality disorder, and antisocial personality disorder. Patients with schizophrenia have higher rates of alcohol, tobacco, and drug use disorders than the general population. As Figure 32.1 shows, the overlap is especially pronounced with serious mental illness (SMI). Serious mental illness among people ages 18 and older is defined at the federal level as having, at any time during the past year a diagnosable mental, behavioral, or emotional disorder that causes serious functional impairment that substantially interferes with or limits one or more major life activities. Serious mental illnesses include major depression, schizophrenia, and bipolar disorder, and other mental disorders that cause serious impairment. Around one in four individuals with SMI also have an SUD.

Data from a large nationally representative sample suggested that people with mental, personality, and substance-use disorders were at increased risk for nonmedical use of prescription opioids. Research

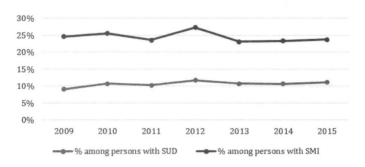

Figure 32.1. *Co-Occurring Substance Use Disorder and Serious Mental Illness in Past Year among Persons Aged 18 or Older* (Source: Substance Abuse and Mental Health Services Administration (SAMHSA), Center for Behavioral Health Statistics and Quality (CBHSQ), National Survey on Drug Use and Health (NSDUH).)

indicates that 43 percent of people in SUD treatment for nonmedical use of prescription painkillers have a diagnosis or symptoms of mental-health disorders, particularly depression and anxiety.

Why Is There Comorbidity between Substance-Use Disorders and Mental Illnesses?

The high prevalence of comorbidity between substance-use disorders and other mental illnesses does not necessarily mean that one caused the other, even if one appeared first. Establishing causality or directionality is difficult for several reasons. For example, behavioral or emotional problems may not be severe enough for a diagnosis (called "subclinical symptoms"), but subclinical mental-health issues may prompt drug use. Also, people's recollections of when drug use or addiction started may be imperfect, making it difficult to determine whether the substance use or mental-health issues came first.

Three main pathways can contribute to the comorbidity between substance-use disorders and mental illnesses:

- Common risk factors can contribute to both mental illness and substance use and addiction.

- Mental illness may contribute to substance use and addiction.

- Substance use and addiction can contribute to the development of mental illness.

Common Risk Factors Can Contribute to Both Mental Illness and Substance Use and Addiction

Both substance-use disorders and other mental illnesses are caused by overlapping factors such as genetic and epigenetic vulnerabilities, issues with similar areas of the brain, and environmental influences such as early exposure to stress or trauma.

Genetic Vulnerabilities

It is estimated that 40 to 60 percent of an individual's vulnerability to substance-use disorders is attributable to genetics. An active area of comorbidity research involves the search for that might predispose individuals to develop both a substance-use disorder and other mental illnesses, or to have a greater risk of a second disorder occurring after the first appears. Most of this vulnerability arises from complex interactions among multiple genes and genetic interactions with environmental influences. For example, frequent marijuana use during adolescence is associated with an increased risk of psychosis in adulthood, specifically among individuals who carry a particular gene variant.

In some instances, a gene product may act directly, as when a protein influences how a person responds to a drug (e.g., whether the drug experience is pleasurable or not) or how long a drug remains in the body. Specific genetic factors have been identified that predispose an individual to alcohol dependence and cigarette smoking, and research is starting to uncover the link between genetic sequences and a higher risk of cocaine dependence, heavy opioid use, and cannabis craving and withdrawal. But genes can also act indirectly by altering how an individual responds to stress or by increasing the likelihood of risk-taking and novelty-seeking behaviors, which could influence the initiation of substance use as well as the development of substance-use disorders and other mental illnesses. Research suggests that there are many genes that may contribute to the risk for both mental disorders and addiction, including those that influence the action of neurotransmitters—chemicals that carry messages from one neuron to another—that are affected by drugs and commonly dysregulated in mental illness, such as dopamine and serotonin.

Epigenetic Influences

Scientists are also beginning to understand the very powerful ways that genetic and environmental factors interact at the molecular level.

Epigenetics refers to the study of changes in the regulation of gene activity and expression that are not dependent on gene sequence; that is, changes that affect how genetic information is read and acted on by cells in the body. Environmental factors such as chronic stress, trauma, or drug exposure can induce stable changes in gene expression, which can alter functioning in neural circuits and ultimately impact behavior.

Through epigenetic mechanisms, the environment can cause long-term genetic adaptations—influencing the pattern of genes that are active or silent in encoding proteins—without altering the deoxyribonucleic acid (DNA) sequence. These modifications can sometimes even be passed down to the next generation. There is also evidence that they can be reversed with interventions or environmental alterations.

The epigenetic impact of the environment is highly dependent on the developmental stage. Studies suggest that environmental factors interact with genetic vulnerability during particular developmental periods to increase the risk for mental illnesses and addiction. For example, animal studies indicate that a maternal diet high in fat during pregnancy can influence levels of key proteins involved in neurotransmission in the brain's reward pathway. Other animal research has shown that poor quality maternal care diminished the ability of offspring to respond to stress through epigenetic mechanisms.

Brain Region Involvement

Many areas of the brain are affected by both substance-use disorders and other mental illnesses. For example, the circuits in the brain that mediate reward, decision making, impulse control, and emotions may be affected by addictive substances and disrupted in substance-use disorders, depression, schizophrenia, and other psychiatric disorders. In addition, multiple neurotransmitter systems have been implicated in both substance-use disorders and other mental disorders including, but not limited to, dopamine, serotonin, glutamate, gamma-aminobutyric acid (GABA), and norepinephrine.

Environmental Influences

Many environmental factors are associated with an increased risk for both substance-use disorders and mental illness including chronic stress, trauma, and adverse childhood experiences, among others. Many of these factors are modifiable and; thus, prevention interventions will often result in reductions in both substance-use disorders and mental illness.

Stress

Stress is a known risk factor for a range of mental disorders and, therefore, provides one likely common neurobiological link between the disease processes of substance-use disorders and mental disorders. Exposure to stressors is also a major risk factor for relapse to drug use after periods of recovery. Stress responses are mediated through the hypothalamic-pituitary-adrenal (HPA) axis, which in turn can influence brain circuits that control motivation. Higher levels of stress have been shown to reduce activity in the prefrontal cortex and increase responsivity in the striatum, which leads to decreased behavioral control and increased impulsivity. Early life stress and chronic stress can cause long-term alterations in the HPA axis, which affects limbic brain circuits that are involved in motivation, learning, and adaptation, and are impaired in individuals with substance-use disorders and other mental illnesses.

Importantly, dopamine pathways have been implicated in the way in which stress can increase vulnerability to substance-use disorders. HPA axis hyperactivity has been shown to alter dopamine signaling, which may enhance the reinforcing properties of drugs. In turn, substance use causes changes to many neurotransmitter systems that are involved in responses to stress. These neurobiological changes are thought to underlie the link between stress and escalation of drug use as well as relapse. Treatments that target stress, such as mindfulness-based stress reduction, have been shown to be beneficial for reducing depression, anxiety, and substance use.

Trauma and Adverse Childhood Experiences

Physically or emotionally traumatized people are at a much higher risk for drug use and SUDs. and the co-occurrence of these disorders is associated with inferior treatment outcomes. People with PTSD may use substances in an attempt to reduce their anxiety and to avoid dealing with trauma and its consequences.

The link between substance-use disorder and PTSD is of particular concern for service members returning from tours of duty in Iraq and Afghanistan. Between 2004 and 2010, approximately 16 percent of veterans had an untreated substance-use disorder, and 8 percent needed treatment for serious psychological distress (SPD). Data from a survey that used a contemporary, national sample of veterans estimated that the rate of lifetime PTSD was 8 percent, while approximately 5 percent reported PTSD. Approximately 1 in 5 veterans with PTSD also has a co-occurring substance-use disorder.

Mental Illnesses Can Contribute to Drug Use and Addiction

Certain mental disorders are established risk factors for developing a substance-use disorder. It is commonly hypothesized that individuals with severe, mild, or even subclinical mental disorders may use drugs as a form of self-medication. Although some drugs may temporarily reduce symptoms of a mental illness, they can also exacerbate symptoms, both acutely and in the long run. For example, evidence suggests that periods of cocaine use may worsen the symptoms of bipolar disorder and contribute to progression of this illness.

When an individual develops a mental illness, associated changes in brain activity may increase the vulnerability for problematic use of substances by enhancing their rewarding effects, reducing awareness of their negative effects, or alleviating the unpleasant symptoms of the mental disorder or the side effects of the medication used to treat it. For example, neuroimaging suggests that ADHD is associated with neurobiological changes in brain circuits that are also associated with drug cravings, perhaps partially explaining why patients with substance-use disorders report greater cravings when they have comorbid ADHD.

Substance Use and Addiction Can Contribute to the Development of Mental Illness

Substance use can lead to changes in some of the same brain areas that are disrupted in other mental disorders, such as schizophrenia, anxiety, mood, or impulse-control disorders. Drug use that precedes the first symptoms of mental illness may produce changes in brain structure and function that kindle an underlying predisposition to develop that mental illness.

Section 32.2

Can Smoking Cause Depression?

This section includes text excerpted from "Smoking and Depression," Smokefree.gov, U.S. Department of Health and Human Services (HHS), July 30, 2013. Reviewed October 2019.

Smokers are more likely to have depression than nonsmokers. Nobody knows for sure why this is. People who have depression might smoke to feel better. Or smokers might get depression more easily because they smoke. No matter what the cause, there are treatments that work for both depression and smoking.

Mood Changes

Mood changes are common after quitting smoking. Some people feel increased sadness. You might be irritable, restless, or feel down or blue. Changes in mood from quitting smoking may be part of withdrawal. Withdrawal is your body getting used to not having nicotine. Mood changes from nicotine withdrawal usually get better in a week or two. If mood changes do not get better in a couple of weeks, you should talk to your doctor. Something else, such as depression, could be the reason.

Smoking may seem to help you with depression. You might feel better in the moment. But, there are many problems with using cigarettes to cope with depression. There are other things you can try to lift your mood:

- **Exercise.** Being physically active can help. Start small and build up over time. This can be hard to do when you are depressed. But, your efforts will pay off.

- **Structure your day.** Make a plan to stay busy. Get out of the house if you can.

- **Be with other people.** Many people who are depressed are cut off from other people. Being in touch or talking with others every day can help your mood.

- **Reward yourself.** Do things you enjoy. Even small things add up and help you feel better.

- **Get support.** Get support If you are feeling down after quitting smoking, it may help to talk about this with friends and family. Your doctor also can help.

Find Help 24/7

If you need help now, call a 24-hour crisis center at 800-273-TALK (800-273-8255) or 800-SUICIDE (800-784-2433) for free, private help or dial 911.

Sometimes people who are feeling depressed think about hurting themselves or dying. If you or someone you know is having these feelings, get help now.

The Substance Abuse and Mental Health Services Administration (SAMHSA)—a part of the U.S. Department of Health and Human Services (HHS)—runs both crisis centers.

Section 32.3

Alcohol Use and Depression among Older Adults

This section includes text excerpted from "Older Adults," National Institute on Alcohol Abuse and Alcoholism (NIAAA), May 17, 2012. Reviewed October 2019.

Older Adults

A national survey found that about 40 percent of adults ages 65 and older drink alcohol. Older adults can experience a variety of problems from drinking alcohol, especially those who:

- Take certain medications

- Have health problems

- Drink heavily

There are special considerations facing older adults who drink, including,

Increased Sensitivity to Alcohol

Aging can lower the body's tolerance for alcohol. Older adults generally experience the effects of alcohol more quickly than when they were

225

younger. This puts older adults at higher risk for falls, car crashes, and other unintentional injuries that may result from drinking.

Increased Health Problems

Certain health problems are common in older adults. Heavy drinking can make these problems worse, including:

- Diabetes
- High blood pressure
- Congestive heart failure
- Liver problems
- Osteoporosis
- Memory problems
- Mood disorders

Bad Interactions with Medications

Many prescription and over-the-counter (OTC) medications, as well as herbal remedies can be dangerous or even deadly when mixed with alcohol. Medications that can interact badly with alcohol include:

- Aspirin
- Acetaminophen
- Cold and allergy medicine
- Cough syrup
- Sleeping pills
- Pain medication
- Anxiety or depression medicine

Drinking Guidelines for Older Adults

Adults over age 65 who are healthy and do not take medications should not have more than:

- 3 drinks on a given day

- 7 drinks in a week

- Drinking more than these amounts puts people at risk of serious alcohol problems

If you have a health problem or take certain medications, you may need to drink less or not at all.

Chapter 33

Other Mental-Health Disorders and the Relationship to Depression

Chapter Contents

Section 33.1

Anxiety Disorders among Women and Children

This section includes text excerpted from "Anxiety Disorders,"
Office on Women's Health (OWH), U.S. Department of Health and
Human Services (HHS), January 30, 2019.

Anxiety is a normal response to stress. But when it becomes hard to control and affects your day-to-day life, it can be disabling. Anxiety disorders affect nearly 1 in 5 adults in the United States. Women are more than twice as likely as men to get an anxiety disorder in their lifetime. Anxiety disorders are often treated with counseling, medicine, or a combination of both. Some women also find that yoga or meditation helps with anxiety disorders.

What Is Anxiety?

Anxiety is a feeling of worry, nervousness, or fear about an event or situation. It is a normal reaction to stress. It helps you stay alert for a challenging situation at work, study harder for an exam, or remain focused on an important speech. In general, it helps you cope.

But anxiety can be disabling if it interferes with daily life, such as making you dread nonthreatening day-to-day activities like riding the bus or talking to a coworker. Anxiety can also be a sudden attack of terror when there is no threat.

What Are Anxiety Disorders?

Anxiety disorders happen when excessive anxiety interferes with your everyday activities such as going to work or school or spending time with friends or family. Anxiety disorders are serious mental illnesses. They are the most common mental disorders in the United States. Anxiety disorders are more than twice as common in women as in men.

What Are the Major Types of Anxiety Disorder?

The major types of anxiety disorder are:

- **Generalized anxiety disorder (GAD).** People with GAD worry excessively about ordinary, day-to-day issues, such as health, money, work, and family. With GAD, the mind often jumps to the worst-case scenario, even when there is little or no reason to worry. Women with GAD may be anxious about just getting through the day. They may have muscle tension and other stress-related physical symptoms, such as trouble sleeping or upset stomach. At times, worrying keeps people with GAD from doing everyday tasks. Women with GAD have a higher risk of depression and other anxiety disorders than men with GAD. They also are more likely to have a family history of depression.

- **Panic disorder.** Panic disorders are twice as common in women as in men. People with panic disorder have sudden attacks of terror when there is no actual danger. Panic attacks may cause a sense of unreality, a fear of impending doom, or a fear of losing control. A fear of one's own unexplained physical symptoms is also a sign of panic disorder. People having panic attacks sometimes believe they are having heart attacks, losing their minds, or dying.

- **Social phobia.** Social phobia, also called "social anxiety disorder," is diagnosed when people become very anxious and self-conscious in everyday social situations. People with social phobia have a strong fear of being watched and judged by others. They may get embarrassed easily and often have panic attack symptoms.

- **Specific phobia.** A specific phobia is an intense fear of something that poses little or no actual danger. Specific phobias could be fears of closed-in spaces, heights, water, objects, animals, or specific situations. People with specific phobias often find that facing, or even thinking about facing, the feared object or situation brings on a panic attack or severe anxiety.

Some other conditions that are not considered anxiety disorders but are similar include:

- **Obsessive-compulsive disorder (OCD).** People with OCD have unwanted thoughts (obsessions) or behaviors (compulsions) that cause anxiety. They may check the oven or iron again and again or perform the same routine over and over to control the anxiety these thoughts cause. Often, the rituals end up controlling the person.

- **Posttraumatic stress disorder (PTSD).** PTSD starts after a scary event that involved physical harm or the threat of physical harm. The person who gets PTSD may have been the one who was harmed, or the harm may have happened to a loved one or even a stranger.

Who Gets Anxiety Disorders

Anxiety disorders affect about 40 million American adults every year. Anxiety disorders also affect children and teens. About 8 percent of teens ages 13 to 18 have an anxiety disorder, with symptoms starting around age 6.

Women are more than twice as likely as men to get an anxiety disorder in their lifetime. Also, some types of anxiety disorders affect some women more than others:

- **Generalized anxiety disorder (GAD)** affects more American Indian/Alaskan Native women than women of other races and ethnicities. GAD also affects more white women and Hispanic women than Asian or African-American women.

- **Social phobia** and panic disorder affect more white women than women of other races and ethnicities.

What Causes Anxiety Disorders

Researchers think anxiety disorders are caused by a combination of factors, which may include:

- Hormonal changes during the menstrual cycle

- Genetics. Anxiety disorders may run in families.

- Traumatic events. Experiencing abuse, an attack, or sexual assault can lead to serious health problems, including anxiety, posttraumatic stress disorder, and depression.

What Are the Signs and Symptoms of an Anxiety Disorder?

Women with anxiety disorders experience a combination of anxious thoughts or beliefs, physical symptoms, and changes in behavior, including avoiding everyday activities they used to do. Each anxiety disorder has different symptoms. They all involve a fear and dread about things that may happen now or in the future.

Physical symptoms may include:

- Weakness

- Shortness of breath

- Rapid heart rate

- Nausea

- Upset stomach

- Hot flashes

- Dizziness

Physical symptoms of anxiety disorders often happen along with other mental or physical illnesses. This can cover up your anxiety symptoms or make them worse.

How Are Anxiety Disorders Diagnosed?

Your doctor or nurse will ask you questions about your symptoms and your medical history. Your doctor may also do a physical exam or other tests to rule out other health problems that could be causing your symptoms.

Anxiety disorders are diagnosed when fear and dread of nonthreatening situations, events, places, or objects become excessive and are uncontrollable. Anxiety disorders are also diagnosed if the anxiety has lasted for at least six months and it interferes with social, work, family, or other aspects of daily life.

How Are Anxiety Disorders Treated?

Treatment for anxiety disorders depends on the type of anxiety disorder you have and your personal history of health problems, violence, or abuse.

Often, treatment may include:

- Counseling (called "psychotherapy")

- Medicine

- A combination of counseling and medicine

How Does Counseling Help Treat Anxiety Disorders?

Your doctor may refer you for a type of counseling for anxiety disorders called "cognitive-behavioral therapy" (CBT). You can talk to a trained mental-health professional about what caused your anxiety disorder and how to deal with the symptoms.

For example, you can talk to a psychiatrist, psychologist, social worker, or counselor. CBT can help you change the thinking patterns around your fears. It may help you change the way you react to situations that may create anxiety. You may also learn ways to reduce feelings of anxiety and improve specific behaviors caused by chronic anxiety. These strategies may include relaxation therapy and problem-solving.

What Types of Medicine Treat Anxiety Disorders?

Several types of medicine treat anxiety disorders. These include:

- **Antianxiety (benzodiazepines).** These medicines are usually prescribed for short periods of time because they are addictive. Stopping this medicine too quickly can cause withdrawal symptoms.

- **Beta-blockers.** These medicines can help prevent the physical symptoms of an anxiety disorder, like trembling or sweating.

- **Selective serotonin reuptake inhibitors (SSRIs).** SSRIs change the level of serotonin in the brain. They increase the amount of serotonin available to help brain cells communicate with each other. Common side effects can include insomnia or sedation, stomach problems, and a lack of sexual desire.

- **Tricyclics.** Tricyclics work like SSRIs. But sometimes they cause more side effects than SSRIs. They may cause dizziness, drowsiness, dry mouth, constipation, or weight gain.

- **Monoamine oxidase inhibitors (MAOIs).** People who take MAOIs must avoid certain foods and drinks (like Parmesan or cheddar cheese and red wine) that contain an amino acid called "tyramine." Taking an MAOI and eating these foods can cause blood pressure levels to spike dangerously. Women who take MAOIs must also avoid certain medicines, such as some types of birth control pills, pain relievers, and cold and allergy medicines. Talk to your doctor about any medicine you take.

All medicines have risks. You should talk to your doctor about the benefits and risks of all medicines.

Section 33.2

Eating Disorders, Anxiety, and Depression

Psychological conditions like depression and anxiety have been found to co-occur frequently in individuals suffering from eating disorders.

Depression

Depression is a mood disorder that comprises acute feelings of distress, helplessness, anxiety, and/or guilt. It is one of the most common mental-health problems, and it can seriously affect the overall well-being and productivity of the individual. Symptoms may include:

- Increased frustration

- Insomnia

- Reckless behavior

- Loss of interest in activities that were previously enjoyed

- Irritability

- Feelings of insignificance or self-hatred

- Tendency to abuse alcohol or drugs

- Frequent feelings of fatigue or pain

- Low energy level

- Fluctuations in eating habits and body weight

- Social withdrawal

- Poor concentration

- Delusions

- Suicidal thoughts

Depression can be caused by a number of factors, including hormonal imbalance, traumatic experiences, previous history of substance abuse, and side-effects of certain medication. It can either co-occur with, or lead to the development of other mental illnesses, such as anxiety, phobias, panic disorders, and eating disorders.

It is not clear whether eating disorders take root in an individual due to existing depression, or whether eating disorders cause depression. Since no two eating disorders are the same, and each is a complex condition on its own, both arguments are considered valid in different cases. For instance, feelings of worthlessness and moodiness are often identified as a sign of an eating disorder, which, on the other hand, may also be symptoms of depression. Likewise, a depressed person can indulge in emotional eating, which can subsequently lead to an eating disorder.

Anxiety

It is quite normal for people to feel anxious in stressful situations, but when an individual experiences an extreme and unreasonable level of anxiety, it is characterized as a disorder. Anxiety disorder is generally identified as a combination of psychological states, such as nervousness, fear, worry, and mistrust, that extends over a long period of time and considerably affects daily activities. Anxiety may be caused by a combination of environmental, social, psychological, genetic, and physiological factors. Some examples include:

- Hormonal imbalance

- Substance abuse, or withdrawal from an illicit drug

- History of mental illness in the family

- Traumatic episodes

- Current physical ailment

Types of anxiety disorders include generalized anxiety disorder (GAD), obsessive-compulsive disorder (OCD), phobias, social anxiety disorder, panic disorder, and posttraumatic stress disorder (PTSD). Each of them has its own unique symptoms, which are further categorized as physical, behavioral, emotional, and cognitive. These symptoms include sweating, irregular heartbeat, difficulty in breathing, headache, irregular sleeping patterns, nervous habits, irritability, restlessness, obsessive and unwanted thoughts, and irrational fear.

Like depression, anxiety disorder can co-occur with eating disorders. And similarly, an individual suffering from an anxiety disorder can develop an eating disorder as a means of coping with anxiety.

In most cases, anxiety precedes the onset of an eating disorder, such as when an individual briefly soothes symptoms of anxiety by trying to gain a sense of control over other aspects of life, such as food, exercise, and weight. This, in the long run, can lead to the development of eating disorders.

Due to the complex nature of eating disorders in conjunction with depression or anxiety, there is a need for an intense treatment plan that analyzes the factors underlying these conditions. Since a number of similar factors can lead to the development of each of these illnesses, successful treatment requires an inclusive strategy that addresses the root cause of all the conditions and helps the individual learn to manage the co-occurring disorder separately and not associate it with food. In addition to medication and nutritional support, the treatment plan may also include various forms of therapy, such as group therapy, cognitive-behavioral therapy (CBT), and music and art therapy.

References

1. "Eating Disorders and Other Health Problems," Eating Disorders Victoria, June 19, 2015.

2. Ekern, Jacquelyn. "Dual Diagnosis and Co-Occurring Disorders," Eating Disorder Hope, April 25, 2012.

Chapter 34

Parental Depression

Evidence from early childhood research and practice shows a strong link between parents health and well-being and their children's development. While raising children is a challenge for any parent, good health and well-being can make it easier for parents to provide sensitive and responsive care, the foundation for healthy brain development. With that care, young children develop the skills they need to succeed in life and in school, such as managing their emotions and behaviors, forming healthy relationships with adults and peers, adjusting to new situations, and resolving conflict. A parent's depression, in particular, can impair parenting quality. In turn, children may develop cognitive, emotional, and behavioral problems that prevent them from entering kindergarten ready and able to learn.

Parental Depression: What We Know

Depression is a common condition that affects people of all backgrounds, classes, and ethnicities. Approximately 15.6 million children live with a depressed parent. Symptoms of depression can come on suddenly (acute) or may be ongoing and long-lasting (chronic). When severe depression is a mental-health disorder that prevents parents from functioning well in everyday aspects of life. It is sometimes accompanied by suicidal thoughts. A number of factors can contribute to

This chapter includes text excerpted from "Family Well-Being: A Focus on Parental Depression," Early Childhood Learning and Knowledge Center (ECLKC), April 15, 2011. Reviewed October 2019.

parental mental illness in general, and to depression in particular, whether biological, familial, personal, or social. Examples include hormonal shifts and experiences during pregnancy and after pregnancy (postpartum), family history of depression, prior depression, life stress (for example, family violence, trauma, substance abuse), poverty, social isolation, and oppression. These risk factors may harm children directly by exposing them to unfavorable conditions, or indirectly by increasing parental depression, which can lead to poor parenting and negative child outcomes.

How Parental Depression Affects Young Children

While not always the case, parents who are depressed are less likely to be responsive and sensitive with their children. They also may be hostile and intrusive or disengaged and neglectful. These negative parenting behaviors increase a child's risk for behavioral, emotional, physical, and cognitive problems. Developmental problems in children are especially likely when a parent's depressive symptoms are severe and long-lasting, and when a parent's depression occurs during periods of rapid brain development in children (e.g., prenatally to age three). Exposure to hardships, such as poverty, child maltreatment, parental substance abuse, and community violence, increase the odds of parental depression while also causing harm to children. Both risk and protective factors interact with depression to affect family well-being and a child's development. The negative effects of depression may be worse when a family lives in poverty. Parents who are depressed and living in poverty may lack the personal resources to access available supports, such as food stamps, transportation, and mental-health services. On the other hand, when professionals and communities offer social support, focus on child and parent strengths, and help parents understand depression, healthy parenting may be supported. Parent-child relationships are a "two-way street," and child factors, such as temperament, physical health, and behavior, also affect parental depression in both positive and negative ways. For example, one study found that healthier child development at ages two and three had a positive influence on mothers' depression. On the other hand, higher levels of child aggression were related to more chronic maternal depression. Another study found that a mother's likelihood of developing postpartum depression increased when newborns were irritable and difficult to console. A child's developmental disability is another factor that can increase the risk of parental depression. Parental factors that increase the risk of depression include physical health problems, unhealthy relationships with intimate partners, and social isolation. Community-level factors include poor neighborhood conditions, poverty, and lack of access to quality early childhood programs. On the other hand, when parents are in good health, have healthy relationships with others, and can access enough community resources, they are less likely to be depressed and more likely to recover when they are already depressed.

Treating Parental Depression and Supporting Children's Development

Fortunately, depression is one of the most treatable of all medical conditions. Decades of research have shown that medication, psycho-therapy, behavioral interventions, alternative medicine, and other approaches can be effective in treating adult depression. Research also clearly shows that poor child outcomes can be avoided with prompt and effective treatment. Early childhood programs can work with parents to reduce depression and its negative effects on children.

Interventions for Identifying Parental Depression and Supporting Positive Parenting

The following approaches are not the only useful, evidence-based interventions in the field, but they represent some good examples of options for programs to consider when working with parents who are depressed. They include:

- Screening

- Postpartum interventions

- Home visits by mental-health workers

- Empowerment, and self-care

- Mental-health services

Screening for Parental Depression

When symptoms emerge during pregnancy or after, in the post-partum period, early detection and treatment can prevent serious disturbances in parent-child relationships. Early detection and prompt treatment of depression in parents of older children can also protect children from its harmful effects. Regular screening is an important strategy to ensure that parents' symptoms are recognized as early as possible. Parents can be encouraged to attend depression screenings in a variety of settings, including pediatricians'offices, obstetrics/gynecology practices, health clinics, and mental-health centers. Nurses, social workers, health workers, clinicians, home visitors, and other professionals are trained to administer standardized, validated screening tools and to follow up with parents about the results. Screening tools are scored and acted upon immediately so that parents in distress are recognized and supported as soon as possible. Emergency services must be identified in advance and used right away when screening results reveal the risk of suicide.

Early Childhood Mental-Health Consultation

Consultation with Infant and Early Childhood Mental-Health (I/ECMH) experts is a promising intervention for parental depression. Skilled I/ECMH consultants in early childhood programs can enhance staff's comfort with and capacity to handle challenging mental-health situations with families through a range of activities:

- Observing and interpreting children's behavior

- Anticipating developmental changes

- Alerting caregivers to a child's needs

- Identifying adult and child strengths and challenges

- Listening to and discussing difficulties that arise

- Creating opportunities for positive change in the program and at home

- Sharing information on how to identify and address mental-health issues in collaboration with community mental-health providers and programs

Home Visiting for Prevention and Treatment of Depression

Home visiting is one of the most widely used services for preventing parental depression and for promoting child and family well-being. It is especially useful for reaching parents who are geographically isolated, have limited mobility, or are too depressed to leave their homes to get treatment. Unfortunately, parental depression can also interfere with providing effective services. Parents experiencing depression may be less able to make use of home visiting. Additional efforts are made to connect with and support these parents. For example, mental-health workers can check in often with parents who are depressed to monitor their progress.

Working with Parents and Building Partnerships with Community Agencies

Strong community partnerships with primary care and mental-health centers that provide treatment for depressed parents. Different treatment approaches, several of which are described below, have been used effectively to support positive parenting for parents struggling with depression.

Interpersonal therapy (IPT), is a well-tested, effective treatment for depressive symptoms. IPT has been modified for postpartum mothers and families from diverse backgrounds. One successful modification is a five-month, home-based IPT program in which community psychiatric mental-health nurses conduct therapy and partner with home visitors. Depressed mothers who participated in this intervention had lower levels of depression and reported less aggression in their children than did depressed mothers who did not participate in it.

Cognitive-behavioral therapy (CBT), widely used as a time-limited intervention, is one of the most studied forms of successful treatments for depression. CBT approaches with depressed parents seek to promote effective parenting by helping parents monitor their harmful thoughts and behaviors and substitute them with positive ones. Often parents are motivated to make positive changes in thoughts and behaviors by their wish to be the best parents they can be. CBT has been used effectively with Black and Latina mothers with low incomes, who are at especially high-risk for postpartum depression.

Chapter 35

Isolation and Depression

Depression Can Get Worse with Isolation

In-person social contact is a uniquely potent tonic against depression, suggests a U.S. Department of Veteran Affairs (VA) study of more than 11,000 older adults.

Isolation can be devastating, so much so that many societies use it as punishment—solitary confinement for prisoners, for example. At the heart of it is the fact that human beings are social creatures. Researchers have long known that lack of social contact and the loneliness that accompanies it are risk factors for depression, particularly in older people.

A few hundred years ago social contact would be easy to define—interacting face-to-face with someone. In this world of virtual connectivity, friends and family can talk or see each other in real time, at any time, regardless of place. Texting, instant messaging, e-mail, Skype, and phone all mean that a friendly face, voice, or message is literally at our fingertips. But is that enough to stave off depression, particularly for older people who may not be fit enough to get out for frequent face-to-face interactions?

New research suggests that technology cannot beat an old-fashioned in-person gab session. A VA study found routine in-person contact could substantially reduce the risk of depression for older adults.

This chapter includes text excerpted from "Depression Study Points to Value of In-Person Social Contact," Office of Research and Development (ORD), U.S. Department of Veteran Affairs (VA), June 25, 2015. Reviewed October 2019.

And generally speaking, the more such contact, the better. Written correspondence—including email—did not have the same effect. Nor did phone contact, although this mode of contact seemed particularly helpful for those with existing depression.

Patterns in Depression Varied by Age

The patterns varied somewhat depending on the age group—50 to 69, or age 70 and older. But, the bottom line, concluded the researchers, is that "infrequent in-person social contact with friends and family is an important predictor for the development of clinically significant depressive symptoms in older adults."

For Dr. Alan Teo, an investigator at VA's Center to Improve Veteran Involvement in Care and a staff psychiatrist at the VA Portland Health Care System, the study has ramifications far beyond mitigating depression in elderly patients. "We know people who are isolated have all sorts of bad mental-health outcomes, not just a higher risk for depression," he says. "And we know social contact acts as a buffer against depression, and not just for older people or people who already have depression, but for everyone."

Teo and colleagues identified more than 11,000 participants who were assessed for depression symptoms and, over the course of two years, asked to identify how often they had met up, telephoned, or had some form of written correspondence with family or friends.

On average, the participants talked on the phone a few times per month, mostly with children and family members. The next most-frequent type of contact was in-person meetings, followed by e-mail or other written contact.

Older Participants: Family Contact Was Most Important

One of the strongest findings: For those age 70 or older, the odds of depression were 53 percent lower after two years if they reported having had in-person contact three or more times per week with children. The odds were 48 percent lower if their regular contact was with other family, not children.

"It is interesting to note that the positive effects we found were tied to contact with friends for those under 70," says Teo. Participants over aged 70 benefited more from contact with family.

Regardless of whom they were contacting, or how, what was clear was that the participants used a variety of methods to communicate.

"In a way it was good news," says Teo. "People were not just shutting themselves up and using e-mail or [other] written correspondence. They have not shunned meeting in person."

The take-home message, says Teo, is that "older Americans should think about specifically incorporating in-person contact with other people. In a way, social contact is like a medicine or a vitamin. It is enjoyable and, as it turns out, it is good for us."

Teo notes that he specifically used the term "in-person" in his research, rather than "face to face," because he realized that "face to face" could include things such as FaceTime or Skype, which allow friends or family to see each other and talk even when thousands of miles apart.

"In future research," he says, "I would like to ask about the use of these specific technologies. My hypothesis is that they would offer some benefit for depression prevention, more modest than in-person but still better than the lack of benefit we saw with the telephone alone."

Chapter 36

Climate Change and Depression

Extreme Weather Events

Many people exposed to climate- or weather-related natural disasters experience stress reactions and serious mental-health consequences, including symptoms of posttraumatic stress disorder (PTSD), depression, and general anxiety, which often occur simultaneously. Mental-health effects include grief or bereavement, increased substance use or misuse, and suicidal thoughts. All of these reactions have the potential to interfere with the individual's functioning and well-being and are especially problematic for certain groups.

Exposure to life-threatening events, such as highly destructive hurricanes (e.g., Hurricane Katrina in 2005) have been associated with acute stress, PTSD, and higher rates of depression and suicide in affected communities. These mental-health consequences are of particular concern for people facing recurring disasters, posing a cumulative psychological toll. Following exposure to Hurricane Katrina, veterans with preexisting mental illness had a 6.8 times greater risk for developing any additional mental illness, compared to those veterans without a preexisting mental illness. Following hurricanes, increased levels of

---

This chapter includes text excerpted from "Climate and Health Assessment—Mental Health and Well-Being," GlobalChange.gov, U.S. Global Change Research Program (USGCRP), April 2016. Reviewed October 2019.

PTSD have been experienced by individuals who perceive members of their community as being less supportive or helpful to one another.

Depression and general anxiety are also common consequences of extreme events (such as hurricanes and floods) that involve a loss of life, resources, or social support and social networks or events that involve extensive relocation and life disruption. For example, long-term anxiety and depression, PTSD, and increased aggression (in children) have been found to be associated with floods. First responders following a disaster also experience increased rates of anxiety and depression.

Increases from predisaster rates have been observed in interpersonal and domestic violence, including intimate partner violence, particularly toward women, in the wake of climate- or weather-related disasters. High-risk coping behaviors, such as alcohol abuse, can also increase following extreme weather events. Individuals who use alcohol to cope with stress and those with preexisting alcohol use disorders are most vulnerable to increased alcohol use following extreme weather events.

Persons directly affected by a climate- or weather-related disaster are at increased incidence of suicidal thoughts and behaviors. Increases in both suicidal thoughts (from 2.8% to 6.4%) and actual suicidal plans (from 1.0% to 2.5%) were observed in residents 18 months after Hurricane Katrina. Following Hurricanes Katrina and Rita, a study of internally displaced women living in temporary housing found reported rates of suicide attempt and completion to be 78.6 times and 14.7 times the regional average, respectively. In the six months following 1992's Hurricane Andrew, the rate of homicide-suicides doubled to two per month in Miami-Dade County, where the hurricane hit, compared to an average of one per month during the prior five-year period that did not include hurricane activity of the same scale.

Climate- or weather-related disasters can strain the resources available to provide adequate mental (or even immediate physical) healthcare, due to the increased number of individuals who experience severe stress and mental-health reactions. Communities adversely affected by these events also have diminished interpersonal and social networks available to support mental-health needs and recovery due to the destruction and disruption caused by the event.

Extreme Heat

The majority (80.7%) of the U.S. population lives in cities and urban areas and urbanization is expected to increase in the future. People in cities may experience greater exposure to heat-related health effects during heat waves. The impact of extreme heat on mental health is associated with increased incidence of disease and death, aggressive behavior, violence, and suicide and increases in hospital and emergency room admissions for those with mental-health or psychiatric conditions.

Individuals with mental illness are especially vulnerable to extreme heat or heat waves. In six case–control studies involving 1,065 heat wave-related deaths, preexisting mental illness was found to triple the risk of death due to heatwave exposure. The risk of death also increases during hot weather for patients with psychosis, dementia, and substance misuse. Hospital admissions have been shown to increase for those with mental illness as a result of extreme heat, increasing ambient temperatures, and humidity. An increased death rate has also been observed in those with mental illness among cases admitted to the emergency department with a diagnosis of heat-related pathology.

People who are isolated and have difficulty caring for themselves — often characteristics of the elderly or those with a mental illness — are also at higher risk for heat-related incidence of disease and death. Fewer opportunities for social interaction and increased isolation, put people at elevated risk for not only heat-related illness and death but also decline in mental health and, in some cases, increases in aggression and violence. Hotter temperatures and poorer air quality limit people's outdoor activities. For many, reductions in outdoor exercise and stress-reducing activities lead to diminished physical health, increased stress, and poor mental health.

There may be a link between extreme heat (climate change related or otherwise) and increasing violence, aggressive motives, and/or aggressive behavior. The frequency of interpersonal violence and intergroup conflict may increase with more extreme precipitation and hotter temperatures. These impacts can include heightened aggression, which may result in increased interpersonal violence and violent crime, negatively impacting individual and societal mental health and well-being. Given projections of increasing temperatures, there is potential for increases in human conflict, but the causal linkages between climate change and conflict are complex and the evidence is still emerging.

Part Five

Chronic Illness and Depression

Chapter 37

Chronic Illness, Pain, and Depression

Chapter Contents

Section 37.1

Chronic Illness Related to Increased Symptoms of Depression

This section includes text excerpted from "Chronic Illness and Mental Health," National Institute of Mental Health (NIMH), December 18, 2015. Reviewed October 2019.

Chronic Illness and Mental Health

Depression is a real illness. Treatment can help you live to the fullest extent possible, even when you have another illness.

It is common to feel sad or discouraged after a heart attack, cancer diagnosis, or if you are trying to manage a chronic condition like pain. You may be facing new limits on what you can do and feel anxious about treatment outcomes and the future. It may be hard to adapt to a new reality and to cope with the changes and ongoing treatment that come with the diagnosis. Your favorite activities, like hiking or gardening, may be harder to do.

Temporary feelings of sadness are expected, but if these and other symptoms last longer than a couple of weeks, you may have depression. Depression affects your ability to carry on with daily life, to enjoy work, leisure, friends, and family. The health effects of depression go beyond mood. Depression is a serious medical illness with many symptoms, including physical ones. Some symptoms of depression are:

- Feeling sad, irritable, or anxious

- Feeling empty, hopeless, guilty, or worthless

- Loss of pleasure in usually enjoyed hobbies or activities, including sex

- Fatigue and decreased energy, feeling listless

- Trouble concentrating, remembering details, and making decisions

- Not being able to sleep, or sleeping too much, or waking too early

- Eating too much or not wanting to eat at all, possibly with unplanned weight gain or loss

- Thoughts of death, suicide, or suicide attempts

- Aches or pains, headaches, cramps, or digestive problems without a clear physical cause and/or that do not ease even with treatment

People with Other Chronic Medical Conditions Have a Higher Risk of Depression

The same factors that increase risk of depression in otherwise healthy people also raise the risk in people with other medical illnesses. These risk factors include a personal or family history of depression or loss of family members to suicide.

However, there are some risk factors directly related to having another illness. For example, conditions such as Parkinson disease (PD) and stroke cause changes in the brain. In some cases, these changes may have a direct role in depression. Illness-related anxiety and stress can also trigger symptoms of depression.

Depression is common among people who have chronic illnesses such as the following:

- Cancer
- Systemic lupus erythematosus (SLE)
- Coronary heart disease (CHD)
- Multiple sclerosis (MS)
- Stroke
- Alzheimer disease (AD)
- HIV/AIDS
- Parkinson disease
- Diabetes
- Epilepsy
- Rheumatoid arthritis (RA)

Sometimes, symptoms of depression may follow a recent medical diagnosis but lift as you adjust or as the other condition is treated. In other cases, certain medications used to treat the illness may trigger depression. Depression may persist, even as physical health improves.

People who have depression and another medical illness tend to have more severe symptoms of both illnesses. They may have more difficulty adapting to their co-occurring illness and medical costs than those who do not have depression. It is still important to seek treatment. It can make a difference in day-to-day life if you are coping with a chronic or long-term illness.

People with Depression Are at Higher Risk for Other Medical Conditions

It is noted that people with a medical illness or condition are more likely to suffer from depression. The reverse is also true: the risk of developing some physical illnesses is higher in people with depression.

People with depression have an increased risk of cardiovascular disease, diabetes, stroke, and AD. People with depression are at higher risk for osteoporosis relative to others. The reasons are not yet clear. One factor with some of these illnesses is that many people with depression may have less access to good medical care. They may have a harder time caring for their health, for example, seeking care, taking prescribed medication, eating well, and exercising.

Ongoing research is also exploring whether physiological changes seen in depression may play a role in increasing the risk of physical illness. In people with depression, scientists have found changes in the way several different systems in the body function, all of which can have an impact on physical health:

- Signs of increased inflammation

- Changes in the control of heart rate and blood circulation

- Abnormalities in stress hormones

- Metabolic changes typical of those seen in people at risk for diabetes

Depression Is Treatable Even When Another Illness Is Present

Do not dismiss depression as a normal part of having a chronic illness. Effective treatment for depression is available and can help even if you have another medical illness or condition. If you or a loved one think you have depression, it is important to tell your healthcare provider and explore treatment options.

You should also inform the healthcare provider about all treatments or medications you are already receiving, including treatment for depression (prescribed medications and dietary supplements). Sharing information can help avoid problems with multiple medications interfering with each other. It also helps the provider stay informed about your overall health and treatment issues.

Section 37.2

Chronic Pain and PTSD

This section includes text excerpted from "Depression and Chronic Pain," National Institute of Mental Health (NIMH). January 30, 2017.

What Is Chronic Pain?

Chronic pain is pain that lasts for weeks, months, or even years. It often does not ease with regular pain medication. Chronic pain can have a distinct cause, such as a temporary injury or infection or a long-term disease. But some chronic pain has no obvious cause. Like depression, chronic pain can cause problems with sleep and daily activities, reducing your quality of life (QOL).

How Are Depression and Chronic Pain Linked?

Depression and chronic pain are known to occur together. Chronic pain can worsen depression symptoms and is a risk factor for suicide in people who are depressed. Bodily aches and pains are a common symptom of depression. People with more severe depression feel more intense pain. People with depression have higher than normal levels of proteins called "cytokines." Cytokines send messages to cells that affect how the immune system responds to infection and disease, including the strength and length of the response. In this way, cytokines can trigger pain by promoting inflammation, which is the body's response to infection or injury. Inflammation helps protect the body by destroying, removing, or isolating the infected or injured area. In addition to pain, signs of inflammation include swelling, redness, heat, and sometimes loss of function occur.

One disorder that has been shown to occur with depression is fibromyalgia. Fibromyalgia causes chronic, widespread muscle pain, fatigue, and multiple tender points on the body that hurt in response to light pressure. People with fibromyalgia are more likely to have depression and other mental illnesses than the general population. Also depression and fibromyalgia share risk factors and treatments.

How Is Depression Treated in People Who Have Chronic Pain?

Depression is diagnosed and treated by a healthcare provider. Treating depression can help you manage your chronic pain and improve your overall health. Recovery from depression takes time but treatments are effective.

At present, the most common treatments for depression include:

- Cognitive-behavioral therapy (CBT), a type of psychotherapy, or talk therapy, that helps people change negative thinking styles and behaviors that may contribute to their depression

- Selective serotonin reuptake inhibitor (SSRI), a type of antidepressant medication that includes citalopram (Celexa®), Sertraline (Zoloft®), and Fluoxetine (Prozac®)

- Serotonin and norepinephrine reuptake inhibitor (SNRI), a type of antidepressant medication similar to SSRI that includes Venlafaxine (Effexor®) and Duloxetine (Cymbalta®).

While the available depression treatments are generally well-tolerated and safe, talk with your healthcare provider about side effects, possible drug interactions, and other treatment options. Not everyone responds to treatment the same way. Medications can take several weeks to work, may need to be combined with ongoing talk therapy, or may need to be changed or adjusted to minimize side effects and achieve the best results. People living with chronic pain may be able to manage their symptoms through lifestyle changes. For example, regular aerobic exercise may help reduce some symptoms of chronic pain. Exercise may also boost your mood and help treat your depression. Talk therapy may also be helpful in treating chronic pain.

Section 37.3

Asthma and Depression in Adolescents

This section includes text excerpted from "Past Year Major
Depressive Episodes More Common among Adolescents
with Asthma," Center for Behavioral Health Statistics and
Quality (CBHSQ) Report, Substance Abuse and Mental Health
Services Administration (SAMHSA), May 4, 2017.

Major Depressive Episodes in Adolescents with Asthma

Asthma and depression are both common health concerns among
adolescents. For example, more than 1 in 12 adolescents have asthma.
Data from a study by the National Survey on Drug Use and Health
(NSDUH) show that about 1 in 11 adolescents aged 12 to 17 years
had a major depressive episode (MDE) in the past year. MDE among
adolescents is defined a period of at least 2 weeks during which they
had either depressed mood or loss of interest in usual activities and
also experienced a change in functioning, such as problems with sleep,
eating, energy, concentration, and self-worth.

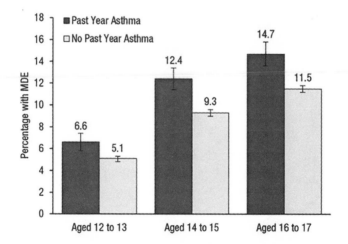

Figure 37.1. *Past Year Major Depressive Episode among Adolescents Aged 12 to 17 by Age Group and Past Year Asthma Status: 2005 to 2014.* (Source: National Survey on Drug Use and Health (NSDUH).)

For each age group, youth with past-year asthma had a significantly higher rate of past year MDE than youth without asthma.

According to the NSDUH research data (Figure 37.1), adolescents aged 12 to 17 years with past-year asthma were more likely to have past year MDE compared to those without asthma (11.4% versus 8.8%). This pattern held true among adolescents aged 12 to 13, 14 to 15, and 16 to 17 years. For example, among 16 to 17-year-olds, those with asthma were more likely to have past year MDE than those without asthma (14.7% versus 11.5%).

Assessing the relationship between asthma and depression is complicated because NSDUH data do not identify which health concern came first. Having asthma may increase the likelihood of developing depressive symptoms, while depression may impact the severity of asthma. Recognizing the association between asthma and depression among adolescents may inform prevention and treatment efforts. For example, understanding this relationship may help parents, schools, and pediatric care providers detect and start treatment.

Chapter 38

Autoimmune Diseases and Depression

Chapter Contents

Section 38.1

Depression Often Coexists with Fibromyalgia

This section contains text excerpted from the following sources:
Text beginning with the heading "What Is Fibromyalgia?" is
excerpted from "Fibromyalgia," National Institute of Arthritis and
Musculoskeletal and Skin Diseases (NIAMS), July 2014. Reviewed
October 2019; Text beginning with the heading "Debilitating Effects"
is excerpted from "Living with Fibromyalgia, Drugs Approved to
Manage Pain," U.S. Food and Drug Administration (FDA),
January 31, 2014. Reviewed October 2019.

What Is Fibromyalgia?

Fibromyalgia is a long-lasting or chronic disorder that causes muscle pain and fatigue. If you have fibromyalgia, you have pain and tenderness throughout your body. Sometimes you may have two or more chronic pain conditions at the same time, such as:

- Chronic fatigue syndrome (CFS)

- Endometriosis

- Irritable bowel syndrome (IBS)

- Interstitial cystitis (IC)

- Temporomandibular joint dysfunction (TMJ)

- Vulvodynia

Who Gets Fibromyalgia

Anyone can get this disorder, though it occurs most often in women and often starts in middle age. If you have certain other diseases such as rheumatoid arthritis (RA), systemic lupus erythematosus (SLE) and ankylosing spondylitis (AS) you may be more likely to have fibromyalgia.

If you have a family member with fibromyalgia, you may be more likely to get the disorder.

Debilitating Effects

People with fibromyalgia can experience pain anywhere, but common sites of pain include the neck, shoulders, back, hips, arms, and legs. In addition to pain and fatigue, other symptoms include difficulty sleeping, morning stiffness, headaches, painful menstrual periods, tingling or numbness of hands or feet, and difficulty thinking and remembering. Some people with the condition may also experience IBS, pelvic pain, restless leg syndrome (RLS), and depression.

What Causes Fibromyalgia

Scientists believe that the condition may be due to injury, emotional distress, or viruses that change the way the brain perceives pain, but the exact cause is unclear. People with rheumatoid arthritis, lupus, and spinal arthritis may be more likely to have the illness.

People with fibromyalgia can have abnormal levels of substance P in their spinal fluid. This chemical helps transmit and amplify pain signals to and from the brain.

Researchers are looking at the role of substance P and other neurotransmitters, and studying why people with fibromyalgia have increased sensitivity to pain and whether there is a gene or genes that make a person more likely to have it.

More than Medicine

People with fibromyalgia may find relief of symptoms with pain relievers, sleep medicines, antidepressants, muscle relaxants, and antiseizure medications. But, medication is just one part of the treatment approach.

A combination of medicines for pain and sleep, treatment for some of the overlapping conditions, such as migraines and IBS, and a combination of water therapy, massage and yoga may be helpful. Walking, jogging, biking, gently stretching muscles, and other exercises also can be helpful.

Emotional support also is essential. It is really about facing chronic pain for the rest of your life. So dealing with the emotional impact and not just the physical side is very important.

Section 38.2

The Arthritis–Mental Health Connection

This section includes text excerpted from "The
Arthritis–Mental Health Connection," Centers for
Disease Control and Prevention (CDC), October 12, 2018.

One in five U.S. adults with arthritis has symptoms of anxiety or depression. People with arthritis are more likely to have symptoms of anxiety and depression than people without arthritis. It is important for people who have arthritis to take care of their mental health. Arthritis, anxiety, and depression can all have a negative impact on the quality of life (QOL).

Some common symptoms of anxiety are:

- Feeling restless or on edge

- Difficulty focusing

- Having your mind go blank

- Feeling worried or irritated

- Trouble sleeping

Some common symptoms of depression are:

- Feeling sad, empty, hopeless, or gloomy

- Feeling guilty or worthless

- Losing interest in hobbies and activities

- Thinking of death or suicide, and/or suicide attempts

- Aches or pains, headaches, cramps, fatigue, or digestive problems without a clear physical cause and/or that do not ease even with treatment

If you have arthritis and are experiencing these symptoms, talk to your healthcare provider. She or he can refer you to mental-health professionals and helpful services. Some of these services may even address your mental health and arthritis together.

Improving Arthritis Patients' Mental Health

Over 54 million U.S. adults have arthritis and about 10 million adults with arthritis reported either anxiety or depression symptoms more often than those without arthritis. 1 in 5 adults with arthritis had anxiety symptoms, and depression symptoms occur twice as often in adults with arthritis as in adults without. Symptoms were more common among adults aged 18 to 44 than among other adults with arthritis.

The U.S. Preventive Services Task Force (USPSTF) recommends depression screening for all adults. The Substance Abuse and Mental Health Services Administration (SAMHSA) encourages universal screening for both anxiety and depression.

When treating mental-health conditions in arthritis patients, care should be taken to address both physical and mental health. Self-management education and physical-activity programs are proven to improve mood, energy, and arthritis symptoms as well. Research has shown that all these can help reduce anxiety and depression symptoms.

Chapter 39

Brain Injury and Depression

Relationship of Traumatic Brain Injury and Depression

Traumatic brain injuries are associated with a range of short and long-term outcomes, including physical, cognitive, behavioral, and emotional impairment. Depression among individuals with traumatic brain injury (TBI) ranges widely, from 15 to 77 percent. The extent to which depression contributes to long-term disability following TBI is still unknown, although depression is one of several potential psychiatric illnesses that may be common following TBI. Major depression may be triggered by physical or emotional distress, and it can deplete the mental energy and motivation needed for both recovering from the depression itself and adapting to the physical, social, and emotional consequences of trauma with brain injury. Depression may be masked by other deficits after a head injury, such as cognitive changes and

This chapter includes text excerpted from the following sources: Text under the heading "Relationship of Traumatic Brain Injury and Depression" is excerpted from "Traumatic Brain Injury and Depression," Effective Health Care Program, Agency for Healthcare Research and Quality (AHRQ), April 2011. Reviewed October 2019; Text under the heading "Veterans and Traumatic Brain Injury" is excerpted from "Study: Veterans with Multiple Brain Injuries Twice as Likely to Consider Suicide," Rehabilitation Research and Development Service (RR&D), U.S. Department of Veterans Affairs (VA), November 20, 2018; Text under the heading "Mental-Health Disorders Common Following Mild Head Injury" is excerpted from "Mental Health Disorders Common Following Mild Head Injury," National Institutes of Health (NIH), January 30, 2019.

flat affect, which may be blamed for lack of progress in posttrauma treatment but actually reflect underlying depression.

Depression associated with TBI can manifest shortly after the injury or well into the future. Depression was noted to coexist with other psychiatric conditions, including addiction or anxiety. Comorbid psychiatric conditions with depression may complicate screening, diagnosis, and management of depression in multiple ways, including masking depression so it remains undiagnosed or affects the individual's follow through or adherence to treatment. It is likely that such comorbid conditions complicate treatment response and recovery. Triggers for depression after TBI may include biological, psychological, and social factors, in the post-TBI population, greater attention is often given to biological factors because of the direct injury to the brain. However, many post-TBI patients do not demonstrate radiological or pathological evidence of brain injury, and in the context of the understanding of depression as a biopsychosocial entity, The psychological impact of decreased occupational and functional abilities and its potential to affect the likelihood of becoming depressed should not be overlooked.

Veterans and Traumatic Brain Injury

Veterans with multiple brain injuries twice as likely to consider suicide, compared with those with one or none. A study finds that veterans with a history of repeated TBIs versus none are at much greater risk for considering suicide.

The researchers found that Iraq and Afghanistan veterans who have suffered multiple TBIs were about twice as likely to report recent suicidal ideation, suicidal thoughts over the past week when compared with vets with one TBI or none at all.

Dr. Robert Shura, a neuropsychologist at the W.G. (Bill) Hefner U.S. Department of Veterans Affairs (VA) Medical Center in North Carolina, led the study. "Suicide is a major concern with veterans," he says. "Right now, the prime point of intervention is at the level of thinking about suicide. Therefore, identifying characteristics of veterans who are more likely to think about suicide is a high priority."

The findings stemmed from interviews with more than 800 veterans who held combat roles in Iraq and Afghanistan. The researchers were mainly interested in whether the vets had experienced suicidal thoughts in the past week. About half of the veterans reported at least one TBI. Of those, nearly 20 percent with a history of multiple TBIs told of recent suicidal ideation, compared with 11 percent with one TBI and nine percent with no history of a TBI.

The veterans with at least one TBI were much younger and more likely to be white and male than those with no brain injuries. The TBI group also reported significantly poorer sleep quality and much higher rates of depression, both of which are risk factors for suicidal ideation. Of the veterans with at least one brain injury, 18 percent met the criteria for major depressive disorder (MDD), which is intense feelings of sadness over long periods of time.

All the participants were enrolled in the Veterans Health Administration (VHA) benefits, but some were not using the VA for care, Shura says. The researchers used specific items in the interviews, such as a positive response on the Beck Scale, to identify those who may need help. In those cases, a licensed mental health professional promptly completed a suicide risk assessment and proceeded based on clinical judgment, he explains.

Mental-Health Disorders Common Following Mild Head Injury

A study reveals that approximately one in five individuals may experience mental health symptoms up to six months after mild traumatic brain injury (mTBI), suggesting the importance of follow-up care for these patients. Scientists also identified factors that may increase the risk of developing posttraumatic stress disorder (PTSD) and/or major depressive disorder following mild TBI or concussion through analysis of the Transforming Research and Clinical Knowledge in Traumatic Brain Injury (TRACK-TBI) study cohort.

"Mental health disorders after concussion have been studied primarily in military populations, and not much is known about these outcomes in civilians," said Patrick Bellgowan, Ph.D., National Institute of Neurological Disorders and Stroke (NINDS) program director. "These results may help guide follow-up care and suggest that doctors may need to pay particular attention to the mental state of patients many months after injury."

In the study, Murray B. Stein, M.D., M.P.H., professor at the University of California (UC) San Diego, and his colleagues investigated mental health outcomes in 1,155 people who had experienced a mild TBI and were treated in the emergency department. At 3, 6, and 12 months after injury, study participants completed various questionnaires related to PTSD and major depressive disorder. For a comparison group, the researchers also surveyed individuals who had experienced orthopedic traumatic injuries, such as broken legs, but did not have a head injury.

The results showed that at 3 and 6 months following injury, people who had experienced mTBI were more likely than orthopedic trauma patients to report symptoms of PTSD and/or major depressive disorder. For example, 3 months after injury, 20 percent of mTBI patients reported mental health symptoms compared to 8.7 percent of orthopedic trauma patients. At 6 months after injury, mental health symptoms were reported by 21.2 percent of people who had experienced head injury and 12.1 percent of orthopedic trauma patients.

Dr. Stein and his team also used the data to determine risk factors for PTSD and major depressive disorder after mTBI. The findings revealed that lower levels of education, self-identifying as African-American, and having a history of mental illness increased risk. In addition, if the head injury was caused by an assault or other violent attacks, that increased the risk of developing PTSD, but not a major depressive disorder. However, the risk of mental health symptoms was not associated with other injury-related occurrences such as duration of loss of consciousness or posttraumatic amnesia.

"Contrary to common assumptions, mild head injuries can cause long-term effects. These findings suggest that follow-up care after a head injury, even for mild cases, is crucial, especially for patients showing risk factors for PTSD or depression," said Dr. Stein.

This study is part of the National Institutes of Health (NIH)-funded TRACK-TBI initiative, which is a large, long-term study of patients treated in the emergency department for mTBI. The goal of the study is to improve understanding of the effects of concussions by establishing a comprehensive database of clinical measures including brain images, blood samples, and outcome data for 3,000 individuals, which may help identify biomarkers of TBI, risk factors for various outcomes, and improve our ability to identify and prevent adverse outcomes of head injury. To date, more than 2,700 individuals have enrolled in TRACK-TBI.

"TRACK-TBI is overturning many of our long-held beliefs around mTBI, particularly in what happens with patients after they leave the emergency department. We are seeing more evidence about the need to monitor these individuals for many months after their injury to help them achieve the best recovery possible," said Geoff Manley, M.D., professor at the University of California (UC) San Francisco, senior author of the current study and principal investigator of TRACK-TBI.

Future research studies will help identify mental health conditions, other than PTSD and major depressive disorder, that may arise following mTBI. In addition, more research is needed to understand the biological mechanisms that lead from mTBI to mental health problems and other adverse outcomes, such as neurological and cognitive difficulties.

Chapter 40

Cancer and Depression

About Depression[1]

Depression is different from normal sadness. Depression is not simply feeling sad. Depression is a disorder with specific symptoms that can be diagnosed and treated. For every 10 patients diagnosed with cancer, about 2 patients become depressed. The numbers of men and women affected are about the same.

A person diagnosed with cancer faces many stressful issues. These may include:

- Fear of death

- Changes in life plans

- Changes in body image and self-esteem

- Changes in day to day living

- Worry about money and legal issues

Sadness and grief are common reactions to a cancer diagnosis. A person with cancer may also have other symptoms of depression, such as:

This chapter includes text excerpted from documents published by two public domain sources. Text under the headings marked 1 are excerpted from "Depression (PDQ®)—Patient Version," National Cancer Institute (NCI), July 9, 2019; Text under the heading marked 2 is excerpted from "Depression (PDQ®)—Health Professional Version," National Cancer Institute (NCI), April 18, 2019.

- Feelings of disbelief, denial, or despair

- Trouble sleeping

- Loss of appetite

- Anxiety or worry about the future

Not everyone who is diagnosed with cancer reacts in the same way. Some cancer patients may not have depression or anxiety, while others may have major depression or an anxiety disorder.

Signs that you have adjusted to the cancer diagnosis and treatment include the following:

- Being able to stay active in daily life

- Continuing in your roles as spouse, parent, or employee

- Being able to manage your feelings and emotions related to your cancer

Some cancer patients may have a higher risk of depression. There are known risk factors for depression after a cancer diagnosis. Anything that increases your chance of developing depression is called a risk factor for depression. Factors that increase the risk of depression are not always related to the cancer.

Risk factors related to cancer that may cause depression include the following:

- Learning you have cancer when you are already depressed

- Having cancer pain that is not well controlled

- Being physically weakened by the cancer

- Having pancreatic cancer

- Having advanced cancer or a poor prognosis

- Feeling you are a burden to others

- Taking certain medicines, such as:
  - Corticosteroids
  - Procarbazine
  - L-asparaginase
  - Interferon alfa
  - Interleukin-2
  - Amphotericin B

Risk factors not related to cancer that may cause depression include the following:

- A personal history of depression or suicide attempts
- A family history of depression or suicide
- A personal history of mental problems, alcoholism, or drug abuse
- Not having enough support from family or friends
- Stress caused by life events other than cancer
- Having other health problems, such as stroke or heart attack that may also cause depression

There are many medical conditions that can cause depression. Medical conditions that may cause depression include the following:

- Pain that doesn't go away with treatment
- Abnormal levels of calcium, sodium, or potassium in the blood.
- Not enough vitamin B_{12} or folate in your diet
- Anemia
- Fever
- Too much or too little thyroid hormone
- Too little adrenal hormone
- Side effects caused by certain medicines

Family members also have a risk of depression. Anxiety and depression may occur in family members who are caring for loved ones with cancer. Family members who talk about their feelings and solve problems together are less likely to have high levels of depression and anxiety.

Screening and Assessment for Depression[2]

Because of the common underrecognition and undertreatment of depression in people with cancer, screening tools can be used to prompt further assessment. Among the physically ill, in general, instruments used to measure depression have not been shown to be more clinically useful than an interview and a thorough examination of mental status.

Simply asking the patient whether she or he is depressed may improve the identification of depression.

The following screening tools are commonly used:

- A single-item interview. In persons with advanced cancer, a single-item interview question has been found to have acceptable psychometric properties and can be useful. One example is to ask "Are you depressed?" Another example is to say, "Please grade your mood during the past week by assigning it a score from 0 to 100, with a score of 100 representing your usual relaxed mood." A score of 60 is considered a passing grade.

- The HADS may have utility in the assessment of depression and anxiety in patients who have comorbid neurovegetative symptoms due to their disease or treatment, helping to avoid false-positive results on the scale caused by these symptoms.

- The nine-item patient health questionnaire (PHQ-9)

- The psychological distress inventory (PDI)

- The Edinburgh Depression Scale (EDS)

- The brief symptom inventory

- The Zung Self-Rating Depression Scale (SDS)

- The distress thermometer

One study of women with newly diagnosed breast cancer (n = 236) successfully utilized brief screening instruments such as the distress thermometer (DT) and the PHQ to identify women requiring further assessment to detect clinically significant levels of distress and psychiatric symptoms.

In a study of 321 women with newly diagnosed stage I to stage III breast cancer, the ability of the single-item Distress Thermometer to specifically predict depression, as measured by a self-report questionnaire of the *Diagnostic and Statistical Manual of Mental Disorders, 4th edition (DSM-IV)* symptoms for major depressive disorder, was investigated. Sensitivity and specificity characteristics were evaluated, and the optimal cutoff score of seven was identified, resulting in a sensitivity of 0.81 and a specificity of 0.85 for detecting depression. Therefore, individuals scoring seven or above should undergo a more thorough psychosocial evaluation.

The Impact Thermometer, a modification of and accompaniment to the Distress Thermometer, has improved specificity for the detection of adjustment disorders and/or major depression, as compared with the distress thermometer. The revised tool has a screening performance comparable to that of the HADS and is brief, potentially making it an effective tool for routine screening in oncology settings. The mood evaluation questionnaire, a cognitive-based screening tool for depression, has a moderate correlation with the structured clinical interview for the *DSM*, third revised edition (*DSM-III-R*) and good acceptability in the palliative care population. With further validation, it may become a useful alternative in this population because it can be used by clinicians who are not trained in psychiatry.

It is important that screening instruments be validated in cancer populations and used in combination with structured diagnostic interviews. A pilot study of 25 patients used a simple, easily reproduced visual analog scale suggesting the benefits of a single-item approach to screening for depression. This scale consists of a 10 cm line with a sad face at one end and a happy face at the other end, on which patients make a mark to indicate their mood. Although the results do suggest that a visual analog scale may be useful as a screening tool for depression, the small patient numbers and lack of clinical interviews limit conclusions. Furthermore, although very high correlations with the HADS were reported ($r = 0.87$), no indication of cut-offs was given. Finally, it is emphasized that such a tool is intended to suggest the need for a further professional assessment. However, if validated further, this simple approach could greatly enhance assessment and management of depression in cognitively intact advanced-cancer patients.

In a study of 2,141 German cancer patients, the HADS and the PHQ-9 had similar sensitivity (89% and 83%, respectively) and specificity (43% and 61%, respectively) for detecting *DSM-IV* major depressive disorder at suggested cutoffs based on receiver operating characteristic curves.

Other brief assessment tools for depression can be used. To help patients distinguish normal anxiety reactions from depression, the assessment includes discussion about common symptoms experienced by cancer patients. Depression is reassessed over time. Because of the increased risk of adjustment disorders and major depression in cancer patients, routine screening with increased vigilance at times of increased stress (e.g., diagnosis, recurrences, progression) is recommended. General risk factors for depression are noted in the list above. Other risk factors may pertain to specific populations, for example, patients with head and neck cancer and women at high risk of developing breast cancer.

Diagnosis of Depression[1]

There are different types of depression.

The type of depression depends in part on the symptoms the patient is having and how long the symptoms have lasted. Major depression is one type of depression. Treatment depends on the type of depression.

Major depression has specific symptoms that last longer than two weeks.

It's normal to feel sad after learning you have cancer, but a diagnosis of major depression depends on more than being unhappy.

Symptoms of major depression include the following:

• Feeling sad most of the time

• Loss of pleasure and interest in activities you used to enjoy

• Changes in eating and sleeping habits

• Slow physical and mental responses

• Feeling restless or jittery

• Unexplained tiredness

• Feeling worthless, hopeless, or helpless

• Feeling a lot of guilt for no reason

• Not being able to pay attention

• Thinking the same thoughts over and over

• Frequent thoughts of death or suicide

• The symptoms of depression are not the same for every patient

Your healthcare provider will talk with you to find out if you have symptoms of depression.

Your healthcare provider will want to know how you are feeling and may want to discuss the following:

• Your feelings about having cancer. Talking with your doctor about this may help you see if your feelings are normal sadness or more serious.

• Your moods. You may be asked to rate your mood on a scale.

• Any symptoms you may have and how long the symptoms have lasted

- How the symptoms affect your daily life, such as your relationships, your work, and your ability to enjoy your usual activities

- Other parts of your life that are causing stress

- How strong your social support system is

- All the medicines you are taking and other treatments you are receiving. Sometimes, side effects of medicines or the cancer seem like symptoms of depression. This is more likely during active cancer treatment or if you have advanced cancer.

This information will help you and your doctor find out if you are feeling normal sadness or have depression.

Checking for depression may be repeated at times when stress increases, such as if cancer gets worse or if it comes back after treatment.

Physical exams, mental exams, and lab tests are used to diagnose depression.

In addition to talking with you, your doctor may do the following to check for depression:

- **Physical exam and history.** An exam of the body to check general signs of health, including checking for signs of disease, such as lumps or anything else that seems unusual. A history of your health habits, past illnesses including depression, and treatments will also be taken. A physical exam can help rule out other causes of your symptoms.

- **Laboratory tests.** Medical procedures that test samples of tissue, blood, urine, or other substances in the body. These tests help to diagnose disease, plan and check treatment, or monitor the disease over time. Lab tests are done to rule out a medical condition that may be causing symptoms of depression.

- **Mental status exam.** An exam done to get a general idea of your mental state by checking the following:

  - How you look and act

  - Your mood

  - Your speech

  - Your memory

  - How well you pay attention and understand simple concepts

Treatment of Depression[1]

The decision to treat depression depends on how long it has lasted and how much it affects your life.

You may have depression that needs to be treated if you are not able to perform your usual activities, have severe symptoms, or the symptoms do not go away. Treatment of depression may include talk therapy, medicines, or both.

Counseling or talk therapy helps some cancer patients with depression.

Your doctor may suggest you see a psychologist or psychiatrist for the following reasons:

- Your symptoms have been treated with medicine for 2 to 4 weeks and are not getting better.

- Your depression is getting worse.

- The antidepressants you are taking are causing unwanted side effects.

- The depression keeps you from continuing with your cancer treatment.

Most counseling or talk therapy programs for depression are offered in both individual and small-group settings. These programs include:

- Crisis intervention

- Psychotherapy

- Cognitive-behavioral therapy

More than one type of therapy program may be right for you. A therapy program can help you learn about the following:

- Coping and problem-solving skills

- Relaxation skills and ways to lower stress

- Ways to get rid of or change negative thoughts

- Giving and accepting social support

- Cancer and its treatment

Talking with a clergy member may also be helpful for some people. Antidepressant medicine helps cancer patients with depression.

Antidepressants may help relieve depression and its symptoms. You may be treated with a number of medicines during your cancer care.

Some anticancer medicines may not mix safely with certain antidepressants or with certain foods, herbals, or nutritional supplements. It's important to tell your healthcare providers about all the medicines, herbals, and nutritional supplements you are taking, including medicines used as patches on the skin, and any other diseases, conditions, or symptoms you have. This can help prevent unwanted reactions with antidepressant medicine.

When you are taking antidepressants, it is important that you use them under the care of a doctor. Some antidepressants take from 3 to 6 weeks to work. Usually, you begin at a low dose that is slowly increased to find the right dose for you. This helps to avoid side effects. Antidepressants may be taken for a year or longer.

There are different types of antidepressants.

Most antidepressants help treat depression by changing the levels of chemicals called neurotransmitters in the brain, while some affect cell receptors. Nerves use these chemicals to send messages to one another. Increasing the amount of these chemicals helps to improve mood. The different types of antidepressants act on these chemicals in different ways and have different side effects.

Several types of antidepressants are used to treat depression:

- **Selective serotonin reuptake inhibitors (SSRIs).** Medicines that stop serotonin (a substance that nerves use to send messages to one another) from being reabsorbed by the nerve cells that make it. This means there is more serotonin for other nerve cells to use. SSRIs include drugs such as citalopram, fluoxetine, and vilazodone.

- **Serotonin-norepinephrine reuptake inhibitors (SNRIs).** Medicines that stop the brain chemicals serotonin and norepinephrine from being reabsorbed by the nerve cells that make it. This means there is more serotonin and norepinephrine for other nerve cells to use. Some SNRIs may also help relieve neuropathy caused by chemotherapy or hot flashes caused by menopause. SNRIs include older drugs, such as tricyclic antidepressants, as well as newer drugs like venlafaxine.

- **Norepinephrine-dopamine reuptake inhibitors (NDRIs).** Medicines that stop the brain chemicals norepinephrine and dopamine from being reabsorbed. This means there is more norepinephrine and dopamine for other nerve cells to use. The only NDRI currently approved to treat depression is bupropion.

The following antidepressants may also be used:

• Mirtazapine

• Trazodone

• Monoamine oxidase inhibitors (MAOIs)

Other medicines may be given along with antidepressants to treat other symptoms. Benzodiazepines may be given to decrease anxiety and psychostimulants may be given to improve energy and concentration.

The antidepressant that is best for you depends on several factors. Choosing the best antidepressant for you depends on the following:

• Your symptoms

• Side effects of the antidepressant

• Your medical history

• Other medicines you are taking

• How you or your family members responded to antidepressants in the past

• The form of medicine you are able to take (such as a pill or a liquid)

You may have to try different treatments to find the one that is right for you.

Your doctor will watch you closely if you need to change or stop taking your antidepressant.

You may need to change your antidepressant or to stop taking it if severe adverse effects occur or your symptoms are not getting better. Check with your doctor before you stop taking an antidepressant. For some types of antidepressants, your doctor will reduce the dose slowly. This is to prevent side effects that can occur if you suddenly stop taking the medicine.

It is important for you to know what to expect when you change or stop antidepressants. Your doctor will watch you closely while lowering or stopping doses of one medicine before starting another.

Suicide Risk in Patients with Cancer[1]

Cancer patients may feel hopeless at times and think about suicide.

Cancer patients sometimes feel hopeless. Talk with your doctor if you feel hopeless. There are ways your doctor can help you.

Feelings of hopelessness may lead to thinking about suicide. If you or someone you know is thinking about suicide, get help as soon as possible.

Certain factors may add to a cancer patient's risk of thinking about suicide.

Some of these factors include the following:

- Having a personal history of depression, anxiety, or other mental health problem, or suicide attempts

- Having a family member who has attempted suicide

- Having a personal history of drug or alcohol abuse

- Feeling hopeless or that you are a burden to others

- Not having enough support from family and friends

- Being unable to live a normal, independent life because of problems with activities of daily living, pain, or other symptoms

- Being within the first 3 to 5 months of your cancer diagnosis

- Having advanced cancer or a poor prognosis

- Having cancer of the prostate, lung, head and neck, or pancreas

- Not getting along well with the treatment team

An assessment is done to find the reasons for feeling hopeless or thoughts of suicide.

Talking about thoughts of hopelessness and suicide with your doctor gives you a chance to describe your feelings and fears, and may help you feel more in control. Your doctor will try to find out what is causing your hopeless feelings, such as:

- Symptoms that are not well controlled

- Fear of having a painful death

- Fear of being alone during your cancer experience

You can find out what may be done to help relieve your emotional and physical pain.

Controlling symptoms caused by cancer and cancer treatment is important to prevent suicide.

Cancer patients may feel desperate to stop any discomfort or pain they have. Keeping pain and other symptoms under control will help to:

- Relieve distress
- Make you feel more comfortable
- Prevent thoughts of suicide

Treatment may include antidepressants. Some antidepressants take a few weeks to work. The doctor may prescribe other medicines that work quickly to relieve distress until the antidepressant begins to work. For your safety, it's important to have frequent contact with a healthcare professional and avoid being alone until your symptoms are controlled. Your healthcare team can help you find social support.

Depression in Children[1]

Some children have depression or other problems related to cancer.

Most children cope well with cancer. However, a small number of children may have:

- Depression or anxiety
- Trouble sleeping
- Problems getting along with family or friends
- Problems following the treatment plan

These problems can affect the child's cancer treatment and enjoyment of life. They can occur at any time from diagnosis to well after treatment ends. Survivors of childhood cancer who have severe late effects from cancer treatment may be more likely to have symptoms of depression.

A mental health specialist can help children with depression.

Assessment for depression includes looking at the child's symptoms, behavior, and health history.

As in adults, children with cancer may feel depressed but do not have the medical condition of depression. Depression lasts longer and has specific symptoms. The doctor may assess a child for depression if a problem, such as not eating or sleeping well, lasts for a while. To assess for depression, the doctor will ask about the following:

- How the child is coping with illness and treatment
- Past illnesses and how the child coped with the illness
- The child's sense of self-worth

- Homelife with family

- The child's behavior, as seen by the parents, teachers, or others

- How the child is developing compared with other children his or her age

The doctor will talk with the child and may use a set of questions or a checklist that helps to diagnose depression in children.

The symptoms of depression are not the same in every child.

A diagnosis of depression depends on the symptoms and how long they have lasted. Children who are diagnosed with depression have an unhappy mood and at least four of the following symptoms every day for two weeks or longer:

- Appetite changes

- Not sleeping or sleeping too much

- Being unable to relax and be still (such as pacing, fidgeting, and pulling at clothing)

- Frequent crying

- Loss of interest or pleasure in usual activities

- Lack of emotion in children younger than 6 years

- Feeling very tired or having little energy

- Feelings of worthlessness, blame, or guilt

- Unable to think or pay attention and frequent daydreaming

- Trouble learning in school, not getting along with others, and refusing to go to school in school-aged children

- Frequent thoughts of death or suicide

Treatment may be talk therapy or medicine such as antidepressants. Talk therapy is the main treatment for depression in children.

Talk therapy is the main treatment for depression in children. The child may talk to the counselor alone or with a small group of other children. Talk therapy may include play therapy for younger children. Therapy will help the child cope with feelings of depression and understand their cancer and treatment.

Antidepressants may be given to children with major depression and anxiety. In some children, teenagers, and young adults, antidepressants may make depression worse or cause thoughts of suicide. The U.S. Food and Drug Administration (FDA) has warned that patients younger than age 25 who are taking antidepressants should be watched closely for signs that the depression is getting worse and for suicidal thinking or behavior.

Chapter 41

Diabetes and Depression

Mental health affects so many aspects of daily life such as how you think and feel, handle stress, relate to others, and make choices. Having a mental-health problem could make it harder to stick to your diabetes care plan.

The Mind–Body Connection

Thoughts, feelings, beliefs, and attitudes can affect how healthy your body is. Untreated mental-health issues can make diabetes worse, and problems with diabetes can make mental-health issues worse. But, fortunately, if one gets better, the other tends to get better, too.

Depression: More than Just a Bad Mood

Depression is a medical illness that causes feelings of sadness and often a loss of interest in activities you used to enjoy. It can get in the way of how well you function at work and home, including taking care of your diabetes. When you are not able to manage your diabetes well, your risk goes up for diabetes complications such as heart disease and nerve damage.

People with diabetes are 2 to 3 times more likely to have depression than people without diabetes. Only 25 to 50 percent of people with diabetes who have depression get diagnosed and treated. Treating

This chapter includes text excerpted from "Diabetes and Mental Health," Centers for Disease Control and Prevention (CDC), August 6, 2018.

depression with therapy or medicine, or both is usually very effective. Without treatment, depression often gets worse, not better.

Symptoms of depression can be mild to severe, and include:

- Feeling sad or empty

- Losing interest in favorite activities

- Overeating or not wanting to eat at all

- Not being able to sleep or sleeping too much

- Having trouble concentrating or making decisions

- Feeling very tired

- Feeling hopeless, irritable, anxious, or guilty

- Having aches or pains, headaches, cramps, or digestive problems

- Having thoughts of suicide or death

If you think you might have depression, get in touch with your doctor right away for help getting treatment. The earlier your depression is treated, the better it is for you, your quality of life (QOL), and your diabetes.

Diabetes Distress

You may sometimes feel discouraged, worried, frustrated, or tired of dealing with daily diabetes care. Maybe you have been trying hard but not seeing results. Or you have developed a health problem related to diabetes in spite of your best efforts.

Those overwhelming feelings, known as "diabetes distress," may cause you to slip into unhealthy habits, stop checking your blood sugar, even skip doctor's appointments. It happens to many people with diabetes, often after years of good management. In any 18 month period, 33 percent to 50 percent of people with diabetes have diabetes distress.

Diabetes distress can look like depression or anxiety, but it cannot be treated effectively with medication. Instead, these approaches have been shown to help:

- Make sure you are seeing an endocrinologist for your diabetes care. She or he is likely to have a deeper understanding of diabetes challenges than your regular doctor.

- Ask your doctor to refer you to a mental-health counselor who specializes in chronic-health conditions.

- Get some one-on-one time with a diabetes educator so you can problem-solve together.

- Focus on 1 or 2 small diabetes management goals instead of thinking you have to work on everything all at once.

- Join a diabetes support group so you can share your thoughts and feelings with people who have the same concerns (and learn from them too).

Chapter 42

Heart Disease and Depression

Heart Disease and Depression: A Two-Way Relationship

For years, scientists have known about the relationship between depression and heart disease. At least a quarter of cardiac patients suffer from depression, and adults with depression often develop heart disease. Researchers have unearthed a treasure trove of important clues, but a definitive explanation on the curious nature of this relationship has yet to emerge

It is a puzzle: Is depression a causal risk factor for heart disease? Is it a warning sign because depressed people engage in behaviors that increase the risks of heart disease? Is depression just a secondary event, prompted by the trauma of major medical problems, such as heart surgery? According to the World Health Organization (WHO), 350 million people suffer from depression worldwide, and 17.3 million die of heart disease each year, making it the number one global cause of death.

Promising insights are emerging because data researchers continue to amass, scientific innovation, and heightened public awareness. It

This chapter includes text excerpted from "Heart Disease and Depression: A Two-Way Relationship," National Heart, Lung, and Blood Institute (NHLBI), April 16, 2017.

was in part because of better diagnostic tools and increased recognition of the prevalence of depression that scientists could establish a connection between depression and heart disease in the first place.

"Thirty years of epidemiological data indicate that depression does predict the development of heart disease," said Jesse C. Stewart, Ph.D., an associate professor of psychology in the School of Science at Indiana University-Purdue University Indianapolis (IUPUI).

Stewart noted that there is "an impressive body of evidence" showing that, compared with people without depression, adults with a depressive disorder or symptoms have a 64 percent greater risk of developing coronary artery disease (CAD); and depressed CAD patients are 59 percent more likely to have a future adverse cardiovascular event, such as a heart attack or cardiac death.

Does Depression Cause Heart Disease?

"Those who have elevated depressive symptoms are at increased risk for heart disease, and this association seems to be largely independent of the traditional risk markers for heart disease," said Karina W. Davidson, Ph.D., professor at Columbia University Medical Center (CUMC). Indeed, she said, the association between depression and heart disease is similar to the association of factors such as high cholesterol, hypertension, diabetes, smoking, and obesity and heart disease.

To establish a true cause-effect relationship between depression and heart disease, according to Stewart, scientists need evidence from randomized controlled trials showing that treating depression reduces the risk of future heart disease. In other words, what needs to be studied is whether treating depression prevents heart disease in the way of treating high cholesterol and blood pressure does.

A 2014 paper by Stewart and his colleagues suggests that early treatment for depression, before the development of the symptomatic cardiovascular disease (CVD), could decrease the risk of heart attacks and strokes by almost half.

In the meantime, the existing evidence prompted the American Heart Association (AHA) to issue a statement in 2015 warning that teens with depression and bipolar disorder stand at increased risk for developing the CVD earlier in life, and urging doctors to actively monitor these patients and intervene to try to prevent its onset.

Just as concerning, say doctors, is the prognosis for older patients who already have heart disease. Researchers have discovered that depression actually worsens the prognosis dramatically. Conversely, people who are diagnosed with heart disease have an increased risk of developing depression. It is a two-way relationship.

The prevalence of depression among cardiac patients range from 20 to 30 percent. With funding from the National Heart, Lung, and Blood Institute (NHLBI), Stewart is conducting the clinical trial he said would help answer this cause-effect question. "Even the lower limit of this range is more than double the prevalence of this treatable condition in the general population," wrote Bruce L. Rollman, M.D. and Stewart in their 2014 study.

A study presented at the American College of Cardiology's (ACCs) 66th Annual Scientific Session shows that patients are twice as likely to die if they develop depression after being diagnosed with heart disease. In fact, depression is the strongest predictor of death in the first decade after a heart disease diagnosis.

"We are confident that depression is an independent risk factor for cardiac morbidity and mortality in patients with established heart disease," said Robert Carney, Ph.D., professor of psychiatry at Washington University School of Medicine (WUSM). "However, depression is also associated with other risk factors, including smoking, so it can be difficult to disentangle its effects from those of other risk factors."

In other words, cardiac patients with depression have worse outcomes, which translates to more deaths and repeated cardiovascular events.

How Does Depression Have Such an Effect?

Researchers agree that while the pathways are not completely understood, there are many likely explanations. Some point to the biology of depression, such as autonomic nervous system dysfunction, elevated cortisol levels, and elevated markers of inflammation.

"There are also plausible behavioral explanations, such as poor adherence to the diet, exercise, and medications, and a higher prevalence of smoking, that have been associated with depression with or without established heart disease," said Ken Freedland, Ph.D., also from Washington University School of Medicine.

Chapter 43

Human Immunodeficiency Virus and Depression

What Is Human Immunodeficiency Virus?

Human immunodeficiency virus (HIV) is a virus that attacks cells that help the body fight infection, making a person more vulnerable to other infections and diseases. It is spread by contact with certain bodily fluids of a person with HIV, most commonly during unprotected sex (sex without a condom or HIV medicine to prevent or treat HIV), or through sharing injection drug equipment.

If left untreated, HIV can lead to the disease AIDS (acquired immunodeficiency syndrome).

The human body cannot get rid of HIV and no effective HIV cure exists. So, once you have HIV, you have it for life.

However, by taking HIV medicine (called "antiretroviral therapy" or "ART"), people with HIV can live long and healthy lives and prevent

This chapter contains text excerpted from the following sources: Text under the heading "What Is Human Immunodeficiency Virus?" is excerpted from "What Are HIV and AIDS?" HIV.gov, U.S. Department of Health and Human Services (HHS), June 17, 2019; Text beginning with the heading "Are People with HIV at Risk for Mental-Health Conditions?" is excerpted from "HIV and Mental Health," AIDS*info*, U.S. Department of Health and Human Services (HHS), January 14, 2019; Text under the heading "Treatments and Therapies" is excerpted from "HIV/AIDS and Mental Health," National Institute of Mental Health (NIMH), November 2016. Reviewed October 2019.

transmitting HIV to their sexual partners. In addition, there are effective methods to prevent getting HIV through sex or drug use, including pre-exposure prophylaxis (PrEP) and post-exposure prophylaxis (PEP).

First identified in 1981, HIV is the cause of one of humanity's deadliest and most persistent epidemics.

Are People with HIV at Risk for Mental-Health Conditions?

Anyone can have mental-health problems. Mental-health conditions are common in the United States. According to MentalHealth.gov, in 2014, about one in five American adults experienced a mental-health issue.

However, people with HIV have a higher risk of mental-health conditions than people who do not have HIV. For example, people living with HIV are twice as likely to have depression as people who do not have HIV.

It is important to remember that mental-health conditions are treatable and that people who have mental-health problems can recover.

The stress of having a serious medical illness or condition, such as HIV infection, may also negatively affect a person's mental health. HIV infection and related opportunistic infections can affect the brain and nervous system. This may lead to changes in how a person thinks and behaves. In addition, some medicines used to treat HIV may have side effects that affect a person's mental health.

What Are the Warning Signs of a Mental-Health Problem?

Changes in how a person feels or acts can be a warning sign of a mental-health problem. Potential signs of a mental-health problem include:

- Losing interest in activities that are usually enjoyable

- Experiencing persistent sadness or feeling empty

- Feeling anxious or stressed

- Having suicidal thoughts

If you have any of these signs of a mental-health problem, it is important to get help.

What Should I Do If I Need Help for a Mental-Health Problem?

Talk to your healthcare provider about how you are feeling. Tell them if you are having any problems with drugs or alcohol.

Your healthcare provider will consider whether any of your HIV medicines may be affecting your mental health. They can also help you find a mental-healthcare provider, for example, a psychiatrist or therapist.

Here are additional ways to improve your mental health:

- Join a support group

- Try meditation, yoga, or deep breathing to relax

- Get enough sleep, eat healthy meals, and stay physically active

HIV Treatments and Mental-Health Problem

Research shows that HIV treatment should be initiated as soon as the infection is detected to achieve the best health outcomes. Once diagnosed, HIV infection is treated using a combination of medicines called "antiretroviral therapy" (ART). Adequate adherence to prescribed treatment regimens, such as taking the medications as prescribed by the healthcare provider, is critical to controlling the virus and to achieving complete viral suppression. Adequate adherence can be difficult but many strategies have been developed to assist individuals living with human immunodeficiency virus infection/acquired immune deficiency syndrome (HIV/AIDS).

Starting ART also can affect your mental health in different ways. Sometimes ART can relieve your anxiety because knowing that you are taking care of yourself can give you a sense of security. However, coping with the reality of living with a chronic illness can be challenging. Depression is one of the most common mental-health conditions experienced by people living with HIV, just as it is in the general population. In addition, some antiretroviral medications may cause symptoms of depression, anxiety, and sleep disturbance, and may make some mental-health issues worse.

For these reasons, it is important to talk to your healthcare provider about your mental health. A conversation about mental health should be part of your complete medical evaluation before starting antiretroviral medications. Continue to discuss your mental health with your healthcare team throughout treatment. Be open and honest with your provider about any changes in the way you are thinking, or how you are feeling about yourself and life in general. Also, discuss any alcohol or substance use with your provider so that she or he can help connect you to treatment if necessary.

In addition, tell your healthcare provider about any over-the-counter (OTC) or prescribed medications you may be taking, including any psychiatric medications, because some of these drugs may interact with antiretroviral medications.

Chapter 44

Multiple Sclerosis and Depression

What Is Multiple Sclerosis?

Multiple sclerosis (MS) is a complex neurologic disease that affects the central nervous system, including the brain, spinal cord, and vision pathways. In MS, the immune system attacks the myelin sheath, the fatty tissue that surrounds and protects nerve fibers, as well as the nerve fibers themselves.

Damage from these attacks is called "demyelination," and the scar tissue that develops when myelin is damaged is called "sclerosis." This scar tissue is also known as "lesions" or "plaques." When any part of the myelin sheath or nerve fiber is damaged or destroyed, nerve impulses traveling to and from the brain and spinal cord are distorted or interrupted, causing a wide variety of symptoms.

Sometimes the myelin can repair itself and the MS symptoms go away after the immune attack. Over time, however, the myelin and underlying nerve fibers cannot recover and suffer permanent damage. This may lead to a gradual decline in function, depending on the disease course. The cause of MS is unknown.

This chapter contains text excerpted from the following sources: Text under the heading "What Is Multiple Sclerosis?" is excerpted from "Multiple Sclerosis," U.S. Department of Veterans Affairs (VA), June 1, 2018; Text under the heading "Psychosocial Aspects of Depression" is excerpted from "Do It Yourself," U.S. Department of Veterans Affairs (VA), April 8, 2018.

Symptoms of MS vary depending on the location of the lesions in the brain and spinal cord. They may include tingling, numbness, painful sensations, slurred speech, and blurred or double vision. Some people experience muscle weakness, poor balance, poor coordination, muscle tightness or spasticity, tremors, or temporary or permanent paralysis. Problems with bladder, bowel, sexual function, or mood (especially depression) are also very common.

Fatigue is a major concern for most people with MS, as a challenge with memory, attention, and concentration. Symptoms may come and go, appear in any combination, and be mild, moderate, or severe.

Many symptoms are very responsive to self-care lifestyle changes such as increased activity. Fatigue, insomnia, mood, cognition, mobility, spasticity, and bowel function may all be improved through regular physical activity. In addition, medication therapies and other interventions are available to help manage MS symptoms.

While some neurological diseases, such as amyotrophic lateral sclerosis, have been associated with military service, this relationship has not been seen with MS. However, veterans who develop symptoms of MS while in the military, or within seven years of their honorable discharge, may be eligible to receive service-connected disability compensation. Medical care for veterans with MS, whether or not their illness was service-connected, can include disease-modifying therapies, other medications, physical and occupational therapy, and other healthcare services and medical equipment.

Psychosocial Aspects of Depression

Multiple sclerosis is often experienced as a debilitating illness that creates many hardships for the millions of people with this disease. MS causes a wide range of symptoms, including physical and sometimes psychological problems. MS can affect the person's self-image and identity: how they look, behave, think, feel, and how others see them.

Since MS has no clear cause or cure, people with MS often wonder, "Why me?" and struggle with existential questions after receiving this diagnosis. Questions such as: "What does my life mean now?" and "Is there any hope?" are common. The difficulty with not knowing how this occurred and how they will deal with it can trigger a sense of hopelessness, unfairness, and even victimization—as if life itself has done them "dirty." Some people experience MS as trauma in their lives. This is especially true given that the attack of symptoms themselves are unpredictable. Dealing with a disability associated with MS can trigger a strong feeling of depression. In addition, MS can cause depression directly, likely because of lesions in the brain and the inflammation associated with the disease.

Depression in people with MS can go less noticed than the physical symptoms. But depression is common with MS and can have more impact on the person's daily functioning than physical symptoms. They can linger in the shadows, influencing the person to see themselves in a negative fashion. And, by the time the person recognizes the depression, it may already have a significant amount of power and influence in their lives, shaping almost every decision they make on a day-to-day basis.

Multiple sclerosis can cause a profound sense of fear that can shake a person's most fundamental beliefs (e.g., belief in a "just world"). And at the root of this fear is an internalized feeling of helplessness which can lead the person to feel like they always need to "be on guard" from future MS attacks and increased disability. This "on guard" behavior can lead people to develop coping mechanisms rooted in avoidance.

To cope, people with MS will often avoid going out in public, being in crowds, or being around others (including family and friends)—preferring to isolate. Isolation can have devastating impacts on a person's life and is one of the main symptoms of depression. Isolation cuts people off from things they used to do for fun, people they love, and those who support them. Isolation stops people from participating in things that make life feel good to them. Over time, isolation also magnifies feelings of anger as life may begin to feel more and more unfair. Trust and intimacy problems are also common, as the person is likely to see herself/himself as a "burden" and feel as if others cannot understand what they are going through.

There are several tell-tale signs of depression. Depression is referred to as "the absence or decrease of positive emotionality." The hallmark sign of depression is a pronounced decrease in the number of positive emotions the person experiences (e.g., pride, joy, happiness, satisfaction). Depression is the absence of the "spark" in the person's life and maybe a byproduct of the isolation and the physical limitations imposed by MS. With depression, as the person loses their "spark" they may begin to feel as if their life has no meaning or is not worth living.

In addition to antidepressant medications, there are things you can do to help with depression associated with MS. There are four main protective factors, grounded in solid research, that can help with depression: diet, exercise, social support, and an emphasis on post-traumatic growth. Specific to diet, eating a balanced, healthy diet can promote healthy brain function. Although exercise may be difficult, it is important to stay as active as you can for as long as you can. Try to set a target to find five really solid people you can learn to trust with what you are going through. Having a few good people in your life can greatly impact your mood.

Lastly, remember that "growth is possible." Many people report positive changes in their lives after traumas, even a diagnosis of MS. Find out what others did, how they approached redefining meaning in their lives, and what their secrets to success were. Therapy or counseling that focuses on these factors can be a "gamechanger" in a person's experience of depression related to MS. Do not be afraid to reach out to improve the quality of you or your loved one's life.

Chapter 45

Depression in Parkinson and Alzheimer Diseases

Neurological Disorders and Depression

Depression often presents in connection with neurological disorders such as Parkinson disease (PD), Alzheimer disease (AD), stroke, multiple sclerosis, and other disorders. It is still unclear to researchers whether neurological disorders essentially lead to a patient getting depressed or if depression is a response to the symptoms of a neurological disease. For example, depressive events appear to be uncommon in amyotrophic lateral sclerosis, which is possibly one of the most critical neurological diagnoses.

Depression in Parkinson Disease

Diagnosing and treating depression in PD patients is necessary for two major reasons. Depression is common in PD, which can cause significant declines in lifestyle, and lead to disability and career stress.

Causes of Depression in Parkinson Disease

People with PD have an imbalance of certain neurotransmitters, a chemical in the brain that influences a person's mood and can be a

---

"Depression in Parkinson and Alzheimer Diseases," © 2020 Omnigraphics. Reviewed October 2019.

factor in depression. Depression can be managed with proper treatment, however. Factors that contribute to depression are listed below.

- **Psychological factors**, such as negative thoughts and withdrawal from socializing

- **Biological factors**, such as alterations in the brain that effect neurotransmitters

- A history of **mental-health issues**. Research indicates that people who suffered from depression before being diagnosed with PD tend to relapse into depression.

- **Environmental factors**, such as stress

- **Side effects** of prescription drugs that may stimulate depression

Symptoms of Depression in Parkinson Disease

A diagnosis of depression in people who have PD can be missed, since the symptoms for both disorders may overlap. The diagnosis may also be overlooked if the depression occurs after the diagnosis of PD. Both these disorders may cause:

- Fatigue

- Weight loss

- Insomnia or excessive sleep

- A slowing of motor function

- Diminished sexual function

- A low mood that prevails for a minimum of two weeks

- Thoughts of death or suicide

- Negative thoughts

Diagnosis of Depression in Parkinson Disease

Most people with PD are either not diagnosed with or are undertreated for depression. Hence, diagnosis is vital so that depressed patients receive effective treatment that leads to recovery from depression.

A person is considered to have depression if she or he experiences the previously outlined symptoms of depression for at least two weeks.

Make an appointment to discuss your symptoms with your doctor when any of these symptoms persist.

Treatment of Depression in Parkinson Disease

The treatment methods used for depression associated with PD may differ from person to person, depending on the individual's medical history, response to the treatment, or the severity of the disorder.

Antidepressant medication and psychological therapy are the two major types of treatment involved. Some of the antidepressant medications are:

- Tricyclic antidepressants (TCAs)

- Selective serotonin reuptake inhibitors (SSRIs)

The psychological therapies include psychotherapy counseling sessions, cognitive behavioral therapy (CBT), and electroconvulsive therapy (ECT).

Depression in Alzheimer Disease

Depression is also common in AD. Studies show that almost 50 percent of people who are affected by AD will experience depressive symptoms at some point.

Symptoms of Depression in Alzheimer Disease

The symptoms of depression found in PD patients are the same as those found in AD patients. Some of these symptoms are listed below:

- Dullness

- Loss of interest in activities and hobbies

- Social withdrawal

- Detachment

- Difficulty concentrating

- Loss of appetite

- Impatience or anger

- Thoughts of suicide

If any of these symptoms prevail, it is necessary to discuss with the doctor who is treating a patient with AD.

Diagnosing Depression with Alzheimer Disease

There is no specific test to diagnose depression in AD patients, since the symptoms of depression and AD tend to overlap. An examination for depression may include:

- Review of the patient's medical history

- Physical and mental evaluations

- Meeting with the patient's close family and friends

A person with AD must experience two or more of the symptoms mentioned above for a minimum of two weeks or longer in order to be diagnosed with depression.

Treating Depression in Alzheimer Disease

The most effective treatment for depression in AD involves a combination of medication and therapy. As with PD, doctors will likely prescribe the antidepressant SSRIs for depression.

Nondrug Approaches for Treating Depression Associated with Parkinson and Alzheimer Diseases

Some nondrug approaches will immensely help in the treatment of people with depression associated with PD and AD, including:

- Light therapy

- Support groups

- Relaxation methods

- Acupuncture

- Massage therapy

- Aromatherapy

- Meditation

- Music therapy

- Preparing a schedule of activities and routines and abiding by them consistently

- Exercise

- Reassurance

Celebrations of small and large successes and achievements

Tips for Coping with Depression Associated with Parkinson and Alzheimer Diseases

Some strategies for coping with depression associated with AD and PD include:

- Learn as much as possible about the disease and its symptoms

- Do not hesitate to ask for help

- Do not blame yourself and keep an open mind about the disorder

- Make short-term goals, such as going for a walk or meeting a friend. Short-term goals lead to long-term achievements.

- Maintain and cultivate social connections

- Restart the hobbies that you stopped enjoying

Find a community of people with the same disorder, which will provide discussions and offer clarity.

Depression associated any neurological disorder is common and can be disabling. Proper diagnosis and treatment makes it possible to prevent depression, though. Effective treatment under the guidance of the doctor will increase the quality of the patient's life.

References

1. Rickards, H. "Depression in Neurological Disorders: Parkinson's Disease, Multiple Sclerosis, and Stroke," BMJ Journals, February 18, 2005.

2. "Depression," The Parkinson's Foundation, October 18, 2017.

3. Gotter, Ana. "Parkinson's and Depression: What's the Connection?" Healthline, October 12, 2017.

4. "Depression," The Alzheimer's Association, June 6, 2012.

Chapter 46

Stroke and Depression

In the United States, more than 700,000 people suffer a stroke each year, and approximately two-thirds of these individuals survive and require rehabilitation. The goals of rehabilitation are to help survivors become as independent as possible and to attain the best possible quality of life. Even though rehabilitation does not "cure" the effects of stroke in that it does not reverse brain damage, rehabilitation can substantially help people achieve the best possible long-term outcome.

What Disabilities Can Result from a Stroke

The types and degrees of disability that follow a stroke depend upon which area of the brain is damaged. Generally, stroke can cause five types of disabilities:

- Paralysis or problems controlling movement

- Sensory disturbances including pain

- Problems using or understanding language

- Problems with thinking and memory

- Emotional disturbances

This chapter contains text excerpted from the following sources: Text in this chapter begins with excerpts from "Post-Stroke Rehabilitation," National Institute of Neurological Disorders and Stroke (NINDS), September 2014. Reviewed October 2019; Text beginning with the heading "What Do You Need to Know?" is excerpted from, "Depression after Stroke," U.S. Department of Veterans Affairs (VA), January 5, 2011. Reviewed October 2019.

Emotional Disturbances

Many people who survive a stroke feel fear, anxiety, frustration, anger, sadness, and a sense of grief for their physical and mental losses. These feelings are a natural response to the psychological trauma of stroke. Some emotional disturbances and personality changes are caused by the physical effects of brain damage. Clinical depression, which is a sense of hopelessness that disrupts an individual's ability to function, appears to be the emotional disorder most commonly experienced by stroke survivors.

Signs of clinical depression include:

- Sleep disturbances

- Radical change in eating patterns that may lead to sudden weight loss or gain

- Lethargy

- Social withdrawal

- Irritability

- Fatigue

- Self-loathing and

- Suicidal thoughts

What Do You Need to Know?

Depression is real—People need help when they have depression.
Physical and emotional changes are common after a stroke—Accept your loved one's changes.
Expect improvements over time—Things often get better.

Why Is It Important to Get Help?

Treatment of depression will help the stroke survivor recover faster. It will make your job as a caregiver easier. For instance, treating depression helps with:

- Thinking skills and memory

- Physical recovery and rehabilitation

- Language and speech

- Emotions and motivation

What Treatments Should You Discuss with Your Healthcare Team?

Get help from your healthcare team quickly. The stroke survivor and family members may explain away the person's depression. Make sure that the stroke survivor receives treatment.

- Medicines, such as antidepressants, improve symptoms.

- Psychotherapy (talk therapy) is used along with medicines. Talk therapy gives your loved one a safe place to talk about feelings.

- Support groups provide help from other stroke survivors and caregivers. They know what you and your loved one are going through. There are support groups for stroke survivors and caregivers like you.

Helpful Tips

- Know the warning signals of depression. Watch for the signs and symptoms of depression. Get help quickly.

- Be patient with your loved one. After a stroke, it will take time for your loved one to understand the changes.

- Help your loved one exercise and take part in fun activities.

- Encourage friends and your family to visit and talk with your loved one.

- Have a good attitude. Focus on how much your stroke survivor can do. Smile and relax about things you can not change.

Part Six

Diagnosis and Treatment of Depression

Chapter 47

Recognizing Signs of Depression in You and Your Loved Ones

Symptoms of Depression

Common signs of depression include:

- An "empty" feeling, ongoing sadness, and anxiety
- Tiredness, lack of energy
- Loss of interest or pleasure in everyday activities
- Sleep problems, including trouble getting to sleep, very early morning waking, and sleeping too much
- Eating more or less than usual
- Crying too often or too much

This chapter contains text excerpted from the following sources: Text beginning with the heading "Symptoms of Depression" is excerpted from "Handling Depression," Smokefree 60+, U.S. Department of Health and Human Services (HHS), April 21, 2016. Reviewed October 2019; Text under the heading "Depression: Conversation Starters" is excerpted from "Depression: Conversation Starters," Office of Disease Prevention and Health Promotion (ODPHP), U.S. Department of Health and Human Services (HHS), June 27, 2019.

- Aches and pains that do not go away when treated

- Difficulty focusing, remembering, or making decisions

- Feeling guilty, helpless, worthless, or hopeless

- Irritability

- Thoughts of death or suicide

The symptoms may seem to go away, but when someone is very depressed, the symptoms usually come back. Do not ignore the warning signs. If left untreated, serious depression may lead to suicide. If you are thinking about harming yourself, tell someone immediately.

Who Gets Depressed, and Why?

Anyone can get depression. In fact, more than 1 in 6 adults will have depression at some point in their lives. Some people are more likely to become depressed than others, including older adults, smokers, people with medical problems, and people who are stressed.

Many things can increase a person's chance of getting depressed. Everyone is different, but here are some common things that can lead to depression:

- The death of a loved one

- Highly stressful situations (for example, acting as a caregiver for a loved one)

- Life-changing health problems (e.g., cancer, diabetes, heart disease)

- Changes in the brain that affect mood

People can also be more likely to have depression if some of their blood relatives have had depression.

Depression and Aging

Important life changes that happen as we get older may cause feelings of uneasiness, stress, and sadness. For example, the death of loved ones, moving from work into retirement, or dealing with a serious illness can understandably leave people feeling sad or anxious. Sometimes it can be difficult to distinguish grief from depression.

Many older adults can regain their emotional balance, but for others, the sadness may continue and they benefit from help.

It is important to remember that while depression is common among older adults, it is not a normal part of aging. In fact, studies show that most older adults feel satisfied with their lives, even if they have health problems. When an older adult does suffer from depression, it may be missed because the person may be less willing to talk about feelings, or they may show different, less obvious symptoms, and doctors may be less likely to suspect or spot it.

Getting Help

You may want to start with your family doctor or mental-health professional.

Treatment options include:

- Psychotherapy/counseling

- Antidepressant drugs

- Support groups to provide new coping skills

Most older adults see an improvement in their symptoms when they are treated with antidepressant medications, counseling, or a combination of both. Treatment is often covered by insurance.

Depression: Conversation Starters

Depression can be hard to talk about. But if a friend or loved one is depressed, having a conversation about getting help can make a big difference. Use these tips to start talking.

Show You Care

- "How are you feeling? I am here to listen to you and support you."

- "I am concerned about you. I think you may need to talk to someone about depression. I want you to get the help you need to feel better."

- "Let me tell you all the things I love about you."

- "I would really like to spend more time with you. Let us take a walk, grab something to eat, or go to a movie."

Offer Hope

- "You are not alone. Many people suffer from depression—it is nothing to be ashamed of."

- "Depression can be treated. Getting help is the best thing you can do."

- "Most people get better with treatment—even people who have severe depression."

- "There are different ways to treat depression, including therapy and medicine. Getting more physical activity might also help you feel better."

Offer to Help

- "Let me help you figure out what is going on. You can start by making an appointment with your doctor—or I can help you find someone else to talk to, such as a counselor, therapist, or social worker."

- "I can give you a ride to your therapy appointment or remind you to take your medicine."

- "You can call or text me at any time if you need support—or if you just want to talk."

Chapter 48

Diagnosing Depression

What Is Depression Screening?

A depression screening also called a "depression test," helps find out if you have depression. Depression is a common, though serious, illness. Everyone feels sad at times, but depression is different than normal sadness or grief. Depression can affect how you think, feel, and behave. Depression makes it hard to function at home and work. You may lose interest in activities you once enjoyed. Some people with depression feel worthless and are at risk for harming themselves.

There are different types of depression. The most common types are:

- **Major depression,** which causes persistent feelings of sadness, anger, and/or frustration. Major depression lasts for several weeks or longer.

- **Persistent depressive disorder (PDD),** which causes depressive symptoms that last two years or more.

- **Postpartum depression.** Many new mothers feel sad, but postpartum depression causes extreme sadness and anxiety after childbirth. It can make it hard for mothers to care for themselves and/or their babies.

This chapter includes text excerpted from "Depression Screening," Medline-Plus, National Institutes of Health (NIH), January 31, 2019.

- **Seasonal affective disorder (SAD).** This form of depression usually happens in winter when there is less sunlight. Most people with SAD feel better in the spring and summer.

- **Psychotic depression** occurs with psychosis, a more serious psychiatric disorder. Psychosis can cause people to lose touch with reality.

- **Bipolar disorder,** formerly called "manic depression." People with bipolar disorder have alternating episodes of mania (extreme highs or euphoria) and depression.

Fortunately, most people with depression feel better after treatment with medicine and/or talk therapy.

Other names: depression test.

What Is It Used For?

A depression screening is used to help diagnose depression. Your primary care provider may give you a depression test if you are showing signs of depression. If the screening shows you have depression, you may need treatment from a mental-health provider. A mental-health provider is a healthcare professional who specializes in diagnosing and treating mental-health problems. If you are already seeing a mental-health provider, you may get a depression test to help guide your treatment.

Why Do I Need Depression Screening?

You may need depression screening if you are showing signs of depression. Signs of depression include:

- Loss of interest or pleasure in daily living and/or other activities, such as hobbies, sports, or sex

- Anger, frustration, or irritability

- Sleep problems: trouble falling asleep and/or staying asleep (insomnia) or sleeping too much

- Fatigue and lack of energy

- Restlessness

- Trouble concentrating or making decisions

- Feelings of guilt or worthlessness

• Losing or gaining a lot of weight

One of the most serious signs of depression is thinking about or attempting suicide. If you are thinking about hurting yourself, or about suicide, seek help right away. There are many ways to get help. You can:

• Call 911 or go to your local emergency room

• Call your mental-health provider or other healthcare providers

• Reach out to a loved one or close friend

• Call a suicide hotline. In the United States, you can call the National Suicide Prevention Lifeline (NSPL) at 800-273-TALK (800-273-8255)

What Happens during Depression Screening

Your primary care provider may give you a physical exam and ask you about your feelings, mood, sleep habits, and other symptoms. Your provider may also order a blood test to find out if a disorder, such as anemia or thyroid disease, may be causing your depression.

During a blood test, a healthcare professional will take a blood sample from a vein in your arm, using a small needle. After the needle is inserted, a small amount of blood will be collected into a test tube or vial. You may feel a little sting when the needle goes in or out. This usually takes less than five minutes.

If you are being tested by a mental-health provider, she or he may ask you more detailed questions about your feelings and behaviors. You may also be asked to fill out a questionnaire about these issues.

Will I Need to Do Anything to Prepare for Depression Screening?

You usually do not need any special preparations for a depression test.

Are There Any Risks to Screening?

There is no risk to having a physical exam or taking a questionnaire.

There is very little risk to having a blood test. You may have slight pain or bruising at the spot where the needle was put in, but most symptoms go away quickly.

What Do the Results Mean?

If you are diagnosed with depression, it is important to get treatment as soon as possible. The sooner you get treatment, the better chance you have of recovery. Treatment for depression may take a long time, but most people who get treated eventually feel better.

If your primary care provider diagnosed you, she or he may refer you to a mental-health provider. If a mental-health provider diagnosed you, she or he will recommend a treatment plan based on the type of depression you have and how serious it is.

Is There Anything Else I Need to Know about Depression Screening?

There are many types of mental-health providers who treat depression. The most common types of mental-health providers include:

- **Psychiatrist,** a medical doctor who specializes in mental health. Psychiatrists diagnose and treat mental-health disorders. They can also prescribe medicine.

- **Psychologist,** a professional trained in psychology. Psychologists generally have doctoral degrees, such as a Ph.D. (Doctor of Philosophy) or a Psy.D. (Doctor of Psychology). But they do not have medical degrees. Psychologists diagnose and treat mental-health disorders. They offer one-on-one counseling and/or group therapy sessions. They cannot prescribe medicine unless they have a special license. Some psychologists work with providers who are able to prescribe medicine.

- **Licensed clinical social worker (L.C.S.W.)** has a master's degree in social work with training in mental health. Some have additional degrees and training. L.C.S.W.s diagnose and provide counseling for a variety of mental-health problems. They cannot prescribe medicine but can work with providers who are able to.

- **Licensed professional counselor. (L.P.C.).** Most L.P.C.s have a master's degree. But training requirements vary by state. L.P.C.s diagnose and provide counseling for a variety of mental-health problems. They cannot prescribe medicine but can work with providers who are able to.

Licensed clinical social workers and L.P.C.s may be known by other names, including "therapist," "clinician," or "counselor."

If you do not know which type of mental-health provider you should see, talk to your primary care provider.

Chapter 49

Psychotherapy For Depression

Chapter Contents

Section 49.1

Elements of Psychotherapy

This section includes text excerpted from "Psychotherapies,"
National Institute of Mental Health (NIMH), November 2016.
Reviewed October 2019.

A variety of different kinds of psychotherapies and interventions
have been shown to be effective for specific disorders. Psychothera-
pists may use one primary approach or incorporate different elements
depending on their training, the condition being treated, and the needs
of the person receiving treatment.

Here are examples of the elements that psychotherapies can include:

- Helping a person become aware of ways of thinking that may
  be automatic but are inaccurate and harmful. (A cognitive-
  behavioral therapy (CBT) example might be someone who has a
  low opinion of her or his own abilities.) The therapist helps the
  person find ways to question these thoughts, understand how
  they affect emotions and behavior, and try ways to change self-
  defeating patterns. This approach is central to (CBT).

- Identifying ways to cope with stress

- Examining in-depth a person's interactions with others and
  offering guidance with social and communication skills, if
  needed

- Relaxation and mindfulness techniques

- Exposure therapy for people with anxiety disorders. In
  exposure therapy, a person spends brief periods, in a supportive
  environment, learning to tolerate the distress of certain items,
  ideas, or imagined scenes cause. Over time, the fear associated
  with these things dissipates.

- Tracking emotions and activities and the impact of each on the
  other

- Safety planning can include helping a person recognize warning
  signs, and thinking about coping strategies, such as contacting
  friends, family, or emergency personnel

- Supportive counseling to help a person explore troubling issues
  and provide emotional support

Section 49.2

Cognitive-Behavioral Therapy

This section includes text excerpted from "Cognitive Behavioral Therapy-Depression (CBT-D)," U.S. Department of Veterans Affairs (VA), April 22, 2019.

Cognitive-behavioral therapy for depression (CBT-D) is an effective treatment for depression in the U.S. Department of Veterans Affairs (VA) healthcare system. CBT-D is a highly recommended treatment for many individuals with depression.

Cognitive-behavioral therapy for depression is a short-term psychotherapy (or "talk therapy") for treating symptoms of depression which may include:

- Feeling sad, depressed or hopeless

- Lack of interest or pleasure in activities

- Feeling worthless or having excessive guilt

- Being irritable or agitated

- Difficulty making decisions or concentrating

- Loss of energy or fatigue

- Increase or decrease in appetite or sleep

The overall goal of CBT-D is to improve the symptoms of depression by helping you to develop balanced and helpful thoughts about yourself, others, and the future and by helping you spend more time engaging in pleasurable or productive activities. CBT-D helps to achieve personal goals and solve problems by learning and practicing new skills. CBT-D can help to improve the quality of your life and overall level of functioning.

Cognitive-behavioral therapy for depression is one of the most studied and effective therapies developed for depression. CBT-D is based on decades of research and has been shown to be very effective with Veterans, specifically. Over 75 percent of people treated for depression show noticeable improvement following CBT-D. This treatment is at least as effective as medications, though both CBT and medications can be helpful in the treatment of depression for some people. Many Veterans with a history of depression continue to enjoy treatment benefits long after completing CBT-D.

In CBT-D, you will work with your therapist to set specific treatment goals that will help you learn new ways of thinking about situations and coping with problems that come up in the future, even after therapy has ended. These skills will relieve your depression and help you move forward in your life.

After you and your therapist have discussed your treatment goals, your therapist may be able to estimate the amount of time that will be required to attain those goals. CBT typically requires 12 to 16 sessions to lead to significant improvement. Sessions last about 50 to 60 minutes when delivered individually and 90 minutes when delivered in a group. You will meet with your therapist regularly until the treatment goals have been reached.

If you decide to participate in CBT, you will be asked to:

- Attend sessions regularly

- Work together with your therapist to set therapy goals

- Address the most important issues during each session

- Practice the new CBT skills in your life outside of session

It will be important for you to use the information that you learn during the therapy sessions and apply them to your everyday life to help you feel better.

Section 49.3

Interpersonal Therapy

This section includes text excerpted from "Interpersonal Psychotherapy (IPT)," U.S. Department of Veterans Affairs (VA), April 22, 2019.

Interpersonal psychotherapy (IPT) is a treatment for depression that focuses on relationship issues that may be the cause or the result of depression. Many studies have been done that support the usefulness of IPT for depression. Also, studies have shown IPT to be useful in the treatment of other issues such as anxiety, bipolar disorder, eating disorders, and borderline personality disorder.

Interpersonal psychotherapy is typically delivered during 16 weekly sessions over three phases of treatment (Initial Sessions, Intermediate Sessions, and Termination). During the Initial Sessions, the therapist will provide you with education about depression, how your life situations may be contributing to depression, and how depression may affect your daily life. The Intermediate Sessions focus on 1 or 2 problem areas that are most concerning to you and may be contributing to your depression. These areas include dealing with major life changes, conflict with others, grief related to the death of a significant person, or problems making or keeping social connections. During Termination, the therapist will work with you to review progress, explore possible stressors that may contribute to depression, discuss how skills learned in IPT can continue to be used, and evaluate the need for further treatment.

Goals are established early in treatment. One of the most important factors in the success of therapy is a commitment to participating in treatment and regularly attending sessions. In IPT, you would typically meet one-on-one with your therapist for 12 to 16 sessions. Sessions are generally held on a weekly basis and last approximately 50 minutes. The information you learn during the therapy sessions will be important to you as you apply it to everyday life in order to feel better.

If you decide to participate in IPT, you will be asked to:

- Attend sessions regularly

- Work with your therapist to set therapy goals

- Discuss relationship issues during each session

- Practice new skills—both in and outside of session

Section 49.4

Acceptance and Commitment Therapy

This section contains text excerpted from the following sources:
Text in this section begins with excerpts from "Acceptance and
Commitment Therapy (ACT)," U.S. Department of Veterans Affairs
(VA), April 22, 2019; Text under the heading "Acceptance and
Commitment Therapy" is excerpted from "Evaluating Acceptance and
Commitment Therapy: An Analysis of a Recent Critique," Education
Resources Information Center (ERIC), U.S. Department of Education
(ED), April 18, 2010. Reviewed October 2019.

Acceptance and commitment therapy (ACT) is a talk therapy for
treating symptoms of depression. ACT for Depression (ACT-D) helps
individuals with depression make changes so that they can have full,
rich, and meaningful lives. The focus in ACT-D is to help you live
closely to your values. It also helps you to accept yourself. Acceptance
and commitment therapy for depression helps individuals to have better relationships with themselves, others, and the world. Individuals
learn to identify and engage in activities that are in line with what
they care about. By participating in ACT-D, the individual learns to:

- A = Accept

- C = Choose

- T = Take Action

Research has shown ACT-D to be effective for the treatment of
depression. ACT-D usually requires 10 to 16 individual sessions
but may take more or less time depending on the goals you set for
treatment.

By participating in ACT-D, you will learn to:

Be present to the "here-and-now." This focus helps to decrease being
caught up in what happened in the past. It also frees individuals from
worrying too much about the future. Being present helps you to fully
connect to and enjoy the moment.

Observe thoughts and feelings in such a way that they no longer
keep you stuck in life. Learning to observe through openness and
acceptance can help you find freedom from negative thoughts and
feelings.

Clarify your values and then take action. Finding what is most
meaningful to you and choosing to act on these values are important

parts of the therapy. This will be part of the process of building a rich and full life.

Acceptance and Commitment Therapy

Acceptance and commitment therapy (ACT) is a novel acceptance/mindfulness-based behavioral treatment that has been increasing in popularity. ACT stems from a philosophy of radical behaviorism. In general, ACT can be described as combining acceptance and mindfulness strategies with overt behavior change efforts to improve what its creators call psychological flexibility.

Psychological flexibility is defined as "the ability to contact the present moment fully as a conscious human being, and to either change or persists when doing so serves valued ends." In other words, healthy psychological functioning is proposed to be related to a person's ability to adaptively respond to changing environmental contingencies. In contrast, psychological inflexibility or rigidity is theorized to be the result of what ACT calls cognitive fusion and experiential avoidance.

Cognitive fusion is defined as "the tendency of human beings to live in a world excessively structured by literal language." For example, when a person is fused with a thought ("I am depressed"), she or he is experiencing that thought literally ("I" = "depression"). This cognitive fusion permits the literal content of thinking to dominate a person's behavior ("I cannot go to work today because I am depressed"). Cognitive fusion also fosters experiential avoidance, which is defined as "the attempt to escape or avoid the form, frequency, or situational sensitivity of private events, even when the attempt to do so causes psychological harm. When engaged in experiential avoidance, the person attempts to avoid or suppress undesirable private material such as thoughts, memories, emotions, and bodily sensations as if they were inherently harmful, even though doing so can paradoxically worsen these problems in the long-run. The coprocesses of fusion and experiential avoidance result in the narrowing of a person's behavioral repertoire (i.e., psychological inflexibility), which is believed to lead to and maintain a wide spectrum of psychopathological behaviors.

Acceptance and commitment therapy targets six core processes for psychological flexibility:

- Promoting acceptance of distressing internal experiences

- Fostering cognitive defusion so the literal content of thought does not dominate over a person's behavior

331

- Practicing awareness of ongoing experience in the present moment

- Establishing a stable sense of self that is broader than merely its evaluative content, developing personal valued life directions to guide behavior

- Committing to actions that are consistent with these personally chosen values

Acceptance and commitment therapy makes heavy use of metaphors, logical paradoxes, and experiential exercises, as well as traditional behavioral techniques (e.g., behavioral activation, exposure). The goal of these strategies is to improve psychological flexibility by fostering acceptance of internal states of distress and cognitive defusion from problematic language-based processes.

Research on ACT suggests that:

- Psychological inflexibility is related to diverse indices of psychopathology as predicted

- Acceptance and commitment therapy has been shown to be potentially efficacious for a variety of clinical conditions based on preliminary trials

- Many of the specific components of ACT show initial evidence of efficacy in experimental studies

- Acceptance and commitment therapy appears to work at least partly through its hypothesized mechanisms of action; although formal statistical mediation has only been demonstrated in a few studies to date

The American Psychological Association's (APA) Division (Clinical Psychology) included ACT for depression on its list of empirically-supported treatments, concluding that it has "moderately strong" empirical support based on clinical trials.

Chapter 50

Mental-Health Medications

Chapter Contents

333

Section 50.1

Understanding Mental-Health Medications

This section includes text excerpted from "Mental Health
Medications," National Institute of Mental Health (NIMH),
October 2016. Reviewed October 2019.

Medications can play a role in treating several mental disorders and conditions. Treatment may also include psychotherapy (also called "talk therapy") and brain stimulation therapies (less common). In some cases, psychotherapy alone may be the best treatment option. Choosing the right treatment plan should be based on a person's individual needs and medical situation and under a mental-health professional's care.

The National Institute of Mental Health (NIMH), a federal research agency, does not provide medical advice or referrals. The NIMH also does not endorse or recommend any particular drug, herb, or supplement.

If you are prescribed a medication, be sure that you:

- Tell the doctor about all medications and vitamin supplements you are already taking

- Remind your doctor about any allergies and any problems you have had with medicines

- Understand how to take the medicine before you start using it and take your medicine as instructed

- Do not take medicines prescribed for another person or give yours to someone else

- Call your doctor right away if you have any problems with your medicine or if you are worried that it might be doing more harm than good. Your doctor may be able to adjust the dose or change your prescription to a different one that may work better for you.

Section 50.2

Ketamine Lifts Depression via Metabolite

This section includes text excerpted from "Ketamine Lifts Depression via a Byproduct of Its Metabolism," National Institutes of Health (NIH), May 4, 2016. Reviewed October 2019.

A chemical byproduct, or metabolite, created as the body breaks down ketamine likely holds the secret to its rapid antidepressant action. This metabolite singularly reversed depression-like behaviors in mice without triggering any of the anesthetic, dissociative, or addictive side effects associated with ketamine.

"This discovery fundamentally changes our understanding of how this rapid antidepressant mechanism works and holds promise for the development of more robust and safer treatments," said Carlos Zarate, M.D., of the National Institutes of Health's (NIH) National Institute of Mental Health (NIMH), a study co-author and a pioneer of research using ketamine to treat depression. "By using a team approach, researchers were able to reverse-engineer ketamine's workings from the clinic to the lab to pinpoint what makes it so unique."

A National Institute of Mental Health, grantee Todd Gould, M.D., of the University of Maryland School of Medicine (UMSOM), in collaboration with Zarate and other colleagues, report on their findings May 4, 2016, in the journal *Nature*. The team also included researchers at the NIH's National Center for Advancing Translational Sciences (NCATS) and National Institute on Aging (NIA) and the University of North Carolina (UNC).

"Now that we know that ketamine's antidepressant actions in mice are due to a metabolite, not ketamine itself, the next steps are to confirm that it works similarly in humans, and determine if it can lead to improved therapeutics for patients," explained Gould.

Clinical trials by Zarate and others have shown that ketamine can lift depression in hours, or even minutes—much faster than the most commonly used antidepressant medications now available, which often require weeks to take effect. Further, the antidepressant effects of a single dose can last for a week or longer. However, despite legitimate medical uses, ketamine also has dissociative, euphoric, and addictive properties, making it a potential drug of abuse and limiting its usefulness as a depression medication.

In hopes of finding leads to a more practical treatment, the research team sought to pinpoint the exact mechanism by which ketamine relieves depression. Ketamine belongs to a class of drugs that block cellular receptors for glutamate, the brain's chief excitatory chemical messenger. Until now, the prevailing view was that ketamine produced its antidepressant effects by blocking N-methyl-D-aspartic acid (NMDA) glutamate receptors.

However, human trials of other NMDA-receptor blockers failed to produce ketamine's robust and sustained antidepressant effects. So the team explored the effects of ketamine on antidepressant-responsive behaviors in mice. Ketamine harbors two chemical forms that are mirror images of each other, denoted (S)-and (R)-ketamine. The investigators found that while (S)-ketamine is more potent at blocking NMDA receptors, it is less effective in reducing depression-like behaviors than the (R) form.

The team then looked at the effects of the metabolites created as the body breaks down (S)-and (R)-ketamine. It was known that ketamine's antidepressant effects are greater in female mice. The National Institute on Aging (NIA) researchers Irving Wainer, Ph.D., and Ruin Moaddel, Ph.D. identified a key metabolite (2S,6S;2R,6R)-HNK (hydroxynorketamine) and showed that it is pharmacologically active. The team then discovered that levels of this metabolite were three times higher in female mice, hinting that it might be responsible for the sex difference in the antidepressant-like effect. To find out, the researchers chemically blocked the metabolism of ketamine. This prevented formation of the metabolite, which blocked the drug's antidepressant-like effects.

Like ketamine, this metabolite includes two forms that mirror each other. By testing both forms, they found that one—(2R,6R)-HNK—had antidepressant-like effects similar to ketamine, lasting for at least three days in mice. Notably, unlike ketamine, the compound does not inhibit NMDA receptors. It instead activates, possibly indirectly, another type of glutamate receptor, α-amino-3-hydroxy-5-methyl-4-isoxazole propionic acid (AMPA). Blocking AMPA receptors prevented the antidepressant-like effects of (2R,6R)-HNK in mice. The experiments confirmed that the rapid antidepressant-like effects require activation of AMPA receptors, not inhibition of NMDA receptors.

Ketamine also has effects in mice that mimic its dissociative, euphoric effects in humans and underlie its abuse and addictive potential; however, these effects were not observed with (2R,6R)-HNK. The

(2R,6R)-HNK did not cause the changes in physical activity, sensory processing, and coordination in mice that occur with ketamine. In an experimental situation where mice were able to self-administer medication, they did so with ketamine but not the (2R,6R)-HNK metabolite, indicating that (2R, 6R)-HNK is not addictive.

"Working in collaboration with NIH and academic researchers, NCATS chemists played a critical role in isolating the specific metabolite of ketamine responsible for fighting depression," said Christopher P. Austin, M.D., NCATS director. "Overall, our collective efforts exemplify how a collaborative, team science approach can help advance the translational process in ways that help get more treatments to more patients more quickly."

"Unraveling the mechanism mediating ketamine's antidepressant activity is an important step in the process of drug development," said Richard J. Hodes, M.D., NIA director. "New approaches are critical for the treatment of depression, especially for older adults and for patients who do not respond to current medications."

Section 50.3

Medications for Treating Depression in Women

This section includes text excerpted from "Depression—Medicines to Help You," U.S. Food and Drug Administration (FDA), March 2008. Reviewed October 2019.

Do you feel depressed? Do not feel ashamed. Women are more likely than men to feel depressed. About 1 woman in 5 has depression in the United States.

Depression can be treated with medicine or counseling. Sometimes both are used. Talk to your doctor to find out what will work best for you.

Talk to your doctor or pharmacist about medicines called "antidepressants" that can help to treat depression. Ask your doctor to tell you about all of the risks of taking different medicines.

The Baby Blues

Having a baby can be a joyful time. However, some women cry a lot and feel sad right after they have a baby. This is called "the baby blues." This feeling usually goes away after about two weeks.

If you still feel sad after two weeks, go to your doctor or clinic. You may be depressed. This type of depression is called "postpartum depression" (PPD) because it starts after a woman has a baby. A woman can have this kind of depression up to one year after she has a baby.

Depression and Your Children

Like adults, kids can also feel depressed. You should watch your children for signs of depression. Talk to your children if you notice changes in their behavior. Talk to your doctor or nurse if you are still concerned.

Children and teens can take medicines for depression. Prozac® (Fluoxetine) is the only U.S. Food and Drug Administration (FDA)-approved antidepressant for children and teens with depression. Talk to your doctor about important warnings for children and teens who take medicines for depression.

Medicines for Depression

There are many different kinds of medicine for depression.

Some general facts about the different kinds of medicine for depression. Tell your doctor about any medicines that you are taking. Do not forget about cold medicines and herbs like St. John's Wort. Some medicines will make you very sick if you take them while you are taking antidepressants.

Like any drug, depression medicines may cause some side effects. Do not stop taking your medicines without first talking to your doctor. Tell your doctor about any problems you are having. Your doctor will help you find the medicine that is best for you.

Selective Serotonin Reuptake Inhibitors

Table 50.1. Tricyclic Antidepressants

Brand Name	Generic Name
Celexa	Citalopram
Lexapro	Escitalopram
Paxil	Paroxetine
Pexeva	Paroxetine
Prozac	Fluoxetine
Zoloft	Sertraline

Warnings

- Do not take with certain other medicines:
  - Monoamine oxidase inhibitors (MAOIs)
  - Thioridazine
  - Orap
- Women should talk to their doctors about the risks of taking paroxetine during pregnancy

Common Side Effects

- Nausea
- Tremor (shaking)
- Nervousness
- Problems sleeping
- Sexual problems

Less Common but Serious Side Effects

- Seizures
- Abnormal bleeding
- Withdrawal symptoms
- Mothers who take these drugs late in pregnancy may have babies with feeding problems and irritability.

Monoamine Oxidase Inhibitors

Table 50.2. Monoamine Oxidase Inhibitors

Brand Name	Generic Name
Emsam (Skin Patch)	Selegiline
Marplan	Isocarboxzaid
Nardil	Parnate
Phenelzine	Tranylcypromine

Warnings

- Do not take MAOIs if you are also taking other medicines for depression or central nervous system stimulants or depressants.

- Do not eat certain foods like cheese, wine, protein foods that have been aged or any food containing tyramine.

- Do not take cold pills or decongestants.

Common Side Effects

- Nausea

- Dizziness

- Restlessness

- Problems sleeping

- Drowsiness

Less Common but Serious Side Effects

- Headache

- Stroke

- Fainting

- Heart palpitations

- Blood pressure changes

Tricyclic Antidepressants

Table 50.3. Tricyclic Antidepressants

Brand Name	Generic Name
	Amitriptyline
	Amoxapine
Norpramin	Desipramine
	Doxepin
Tofranil	Imipramine
Pamelor	Nortriptyline
Vivactil	Protriptyline
Surmontil	Trimipramine

Warnings

- Do not take tricyclic antidepressants if you are also taking MAO inhibitors (MAOIs).
- Do not take tricyclic antidepressants if you have narrow-angle glaucoma.

Common Side Effects

- Dry mouth constipation
- Blurred vision drowsiness
- Low blood pressure

Less Common but Serious Side Effects

- Problems urinating
- Confusion
- Fainting
- Seizures
- Life-threatening irregular heartbeat

Atypical Antidepressants

Table 50.4. Maprotiline

Brand Name	Generic Name
	Maprotiline

Warnings

- Do not take if you have narrow-angle glaucoma or seizures.

- Be careful if you have liver or cardiovascular disease.

- Use caution if you drink alcohol or take barbiturates while taking this medicine.

Common Side Effects

- Blurred vision

- Feeling dizzy or lightheaded

- Drowsiness

- Feeling tired or weak

- Dry mouth

- Headache

Less Common but Serious Side Effects

- Confusion

- Problems urinating

- Fainting

Table 50.5. Trazodone

Brand Name	Generic Name
	Trazodone

Warnings

- Do not take Trazodone if you are also taking MAO inhibitors (MAOIs).

- Use caution if you drink alcohol or take barbiturates while taking this medicine.

- Be careful if you have cardiovascular disease.

Common Side Effects

- Dry Mouth

- Dizziness

- Blurred Vision
- Feeling Drowsy or Sleepy

Less Common but Serious Side Effects

- Painful Erection that lasts a long time
- Low Blood Pressure
- Fainting

Table 50.6. Nefazodone

Brand Name	Generic Name
	Nefazodone

Warnings

- Do not take Nefazodone if you are also taking MAO inhibitors, Triazolam, or Alprazolam.
- Use caution if you drink alcohol while taking this medicine.

Common Side Effects

- Dizziness
- Constipation
- Nausea
- Dry mouth
- Feeling drowsy or sleepy

Less Common but Serious Side Effects

- Confusion
- Fainting
- Liver failure

Table 50.7. Mirtazapine

Brand Name	Generic Name
Remeron	Mirtazapine

Warnings

• Do not take with MAO inhibitors (MAOIs).

Common Side Effects

• Feeling drowsy or sleepy
• Weight gain
• Dizziness

Less Common but Serious Side Effects

• Agranulocytosis (drop in white blood cells)
• Increase in cholesterol
• Increase in liver enzymes

Table 50.8. Bupropion

Brand Name	Generic Name
Wellbutrin	Bupropion

Warnings

• Use caution if you drink alcohol while taking this medicine.
• Use caution if you take levodopa.
• Use caution if you have seizures or take medicines that raise your chance of having a seizure.

Common Side Effects

• Dizziness
• Constipation
• Nausea
• Vomiting
• Blurred vision

Less Common but Serious Side Effects

• Seizures

Table 50.9. Venlafaxine

Brand Name	Generic Name
Effexor	Venlafaxine

Warnings

- Do not take with MAO inhibitors (MAOIs).

- Use with care if you have heart disease, liver disease, kidney problems, or seizures.

Common Side Effects

- Sweating

- Nausea

- Constipation

- Dizziness

- Feeling nervous or anxious

- Problems sleeping

- Feeling drowsy

Less Common but Serious Side Effects

- High blood pressure

- Seizures

- Mothers who take these drugs late in pregnancy may have babies with feeding problems and irritability.

Selective Serotonin and Norepinephrine Reuptake Inhibitors

Table 50.10. Duloxetine

Brand Name	Generic Name
Cymbalta	Duloxetine

Warnings

Do not take Pristiq® if you have taken a MAOI medicine within the last 14 days.

Tell your doctor if you have any health problems especially seizures, mania, bipolar disorder, and heart, liver or kidney problems.

Common Side Effects

- Nausea
- Headache
- Dry mouth
- Sweating
- Dizziness
- Feeling sleepy or tired
- Trouble sleeping
- Constipation
- Diarrhea
- Vomiting
- Sexual problems
- Do not feel like eating

Less Common but Serious Side Effects

- New or worsened high blood pressure
- Abnormal bleeding or bruising
- Glaucoma
- High cholesterol
- Seizures
- Low sodium in your blood
- Ask your doctor about serotonin syndrome

Section 50.4

Medications for Treating Depression in Elders

This section contains text excerpted from the following sources:
Text in this section begins with excerpts from "Mental Health
Medications," National Institute of Mental Health (NIMH), October
2016. Reviewed October 2019; Text beginning with the heading
"What You Need to Know about Your Medicines" is excerpted from
"Safe Use of Medicines for Older Adults," National Institute on Aging
(NIA), National Institutes of Health (NIH), June 26, 2019.

All types of people take psychiatric medications, but some groups
have special needs which includes the elderly. People over 65 have to
be careful when taking medications, especially when they are taking
many different drugs. Older adults have a higher risk for experiencing
bad drug interactions, missing doses, or overdosing.

Older adults also tend to be more sensitive to medications. Even
healthy older people react to medications differently than younger
people because older people's bodies process and eliminate medications
more slowly. Therefore, lower or less frequent doses may be needed
for older adults. Before starting a medication, older people and their
family members should talk carefully with a physician about whether
a medication can affect alertness, memory, or coordination, and how
to help ensure that prescribed medications do not increase the risk
of falls.

Sometimes memory problems affect older people who take medications for mental disorders. An older adult may forget her or his
regular dose and take too much or not enough. A good way to keep
track of medicine is to use a seven-day pillbox, which can be bought at
any pharmacy. At the beginning of each week, older adults and their
caregivers fill the box so that it is easy to remember what medicine to
take. Many pharmacies also have pillboxes with sections for medications that must be taken more than once a day.

What You Need to Know about Your Medicines

Talk with your doctor, nurse, or other healthcare provider before
starting a new medicine. Go over your allergies and any problems you
have had with other medicines, such as rashes, trouble breathing,
indigestion, dizziness, or mood changes.

347

You will also want to find out whether you will need to change or stop taking any of your other prescriptions or over-the-counter (OTC) drugs while using this new medicine. Mixing some drugs can cause unpleasant and sometimes serious problems.

When starting a new medication, make sure to write down the name of the drug and why it is being prescribed for you. Also, make a note of any special instructions for how to take the medicine.

Keeping Track of Your Medicines

Here are some tips to help you keep track of all your medicines:

- **Make a list.** Write down all the medicines you take, including OTC drugs and dietary supplements. The list should include the name of each medicine, amount you take, and time(s) you take it. If it is a prescription, also note the doctor who prescribed it and reason it was prescribed. Show the list to all of your healthcare providers, including physical therapists and dentists. Keep one copy in a safe place at home and one in your wallet or pocketbook.

- **Create a file.** Save all the written information that comes with your medicine and keep it somewhere you can easily refer to it.

- **Check expiration dates on bottles.** If a medicine is past its expiration date, you may be able to dispose of it at your pharmacy, or, check with your doctor about how to safely discard it. Your doctor can also tell you if you will need a refill.

- **Keep medicines out of reach of young children.** Avoid taking medicines in front of them, as they might try to copy you. Also, if your medicines are kept in bottles without child safety caps because they are hard to open, be extra careful about where you store medicines.

Taking Medicines Safely

Here are some tips to help you take your medicines safely:

- **Follow instructions.** Read all medicine labels. Make sure to take your medicines the right way.

- **Use the right amount.** Do not take a larger dose of medicine thinking it will help you more. It can be very dangerous, even deadly. And, do not skip or take half doses of a prescription drug to save money. (Talk with your doctor or pharmacist if you cannot afford the medicine. There may be help.)

- **Take medicine on time.** Some people use meals or bedtime as reminders to take their medicine. Other people use charts, calendars, or weekly pillboxes. You can also set timers and write reminders to take your medication.

- **Turn on a light.** Do not take medicine in the dark; otherwise, you might make a mistake.

- **Report problems.** Call your doctor right away if you have any trouble with your prescription, or if you are worried that it might be doing more harm than good. There may be something else you can take.

- **Tell your doctor about alcohol, tobacco, and drug use.** Alcohol, tobacco, and other drugs can affect how well your medicines work. Be honest with your doctor about how much you use.

- **Check before stopping.** Take prescription medicine until it is finished or until your doctor says it is all right to stop. Note that some medicines are supposed to be taken only "as needed."

- **Do not share.** Do not take medicines prescribed for another person or give yours to someone else.

Chapter 51

Combined Interventions for Depression

Depression is a complex mental illness that can result in significant disability, reduced quality of life, and societal burden. Pharmacological agents are one of several initial treatment modalities used for depression and one of the most frequently utilized classes of drugs are the selective serotonin reuptake inhibitors (SSRIs). However, the rate of treatment response from baseline symptoms following first-line treatment with SSRIs is moderate, varying from 40 to 60 percent; remission rates vary from 30 to 45 percent. Up to one-third of persons on drug treatment will develop recurrent symptoms of depression while on therapy. Moreover, there is limited evidence identifying reliable predictors (demographic, clinical, or genetic characteristics) of individual response. Adequate response to SSRI interventions is not consistently operationalized, but it is generally accepted that a 50 percent decrease in symptom severity from baseline is sufficient. Remission from depression is defined as being free or nearly free of symptoms for the current episode.

Given the large proportion of patients who do not respond adequately to SSRIs as first-line therapy, the practitioner is faced with

This chapter contains text excerpted from "Depression Treatment after Unsatisfactory Response to SSRIs When Used as First-Line Therapy," Effective Health Care Program, Agency for Healthcare Research and Quality (AHRQ), June 15, 2010. Reviewed October 2019.

the dilemma of determining the presence of inadequacy of the response and then selecting a new course of action. The new course of action may vary and can include:

1. An optimization strategy (altering dose or duration of the SSRI)

2. Switching to other SSRIs

3. Switching to other classes of antidepressants

4. Combining SSRIs with other medications or nonpharmacological therapies

5. Switching to nonpharmacological interventions alone or

6. Combinations of these

There is a need to examine the evidentiary base for these varying management strategies for patients who have failed to adequately respond to SSRI used as first-line therapy for the index episode. For the purposes of this systematic review treatment failure (TF) is a response of less than 50 percent change relative to baseline and primarily reflects the perspective of the clinician and researcher; It marks the threshold of change by which a clinician will seek to progress or modify treatment for the patient. We use the terms "failure to respond" or "nonresponder" in this same context. The unsatisfactory response is used in this review to capture the perspective of the patient being treated for depression; An unsatisfactory response may include other aspects of concern not captured by a change score relative to baseline.

TF can encompass a number of subgroups of patients who do not adequately respond to interventions for their current episode of depression. TF is not consistently defined within the literature, but is generally understood to reflect patients with depression who have not responded to one course of therapy. TF populations may include patients who would meet criteria for treatment resistance (> 2 inadequate responses) subgroups based on past treatment for prior episodes of depression. A portion of patients who have experienced TF will also go on to be defined as treatment-resistant if they also fail to respond to subsequent treatment strategies. Treatment resistance is variably defined but usually refers to patients who have failed at least two trials of medication that have been of adequate dose and duration. Some definitions suggest that the failures should be to medications of different classes, but this is not universally accepted.

Monitoring adherence to antidepressants is sometimes difficult, but nonadherence may account for up to 20 percent of patients classified as having treatment-resistant depression. Similarly, there is the potential for pseudo-resistance (nonresponse to inadequate treatment). All this would suggest the difficulty of defining and capturing subjects who have had TF and related subgroups. It may also reflect heterogeneity across studies evaluating the efficacy of SSRIs within this patient population.

Previous literature reviews would suggest that some of the strategies to treat patients following inadequate response may not be based on evidence; this is partially attributable to the small number of studies that have evaluated the different strategies. Rhue et al. evaluated the evidence for switching SSRIs in studies where 50 percent of subjects had previously used an SSRI and not responded adequately. This review found eight randomized trials and 23 open studies (with and without comparator groups). Response rates after switching to a new therapy varied from 12 to 86 percent and remission rates varied between 7 and 82 percent. Rates of dropouts due to harms varied from 9 to 39 percent. This review also identified some evidence showing that the number of failed responses to previous treatment with antidepressants was negatively associated with a positive response or outcome. Overall, this review showed that there was limited high-quality evidence describing optimal strategies to switch medications in persons with previous SSRI use. In addition, there were limited studies that recruited prospectively determined SSRI nonresponders. Papakostas et al. undertook a meta-analysis of four trials in subjects with TF who were randomized to switch to a non-SSRI versus another SSRI. The results suggest a modest and statistically significant advantage for remission rates when switching to non-SSRI rather than another SSRI. This review restricted eligible studies to those using three outcomes (Hamilton Depression Rating Scale, Montgomery-Asberg Depression Rating Scale, Quick Inventory of Depressive Symptomology) and to those evaluating the acute phase of Major Depressive Disorder (MDD). Williams et al. completed a systematic review on the treatment of depression in adolescents and children. Although this review did not focus on subjects who had failed to respond, the eligible studies did show that the rate at which children failed to respond to an initial trial of SSRIs varied from 31 to 64 percent. There was also some evidence that not all SSRIs were efficacious and that combined therapy (including an SSRI) is effective in this population.

A variety of treatment strategies aimed at helping individuals who have inadequate responses to first-line therapy with an SSRIs have been developed and applied in patients with depression. The primary goal of this CER is to examine the evidence guiding clinical treatment decisions and ultimately to aid clinicians in their care of patients in whom SSRI use as a first-line therapy for the index episode fails to bring about either complete or partial response or remission of depression.

Chapter 52

Brain Stimulation Therapies for Severe Depression

What Are Brain Stimulation Therapies?

Brain stimulation therapies can play a role in treating certain mental disorders. Brain stimulation therapies involve activating or inhibiting the brain directly with electricity. The electricity can be given directly by electrodes implanted in the brain, or noninvasively through electrodes placed on the scalp. The electricity can also be induced by using magnetic fields applied to the head. While these types of therapies are less frequently used than medication and psychotherapies, they hold promise for treating certain mental disorders that do not respond to other treatments.

Electroconvulsive therapy is the best-studied brain stimulation therapy and has the longest history of use. Other stimulation therapies discussed here are newer, and in some cases still experimental methods. These include:

- Vagus nerve stimulation (VNS)

- Repetitive transcranial magnetic stimulation (rTMS)

- Magnetic seizure therapy (MST)

- Deep brain stimulation (DBS)

This chapter includes text excerpted from "Brain Stimulation Therapies," National Institute of Mental Health (NIMH), June 2016. Reviewed October 2019.

A treatment plan may also include medication and psychotherapy. Choosing the right treatment plan should be based on a person's individual needs and medical situation and under a doctor's care.

Electroconvulsive Therapy

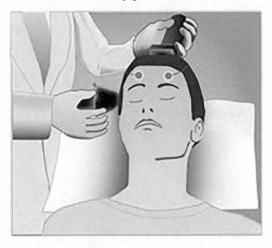

Figure 52.1. *Electroconvulsive Therapy*

Electroconvulsive therapy (ECT) uses an electric current to treat serious mental disorders. This type of therapy is usually considered only if a patient's illness has not improved after other treatments (such as antidepressant medication or psychotherapy) are tried, or in cases where rapid response is needed (as in the case of suicide risk and catatonia, for example).

Why Electroconvulsive Therapy Is Done?

Electroconvulsive therapy is most often used to treat severe, treatment-resistant depression, but it may also be medically indicated in other mental disorders, such as bipolar disorder or schizophrenia. It also may be used in life-threatening circumstances, such as when a patient is unable to move or respond to the outside world (e.g., catatonia), is suicidal, or is malnourished as a result of severe depression.

Electroconvulsive therapy can be effective in reducing the chances of relapse when patients undergo follow-up treatments. Two major advantages of ECT over medication are that ECT begins to work quicker, often starting within the first week, and older individuals respond especially quickly.

How Electroconvulsive Therapy Works

Before ECT is administered, a person is sedated with general anesthesia and given a medication called a "muscle relaxant" to prevent movement during the procedure. An anesthesiologist monitors breathing, heart rate and blood pressure during the entire procedure, which is conducted by a trained medical team, including physicians and nurses. During the procedure:

- Electrodes are placed at precise locations on the head.

- Through the electrodes, an electric current passes through the brain, causing a seizure that lasts generally less than one minute. Because the patient is under anesthesia and has taken a muscle relaxant, it is not painful and the patient cannot feel the electrical impulses.

- 5 to 10 minutes after the procedure ends, the patient awakens. She or he may feel groggy at first as the anesthesia wears off. But after about an hour, the patient usually is alert and can resume normal activities.

A typical course of ECT is administered about three times a week until the patient's depression improves (usually within 6 to 12 treatments). After that, maintenance ECT treatment is sometimes needed to reduce the chances that symptoms will return. ECT maintenance treatment varies depending on the needs of the individual and may range from one session per week to one session every few months. Frequently, a person who undergoes ECT also takes antidepressant medication or a mood-stabilizing medication.

Side Effects of Electroconvulsive Therapy

The most common side effects associated with ECT include:

- Headache

- Upset stomach

- Muscle aches

- Memory loss

Some people may experience memory problems, especially of memories around the time of the treatment. Sometimes the memory problems are more severe, but usually, they improve over the days and weeks following the end of an ECT course.

Research has found that memory problems seem to be more associated with the traditional type of ECT called "bilateral ECT," in which the electrodes are placed on both sides of the head.

In unilateral ECT, the electrodes are placed on just one side of the head—typically the right side because it is opposite the brain's learning and memory areas. Unilateral ECT has been found to be less likely to cause memory problems and, therefore, is preferred by many doctors, patients and families.

Vagus Nerve Stimulation

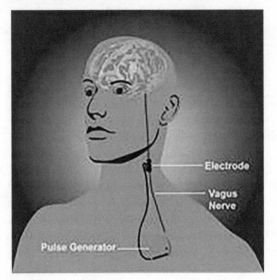

Figure 52.2. *Vagus Nerve Stimulation*

Vagus nerve stimulation (VNS) works through a device implanted under the skin that sends electrical pulses through the left vagus nerve, half of a prominent pair of nerves that run from the brainstem through the neck and down to each side of the chest and abdomen. The vagus nerves carry messages from the brain to the body's major organs (e.g., heart, lungs, and intestines) and to areas of the brain that control mood, sleep, and other functions.

Why Vagus Nerve Stimulation Is Done

Vagus nerve stimulation was originally developed as a treatment for epilepsy. However, scientists noticed that it also had favorable effects on mood, especially depressive symptoms. Using brain scans, scientists found that the device affected areas of the brain that are involved in mood regulation. The pulses appeared to alter the levels of certain neurotransmitters (brain chemicals) associated with mood, including serotonin, norepinephrine, gamma-aminobutyric acid (GABA), and glutamate.

In 2005, the U.S. Food and Drug Administration (FDA) approved VNS for use in treating treatment-resistant depression in certain circumstances:

- If the patient is 18 years of age or over

- If the illness has lasted 2 years or more

- If it is severe or recurrent

- If the depression has not eased after trying at least 4 other treatments

According to the FDA, it is not intended to be a first-line treatment, even for patients with severe depression. And, despite the FDA's approval, VNS remains an infrequently used because results of early studies testing its effectiveness for major depression were mixed. But a newer study, which pooled together findings from only controlled clinical trials, found that 32 percent of depressed people responded to VSN and 14 percent had full remission of symptoms after being treated for nearly 2 years.

How Vagus Nerve Stimulation Works

A device called a "pulse generator," about the size of a stopwatch is surgically implanted in the upper left side of the chest. Connected to the pulse generator is an electrical lead wire, which is connected from the generator to the left vagus nerve.

Typically, 30-second electrical pulses are sent about every five minutes from the generator to the vagus nerve. The duration and frequency of the pulses may vary depending on how the generator is programmed. The vagus nerve, in turn, delivers those signals to the brain. The pulse generator, which operates continuously, is powered by a battery that lasts around 10 years, after which it must be replaced. Normally, people do not feel pain or any other sensations as the device operates.

The device also can be temporarily deactivated by placing a magnet over the chest where the pulse generator is implanted. A person may want to deactivate it if side effects become intolerable, or before engaging in strenuous activity or exercise because it may interfere with breathing. The device reactivates when the magnet is removed.

Vagus nerve stimulation treatment is intended to reduce symptoms of depression. It may be several months before the patient notices any benefits and not all patients will respond to VNS. It is important to remember that VNS is intended to be given along with other traditional therapies, such as medications, and patients should not expect to discontinue these other treatments, even with the device in place.

Side Effects of Vagus Nerve Stimulation

Vagus nerve stimulation is not without risk. There may be complications such as infection from the implant surgery, or the device may come loose, move around or malfunction, which may require additional surgery to correct. Some patients have no improvement in symptoms and some actually get worse.

Other potential side effects include:

- Voice changes or hoarseness

- Cough or sore throat

- Neck pain

- Discomfort or tingling in the area where the device is implanted

- Breathing problems, especially during exercise

- Difficulty swallowing

Long-term side effects are unknown.

Repetitive Transcranial Magnetic Stimulation

Repetitive transcranial magnetic stimulation (rTMS) uses a magnet to activate the brain. First developed in 1985, rTMS has been studied as a treatment for depression, psychosis, anxiety, and other disorders.

Unlike ECT, in which electrical stimulation is more generalized, rTMS can be targeted to a specific site in the brain. Scientists believe that focusing on a specific site in the brain reduces the chance for the types of side effects associated with ECT. But opinions vary as to what site is best.

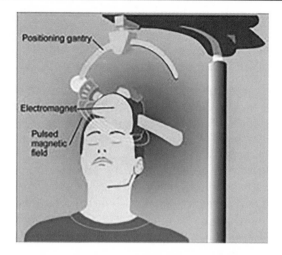

Figure 52.3. *Repetitive Transcranial Magnetic Stimulation*

Why Repetitive Transcranial Magnetic Stimulation Is Done

In 2008, rTMS was approved for use by the FDA as a treatment for major depression for patients who do not respond to at least one antidepressant medication in the current episode. It is also used in other countries as a treatment for depression in patients who have not responded to medications and who might otherwise be considered for ECT.

The evidence supporting rTMS for depression was mixed until the first large clinical trial, funded by NIMH, was published in 2010. The trial found that 14 percent achieved remission with rTMS compared to 5 percent with an inactive (sham) treatment. After the trial ended, patients could enter a second phase in which everyone, including those who previously received the sham treatment, was given rTMS. Remission rates during the second phase climbed to nearly 30 percent. A sham treatment is such as a placebo, but instead of being an inactive pill, it is an inactive procedure that mimics real rTMS.

How Repetitive Transcranial Magnetic Stimulation Works

A typical rTMS session lasts 30 to 60 minutes and does not require anesthesia.

During the procedure:

• An electromagnetic coil is held against the forehead near an area of the brain that is thought to be involved in mood regulation.

• Then, short electromagnetic pulses are administered through the coil. The magnetic pulses easily pass through the skull and cause small electrical currents that stimulate nerve cells in the targeted brain region.

Because this type of pulse generally does not reach further than two inches into the brain, scientists can select which parts of the brain will be affected and which will not be. The magnetic field is about the same strength as that of a magnetic resonance imaging (MRI) scan. Generally, the person feels a slight knocking or tapping on the head as the pulses are administered.

Not all scientists agree on the best way to position the magnet on the patient's head or give the electromagnetic pulses. They also do not yet know if rTMS works best when given as a single treatment or combined with medication and/or psychotherapy.

Side Effects of Repetitive Transcranial Magnetic Stimulation

Sometimes a person may have discomfort at the site on the head where the magnet is placed. The muscles of the scalp, jaw or face may contract or tingle during the procedure. Mild headaches or brief lightheadedness may result. It is also possible that the procedure could cause a seizure, although documented incidences of this are uncommon. Two large-scale studies on the safety of rTMS found that most side effects, such as headaches or scalp discomfort, were mild or moderate, and no seizures occurred. Because the treatment is relatively new, however, long-term side effects are unknown.

Magnetic Seizure Therapy
How Magnetic Seizure Therapy Works

Magnetic seizure therapy (MST) borrows certain aspects from both ECT and rTMS. Like rTMS, MST uses magnetic pulses instead of electricity to stimulate a precise target in the brain. However, unlike rTMS, MST aims to induce seizure-like ECT. So the pulses are given at a higher frequency than that used in rTMS. Therefore, like ECT, the patient must be anesthetized and given a muscle relaxant to prevent movement. The goal of MST is to retain the effectiveness of ECT while reducing its cognitive side effects.

Magnetic seizure therapy is in the early stages of testing for mental disorders, but initial results are promising. A review article that examined the evidence from 8 clinical studies found that MST triggered remission from major depression or bipolar disorder in 30 to 40 percent of individuals.

Side Effects of Magnetic Seizure Therapy

Like ECT, MST carries the risk of side effects that can be caused by anesthesia exposure and the induction of a seizure. Studies in both animals and humans have found that MST produces

- Fewer memory side effects

- Shorter seizures

- Allows for a shorter recovery time than ECT

Deep Brain Stimulation

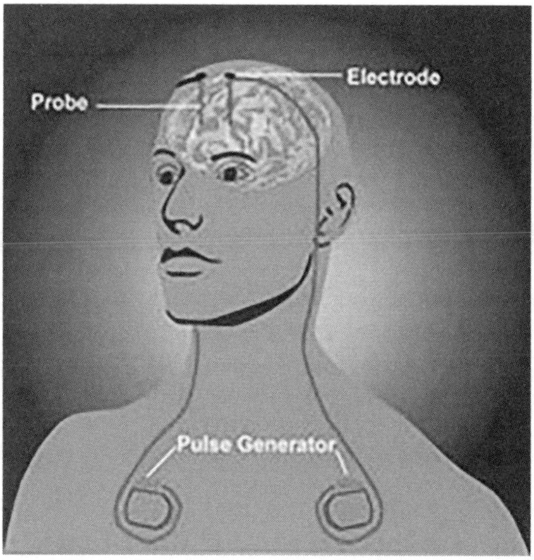

Figure 52.4. *Deep Brain Stimulation*

Deep brain stimulation (DBS) was first developed as a treatment for Parkinson disease to reduce tremor, stiffness, walking problems and uncontrollable movements. In DBS, a pair of electrodes is implanted in the brain and controlled by a generator that is implanted in the chest.

Stimulation is continuous and its frequency and level are customized to the individual.

Deep brain stimulation has been studied as a treatment for depression or obsessive-compulsive disorder (OCD). There is a Humanitarian Device Exemption (HDE) for the use of DBS to treat OCD, but its use in depression remains only on an experimental basis. A review of all 22 published studies testing DBS for depression found that only three of them were of high quality because they not only had a treatment group but also a control group that did not receive DBS. The review found that across the studies, 40 to 50 percent of people showed receiving DBS greater than 50 percent improvement.

How Deep Brain Stimulation Works

Deep brain stimulation requires brain surgery. The head is shaved and then attached with screws to a sturdy frame that prevents the head from moving during the surgery. Scans of the head and brain using MRI are taken. The surgeon uses these images as guides during the surgery. Patients are awake during the procedure to provide the surgeon with feedback, but they feel no pain because the head is numbed with a local anesthetic and the brain itself does not register pain.

Once ready for surgery, 2 holes are drilled into the head. From there, the surgeon threads a slender tube down into the brain to place electrodes on each side of a specific area of the brain. In the case of depression, the first area of the brain targeted by DBS is called "Area 25," or the subgenual cingulate cortex. This area has been found to be overactive in depression and other mood disorders. But later research targeted several other areas of the brain affected by depression. So DBS is now targeting several areas of the brain for treating depression. In the case of OCD, the electrodes are placed in an area of the brain (the ventral capsule/ventral striatum) believed to be associated with the disorder.

After the electrodes are implanted and the patient provides feedback about their placement, the patient is put under general anesthesia. The electrodes are then attached to wires that are run inside the body from the head down to the chest, where a pair of battery-operated generators are implanted. From here, electrical pulses are continuously delivered over the wires to the electrodes in the brain. Although it is unclear exactly how the device works to reduce depression or OCD, scientists believe that the pulses help to "reset" the area of the brain that is malfunctioning so that it works normally again.

Side Effects of Deep Brain Stimulation

Deep brain stimulation carries risks associated with any type of brain surgery. For example, the procedure may lead to:

- Bleeding in the brain or stroke
- Infection
- Disorientation or confusion
- Unwanted mood changes
- Movement disorders
- Lightheadedness
- Trouble sleeping

Because the procedure is still being studied, other side effects not yet identified may be possible. Long-term benefits and side effects are unknown.

Chapter 53

Light Therapy for Seasonal Affective Disorder

Seasonal affective disorder (SAD) is a condition associated with feeling sad or blue during certain times of the year. It is a disorder that triggers symptoms of depression, most commonly in the fall or winter. In the fall and winter, there is less sunlight, hence it is sometimes called "winter depression."

Psychiatrists and other mental-health clinicians diagnose depression by documenting the low or sad mood, irritability, feelings of guilt or shame, problems with sleep, poor concentration or attention (memory problems), low energy or motivation, poor appetite and thoughts of self-harm.

Seasonal affective disorder can mimic other medical conditions, such as anemia, hypothyroidism, diabetes, infections. Hence a medical workup may be needed including levels of some vitamins, such as vitamin D.

You may have SAD if, in the last two years, you feel depressed during this season and normal during the rest of the year. You may

This chapter contains text excerpted from the following sources: Text in this chapter begins with excerpts from "Help for Veterans with Seasonal Affective Disorder," U.S. Department of Veterans Affairs (VA), February 6, 2018; Text under the heading "Get More Sun, Stay Active, and Get to a Brighter Place" is excerpted from "Seasonal Affective Disorder and Complementary Health Approaches: What the Science Says," National Center for Complementary and Integrative Health (NCCIH), January 18, 2019.

also have SAD if your depression for which you are being treated gets worse in this season.

Your symptoms will get better on their own when a new season arrives, often in spring or summer. But, treatment can make you feel better sooner.

Light Therapy

Light therapy, also called "phototherapy" generally works well for SAD. You need to sit in front of a box or lamp that gives out up to 10,000 lux of fluorescent light—more than 20 times brighter than most indoor light. Researchers think that light helps your brain make more serotonin, a neurotransmitter that affects your mood. You have to sit 12 to 18 inches in front of the light for 30 minutes or more a day, 3 times per week at least. The light must shine on your back or chest. You can read a book to pass the time. Do not stare at the light. You will feel better after 1 or 2 weeks.

You may also want to see a medical provider to consider taking medications to increase serotonin levels. Your doctor may also recommend talk therapy such as cognitive-behavioral therapy. You will learn behavioral skills to do pleasurable things during the winter, notice and change negative thoughts or manage stress.

It is important to consider all types of treatment. Get more sun, stay active, get to a brighter place and work toward sleeping the right amount of time.

Consider talking to a professional to identify ways of coping with SAD. Counselors are available to guide you during this time. Do not feel frightened to talk about your problems. They are there to help you.

Get More Sun, Stay Active, and Get to a Brighter Place

There is some evidence that light therapy may be useful as a preventive treatment for people with a history of seasonal affective disorder. The idea behind light therapy is to replace the diminished sunshine of the fall and winter months using daily exposure to a lightbox. Most typically, light boxes filter out the ultraviolet rays and require 20 to 60 minutes of exposure to 10,000 lux of cool-white fluorescent light, an amount that is about 20 times greater than ordinary indoor lighting.

Chapter 54

Alternative and Complementary Therapies Used for Depression

Chapter Contents

Section 54.1

Complementary and Alternative Medicine for Depression

This section includes text excerpted from "5 Tips: What You Should Know about the Science behind Depression and Complementary Health Approaches," National Center for Complementary and Integrative Health (NCCIH), May 3, 2018.

Depression is a medical condition that affects about 1 in 10 adults in the United States. Depression can be treated with conventional medicine, including antidepressants and certain types of psychotherapy. Still, many people turn to complementary health approaches in addition to conventional treatment. Although complementary approaches are commonly used and readily available in the marketplace, many of these treatments have not been rigorously studied for depression. For this reason, it is important that you understand the benefits and risks of these complementary approaches to making informed decisions about your health.

Here are 5 things you should know about some complementary health approaches for depression:

1. Some studies suggest that omega-3 fatty acid supplements may provide a small improvement along with conventional treatment, such as antidepressants, in patients with major depressive disorder (MDD) and in depressed patients without a diagnosis of MDD. However, a lot of questions remain about how, or if, omega-3 supplements work in the body to produce such an effect.

2. Although some studies of St. John's wort (*Hypericum perforatum*) have shown benefits similar to standard antidepressants for depression in a limited number of patients, others have not. Research has shown that St. John's wort interacts with many medications in ways that can interfere with their intended effects, making its safety risks outweigh the benefit of any use of St. John's wort.

3. Current scientific evidence does not support the use of other dietary supplements, including S-Adenosyl methionine (SAMe) or inositol, for depression.

4. Some studies on mind and body practices, when used along with standard treatment for depression in adults, have had modestly promising results. For example, there is limited evidence that music therapy may provide an improvement in mood. In addition, studies indicate that relaxation training is better than no treatment in reducing

symptoms of depression, but is not as beneficial as psychological therapies, such as cognitive-behavioral therapy.

5. Take charge of your health—talk with your healthcare providers about any complementary health approaches you use. Together, you can make shared, well-informed decisions.

Section 54.2

St. John's Wort and Depression

This section includes text excerpted from "St. John's Wort and Depression: In Depth," National Center for Complementary and Integrative Health (NCCIH), January 4, 2018.

What Is St. John's Wort?

- St. John's wort (*Hypericum perforatum*), a plant that grows in the wild, has been used for centuries for mental-health conditions. It is widely prescribed for depression in Europe.

- St. John's wort is sold as a dietary supplement in the United States, where the standards for selling supplements are less strict than the standards for prescription or over-the-counter drugs.

What the Science Says about the Effectiveness of St. John's Wort for Depression

The results of studies on the effectiveness of St. John's wort for depression are mixed.

- In a 12-week, 2011 clinical trial with 73 participants, neither St. John's wort nor a standard antidepressant medication called "citalopram," a selective serotonin reuptake inhibitor (SSRI), decreased symptoms of minor depression better than a placebo. The study was funded by the National Center for Complementary and Integrative Health (NCCIH) and the National Institute of Mental Health (NIMH).

- In a 26-week clinical trial with 124 participants, St. John's wort, a standard antidepressant (sertraline, an SSRI)), and placebo were similarly effective in treating major depression of moderate severity. The NCCIH and NIMH funded this 2012 analysis of data collected in 2002.

- A review of 29 international studies suggested that St. John's wort may be better than a placebo and as effective as different standard prescription antidepressants for major depression of mild to moderate severity. St. John's wort also appeared to have fewer side effects than standard antidepressants. The studies conducted in German-speaking countries—where St. John's wort has a long history of use by medical professionals—reported more positive results than those done in other countries, including the United States.

- St. John's wort was no more effective than placebo in treating major depression of moderate severity, an NCCIH- and NIMH-funded study of 340 participants reported in 2002.

- The placebo effect is when patients' health improves because they think that an intervention—a pill, procedure, or injection, for example—will help. In a clinical trial of St. John's wort for major depression, what participants guessed they were taking may have affected their recovery from depression more than what they actually received. A healthcare provider's style in talking with patients also may have a positive effect on patient health that is separate from the treatment.

What the Science Says about the Safety and Side Effects of St. John's Wort for Depression

- Combining St. John's wort with certain antidepressants can lead to a potentially life-threatening increase of serotonin, a brain chemical targeted by antidepressants. Symptoms occur within minutes to hours and may include agitation, diarrhea, fast heartbeat, high blood pressure, hallucinations, increased body temperature, and more.

- There are case reports of St. John's wort having dangerous side effects, such as worsening of psychotic symptoms in people with bipolar disorder or schizophrenia.

- Taking St. John's wort can weaken many prescription medicines, such as:

- Antidepressants

- Birth control pills

- Cyclosporine used to prevent the body from rejecting transplanted organs

- Digoxin, a heart medication

- Oxycodone, a pain medicine

- Some HIV drugs, including indinavir

- Some cancer medications, including irinotecan

- Warfarin, an anticoagulant (blood thinner)

- Other side effects of St. John's wort are usually minor and uncommon. They may include upset stomach, dry mouth, headache, fatigue, dizziness, confusion, sexual dysfunction, or sensitivity to sunlight. Also, St. John's wort is a stimulant and may worsen feelings of anxiety in some people.

More to Consider

- Depression can be a serious illness and lead to an increased risk of suicide. If you or someone you know may have depression, talk to a healthcare provider. Do not try to treat depression on your own.

- Do not use St. John's wort to replace conventional care or to postpone seeing a healthcare provider about a mental health problem.

- Dietary supplements can cause medical problems if you use them incorrectly or in large amounts. Some may interact with the medications you take. Your healthcare provider can advise you.

- Many dietary supplements have not been tested in pregnant women, nursing mothers, or children. We have little safety information on St. John's wort for pregnant women or children. Talk with healthcare providers if you are pregnant or nursing or are considering giving a dietary supplement to a child.

- Take charge of your health—talk with your healthcare providers about any complementary health approaches you use. Together, you can make shared, well-informed decisions.

Section 54.3

Valerian

This section includes text excerpted from "Valerian,"
National Center for Complementary and Integrative
Health (NCCIH), December 1, 2016. Reviewed October 2019.

What Is Valerian?

- Valerian is a plant native to Europe and Asia; it also grows in North America.

- Valerian has been used medicinally since the times of early Greece and Rome; Hippocrates wrote about its uses. Historically, valerian was used to treat nervousness, trembling, headaches, and heart palpitations.

- Valerian is used as a dietary supplement for insomnia, anxiety, and other conditions, such as depression and menopause symptoms.

- The roots and rhizomes (underground stems) of valerian are used to make capsules, tablets, and liquid extracts, as well as teas.

How Much Do We Know?

Knowledge about valerian is limited because there have been only a small number of high-quality studies in people.

What Have We Learned?

- The evidence on whether valerian is helpful for sleep problems is inconsistent.

- There is not enough evidence to allow any conclusions about whether valerian can relieve anxiety, depression, or menopausal symptoms.

What Do We Know about Safety?

- Studies suggest that valerian is generally safe for use by most healthy adults for short periods of time.

- No information is available about the long-term safety of valerian or its safety in children younger than age 3, pregnant women, or nursing mothers.

- Few side effects have been reported in studies of valerian. Those that have occurred include headache, dizziness, itching, and digestive disturbances.

- Because it is possible (though not proven) that valerian might have a sleep-inducing effect, it should not be taken along with alcohol or sedatives.

Keep in Mind

Tell all your healthcare providers about any complementary or integrative health approaches you use. Give them a full picture of what you do to manage your health. This will help ensure coordinated and safe care.

Section 54.4

Meditation Can Help in Conquering Depression

This section includes text excerpted from "Meditation: In Depth," National Center for Complementary and Integrative Health (NCCIH), April 2016. Reviewed October 2019.

What Is Meditation?

Meditation is a mind and body practice that has a long history of use for increasing calmness and physical relaxation, improving psychological balance, coping with illness, and enhancing overall health and well-being. Mind and body practices focus on the interactions among the brain, mind, body, and behavior. A report based on data from the 2017 National Health Interview Survey (NHIS) found that U.S. adults' use of meditation in the past 12 months tripled between 2012 and 2017 (from 4.1 percent to 14.2%). The use of meditation by

U.S. children (aged 4 to 17 years) also increased significantly (from 0.6% in 2012 to 5.4% in 2017).

There are many types of meditation, but most have four elements in common: a quiet location with as few distractions as possible; a specific, comfortable posture (sitting, lying down, walking, or in other positions); a focus of attention (a specially chosen word or set of words, an object, or the sensations of the breath); and an open attitude (letting distractions come and go naturally without judging them).

What the Science Says about the Effectiveness of Meditation

Many studies have investigated meditation for different conditions, and there is evidence that it may reduce blood pressure as well as symptoms of irritable bowel syndrome and flare-ups in people who have had ulcerative colitis. It may ease symptoms of anxiety and depression and may help people with insomnia.

For Anxiety, Depression, and Insomnia

- A 2014 literature review of 47 trials in 3,515 participants suggests that mindfulness meditation programs show moderate evidence of improving anxiety and depression. But the researchers found no evidence that meditation changed health-related behaviors affected by stress, such as substance abuse and sleep.

- A 2012 review of 36 trials found that 25 of them reported better outcomes for symptoms of anxiety in the meditation groups compared to control groups.

- In a small, NCCIH-funded study, 54 adults with chronic insomnia learned mindfulness-based stress reduction (MBSR), a form of MBSR specially adapted to deal with insomnia (mindfulness-based therapy for insomnia, or MBTI), or a self-monitoring program. Both meditation-based programs aided sleep, with MBTI providing a significantly greater reduction in insomnia severity compared with MBSR.

What the Science Says about Safety and Side Effects of Meditation

- Meditation is generally considered to be safe for healthy people.

- People with physical limitations may not be able to participate in certain meditative practices involving movement. People with physical health conditions should speak with their healthcare providers before starting a meditative practice, and make their meditation instructor aware of their condition.

- There have been rare reports that meditation could cause or worsen symptoms in people with certain psychiatric problems, such as anxiety and depression. People with existing mental-health conditions should speak with their healthcare providers before starting a meditative practice, and make their meditation instructor aware of their condition.

More to Consider

- Do not use meditation to replace conventional care or as a reason to postpone seeing a healthcare provider about a medical problem.

- Ask about the training and experience of the meditation instructor you are considering.

- Tell all your healthcare providers about any complementary or integrative health approaches you use. Give them a full picture of what you do to manage your health. This will help ensure coordinated and safe care.

Chapter 55

Treating Depression in Children and Adolescents

Chapter Contents

Section 55.1

Do Not Leave Childhood Depression Untreated

This section includes text excerpted from "FDA: Don't Leave
Childhood Depression Untreated," U.S. Food and Drug
Administration (FDA), September 10, 2014. Reviewed October 2019.

Every psychological disorder, including depression, has some behavioral components.

Depressed children often lack energy and enthusiasm. They become withdrawn, irritable and sulky. They may feel sad, anxious and restless. They may have problems in school, and frequently lose interest in activities they once enjoyed.

Some parents might think that medication is the solution for depression-related problem behaviors. In fact, that is not the case. The Food and Drug Administration (FDA) has not approved any drugs solely for the treatment of "behavior problems." When the FDA approves a drug for depression—whether for adults or children—it is to treat the illness, not the behavior associated with it.

"There are multiple parts to mental illness, and the symptoms are usually what drug companies study and what parents worry about. But it is rare for us at FDA to target just one part of the illness," says Mitchell Mathis, M.D., a psychiatrist who is the Director of the FDA's Division of Psychiatry Products (DPP).

Depression Is Treatable

The first step to treating depression is to get a professional diagnosis; most children who are moody, grouchy or feel that they are misunderstood are not depressed and do not need any drugs.

Only about 11 percent of adolescents have a depressive disorder by age 18, according to the National Institute of Mental Health (NIMH). Before puberty, girls and boys have the same incidence of depression. After adolescence, girls are twice as likely to have depression as boys. The trend continues until after menopause. "That's a clue that depression might be hormonal, but so far, scientists have not found out exactly how hormones affect the brain," says the child and adolescent psychiatrist Tiffany R. Farchione, M.D., the Acting Deputy Director of the FDA's DPP.

It is hard to tell if a child is depressed or going through a difficult time because the signs and symptoms of depression change as children grow and their brains develop. Also, it can take time to get a correct diagnosis because doctors might be getting just a snapshot of what is going on with the young patient.

"In psychiatry, it's easier to take care of adults because you have a lifetime of patient experience to draw from, and patterns are more obvious," says Mathis. "With kids, you don't have that information. Because we don't like to label kids with lifelong disorders, we first look for any other reason for those symptoms. And if we diagnose depression, we assess the severity before treating the patient with medications."

Getting the Proper Care

The second step is to decide on a treatment course, which depends on the severity of the illness and its impact on the child's life. Treatments for depression often include psychotherapy and medication. The FDA has approved two drugs—fluoxetine (Prozac®) and escitalopram (Lexapro®)—to treat depression in children. Prozac® is approved for ages 8 and older; Lexapro® for kids 12 and older.

"We need more pediatric studies because many antidepressants approved for adults have not been proven to work in kids," Farchione says. "When we find a treatment that has been shown to work in kids, we're encouraged because that drug can have a big impact on a child who doesn't have many medication treatment options."

The FDA requires that all antidepressants include a boxed warning about the increased risks of suicidal thinking and behavior in children, adolescents and young adults up to age 24. "All of these medicines work in the brain and the central nervous system, so there are risks. Patients and their doctors have to weigh those risks against the benefits," Mathis says.

Depression can lead to suicide. Children who take antidepressants might have more suicidal thoughts, which is why the labeling includes a boxed warning on all antidepressants. But the boxed warning does not say not to treat children, just to be aware of, and to monitor them for signs of suicidality.

"A lot of kids respond very well to drugs. Oftentimes, young people can stop taking the medication after a period of stability, because some of these illnesses are not a chronic disorder, such as major depression," Mathis adds. "There are many things that help young psychiatric patients get better, and drugs are just one of them."

It is important that patients and their doctors work together to taper off the medications. Abruptly stopping treatment without gradually reducing the dose might lead to problems, such as mood disturbances, agitation, and irritability.

Depression in children should not be left untreated. Untreated acute depression may get better on its own, but it relapses and the patient is not cured. Real improvement can take six months or more, and may not be complete without treatment. And the earlier the treatment starts, the better the outcome.

"Kids just don't have time to leave their depression untreated," Farchione says. "The social and educational consequences of a lengthy recovery are huge. They could fail a grade. They could lose all of their friends."

Medications help patients recover sooner and more completely.

Section 55.2

Antidepressant Medication and Psychotherapy for Children and Teens

This section contains text excerpted from the following sources:
Text beginning with the heading "What Is Child and Adolescent
Mental Health?" is excerpted from "Child and Adolescent Mental
Health," National Institute of Mental Health (NIMH), May 2019;
Text beginning with the heading "Antidepressants" is excerpted from
"Mental Health Medications," National Institute of Mental Health
(NIMH), October 2016. Reviewed October 2019; Text under the
heading "Treatment Options" is excerpted from "Children and Mental
Health," National Institute of Mental Health (NIMH), 2018.

What Is Child and Adolescent Mental Health?

Mental health is an important part of overall health for children as well as adults. For many adults who have mental disorders, symptoms were present—but often not recognized or addressed—in childhood and adolescence. For a young person with symptoms of a mental disorder, the earlier treatment is started, the more effective it can be. Early treatment can help prevent more severe, lasting problems as a child grows up.

Warning Signs

It can be tough to tell if troubling behavior in a child is just part of growing up or a problem that should be discussed with a health professional. But if there are behavioral signs and symptoms that last weeks or months, and if these issues interfere with the child's daily life at home and at school, or with friends, you should contact a health professional.

Young children may benefit from an evaluation and treatment if they:

- Have frequent tantrums or are intensely irritable much of the time

- Often talk about fears or worries

- Complain about frequent stomach aches or headaches with no known medical cause

- Are in constant motion and cannot sit quietly (except when they are watching videos or playing video games)

- Sleep too much or too little, have frequent nightmares or seem sleepy during the day

- Are not interested in playing with other children or have difficulty making friends

- Struggle academically or have experienced a recent decline in grades

- Repeat actions or check things many times out of fear that something bad may happen

Older children and adolescents may benefit from evaluation if they:

- Have lost interest in things that they used to enjoy

- Have low energy

- Sleep too much or too little, or seem sleepy throughout the day

- Are spending more and more time alone, and avoid social activities with friends or family

- Fear gaining weight, or diet or exercise excessively

- Engage in self-harm behaviors (e.g., cutting or burning their skin)

- Smoke, drink alcohol or use drugs

- Engage in risky or destructive behavior alone or with friends

- Have thoughts of suicide

- Have periods of highly elevated energy and activity, and require much less sleep than usual

- Say that they think someone is trying to control their mind or that they hear things that other people cannot hear.

Antidepressants
What Are Antidepressants?

Antidepressants are medications commonly used to treat depression. Antidepressants are also used for other health conditions, such as anxiety, pain, and insomnia. Although antidepressants are not U.S. Food and Drug Administration (FDA)-approved specifically to treat attention deficit hyperactivity disorder (ADHD), antidepressants are sometimes used to treat ADHD in adults.

The most popular types of antidepressants are called "selective serotonin reuptake inhibitors" (SSRIs). Examples of SSRIs include:

- Fluoxetine

- Citalopram

- Sertraline

- Paroxetine

- Escitalopram

Other types of antidepressants are serotonin and norepinephrine reuptake inhibitors (SNRIs). SNRIs are similar to SSRIs and include venlafaxine and duloxetine.

Another antidepressant that is commonly used is bupropion. Bupropion is a third type of antidepressant that works differently than either SSRIs or SNRIs. Bupropion is also used to treat the seasonal affective disorder (SAD) and to help people stop smoking.

Selective serotonin reuptake inhibitors, SNRIs, and bupropion are popular because they do not cause as many side effects as older classes of antidepressants, and seem to help a broader group of depressive and anxiety disorders. Older antidepressant medications include tricyclics, tetracyclic, and monoamine oxidase inhibitors (MAOIs). For some people, tricyclics, tetracyclic, or MAOIs may be the best medications.

How Do People Respond to Antidepressants?

According to a research review by the Agency for Healthcare Research and Quality, all antidepressant medications work about as well as each other to improve symptoms of depression and to keep depression symptoms from coming back. For reasons not yet well understood, some people respond better to some antidepressant medications than to others.

Therefore, it is important to know that some people may not feel better with the first medicine they try and may need to try several medicines to find the one that works for them. Others may find that medicine helped for a while, but their symptoms came back. It is important to carefully follow your doctor's directions for taking your medicine at an adequate dose and over an extended period of time (often 4 to 6 weeks) for it to work.

Once a person begins taking antidepressants, it is important to not stop taking them without the help of a doctor. Sometimes people taking antidepressants to feel better and stop taking the medication too soon, and the depression may return. When it is time to stop the medication, the doctor will help the person slowly and safely decrease the dose. It is important to give the body time to adjust to the change. People do not get addicted (or "hooked") on these medications, but stopping them abruptly may also cause withdrawal symptoms

What Are the Possible Side Effects of Antidepressants?

Some antidepressants may cause more side effects than others. You may need to try several different antidepressant medications before finding the one that improves your symptoms and that causes side effects that you can manage.

The most common side effects listed by the FDA include:

- Nausea and vomiting
- Weight gain
- Diarrhea
- Sleepiness
- Sexual problems

Call your doctor right away if you have any of the following symptoms, especially if they are new, worsening, or worry you:

- Thoughts about suicide or dying

- Attempts to commit suicide
- New or worsening depression
- New or worsening anxiety
- Feeling very agitated or restless
- Panic attacks
- Trouble sleeping (insomnia)
- New or worsening irritability
- Acting aggressively, being angry, or violent
- Acting on dangerous impulses
- An extreme increase in activity and talking (mania)
- Other unusual changes in behavior or mood

Combining the newer SSRI or SNRI antidepressants with one of the commonly-used "triptan" medications used to treat migraine headaches could cause a life-threatening illness called "serotonin syndrome." A person with serotonin syndrome may be agitated, have hallucinations (see or hear things that are not real), have a high temperature, or have unusual blood pressure changes. Serotonin syndrome is usually associated with the older antidepressants called "monoamine oxidase inhibitors" MAOIs, but it can happen with the newer antidepressants as well if they are mixed with the wrong medications.

Children and Adolescents

Many medications used to treat children and adolescents with mental illness are safe and effective. However, some medications have not been studied or approved for use with children or adolescents.

Still, a doctor can give a young person an FDA-approved medication on an "off-label" basis. This means that the doctor prescribes the medication to help the patient even though the medicine is not approved for the specific mental disorder that is being treated or for use by patients under a certain age. Remember:

- It is important to watch children and adolescents who take these medications on an "off-label" basis.
- Children may have different reactions and side effects than adults.
- Some medications have current FDA warnings about potentially dangerous side effects for younger patients.

In addition to medications, other treatments for children and adolescents should be considered, either to be tried first, with medication added later if necessary or to be provided along with medication. Psychotherapy, family therapy, educational courses, and behavior management techniques can help everyone involved cope with disorders that affect a child's mental health.

Treatment Options

Assessment results may suggest that a child's behavior is related to changes or stresses at home or school, or is the result of a disorder for which treatment would be recommended. Treatment recommendations may include:

Psychotherapy ("Talk Therapy")

There are many different approaches to psychotherapy, including structured psychotherapies directed at specific conditions. Effective psychotherapy for children always includes:

- Parent involvement in the treatment (especially for children and adolescents

- Teaching skills and practicing skills at home or at school (between-session "homework assignments")

- Measures of progress (e.g., rating scales, improvements on homework assignments) that are tracked over time.

Medications

- Medication may be used along with psychotherapy. As with adults, the type of medications used for children depends on the diagnosis and may include antidepressants, stimulants, mood stabilizers, and others. Medications are often used in combination with psychotherapy. If different specialists are involved, treatment should be coordinated.

Family Counseling

- Including parents and other members of the family in treatment can help families understand how a child's individual challenges may affect relationships with parents and siblings and vice versa.

Support for Parents

- Individual or group sessions that include training and the opportunity to talk with other parents can provide new strategies for supporting a child and managing difficult behavior in a positive way. The therapist can also coach parents on how to deal with schools.

Chapter 56

Treatment-Resistant and Relapsed Depression

Chapter Contents

Section 56.1

Treatment-Resistant Depression: An Overview

This section contains text excerpted from the following sources: Text in this section begins with excerpts from "Definition of Treatment-Resistant Depression in the Medicare Population," Centers for Medicare and Medicaid Services (CMS), February 9, 2018; Text under the heading "Rapidly-Acting Treatments for Treatment-Resistant Depression" is excerpted from, "Rapidly-Acting Treatments for Treatment-Resistant Depression (RAPID)," National Institute of Mental Health (NIMH), November 19, 2012. Reviewed October 2019.

Depressive episodes can be seen in patients with either major depressive disorder (MDD) or bipolar disorder. The bulk of these episodes are part of MDD, experienced by more than 13 million U.S. residents each year. Of these individuals, one-half seek help for this condition; one in five of those seeking help receive adequate acute-phase treatment. Even for patients receiving adequate treatment, only 30 percent of patients with MDD reach the treatment goal of full recovery or remission. The remaining 70 percent of MDD patients will either respond without remission or not respond at all. Patients whose depressive disorder does not respond satisfactorily to adequate treatment is generally referred to as treatment-resistant depression (TRD). Although often broadly defined this way, TRD is a complex phenomenon that is influenced by heterogeneity in depressive subtypes, psychiatric comorbidity, and coexisting medical illnesses.

Treatment-resistant depression has substantial effects on patients and major impacts on families, communities, and society at large. TRD represents the highest direct and indirect medical costs among those with MDD. These costs increase with the severity of TRD. Individuals with TRD are twice as likely to be hospitalized; the cost of this hospitalization is more than six times the mean total cost for depressed patients who are not treatment-resistant. TRD can nearly double both direct and indirect employer medical expenditures relative to expenditures for patients whose MDD responds to treatment.

Risk Factors of Treatment-Resistant Depression

Risk and prognostic factors that can act as potential confounders are:

- Age
- Chronic pain

- Class(es) of previous antidepressant(s)

- Medical comorbidities

- Psychiatric conditions

- Disease severity

- Dose of the previous antidepressant

- Duration of the current episode

- Family history of depressive disorder

- History of bipolar disorder

- Interferon or glucocorticoid treatment

- Marital status

- Melancholic features

- Number of previous hospitalizations

- Number of prior (failed) treatments

- The onset of disease before age 20

- Race and ethnicity

- Severe, sudden depression during the past three years

- Sex or gender

- Socioeconomic status

- Suicidal ideation or attempts

Rapidly-Acting Treatments of Treatment-Resistant Depression

Rapidly-acting treatments for treatment-resistant depression (RAPID) is a National Institute of Mental Health (NIMH)-funded research project that promotes the development of speedier therapies for severe, treatment-resistant depression. The initiative is supporting a team of researchers, who are identifying and testing promising pharmacological and/or nonpharmacological treatments that lift depression within a few days.

By contrast, antidepressant medications usually take a few weeks to work—and half of the patients fail to fully respond. While a proven brain stimulation technique, electroconvulsive therapy (ECT), works faster, it runs the risk of cognitive side-effects and requires anesthesia and a surgical setting. The urgent need for improved, faster-acting antidepressant treatments is underscored by the fact that severe depression can be life-threatening, due to the heightened risk of suicide.

Ketamine, a drug known previously as an "anesthetic," can lift depression in many patients within hours. Researchers are making significant progress in pinpointing its mechanism of action and in identifying biomarkers that predict response.

It is unlikely that ketamine itself will become a practical treatment for most cases of depression. It must be administered through infusion, requiring a hospital setting, and can potentially trigger adverse side effects. Patients also typically relapse after treatment ends.

Section 56.2

Teens Who Recover from Hard-to-Treat Depression Are Still at Risk for Relapse

Relapse of depression means that the symptoms of depression have come back. A relapse can happen at any time, even while taking medications for depression and during ongoing treatment. Proper treatment can help reduce and control the symptoms of depression, but cannot cure them permanently or eliminate the possibility of a relapse. A relapse is defined by symptoms of depression that occur after a minimum of four months of being depression-free.

Causes of Depression Relapse

Many reasons make a person to have a depression relapse. Teens who had recovered from hard-to-treat depression are known to relapse due to many external and internal forces. Some of the most important and common causes are listed below:

- Death of a family member or friend

- Reliving on one's previous negative experiences, mistakes, or memories
- Stressful circumstances, such as an upcoming exams
- Familial changes, such as the divorce of parents or going away to college
- Hormonal shifts, such as those that occur during puberty or pregnancy
- Dealing with a serious medical condition
- Drug or alcohol abuse

Symptoms of a Relapse

Some people may be more at high risk for relapsing depression than others. And sometimes the symptoms that a person experiences during a relapse will not be the same as the symptoms experienced during the first depressive episode. Hence, one has to be cognizant of and watch for the symptoms of relapse. The most common signs of relapse are feeling sad, worthless, or hopeless, and a loss of interest in daily activities. A person can be at risk for relapse if they experience any of the other symptoms listed below.

Irritability

Irritability is a sign of relapse if a person is getting annoyed more easily than normal. Getting quickly irritated and infuriated at family and friends can be a sign that a person is at risk of a relapse.

Difficulty Concentrating

A common symptom of depression is brain fog, or problems concentrating. Many people have difficulties concentrating in class or experience a slowed-down thought process that feels as if they are thinking through a haze.

Sleep Changes and Fatigue

An early symptom of depression relapse is difficulties in sleeping. The reasons associated with difficulty sleeping may be due to a person fixating on what happened during the day or on what is making them unhappy. Similarly, if a person sleeps more than usual, this is also considered a sign of depression relapse.

Another common sign of depression relapse is experiencing fatigue. If a person is experiencing frequent exhaustion, then it is necessary to seek immediate help.

Social Withdrawal

Social withdrawal can either be avoiding a social experience or being withdrawn or secluded while attending a social gathering. Social withdrawal can influence a person negatively and result in depression relapse.

Weight Changes

Depression usually affects eating habits. It can cause a lack of interest in food, resulting in weight loss. It might cause a lack of interest in eating healthy food and maintaining a good fitness routine, or in overeating, which then causes weight gain.

Treatment of Depression Relapse

The treatments for depression relapse can include medications such as serotonin, norepinephrine, and dopamine. Cognitive-behavioral therapy (CBT) and interpersonal therapy (IPT) may be included in treatment.

If treatment for depression is already in place and being followed when a person experiences relapse, the doctor might look for a change in medication, including an increase in dosage or the addition of other medications.

In addition to these treatments, there are coping strategies that can improve the symptoms of relapse.

- Seeking help from family and friends
- Practicing self-care
- Trying to focus on the positive
- Being active, such as exercising daily
- Getting enough sleep. A minimum of eight hours of sleep is required nightly.

Preventing Depression Relapse

It is always better to prevent depression from reoccurring rather than curing it after it recurs. Some of the best ways to prevent depression relapse are listed below.

- Take all medications as prescribed and follow the treatment plan.

- Continue with counseling even after you stop the medications.

- Always eat healthily and get adequate exercise.

- Visit the doctor immediately when experiencing new depression symptoms.

- Maintain a regular sleep schedule.

- Avoid using illegal drugs or drinking alcohol.

- Build strong relationships.

- Do not stop any medication without discussing this with the doctor first.

The symptoms outlined above could mean a depression relapse. It is necessary to consult with the doctor immediately if any of the symptoms are present.

References

1. Gotter, Ana "15 Ways to Avoid Depression," Healthline, June 2, 2017.

2. Gotter, Ana "Recognizing Depression Relapse: How to Cope," Healthline, May 19, 2017.

3. "Preventing a Relapse of Depression in Teens: After Your Visit," Alberta Health Services (AHS), MyHealth.Alberta.ca, September 30, 2015.

4. "Patient Education: Depression in Children and Adolescents (Beyond the Basics)," UpToDate, February 21, 2018.

Chapter 57

Finding and Choosing a Therapist

Chapter Contents

Section 57.1

Types of Therapists

This section includes text excerpted from "Types of Therapist," National Center for Posttraumatic Stress Disorder (NCPTSD), U.S. Department of Veterans Affairs (VA), October 4, 2018.

There are many types of professionals who provide evidence-based psychotherapy and medication to people who have experienced trauma. The information below reviews the most common types of licensed mental-health providers and generally explains their education, training, and services offered.

Mental-health professionals can have different training, credentials, or licenses. Providers can also offer different services, based upon their expertise. If you are looking for a particular type of treatment (such as medications) or expert focus, the license and specialized training of the mental-health provider is important. Your health insurance provider may also allow you to see only certain types of mental-health providers. Check your policy for details.

Who Is Licensed to Provide Psychotherapy for Posttraumatic Stress Disorder?

The mental-health professionals below provide psychotherapy for posttraumatic stress disorder (PTSD), and in most states, they are not licensed to prescribe medications.

Psychologists

Licensed clinical psychologists focus on mental-health assessment and treatment. They have a doctoral degree (e.g., Ph.D., Psy.D., EdD) from four or more years of graduate training in clinical or counseling psychology. To be licensed to practice, psychologists must have another one to two years of supervised clinical experience. Psychologists have the title of "doctor" because of their doctoral degree, but they cannot prescribe medicine.

Clinical Social Workers

The purpose of social work is to enhance human well-being by helping people meet basic human needs. Licensed social workers also focus on diagnosis and treatment, and specialize in areas, such as mental health, aging, family, and children. Most licensed social workers have a master's degree from two years of graduate training (e.g., MSW) or a doctoral degree in social work (e.g., DSW or Ph.D.).

Master's Level Clinicians

Master's level clinicians have a master's degree in counseling, psychology, or marriage and family therapy (e.g., MA, MFT). To be licensed to provide individual and/or group counseling, master's level clinicians must meet requirements that vary by state.

Who Is Licensed to Provide Medications for Posttraumatic Stress Disorder?

Working with a specialist who commonly sees patients with PTSD is ideal. However, in addition to the mental-health providers listed below, primary care physicians, physician's assistants, and nurse practitioners are usually qualified to prescribe medications for PTSD.

Psychiatrists

Psychiatrists have either a Doctor of Allopathic Medicine (MD) or Doctor of Osteopathic Medicine (DO) degree in addition to specialized training in the diagnosis and treatment of mental-health problems. Since they are medical doctors, psychiatrists can prescribe medicine. Some may also provide psychotherapy.

Psychiatric Nurses or Nurse Practitioners

Psychiatric mental-health nurses (PMHN) can have different levels of training. Most are registered nurses (RN) with additional training in psychiatry or psychology. Psychiatric mental health advanced practice registered nurses (PMH-APRN) have a graduate degree. Psychiatric nurse practitioners are registered nurse practitioners with specialized training in the diagnosis and treatment of mental-health problems. In most states, psychiatric nurses and psychiatric nurse practitioners can prescribe medicine.

Section 57.2

Finding a Therapist

This section includes text excerpted from "Help for Mental Illnesses,"
National Institute of Mental Health (NIMH), August 31, 2019.

If you or someone you know has a mental illness, there are ways to
get help. Use these resources to find help for you, a friend, or a family
member.

Get Immediate Help

If you are in crisis, and need immediate support or intervention,
call, or go the website of the National Suicide Prevention Lifeline
(NSPL) (suicidepreventionlifeline.org) 800-273-TALK (800-273-8255).
Trained crisis workers are available to talk 24 hours a day, 7 days a
week. Your confidential and toll-free call goes to the nearest crisis
center in the Lifeline national network. These centers provide crisis
counseling and mental-health referrals. If the situation is potentially
life-threatening, call 911 or go to a hospital emergency room.

Find a Healthcare Provider or Treatment

For general information on mental health and to locate treatment
services in your area, call the Substance Abuse and Mental Health
Services Administration (SAMHSA) Treatment Referral Helpline at
800-662-HELP (800-662-4357). SAMHSA also has a Behavioral Health
Treatment Locator (findtreatment.samhsa.gov) its website that can be
searched by location.

National agencies and advocacy and professional organizations
have information on finding a mental-health professional and sometimes practitioner locators on their websites. Examples include but
are not limited to:

- Anxiety and Depression Association of America (ADAA)

- Depression and Bipolar Support Alliance (DBSA)

- Mental Health America (MHA)

- National Alliance on Mental Illness (NAMI)

University or medical school-affiliated programs may offer treatment options. Search on the website of local university health centers
for their psychiatry or psychology departments.

You can also go to the website of your state or county government and search for the health services department.

Some federal agencies offer resources for identifying practitioners and assistance in finding low-cost health services. These include:

- **Health Resources and Services Administration (HRSA).** HRSA works to improve access to healthcare. Visit HRSA website (www.hrsa.gov) for more information on finding affordable healthcare, including health centers that offer care on a sliding fee scale.

- **Centers for Medicare & Medicaid Services (CMS).** CMS has information on its website (www.cms.gov) about benefits and eligibility for mental health programs and how to enroll.

- **The U.S. National Library of Medicine (NLM) MedlinePlus.** NLM has directories and lists of organizations that can help in identifying a health practitioner.

- **Mental Health and Addiction Insurance Help.** This agency from the U.S. Department of Health and Human Services (HHS) offers resources to help answer questions about insurance coverage for mental-healthcare.

Chapter 58

Paying for Mental-Healthcare

Chapter Contents

Section 58.1

Finding Low-Cost Mental-Healthcare and Help Paying for Prescriptions

This section contains text excerpted from the following sources: Text beginning with the heading "Does the Affordable Care Act Require Insurance Plans to Cover Mental-Health Benefits?" is excerpted from "Health Insurance and Mental Health Services," MentalHealth.gov, U.S. Department of Health and Human Services (HHS), March 22, 2019; Text under the heading "Advances in Mental-Healthcare" is excerpted from "Recent Advances in Mental Health Care," U.S. Department of Health and Human Services (HHS), January 15, 2019.

Does the Affordable Care Act Require Insurance Plans to Cover Mental-Health Benefits?

As of 2014, most individual and small group health insurance plans, including plans sold on the Marketplace are required to cover mental health and substance-use disorder (SUD) services. Medicaid Alternative Benefit Plans (ABP) also must cover mental health and SUD services. These plans must have coverage of essential health benefits, which include 10 categories of benefits as defined under the healthcare law. One of those categories is mental health and SUD services. Another is rehabilitative and habilitative services. Additionally, these plans must comply with mental health and substance use parity requirements, as set forth in Mental Health Parity and Addiction Equity Act of 2008 (MHPAEA), meaning coverage for mental health and substance-abuse services generally cannot be more restrictive than coverage for medical and surgical services.

How to Find Out If the Health Insurance Plan Is Supposed to Be Covering Mental Health or Substance-Use Disorder Services in Parity with Medical and Surgical Benefits? What to Do If You Think Your Plan Is Not Meeting Parity Requirements?

In general, for those in large employer plans, if mental health or SUD services are offered, they are subject to the parity protections required under MHPAEA. And, as of 2014, for most small employer and individual plans, mental health and SUD services must meet MHPAEA requirements.

If you have questions about your insurance plan, we recommend you first look at your plan's enrollment materials, or any other information you have on the plan, to see what the coverage levels are for all benefits. Because of the Affordable Care Act (ACA), health insurers are required to provide you with an easy-to-understand summary about your benefits including mental-health benefits, which should make it easier to see what your coverage is.

Does Medicaid Cover Mental Health or Substance-Use Disorder Services?

All state Medicaid programs provide some mental-health services and some offer substance use disorder services to beneficiaries, and Children's Health Insurance Program (CHIP) beneficiaries receive a full-service array. These services often include counseling, therapy, medication management, social work services, peer supports, and substance use disorder treatment. While states determine which of these services to cover for adults, Medicaid and CHIP requires that children enrolled in Medicaid receive a wide range of medically necessary services, including mental-health services. In addition, coverage for the new Medicaid adult expansion populations is required to include essential health benefits, including mental health and SUD benefits, and must meet mental health and substance abuse parity requirements under MHPAEA in the same manner as health plans.

Does Medicare Cover Mental Health or Substance-Use Disorder Services?

Medicare covers a wide range of mental-health services.

Medicare Part A (hospital insurance) covers inpatient mental-healthcare services you get in a hospital. Part A covers your room, meals, nursing care, and other related services and supplies.

Medicare Part B (medical insurance) helps cover mental-health services that you would generally get outside of a hospital, including visits with a psychiatrist or other doctor, visits with a clinical psychologist or clinical social worker, and lab tests ordered by your doctor.

Medicare Part D (prescription drug) helps cover drugs you may need to treat a mental-health condition. Each Part D plan has its own list of covered drugs, known as a "formulary."

If you get your Medicare benefits through a Medicare Advantage Plan (such as Health Maintenance Organizations (HMO) or Preferred

Provider Organization (PPO) or other Medicare health plan, check your plan's membership materials or call the plan for details about how to get your mental-health benefits.

What Is Health Insurance Marketplace?

The Health Insurance Marketplace is designed to make buying health coverage easier and more affordable. The Marketplace allows individuals to compare health plans, get answers to questions, find out if they are eligible for tax credits to help pay for private insurance or health programs, such as the CHIP, and enroll in a health plan that meets their needs. The Marketplace Can Help You:

- Look for and compare private health plans.

- Get answers to questions about your health coverage options.

- Get reduced costs, if you are eligible.

- Enroll in a health plan that meets your needs.

Advances in Mental-Healthcare

The Mental Health Parity and Addiction Equity Act (MHPAEA) and the Affordable Care Act (ACA), and the Medicaid expansion in many states have helped improve access to mental-health services for Americans of all ages. Parity, in health-insurance plans, means that mental-health services are covered and reimbursed at the same levels as physical healthcare. Several laws address parity and equity in how health-insurance plans cover mental-health services.

The Mental Health Parity Act and Mental Health Parity and Addiction Equity Act

The Mental Health Parity Act of 1996 (MHPA) prohibited large group health plans from putting annual or lifetime dollar limits on mental-health benefits that are less than those put on medical/surgical benefits. The MHPAEA added new protections, such as requiring that substance use disorders also have comparable coverage. However, MHPAEA does not require health insurance plans to include mental-health disorders and SUDs benefits; its requirements apply only to insurers that include mental health and SUDs in their existing benefit packages.

The Affordable Care Act

The ACA builds on the earlier parity legislation by requiring that most individual and small-employer health insurance plans—including all plans offered through the Health Insurance Marketplace—cover mental health and substance use disorders services. The ACA also requires coverage of rehabilitative services that support people with behavioral health challenges. Together, these protections expand benefits for an estimated 174 million Americans. Because of the ACA, most health plans must now cover preventive services (e.g., depression screening for adults and behavioral assessments for children) at no additional cost. Most health plans cannot deny coverage, or charge more, for preexisting health conditions, including mental illnesses.

Finally, under the ACA, participants can now add or keep their children on their health insurance policy until they turn 26. Children can join or remain on a parent's plan, even if they are married, live separately from their parents, or are financially independent. In addition, those who are attending a school or are eligible to enroll in their employer's plan can still be on their parent's health-insurance policy. Upon turning 26, children do not have to wait for a plan's open enrollment period but can sign up at any time.

Medicaid

All states provide some mental health/substance use disorders services to children who receive Medicaid. In addition, the CHIP, which works with Medicaid for eligible children, provides a variety of services including counseling, therapy, medication management, social work services, peer supports, and substance use disorder treatment. In all states, eligible children through age 18 can be covered by Medicaid and/or CHIP, and they can enroll at any time.

In addition, states can agree to a Medicaid expansion that provides coverage for eligible individuals under age 65. As of July 1, 2016, 31 states and the District of Columbia (DC) have done so. The Medicaid expansion includes benefits for people with mental health and SUDs, and coverage must meet the same parity requirements required under MHPAEA for other health plans.

Section 58.2

Medicare and Your Mental-Healthcare Benefits

This section includes text excerpted from "Medicare and Your Mental Health Benefits," Centers for Medicare & Medicaid Services (CMS), January 9, 2019.

Mental-Healthcare and Medicare

Mental-health conditions, such as depression or anxiety, can happen to anyone at any time. If you think you may have problems that affect your mental health, you can get help. Talk to your doctor or other healthcare providers if you have:

- Thoughts of ending your life (such as a fixation on death or suicidal thoughts or attempts)
- Sad, empty, or hopeless feelings
- Loss of self-worth (such as worries about being a burden, feelings of worthlessness, or self-loathing)
- Social withdrawal and isolation (such as you do not want to be with friends, engage in activities, or leave home)
- Little interest in things you used to enjoy
- A lack of energy
- Trouble concentrating
- Trouble sleeping (such as difficulty falling asleep or staying asleep, oversleeping, or daytime sleepiness)
- Weight loss or loss of appetite
- Increased use of alcohol or other drugs

Mental-healthcare includes services and programs to help diagnose and treat mental-health conditions. These services and programs may be provided in outpatient and inpatient settings. Medicare helps cover outpatient and inpatient mental-healthcare, as well as prescription drugs you may need to treat a mental-health condition.

Medicare Helps Cover Mental-Health Services

Medicare Part A (hospital insurance) helps cover mental-healthcare if you are a hospital inpatient. Part A covers your:

408

- Room

- Meals

- Nursing care

- Therapy or other treatment for your condition

- Lab tests

- Medications

- Other related services and supplies

Medicare Part B (medical insurance) helps cover mental-health services that you would get from a doctor and services that you generally get outside of a hospital, such as:

- Visits with a psychiatrist or other doctor

- Visits with a clinical psychologist or clinical social worker

- Lab tests ordered by your doctor

Part B may also pay for partial hospitalization services if you need intensive coordinated outpatient care.

Medicare prescription drug coverage (Part D) helps cover drugs you may need to treat a mental-health condition.

Outpatient Mental-Healthcare and Professional Services
What Original Medicare Covers

Medicare Part B (medical insurance) helps cover mental-health services and visits with these types of health professionals (deductibles and coinsurance may apply):

- Psychiatrist or other doctors

- Clinical psychologist

- Clinical social worker

- Clinical nurse specialist

- Nurse practitioner

- Physician assistant

Psychiatrists and other doctors must accept an assignment if they participate in Medicare. Ask your doctor or psychiatrist if they accept the assignment before you schedule an appointment. The other health professionals listed above must always accept the assignment.

Part B covers outpatient mental-health services, including services that are usually provided outside a hospital (such as in a clinic, doctor's office, or therapist's office) and services provided in a hospital's outpatient department. Part B also covers outpatient mental-health services for the treatment of inappropriate alcohol and drug use. Part B helps pay for these covered outpatient services (deductibles and coinsurance may apply):

- One depression screening per year. The screening must be done in a primary care doctor's office or primary care clinic that can provide follow-up treatment and referrals. You pay nothing for your yearly depression screening if your doctor or healthcare provider accepts an assignment.

- Individual and group psychotherapy with doctors or certain other licensed professionals allowed by the state where you get the services

- Family counseling, if the main purpose is to help with your treatment

- Testing to find out if you are getting the services you need and if your current treatment is helping you

- Psychiatric evaluation

- Medication management

- Certain prescription drugs that are not usually "self-administered" (drugs you would normally take on your own), such as some injections

- Diagnostic tests

- Partial hospitalization

- A one-time "Welcome to Medicare" preventive visit. This visit includes a review of your potential risk factors for depression. You pay nothing for this visit if your doctor or other healthcare provider accepts an assignment.

- A yearly "Wellness" visit. Medicare covers a yearly "Wellness" visit once every 12 months (if you have had Part B for longer than 12 months). This is a good time to talk to your doctor or other healthcare providers about changes in your mental health so they can evaluate your changes year to year. You pay nothing for your yearly "Wellness" visit if your doctor or other healthcare provider accepts an assignment.

What You Pay

In general, after you pay your yearly Part B deductible for visits to a doctor or other healthcare provider to diagnose or treat your condition, you pay 20 percent of the Medicare-approved amount if your healthcare provider accepts an assignment. If you get your services in a hospital outpatient clinic or hospital outpatient department, you may have to pay an additional copayment or coinsurance amount to the hospital.

If you have a Medicare Supplement Insurance (Medigap) policy or other health coverage, tell your doctor or other healthcare providers so your bills get paid correctly.

Medicare May Cover Partial Hospitalization

Part B covers partial hospitalization in some cases. Partial hospitalization is a structured program of outpatient psychiatric services provided to patients as an alternative to inpatient psychiatric care. It is more intense than the care you get in a doctor's or therapist's office. This type of treatment is provided during the day and does not require an overnight stay.

Medicare helps cover partial hospitalization services when they are provided through a hospital outpatient department or community mental-health center. As part of your partial hospitalization program, Medicare may cover occupational therapy that is part of your mental-health treatment and/or individual patient training and education about your condition.

For Medicare to cover a partial hospitalization program, you must meet certain requirements, and your doctor must certify that you would otherwise need inpatient treatment. Your doctor and the partial hospitalization program must accept Medicare payment.

What You Pay

You pay a percentage of the Medicare-approved amount for each service you get from a doctor or certain other qualified mental-health professionals if your healthcare professional accepts an assignment. You also pay coinsurance for each day of partial hospitalization services provided in a hospital outpatient setting or community mental-health center.

What Original Medicare Does Not Cover

- Meals.

- Transportation to or from mental-healthcare services.

- Support groups that bring people together to talk and socialize.

- Testing or training for job skills that are not part of your mental-health treatment.

Inpatient Mental-Healthcare
What Original Medicare Covers

Medicare Part A (Hospital Insurance) helps pay for mental-health services you get in a hospital that require you to be admitted as an inpatient. You can get these services either in a general hospital or in a psychiatric hospital that only cares for people with mental-health conditions. No matter which type of hospital you choose, Part A will help cover inpatient mental-health services.

If you are in a psychiatric hospital (instead of a general hospital), Part A only pays for up to 190 days of inpatient psychiatric hospital services during your lifetime.

What You Pay

Medicare measures your use of hospital services (including services you get in a psychiatric hospital) in benefit periods. A benefit period begins the day you are admitted as an inpatient in a general or psychiatric hospital. The benefit period ends after you have not had any inpatient hospital care for 60 days in a row. If you go into a hospital again after 60 days, a new benefit period begins, and you must pay a new deductible for any inpatient hospital services you get.

There is no limit to the number of benefit periods you can have when you get mental-healthcare in a general hospital. You can also have multiple benefit periods when you get care in a psychiatric hospital, but there is a lifetime limit of 190 days.

As a hospital inpatient, you pay these amounts in 2017:

Part B also helps cover mental-health services provided by doctors and other healthcare professionals if you are admitted as a hospital inpatient. You pay 20 percent of the Medicare-approved amount for these mental-health services while you are a hospital inpatient.

If you have a Medicare Supplement Insurance (Medigap) policy or other health coverage, tell your doctor or other healthcare providers so your bills get paid correctly.

What Original Medicare Does Not Cover

- Private duty nursing

- Phone or television in your room

- Personal items (such as toothpaste, socks, or razors)

- A private room (unless medically necessary)

Medicare Prescription Drug Coverage (Part D)

To get Medicare prescription drug coverage, you must join a Medicare prescription drug plan. Medicare drug plans are run by insurance companies and other private companies approved by medicare. Each Medicare drug plan can vary in cost and in the specific drugs it covers. It is important to know your plan's coverage rules and your rights.

Medicare Drug Plans Have Special Rules
Will My Plan Cover the Drugs I Need?

Most Medicare drug plans have a list of drugs that the plan covers, called a "formulary." Medicare drug plans are not required to cover all drugs, but they are required to cover all (with limited exceptions) antidepressant, anticonvulsant, and antipsychotic medications, which you may need to keep you mentally healthy. Medicare reviews each plan's formulary to make sure it contains a wide range of drugs and that it does not discriminate against certain groups (such as people with disabilities or mental-health conditions).

Can My Drug Plan's Formulary Change?

A Medicare drug plan can make some changes to its formulary during the year within guidelines set by Medicare. If the change involves a drug you are currently taking, your plan must do one of these:

Provide written notice to you at least 60 days prior to the date the change becomes effective.

413

At the time you ask for a refill, provide written notice of the change and a 60-day supply of the drug under the same plan rules as before the change.

What If My Prescriber Thinks I Need a Certain Drug That My Plan Does Not Cover?

If you belong to a Medicare drug plan, you have the right to ask for a coverage determination (including an exception). You can appoint a representative to help you. Your representative can be a family member, friend, advocate, attorney, doctor, or someone else you trust who will act on your behalf. You, your representative, or your doctor or other prescribers must contact your plan to ask for a coverage determination.

Your Medicare Rights

No matter how you get Medicare, you generally have certain rights and protections. All people with Medicare have the right to:

- Be treated with dignity and respect at all times.
- Be protected from discrimination.
- Have their personal and health information kept private.
- Get a decision about healthcare payment, coverage of services, or prescription drug coverage.

Your Medicare Appeal Rights

An appeal is an action you can take if you disagree with a coverage or payment decision by Medicare, your Medicare health plan, or your Medicare Prescription Drug Plan. If you decide to file an appeal, ask your doctor, healthcare provider, or supplier for any information that may help your case. Keep a copy of everything you send to Medicare or your plan as part of the appeal.

Part Seven

Strategies for Managing Depression

Chapter 59

Understanding Mental Illness Stigma and Depression Triggers

Chapter Contents

417

Section 59.1

Perception and Attitude toward Mental Illness

This section includes text excerpted from "Attitudes toward Mental
Illness: Results from the Behavioral Risk Factor Surveillance
System," Centers for Disease Control and Prevention
(CDC), 2012. Reviewed October 2019.

Stigmas about Mental Illness Contribute to Depression

People's beliefs and attitudes toward mental illness set the stage
for how they interact with, provide opportunities for, and help support
a person with mental illness. People's beliefs and attitudes toward
mental illness also frame how they experience and express their own
emotional problems and psychological distress and whether they disclose these symptoms and seek care. About one in four U.S. adults
(26.2%) age 18 and older, in any given year, has a mental disorder
(e.g., mood disorder, anxiety disorder, impulse control disorder, or
substance-abuse disorder), meaning that mental disorders are common and can affect anyone. Many adults with common chronic conditions, such as arthritis, cancer, diabetes, heart disease, and epilepsy
experience concurrent depression and anxiety—further complicating
self-management of these disorders and adversely affecting the quality
of life.

Attitudes and beliefs about mental illness are shaped by personal
knowledge about mental illness, knowing and interacting with someone
living with mental illness, cultural stereotypes about mental illness,
media stories, and familiarity with institutional practices and past
restrictions. When such attitudes and beliefs are expressed positively,
they can result in supportive and inclusive behaviors (e.g., willingness
to date a person with mental illness or to hire a person with mental
illness). When such attitudes and beliefs are expressed negatively,
they may result in avoidance, exclusion from daily activities, and, in
the worst case, exploitation and discrimination.

Stigma has been described as a cluster of negative attitudes and
beliefs that motivate the general public to fear, reject, avoid, and discriminate against people with mental illnesses. When stigma leads to
social exclusion or discrimination ("experienced" stigma), it results in
unequal access to resources that all people need to function well: educational opportunities, employment, a supportive community, including

friends and family, and access to quality healthcare. These types of disparities in education, employment, and access to care can have cumulative long-term negative consequences.

For example, a young adult with untreated mental illness who is unable to graduate from high school is less likely to find a good-paying job that can support her or his basic needs, including access to healthcare. These disadvantages can cause a person to experience more negative outcomes. Being unemployed, living at or below the poverty line, being socially isolated, and living with other social disadvantages can further deflate self-esteem, compounding mental illness symptoms, and add to the burden of stigma. Sometimes stigma is simply felt in the absence of being discriminated against and results from internalizing perceived negative attitudes associated with a characteristic (e.g., age), a disorder (e.g., Human immunodeficiency virus-Acquired immunodeficiency syndrome (HIV-AIDS)), a behavior (e.g., smoking), or other factors (e.g., place of birth).

Whether stigma is experienced as social exclusion or discrimination or felt as a pervasive and underlying sense of being different from others, it can be debilitating for people and poses a challenge for public health prevention efforts. Different opinions exist regarding the implications of different labels associated with describing mental illness (e.g., brain disease) and felt or experienced stigma. However, the prevailing view of health-related stigma is that it refers to perceived, enacted, or anticipated avoidance or social exclusion, and not to an individual blemish or mark. Different methods exist for measuring health-related stigma, and challenges and limitations associated with distinguishing between felt versus experienced stigma in attitudinal research have been described.

What Are the Consequences of Negative Attitudes toward Mental Illness and Stigma?

Only about 20 percent of adults with a diagnosable mental disorder or with a self-reported mental-health condition saw a mental-health provider in the previous year. The embarrassment associated with accessing mental-health services is one of the many barriers that cause people to hide their symptoms and to prevent them from getting the necessary treatment for their mental illness symptoms. Stigma poses a barrier for public health primary prevention efforts designed to minimize the onset of mental illness, as well as with secondary prevention efforts aimed at promoting early treatment to prevent worsening of symptoms over time.

Stigma can also interfere with the self-management of mental disorders (tertiary prevention). Untreated symptoms can have grave consequences for people living with mental illness and negatively impact families affected by these disorders. For example, most people with serious and persistent mental illness (mental disorders that interfere with some area of social functioning) are unemployed and live below the poverty line, and many face major barriers to obtaining decent, affordable housing. These individuals may need a number of additional social supports (e.g., job training, peer-support networks) to live successfully in the community, but such support may not be available. Other individuals with depression and anxiety might avoid disclosing their symptoms and instead adopt unhealthy behaviors to help them cope with their distress (e.g., smoking, excessive alcohol use, binge-eating). These behaviors can increase their risk for developing chronic diseases, worsening their overall health over time. Studies have found an increased risk of death at younger ages for people with mental illness.

Attitudes toward mental illness can also influence how policymakers allocate public resources to mental-health services, pose challenges for staff retention in mental-health settings, result in poorer quality of medical care administered to people with mental illness, and create fundraising challenges for organizations who serve people with mental illness and their families. State-level factors such as unemployment levels and access to mental-health services and the presence or absence of other state resources may affect public attitudes and merit study.

Why Is It Important to Track Attitudes toward Mental Illness?

People's attitudes and beliefs predict their behavior. People's beliefs and attitudes about mental illness might predict whether they disclose their symptoms and seek treatment and support. Knowledge and beliefs that can aid in the recognition, management, or prevention of mental-health disorders are defined as mental-health literacy. Tracking attitudes toward mental illness can serve as an indicator of the public's mental-health literacy. For example, in a 1996 study, 54 percent of the U.S. public attributed major depression to neurobiological causes, and this increased to 67 percent in 2006. Similarly, a larger percentage of people endorsed the benefits of treatment by a physician for people with major depression in 2006 (91%) than in 1996 (78%). However, improvements in neurobiological understanding of mental illness were unrelated to negative attitudes and, in some cases, increased the odds of negative attitudes (e.g., need for social distance, perceived dangerousness). In another study of U.S. adults, only about one fourth agreed that people are caring and sympathetic to people with mental illness. When asked about how much it would be worth to avoid mental illness compared to general medical illnesses, the public was less willing to pay to avoid mental-health treatment than they were to pay to avoid physical health treatment. These studies provide important snapshots of attitudes toward mental illness across the country; however, studies that examine attitudes in-depth, such as distinguishing between attitudes relative to perceived or experienced stigma, studies that link attitudes to actual behavior, or studies that track attitudes toward mental illness at the state level do not occur routinely. These limited, cross-sectional studies tell us little about how attitudes shift in relation to historical events (e.g., media over-sensationalization of the rare violence associated with a person with mental illness), how attitudes shift over time in the same people, and how these attitudes differ within a state relative to characteristics of the state, such as the average unemployment rate or per capita expenditures on state mental-health agencies.

Section 59.2

Depression Triggers: How to Prevent Them

"Depression Triggers and How to Avoid Them," © 2017 Omnigraphics. Reviewed October 2019.

Depression affects between 15 and 20 million Americans each year. It is a medical condition that should be taken seriously. Some forms of depression are related to malfunctions in brain circuits that transmit signal-carrying chemicals called "neurotransmitters," which help regulate mood. Although these cases may not be preventable, they often respond well to treatment. However, studies suggest that it may be possible to prevent some depressive episodes by learning to recognize and avoid common situations that serve as depression triggers.

Potential environmental triggers include stressful life events, such as divorce or job loss, as well as unexpected factors that can impact emotional well-being, such as being a caregiver or spending too much time on social media. The following list describes situations that have been shown to correlate with depression and offers tips for how to avoid or cope with them.

Stress

Nearly 25 percent of American adults reported feeling "extreme stress" in 2015, according to the American Psychological Association (APA), ranking their overall stress levels above 5 on a 10-point scale. Some of the main sources of stress included economic worries, job security, family responsibilities, health concerns, and discrimination or harassment. Many other people simply feel overwhelmed by daily chores, obligations, and deadlines that seem to get in the way of their enjoyment of life. To prevent stress from turning into depression, experts recommend keeping a positive attitude, recognizing your own limits, and setting and enforcing personal boundaries. When tasks seem overwhelming, breaking them down into steps may make them seem more manageable. Finally, building an emotional support network, discussing problems and concerns, and leaning on others for help as needed are important means of coping with stress.

Job Loss

Losing a job can cause a serious blow to a person's sense of identity and self-esteem, especially for older and highly paid workers who are likely to have more trouble finding equivalent positions. People who are fired or laid off may feel rejected, frightened, and uncertain about the future. In addition, unemployment often causes financial difficulties, which in turn can create strain in family relationships. The combination of these factors means that job loss is a leading trigger for depression. Experts recommend that people affected by job loss build a support network consisting of friends and colleagues, and take advantage of career-related courses and job-search resources. It is also important to stay busy and connected, structuring free time by scheduling lunches, walks, classes, or volunteer activities. Finally, after taking time to process the emotional impact of job loss, it may be helpful to identify its positive aspects. For instance, losing a job might offer an unexpected opportunity to make a career change, pursue a new business idea, or move to a different geographic area.

Financial Problems

Money concerns and accumulated debts are a source of stress and worry for many people, especially those who feel as if they are struggling with financial problems alone. Common emotions associated with financial stress—such as shame, fear, anxiety, uncertainty—can negatively impact self-esteem and trigger depression. Research has shown that one of the key methods of combating financial stress involves formulating a plan and taking positive action. Reviewing sources of income and expenses and establishing a budget are important first steps toward increasing financial stability. People who are not good with money can take advantage of free financial services offered by many communities or borrow books on financial management from a local library. To avoid becoming overwhelmed, experts recommend focusing on areas you can control and creating a long-term plan to pay down debt and build savings. Finally, it is important to remain active and stay connected to friends and family by enjoying free activities, such as a concert in a park.

Divorce

Divorce creates a complicated mix of emotions for those affected by it, including anger, resentment, sadness, regret, guilt, and failure. It also causes a sudden change in social status from couple to single, which can generate feelings of loneliness, fear, and uncertainty. Finally, many divorces involve a stressful conflict over financial settlements and custody of children. Taken together, the emotional upheaval of divorce becomes a potent depression trigger. Therapy—whether individual, couples, family, or support groups—can help people navigate the complicated emotions of divorce and move forward with greater confidence. It can also help resolve conflicts, reduce bitterness, and promote effective coparenting.

Sexual Dysfunction

Active sex life is a proven outlet that helps relieve stress and improve mood. In addition, sexual performance is intricately tied to self-esteem and identity, especially for men. As a result, sexual dysfunction, loss of libido, and sexual health issues can trigger depression. These issues can arise due to age, underlying health problems, or even as side effects of common antidepressant medications, such as selective serotonin reuptake inhibitors (SSRIs). To address sexual problems that

423

may trigger depression, see a healthcare professional for a complete medical examination. Although discussing sex is uncomfortable for many people, it is important not to allow shame or embarrassment to prevent you from getting help. Studies have shown that satisfying sex life can improve relationships as well as release chemicals in the brain that improve mood.

Infertility

The inability to have a much-desired baby is a powerful depression trigger, especially for women who suffer multiple miscarriages or have age or health-related fertility issues. Experts suggest that people who feel despair over infertility try to take charge of the situation by investigating alternative routes to parenthood, such as adoption. Single women whose fertility window is closing due to age or health might explore such options as preserving eggs or using a sperm donor. Even if you ultimately decide not to pursue the matter, simply researching the steps involved can make you feel less vulnerable and more empowered.

Caregiving

Serving as a caregiver for a person who is elderly or afflicted with a debilitating illness is another potential depression trigger. Caregiving demands tremendous time and energy creates stress and depletes emotional resources. Oftentimes caregivers struggle with conflicting emotions, such as love, concern, and compassion coupled with resentment, guilt, and inadequacy. People who must manage multiple responsibilities, such as job and family pressures, along with caregiving are most at risk for stress and depression. Experts recommend that caregivers establish firm boundaries around how much they can handle and ask for help as needed. In addition, it is vital for caregivers to build a support system, delegate or outsource some tasks, arrange for occasional breaks to replenish their reserves of energy and compassion, and take care of their own health and well-being.

"Empty Nest" Syndrome

Although a child leaving home to begin college or adult life can be a joyous event, it is also a major life change for parents who suddenly must face an empty nest. Many parents struggle with feelings of loss and uncertainty as they adjust to a new daily routine and a different self-identity. Divorced or single parents are particularly vulnerable to loneliness and depression, although it also affects married couples who built their lives around their children and suddenly find that they do not share many common interests. Experts suggest that parents plan in advance to help reduce the emotional impact of empty nest syndrome. Beginning a year or more before the child leaves home, it may be helpful to sign up for a class, join a book group, plan a vacation, or schedule regular activities with friends. Although taking time to adjust is normal, the key to avoiding depression is to remain active, discover new interests, and have things to look forward to outside of the parental role.

Serious Illness

Being diagnosed with a serious illness is a frightening and disorienting experience that can profoundly affect a person's sense of self and outlook for the future. While the physical symptoms can be difficult enough to deal with, the emotional impact can shake the foundations of relationships and trigger depression. One of the most important steps in coping with a serious illness diagnosis is taking a proactive role in establishing a treatment plan. Patients should seek second opinions, ask for referrals to specialists, and build an effective team that includes a patient advocate or social worker as well as doctors. Experts also recommend joining a support group to gain access to the insights and understanding of people who have dealt with the same illness or condition.

Alcohol Abuse

Research has shown that alcoholism and depression are intricately linked. Although many people use alcohol as a way of relaxing and forgetting their troubles, it actually serves as a depressant on the central nervous system. As a result, using alcohol to cope with depression symptoms only makes them worse. Depression can promote alcohol abuse in people who are susceptible to it, while alcohol abuse can trigger depression in people who are prone to it. In fact, studies have shown that up to 50 percent of alcoholics suffer from major depression. The only way to break the connection is to cut back on drinking and see whether depression symptoms improve over time. People who hide or deny their drinking, repeatedly try and fail to quit drinking or find that their drinking has negative effects on their lives may need to seek help for alcohol addiction. Treatment options range from Alcoholics

Anonymous (AA) to residential treatment programs and inpatient medical detoxification.

Hormone Imbalance

As people age, they experience fluctuation and decline in the levels of key hormones in the bloodstream. This natural process can cause a number of unpleasant symptoms, including fatigue, weight gain, hot flashes, low libido, anxiety, and depression. While the experiences of women undergoing menopause receive the most attention, men also go through midlife hormonal changes that can affect mood, energy, and sexual performance. Experts suggest that people age 45 and older keep a record of their symptoms and discuss them with a doctor. Hormonal imbalances can often be stabilized with hormone supplementation or replacement therapy. Some people also find that vitamins, herbal remedies, and stress-management techniques such as meditation and yoga can help combat mood swings associated with hormone fluctuations. Treating underlying conditions such as thyroid disorders can also help regulate hormone levels and reduce the risk of depression.

Unhealthy Habits

Obesity, an unhealthy diet full of refined carbohydrates, and poor sleep habits can also trigger depression. Fortunately, these triggers are among the easiest to avoid. Experts recommend evaluating your lifestyle and making gradual, long-term changes to improve your overall health and well-being. They warn against fad diets and instead suggest a diet that emphasizes fresh fruits and vegetables, whole grains, lean proteins, healthy fats, and drinking plenty of water. Consuming foods high in saturated fat or sugar—such as chips, cookies, white bread, and soda—has been shown to increase the risk of depressive episodes, so these should be avoided. In addition, experts recommend increasing physical fitness by walking or doing other activities to help maintain a healthy weight, improve mood, and stave off depression. Exercise also helps improve sleep, which is another aspect of general health that correlates to depression. Studies have shown that people who get the recommended six to eight hours of sleep per night are less likely to experience depression than those who receive more or less than the recommended amount. Some tips for improving sleep include maintaining a consistent schedule, avoiding the use of electronics in the bedroom, creating a calm, relaxing sleep environment, and employing techniques such as reading or meditation to wind down after a busy day.

News and Social Media

Smartphones and other mobile devices make it easier to keep connected and up to date than ever before. Yet studies have shown that excessive consumption of bad news—which outweighs coverage of good news by a 17 to 1 margin in the modern media—can trigger anxiety and depression. Similarly, obsessive checking of social media like Facebook, where others tend to highlight only the best aspects of their lives, can create feelings of envy, loneliness, frustration, and guilt that can trigger or worsen depression symptoms. To reduce the impact of news and social media on mood, experts suggest spending less time online and more time socializing in real life with friends and family. Spending time talking with people who care has been shown to improve mood and increase life satisfaction.

References

1. Brabaw, Kasandra. "Five Strange, Surprising Depression Triggers," Prevention, October 26, 2015.

2. Haiken, Melanie. "Ten Biggest Depression Triggers, and How to Turn Them Off," Caring.com, September 5, 2016.

3. Theobald, Mikel. "Avoiding Ten Common Depression Triggers," EverydayHealth, 2016.

Chapter 60

Well-Being Concepts

Chapter Contents

Section 60.1

Well-Being and Satisfaction with Life

This section includes text excerpted from "Well-Being Concepts,"
Centers for Disease Control and Prevention (CDC), October 31, 2018.

Well-being is a positive outcome that is meaningful for people and
for many sectors of society because it helps people perceive that their
lives are going well. Good living conditions (e.g., housing, employment)
are fundamental to well-being. Tracking these conditions is important
for public policy. However, many indicators that measure living conditions fail to measure what people think and feel about their lives,
such as the quality of their relationships, their positive emotions, and
resilience, the realization of their potential, or their overall satisfaction
with life i.e., their "well-being." Well-being generally includes global
judgments of life satisfaction and feelings ranging from depression
to joy.

Why Is Well-Being Useful for Public Health?

Well-being integrates mental health (mind) and physical health
(body) resulting in holistic approaches to disease prevention and health
promotion. Well-being is a valid population outcome measure beyond
morbidity, mortality, and economic status that tells how people perceive their life is going from their own perspective. Well-being is an
outcome that is meaningful to the public. Advances in psychology,
neuroscience, and measurement theory suggest that well-being can
be measured with some degree of accuracy. Results from studies find
that well-being is associated with:

- Self-perceived health

- Longevity

- Healthy behaviors

- Mental and physical illness

- Social connectedness

- Productivity

- Factors in the physical and social environment

Well-being is associated with numerous health, job, family, and
economically-related benefits. For example, higher levels of well-being

are associated with decreased risk of disease, illness, and injury; better immune functioning; speedier recovery; and increased longevity. Individuals with high levels of well-being are more productive at work and are more likely to contribute to their communities.

How Does Well-Being Relate to Health Promotion?

Health is more than the absence of disease; it is a resource that allows people to realize their aspirations, satisfy their needs and to cope with the environment in order to live a long, productive, and fruitful life. In this sense, health enables social, economic and personal development fundamental to well-being. Health promotion is the process of enabling people to increase control over and to improve their health.

Environmental and social resources for health can include:

- Peace
- Economic security
- A stable ecosystem and
- Safe housing

Individual resources for health can include:

- Physical activity
- Healthful diet
- Social ties
- Resiliency
- Positive emotions and
- Autonomy

Health promotion activities aimed at strengthening such individual, environmental, and social resources may ultimately improve well-being.

How Is Well-Being Defined?

Well-being includes the presence of positive emotions and moods (e.g., contentment, happiness), the absence of negative emotions (e.g., depression, anxiety), satisfaction with life, fulfillment and positive functioning. In simple terms, well-being can be described as judging life positively and feeling good. For public health purposes, physical well-being (e.g., feeling very healthy and full of energy) is also viewed as critical to overall well-being.

Different aspects of well-being are:

- Physical well-being

- Economic well-being

- Social well-being

- Development and activity

- Emotional well-being

- Psychological well-being

- Life satisfaction

- Domain-specific satisfaction

- Engaging activities and work

Section 60.2

Self-Management

This section includes text excerpted from "Depression,"
U.S. Department of Veterans Affairs (VA),
September 13, 2010. Reviewed October 2019.

It can often take a few weeks before you feel an improvement from counseling or medications. In the meantime, there are a number of things you can do to help yourself.

Twelve activities that can help your depression, such as:

- **Engage in fun physical activities and exercise.** Regular exercise can improve your mood. Even taking a short walk every day may help you feel a little better.

- **Make time for activities you enjoy.** Even though you may not feel as motivated or happy as you used to, commit to scheduling a fun activity (such as a favorite hobby) at least a few times a week.

- **Spend time with people who can support you.** It is easy to avoid contact with people when you are feeling down. But, it is during these times that you actually need the support of friends and family. Try explaining to them what you are feeling. If you do not feel comfortable talking about it, that is all right. Just asking them to be with you, maybe during an activity, is a good first step. Suggestions: Meet a friend for coffee or to play cards, take a walk with a neighbor, or work in the garden with your spouse.

- **Practice relaxation.** For many people, the changes that come with depression can be stressful. Since physical relaxation can lead to mental relaxation, try deep breathing; taking a hot shower; or just finding a quiet, comfortable, and peaceful place. Say comforting things to yourself such as, "It is going to get better."

- **Pace yourself.** Set simple goals and take small steps. It is easy to feel overwhelmed by problems and decisions, and it can be hard to deal with them when you are feeling sad, have little energy, or are not thinking as clearly as usual. Some problems and decisions can be delayed, but others cannot. Try breaking down a large problem into smaller ones and then taking one small step at a time to solve it. Give yourself credit for each step you take.

- **Avoid making major life decisions while feeling depressed.** Major decisions might include changing jobs, making a financial investment, moving, divorcing, or making a major purchase. If you feel you must make a major decision about your life, ask your care provider or someone you trust to help you.

- **Eat nutritious, balanced meals.** Many people find that when they eat more nutritious, balanced meals, they not only feel better physically but also emotionally and mentally. To learn about choosing healthy foods, talk with a Nutritionist. Avoid using alcohol and drugs of abuse. Alcohol is a depressant and can add to feeling down and alone. It can also interfere with the help you may receive from antidepressant medication.

- **Develop healthy sleep habits.** Sleep problems are common for those with depression. Getting enough sleep can help you feel better and more energetic.

- **Follow your care provider's instructions about your treatment and communicate openly.** It is very important to take your medicine as prescribed each day and to keep your appointments with your provider, even when you begin to feel better. Ask your provider if you have any questions or concerns about your treatment. Tell your provider about your feelings, activities, sleep and eating patterns, unusual symptoms, or physical problems.

- **Tell someone if you are thinking about death or hurting yourself Thoughts of death may accompany depression.** Always discuss this symptom with your care provider. If you are thinking about hurting yourself, tell your provider or a trusted friend, your spouse, or a relative who can get you immediate emergency professional help.

- **Remain hopeful—depression is treatable.** With treatment, most people with depression can begin to feel better, but it may take some time. Remember that negative thinking (blaming yourself, feeling hopeless, expecting failure, and other similar thoughts) is part of depression. As the depression lifts, negative thinking will also lift.

You do not have to do all of these things right away! Start slowly and take small steps on your way to feeling better. Work with your provider(s) to select the activities that fit your own situation, lifestyle, and needs.

Chapter 61

Building Resilience

Chapter Contents

Section 61.1

Understanding Resilience

This section includes text excerpted from "Individual Resilience," Office of the Assistant Secretary for Preparedness and Response (ASPR), U.S. Department of Health and Human Services (HHS), January 29, 2018.

What Is Individual Resilience?

Individual resilience involves behaviors, thoughts, and actions that promote personal wellbeing and mental health. People can develop the ability to withstand, adapt to, and recover from stress and adversity—and maintain or return to a state of mental health well-being—by using effective coping strategies. We call this individual resilience.

A disaster can impair resilience due to stress, traumatic exposure, distressing psychological reactions, and disrupted social networks. Feelings of grief, sadness, and a range of other emotions are common after traumatic events. Resilient individuals, however, are able to work through the emotions and effects of stress and painful events and rebuild their lives.

What Contributes to Individual Resilience

People develop resilience by learning better skills and strategies for managing stress and better ways of thinking about life's challenges. To be resilient one must tap into personal strengths and the support of family, friends, neighbors, and/or faith communities.

What Are the Characteristics That Support Individual Resilience?

Age, gender, health, biology, education level, cultural beliefs and traditions, and economic resources can play important roles in psychological resilience. The following characteristics also contribute to individual resilience:

- **Social support and close relationships with family and friends.** People who have close social support and strong connections with family and friends are able to get help during tough times and also enjoy their relationships during everyday life.

- **The ability to manage strong feelings and impulses.** People who are able to manage strong emotions are less likely to get overwhelmed, frustrated, or aggressive. People who are able to manage feelings can still feel sadness or loss, but they are also able to find healthy ways to cope and heal.

- **Good problem-solving skills.** People problem-solve daily. Thinking, planning, and solving problems in an organized way are important skills. Problem-solving skills contribute to feelings of independence and self-competence.

- **Feeling in control.** People problem-solve daily. Thinking, planning, and solving problems in an organized way are important skills. Problem-solving skills contribute to feelings of independence and self-competence.

- **Asking for help and seeking resources.** Resourceful people will get needed help more quickly if they know how to ask questions, are creative in their thinking about situations, are good problem solvers and communicators, and have a good social network to reach out to.

- **Seeing yourself as resilient.** After a disaster, many people may feel helpless and powerless, especially when there has been vast damage to the community. Being able to see yourself as resilient, rather than as helpless or as a victim, can help build psychological resilience.

- **Coping with stress in healthy ways.** People get feelings of pleasure and self-worth from doing things well. Strategies that use positive and meaningful ways to cope are better than those which can be harmful, such as drinking too much or smoking.

- **Helping others and finding positive meaning in life.** Positive emotions such as gratitude, joy, kindness, love, and contentment can come from helping others. Acts of generosity can add meaning and purpose to your life, even in the face of tragedy.

What Resilient Individuals Are Able to Do

- Care for themselves and others day-to-day and during emergency situations.

- Actively support their neighborhoods, workplaces, and communities to recover after a disaster.

- Be confident and hopeful about overcoming present and future difficulties.

- Get needed resources more effectively and quickly.

- Be physically and mentally healthier and have overall lower recovery expenses and service needs.

- Miss fewer days of work

- Maintain stable family and social connections.

- Reestablish routines more quickly, which helps children and adults alike.

Ways to Strengthen Resilience

You can build your resilience by taking care of your health, managing stress, and being an active participant in the life of your community. For example, try to:

- Develop coping skills and practice stress management activities, such as yoga, exercise, and meditation.

- Healthy eating and exercise.

- Get plenty of sleep.

- Maintain social connections to people and groups that are meaningful for you.

- Volunteer in your community.

- Get training in first aid, cardiopulmonary resuscitation (CPR), Computer Emergency Response Team (CERT), and psychological first aid.

- Create evacuation and family reunification plans.

- Make a disaster kit and stock supplies to shelter in place for up to three days.

- Find things that bring you pleasure and enjoyment such as reading a book or watching a movie, writing in a journal, or engaging in an art activity.

Does Individual Resilience Help Build Community Resilience?

Yes! Individual resilience is important to community resilience in that healthy people make for a healthier community. Healthy communities are better able to manage and recover from disasters and other emergencies.

Section 61.2

Building Resilience in Children and Youth Dealing with Trauma

This section contains text excerpted from the following sources:
Text beginning with the heading "What Is Happening?" is excerpted
from "Building Resilience in Children and Teens," Child Welfare
Information Gateway, U.S. Department of Health and Human
Services (HHS), April 18, 2016. Reviewed October 2019; Text
beginning with the heading "Factors that Contribute to Childhood
Resilience" is excerpted from "Childhood Resilience,"
Substance Abuse and Mental Health Services
Administration (SAMHSA), July 31, 2019.

What Is Happening?

All youth face difficulties, which can range from traumatic losses to everyday disappointments. The ability to cope and recover (or "bounce back") after a setback is important to their success. Experts call this "resilience," and it is a skill that can be learned.

What You Can Do

You can help your children develop resilience by taking the following steps:

- **Model a positive outlook.** Children will learn from your ability to bounce back from difficulties. When faced with a challenge yourself, model an "I can do it" attitude. Remind yourself and your child that the current problem is temporary, and "things will get better."

- **Build confidence.** Comment frequently on what your child does well. Point out when he demonstrates qualities such as kindness, persistence, and integrity.

- **Build connections.** Create a strong, loving family and encourage your child to make good friends. This will help ensure that she has plenty of support in times of trouble.

- **Encourage goal-setting.** Teach children to set realistic goals and work toward them one step at a time. Even small steps can build confidence and resilience.

- **See challenges as learning opportunities.** Tough times are often when we learn the most. Resist the urge to solve your child's problem for him—this can send a message that you do not believe he can handle it. Instead, offer love and support, and show faith in his ability to cope. Remind him of times when he has solved problems successfully in the past.

- **Teach self-care.** Many challenges are easier to face when we eat well and get enough exercise and rest. Self-care can also mean taking a break from worrying to relax or have some fun.

- **Help others.** Empower your child by giving her opportunities to help out at home or do age-appropriate volunteer work for her school, neighborhood, or place of worship.

Factors That Contribute to Childhood Resilience

While many factors contribute to resilience, three stands out:

- Cognitive development/problem-solving skills

- Self-regulation

- Relationships with caring adults

Cognitive Development / Problem-Solving Skills

As a species, we have been solving problems since the beginning of time. Watch a child play and you will see that her/his problem-solving skills are nearly always at work. Infants attempt to soothe themselves by figuring out how to put their thumbs in their mouths or crying for a caregiver. Toddlers try to fit shapes into shape sorters. As children mature, the problems they solve get more complex. Solving problems engage our prefrontal cortex, sometimes called the "thinking brain," which is the seat of our executive function. During times of stress and trauma, this part of our brain is typically shut down so that our body can respond to the threats it is facing. By helping children engage in problem-solving activities, they not only gain a sense of self-efficacy and mastery they also reengage the parts of their brain that may have been offline. Because the neural pathways of young brains are still being wired, the more we can engage and reinforce healthy pathways, the better. Developing problem-solving skills also helps children with self-regulation skills, another key quality that fosters resilience.

Self-Regulation

Self-regulation is the ability to control oneself in a variety of ways. Infants develop regular sleep-wake patterns. School children learn to raise their hands and wait patiently to be called on, rather than shouting out an answer. College students concentrate for hours on a research paper, delaying the gratification that might come with being outdoors on a sunny day. Self-regulation has been identified as "the cornerstone" of child development. In the seminal publication From Neurons to Neighborhoods, experts conclude, "Development may be viewed as an increased capacity for self-regulation, seen particularly in the child's ability to function more independently in a personal and social context." It involves working memory, the ability to focus on a goal, tolerance for frustration, and controlling and expressing one's emotions appropriately and in context. Self-regulation is key for academic and social success and plays a significant role in mental-health outcomes—all things that can be a challenge for children experiencing homelessness and other stressors.

Relationships with Caring Adults

Ideally, we form close attachment relationships with our primary caregiver(s) beginning at birth. As we get older, those relationships extend to teachers, neighbors, family, friends, coaches, and others. Disrupted attachment relationships can be devastating for young children because they are still developing an internal working model of what relationships look like and because they rely so intensively on their caregivers to get their basic needs met.

By developing relationships with caring adults, whether they be parents, family members, coaches, teachers, or neighbors, children learn about healthy relationships—ones that are consistent, predictable, and safe. They receive guidance, comfort, and mentoring.

Play: A Key Strategy for Developing Resilience

What strategies can we use to draw out children's resilience? The short answer is playing. According to the Life Is Good Playmakers

Blog, "Children who grow up afraid don't learn how to play. They learn how to survive." One of our jobs then becomes to draw out children's natural playfulness, which gives them an opportunity to discover, learn, and heal. As the iconic Fred Rogers tells us, "Play gives children a chance to practice what they are learning. They have to play with what they know to be true in order to find out more, and then they can use what they learn in new forms of play." We can create play experiences for children of all ages that give them ways to engage in solving problems, develop self-regulation skills, and form relationships. Here are some ideas:

- "Simon Says" helps children practice several self-regulation skills (for example, working memory and inhibitory control)

- Legos, blocks, and other tactile toys give children opportunities to solve problems and focus on a goal ("I want to build a tower. How can I build the tower really high without it falling?"). If they are playing with an adult (especially one who lets the child direct the play), they are also building a relationship.

- Breathing exercises and bodywork (yoga, stretching)

- Reading books, playing games, and having conversations about identifying emotions

- Letting children talk aloud (and/or hear you talk aloud) about solving a problem. What are the pros and cons of possible solutions?

- Dancing, singing, listening to music, and playing musical instruments and experimenting with speed (fast song, slow song), volume (sing loudly, sing quietly), and breath (play your instrument and hold the note as long as you can...now try making short, staccato notes)

- Any activity that strengthens the relationship between the child and her/his primary caregiver

The Art of Resilience at Psychology found that it is important to remember that "Resilient people do not walk between the raindrops; they have scars to show for their experience. They struggle—but keep functioning anyway. Resilience is not the ability to escape unharmed." Trauma can undermine resilience because it challenges the very things that make us strong. "Traumatic events overwhelm the ordinary systems of care that give people a sense of control, connection, and meaning," writes Judith Herman. By helping children restore and enhance their sense of control, connection, and meaning—through the skills described above and in many other ways—we can give them opportunities to persevere and thrive.

Chapter 62

Building a Healthy Body Image and Self-Esteem

Chapter Contents

Section 62.1

Healthy Body Image

This section includes text excerpted from "Body Image," Office on Women's Health (OWH), U.S. Department of Health and Human Services (HHS), March 27, 2019.

A healthy body image means you feel comfortable in your body and you feel good about the way you look. This includes what you think and feel about your appearance and how you judge your own self-worth. A negative body image can put you at higher risk of certain mental-health conditions, such as eating disorders and depression.

What Is Body Image?

Your body image is what you think and how you feel when you look in the mirror or when you picture yourself in your mind. This includes how you feel about your appearance; what you think about your body itself, such as your height and weight; and how you feel within your own skin. Body image also includes how you behave as a result of your thoughts and feelings. You may have a positive or negative body image. Body image is not always related to your weight or size.

Why Is a Healthy Body Image Important?

People with a positive body image are more likely to have good physical and mental health. People with negative thoughts and feelings about their bodies are more likely to develop certain mental-health conditions, such as eating disorders and depression. Researchers think that dissatisfaction with their bodies may be part of the reason more women than men have depression.

A negative body image may also lead to low self-esteem, which can affect many areas of your life. You may not want to be around other people or may obsess constantly about what you eat or how much you exercise. But, you can take steps to develop a healthier body image.

Are Some People More Likely to Develop a Negative Body Image?

Women are more likely to have a negative body image. This may be because many women in the United States feel pressured to measure up to strict and unrealistic social and cultural beauty ideals, which can lead to a negative body image.

Children of parents who diet or who have a negative body image are also more likely to develop unhealthy thoughts about their own bodies.

What Causes a Negative Body Image

Past events and circumstances can cause you to have a negative body image, including:

- Being teased or bullied as a child for how you looked
- Being told you are ugly, too fat, or too thin or having other aspects of your appearance criticized
- Seeing images or messages in the media (including social media) that make you feel bad about how you look
- Having underweight, overweight, or obesity

In rare cases, people can have such a distorted view of their bodies that they have a mental-health condition called "body dysmorphic disorder" (BDD). BDD is a serious illness in which a person is preoccupied with minor or imaginary physical flaws.

How Does Overweight or Obesity Affect Body Image?

People who have obesity are more likely to have a negative body image, but not all who have obesity or overweight are dissatisfied with their bodies. Those with a healthy weight can also have a negative body image, although obesity can make a person's negative body image more severe.

Weight is not the only part of a person's body that determines body image. Self-esteem, past history, daily habits such as grooming, and the particular shape of your body all contribute to body image. Weight is an important part of body image, but it is not the only part.

How Does Underweight Affect Body Image?

People who are underweight due to a health condition such as an eating disorder, cancer, or Crohn disease may have a negative body image due to the effects of their condition. People who are underweight without another health condition may also have a negative body image if others comment negatively on their weight or express other negative attitudes.

How Can I Have a Healthy Body Image?

Research shows that if you have overweight or obesity, your body image may improve if you participate in a weight loss program, even if you do not lose as much weight as you hoped. The weight loss program should include a focus on healthy eating and physical activity.

If you are underweight and have a negative body image, you can work with a doctor or nurse to gain weight in a healthy way and treat any other health problems you have. If you are eating healthy and getting enough exercise, your weight may matter less in your body image.

The more you practice thinking positive thoughts about yourself and the fewer negative thoughts you have about your body, the better you will feel about who you are and how you look. While very few people are 100 percent positive about every aspect of their body, it can help to focus on the things you do like. Also, most people realize as they get older that how you look is only one part of who you are. Working on accepting how you look is healthier than constantly working to change how you look.

Section 62.2

Ways to Build a High Self-Esteem

This section includes text excerpted from "Ways to Build Self-Esteem," girlshealth.gov, Office on Women's Health (OWH), December 22, 2015. Reviewed October 2019.

Having healthy or high self-esteem means that you feel good about yourself and are proud of what you can do. Having high self-esteem can help you to think positively, deal better with stress, and boost your drive to work hard. Having high self-esteem can also make it easier to try new things. Before you try something new, you think, "I can do this," and not, "This is too hard. I will never be able to do this."

If you have an illness or disability, how does it affect your self-esteem? Do you find your self-esteem is affected by how you think others see you? Do people put you down or bully you? This can put your self-esteem at risk. If you need a self-esteem boost, take these steps:

- **Ask yourself what you are really good at and enjoy doing.** Everyone is good at something. When you are feeling bad about yourself, just think, "I am good at art" (or computers or playing an instrument or whatever you are good at). You might make a list of your great traits and talents, too. And remember that it is okay not to be great at everything.

- **Push yourself to try new things.** If you try something new and fail, that is okay. Everyone fails sometime. Try to figure out what went wrong, so you can try again in a new way. Keep trying, and do not give up. In time, you will figure out how to succeed.

- **Always give your best effort, and take pride in your efforts.** When you accomplish a goal, celebrate over a family meal or treat yourself to a fun outing.

- **If you need help, ask for it.** Talking to a friend can help you come up with different ways to solve a problem. This is called "brainstorming." Make a list of your possible solutions. Put the ones that you think will work the best at the top. Then rehearse them ahead of time so that you will know exactly what you are going to do or say when the problem comes up. If your first plan does not work, then go on to Plan B. If Plan B does not work, go on to Plan C, and so on.

- **Join a support group.** Finding out how other people deal with illnesses or disabilities can help you cope. Ask your doctor for help finding a support group in your community or online.

- **Volunteer to do something in your community.** For instance, you could tutor a young child or take care of the plants in the community center lobby.

- **Look for ways to take more control over your life.**

- **Speak up for yourself.** This can be difficult if you are shy. But, it can get easier with practice. Learn to communicate your needs and do not hesitate to ask for something.

- **Work on trying to feel good about how you look.** Everyone has some things they like and do not like about their bodies. It pays to focus on the positives since your body image, or how you feel about your looks, can affect your self-esteem. And remember that real beauty comes from the inside!

- **If you still find that you are not feeling good about yourself, talk to your parents, a school counselor, or your doctor because you may be at risk for depression.** You can also ask the school nurse if your school offers counseling for help through tough times.

Chapter 63

Dealing with the Effects of Trauma

What Is Trauma?

"Most people associate posttraumatic stress symptoms with veterans and combat situations," says Dr. Amit Etkin, a National Institutes of Health (NIH)-funded mental-health expert at Stanford University. "However, all sorts of trauma happen during one's life that can lead to posttraumatic stress disorder (PTSD) and PTSD-like symptoms."

This includes people who have been through a physical or sexual assault, abuse, an accident, a disaster, or many other serious events.

Anyone can develop PTSD, at any age. According to the National Center for Posttraumatic Stress Disorder (NCPTSD), about 7 or 8 out of every 100 people will experience PTSD at some point in their lives.

"We don't have a blood test that would tell you or question you can ask somebody to know if they're in the highest risk group for developing PTSD," Tuma says. "But we do know that there are some things that increase risk in general and some things that protect against it."

This chapter includes text excerpted from "Dealing with Trauma," *NIH News in Health*, National Institutes of Health (NIH), June 2018.

Coping with Trauma

How you react when something traumatic happens, and shortly afterward, can help or delay your recovery.

"It's important to have a coping strategy for getting through the bad feelings of a traumatic event," Tuma says. A good coping strategy, he explains, is finding somebody to talk with about your feelings. A bad coping strategy would be turning to alcohol or drugs.

Having a positive coping strategy and learning something from the situation can help you recover from a traumatic event. So can seeking support from friends, family, or a support group.

Talking with a mental-health professional can help someone with posttraumatic stress symptoms learn to cope. It is important for anyone with PTSD-like symptoms to be treated by a mental-health professional who is trained in trauma-focused therapy.

"For those who start therapy and go through it, a large percentage of those will get better and will get some relief," Tuma says. Some medications can help treat certain symptoms, too.

Posttraumatic stress disorder affects people differently, so a treatment that works for one person may not work for another. Some people with PTSD need to try different treatments to find what works for their symptoms.

Finding Treatments

"While we currently diagnose this as one disorder in psychiatry, in truth, there's a lot of variation between people and the kinds of symptoms that they have," Etkin says.

These differences can make it difficult to find a treatment that works. Etkin's team is trying to understand why some people's brains respond to treatment and others do not.

"PTSD is very common. But the variety of ways that it manifests in the brain is vast," Etkin explains. "We don't know how many underlying conditions there are, or distinct brain problems there are, that lead to PTSD. So we are trying to figure that part out."

His team has identified brain circuits that show when therapy is working. They have found a separate brain circuit that can predict who will respond to treatment.

His group is now testing a technique called "noninvasive brain stimulation" for people who do not respond to treatment. They hope that stimulating certain brain circuits will make therapy more effective.

Most people recover naturally from trauma. But it can take time. If you are having symptoms for too long—or that are too intense—talk with your healthcare provider or mental-health professional. In times of crisis, call the National Suicide Prevention Lifeline at 800-273-TALK (800-273-8255) or visit the emergency room.

"PTSD is real. This is not a weakness in any way," Tuma explains. "People shouldn't struggle alone and in silence."

Chapter 64

Stress in Disaster Responders and Recovery Workers

Chapter Contents

Section 64.1

Depression and Emergency Medical Services Personnel

This section includes text excerpted from "First Responders:
Behavioral Health Concerns, Emergency Response, and Trauma,"
Substance Abuse and Mental Health Services Administration
(SAMHSA), May 2018.

Research into the behavioral health conditions in emergency medical services (EMS) personnel reveals that one of the core risk factors for first responders is the pace of their work. First responders are always on the front line facing highly stressful and risky calls. This tempo can lead to an inability to integrate work experiences. For instance, according to a study, 69 percent of EMS professionals have never had enough time to recover between traumatic events. As a result, depression, stress and posttraumatic stress symptoms, suicidal ideation, and a host of other functional and relational conditions have been reported.

Depression is commonly reported in first responders, and rates of depression as well as severity vary across studies. For instance, in a case-control study of certified EMS professionals, depression was reported in 6.8 percent, with mild depression the most common type (3.5%). Among medical team workers responding to the great East Japan earthquake, 21.4 percent were diagnosed with clinical depression. In a study in Germany, 3.1 percent of emergency physicians had clinical depression.

Depression and Firefighters

The nature of the work of firefighters, including repeated exposure to painful and provocative experiences and erratic sleep schedules, can pose significant risk to firefighters' mental health. To add to that risk, firefighters face many barriers to seeking help, including stigma and the cost of treatment. For instance, according to a study, volunteer firefighters have greater structural barriers to use of mental-health services (including cost, inadequate transportation, difficulty getting time off from work, and availability of resources) than career firefighters and the general population.

As with EMS professionals, depression is commonly reported in firefighters, and studies have found various rates and severity of depression. One study found that volunteer firefighters reported markedly elevated levels of depression as compared to career firefighters (with an odds radio for volunteer firefighters of 16.85 and for career firefighters of 13.06). The researchers observed that greater structural barriers to mental-healthcare (such as cost and availability of resources) may explain the increased levels of depression observed among volunteer firefighters. Additionally, competing demands for volunteer firefighters (having a separate job) create stress vulnerabilities that contribute to the development or exacerbation of behavioral health conditions. Organizational factors (such as more systematic and stringent recruitment and screening within career departments relative to volunteer departments) may contribute to the difference in the levels of behavioral health symptoms. In another study, 22.2 percent of female career firefighters were at risk of depression, while 38.5 percent of the female volunteer firefighters were at risk of depression. This could be attributed to social pressures associated with working in a male-dominated profession. Additionally, although women firefighters reported similar job stressors to men, they also reported experiencing significantly more occupational discrimination than their male peers.

Depression and Police Officers

Police officers are at increased risk of negative mental-health consequences due to the dangerous nature of their jobs as well as the greater likelihood that they experience critical incidents, environmental hazards, and traumatic events. In a study, about three-fourths of the surveyed officers reported having experienced a traumatic event, but less than half of them had told their agency about it. Additionally, about half of the officers reported personally knowing one or more law enforcement officers who changed after experiencing a traumatic event, and about half reported knowing an officer in their agency or another agency who had committed suicide. Depression in police officers after the 9/11 attacks was found at 24.7 percent prevalence, and at 47.7 percent prevalence of both depression and anxiety.

Behavioral Health and First Responders

First responders are always at the forefront of each incident or disaster, and they ensure the safety and well-being of the population. They are, however, at great danger of being exposed to potentially traumatic situations that pose risk of harm to them or the people under their care. This constitutes a great risk for the behavioral health of first responders, putting them at risk for stress, posttraumatic stress disorder (PTSD), depression, substance use, and suicide ideation and attempts. Both natural and technological disasters were found to be associated with increased risk of these conditions, as were factors such as resiliency, trust in self and team, duration on the disaster scene, individual coping style, and post disaster mental-health support.

To improve the behavioral health of the first responders, a cooperative effort is needed between organizational leadership and coworkers to establish a work environment that provides adequate training and ensures the resiliency and health of first responders by protecting them from overwork and excessive stress and supporting them in seeking help when needed. First responders carry the weight of their own safety and well being as well as those they serve, and thus making programmatic changes to educate them, offer them support, and protect their health and well being would reduce the risk of burnout, fatigue, or other behavioral health issues associated with being overworked, uncertain, or stressed. Behavioral and public health agencies can help prevent or alleviate behavioral health issues in first responders through preventive training on resiliency and behavioral health prior to disasters or other events, interventions to address burnout, and peer support programs. As noted, such efforts and programs are a cultural shift in fields in which professionals sometimes have coped with disastrous and traumatic experiences on the job by trying to disregard their reactions or using other maladaptive techniques such as substance misuse. As more first responders discover the resilience they can access through others, and particularly their peers, they become better able to maintain their own behavioral health while addressing the myriad challenges of disaster response.

Section 64.2

About Compassion Fatigue

This section includes text excerpted from "Tips for Disaster Responders—Understanding Compassion Fatigue," Substance Abuse and Mental Health Services Administration (SAMHSA), 2014. Reviewed October 2019.

Disaster behavioral health response work can be very satisfying, but it can also take its toll on you. Research indicates that compassion fatigue (CF) is made up of two main components: burnout and secondary traumatic stress. When experiencing burnout, you may feel exhausted and overwhelmed, such as nothing you do will help make the situation better. For some responders, the negative effects of this work can make them feel like the trauma of the people they are helping is happening to them or the people they love. This is called "secondary traumatic stress." When these feelings go on for a long time, they can develop into "vicarious trauma." This type of trauma is rare but can be so distressing that the way a person views the world changes for the worse.

Risks of Being a Disaster Behavioral Health Responder

Willingness to be in the trenches when responding to a disaster is one of the things that makes you credible and trustworthy to survivors. This usually means you live in conditions similar to those of disaster survivors. For example, you may have trouble finding enough food, let alone nutritious food. You may struggle with lack of personal space and privacy. You are likely to experience disruptions in sleep due to hectic work schedules or surrounding noise. These things can wear you down behaviorally, cognitively, physically, spiritually, and emotionally. You may also become more vulnerable to feeling the acute traumatic stress, sorrow, and anger of the people you help. You may even experience feelings of guilt for surviving the disaster. When this happens, you may have trouble understanding the risks to your own health and safety.

Signs of Burnout and Secondary Traumatic Stress

It is important to acknowledge the limitations of your skills and your own personal risks (such as a history of trauma) and other negative aspects of the disaster response experience (e.g., gruesome scenes or intense grieving) so that you recognize how they may be affecting your feelings as well as your behavior. Some responders may experience several of the following signs of burnout and the more serious component of CF, secondary traumatic stress. Remember, not all disaster behavioral health responders will experience every symptom.

When you experience burnout, a symptom of CF, you may have some of the following feelings:

- As if nothing you can do will help
- Tired—even exhausted—and overwhelmed
- Like a failure
- As though you are not doing your job well
- Frustrated
- Cynical
- Disconnected from others, lacking feelings, indifferent
- Depressed
- As if you need to use alcohol or other mind-altering substances to cope

Signs of secondary traumatic stress, a more serious component of CF, may include the following:

- Fear in situations that others would not think were frightening
- Excessive worry that something bad will happen to you, your loved ones, or colleagues
- Easily startled, feeling "jumpy" or "on guard" all of the time
- Wary of every situation, expecting a traumatic outcome
- Physical signs such as a racing heart, shortness of breath, and increased tension headaches
- Sense of being haunted by the troubles you see and hear from others and not being able to make them go away
- The feeling that others' trauma is yours

If you are experiencing any of these signs of stress, talk with a friend or colleague, seek wise counsel from a trusted mentor, or ask your supervisor to help you determine a course of action.

You may also consider seeking help from a qualified mental-health professional.

Coping with Compassion Fatigue

Traditionally, disaster workers have been trained to screen survivors for negative behavioral health effects. More recently, the field is also focusing on identifying survivor resilience, fostering strengths, and encouraging self-care. Just as you assist survivors in this process, you can apply this approach to yourself on a routine basis—even when not on a disaster assignment—to avoid CF. By focusing on building your strengths and carrying out self-care activities, you are contributing to your behavioral, cognitive, physical, spiritual, and emotional resilience. The following strategies can help you do just that:

- Focus on the four core components of resilience: adequate sleep, good nutrition, regular physical activity, and active relaxation (e.g., yoga or meditation).

- Get enough sleep or at least rest. This is of great importance, as it affects all other aspects of your work—your physical strength, your decision making, your temperament.

- Drink enough fluids to stay hydrated, and eat the best quality food that you can access.

- Complete basic hygiene tasks such as combing your hair, brushing your teeth, and changing clothes when possible. Wearing clean clothes can make you feel better.

- Try to wash up, even just your hands and face, after you leave your work shift. Think of it as a symbolic "washing away" of the hardness of the day.

- Make time to learn about the people with whom you work. Taking time for conversations will help foster feelings of positive regard toward yourself and others.

- Engage with your fellow workers to celebrate successes and mourn sorrows as a group.

- Take time to be alone so you can think, meditate, and rest.

- Practice your spiritual beliefs or reach out to a faith leader for support.

- Take time away from the work when possible. Removing yourself from the disaster area can help you remember that not every place is so troubled.

- Try to find things to look forward to.

- Communicate with friends and family as best you can. If you do not have Internet or cell phone access or ways to mail letters, write to loved ones anyway and send the letters later.

- Create individual ceremonies or rituals. For example, write down something that bothers you and then burn it as a symbolic goodbye. Focus your thoughts on letting go of stress or anger or on honoring the memory, depending on the situation.

Prevention of Compassion Fatigue

When combined, the self-care practices mentioned above can help prevent the development of CF. Once you begin to routinely practice these healthy habits, they become part of your overall prevention plan. Not only do healthy habits strengthen your ability to cope while in the moment, they can help your body remember how to bounce back to a healthier state. Remember, prevention is part of a good preparedness plan.

Section 64.3

Disaster Response and Depression

This section includes text excerpted from "Helping Staff Manage Stress When Returning to Work," Substance Abuse and Mental Health Services Administration (SAMHSA), 2014. Reviewed October 2019.

Many people who are involved in disaster response work find that it has a unique blend of stressors and rewards, both of which are powerful parts of the response experience. Upon completing a disaster response assignment, many responders find their return to regular duties to be a complicated, prolonged, and difficult process. In addition, coworkers who maintained the ongoing operation of the office during the response period may have experienced unwelcome demands, causing them to experience stress, as well. Supervisors can help manage the stress of returning disaster response team members and encourage them to gain perspective on their experience, contributing to their employees' personal and professional growth. This section can help supervisors ease the transition for disaster responders returning to work, recognize and reduce potential difficulties in the workplace, and enhance positive consequences for all of their staff.

Strengthening Stress Management Skills before and during a Disaster Response

The ideal time to strengthen stress management skills, both for you and your employees, is before a disaster occurs. These skills are also important for employees who stay behind when their coworkers are engaged in offsite disaster response work. You can offer the following self-care tips to your employees, and practice them yourself, to prevent and manage stress in your workplace both before and during disaster response and recovery efforts:

- Maintain a healthy diet, and get routine exercise and adequate rest

- Spend time with family and friends

- Pay attention to health concerns, and schedule routine checkups to ensure you are ready when called for an assignment

- Keep up with personal tasks (e.g., pay bills, mow the lawn, shop for groceries). This can help you avoid having to complete last-minute tasks that can take away from time spent preparing for your response assignment

- Think about your goals for upcoming assignments, and how you can apply lessons learned from past assignments to future situations

- Reflect upon what your disaster response experiences have meant personally and professionally

- Get involved in personal and family disaster preparedness activities

Preparing Your Organization for Returning Employees

Supporting your returning employees starts with organizational policies and priorities. You can work with other leaders of your organization to:

- Create an atmosphere where people can be open with supervisors about their experiences, feelings, and concerns

- Create structured forums for responders to present their lessons learned or recommendations for organization-wide preparedness activities

- Optimize liberal or flexible leave policies for returning employees

- Be candid about the complex and potentially difficult job that supervisors and managers face—meeting both individual needs and the need to maintain ongoing work

Helping Your Returning Employees Transition to Routine Work

Upon returning to their duties, some employees may face difficulties readjusting. Many of these challenges typically subside over time as staff return to previous routines. A few potential difficulties are described below, along with some tips on how you can help.

Unrelenting fatigue. Sometimes excessive stress results in never feeling rested. Some employees may experience extreme fatigue, even when they are getting a sufficient amount of sleep each night. Encourage your employees to get a medical evaluation if the problem persists.

Pace change. Disaster responders grow accustomed to the rapid pace of the disaster environment, and for some employees, returning to a more typical rhythm of work may be challenging. It may appear as though people are moving at a much slower pace than they remember. Encourage returning responders to refrain from judging colleagues or criticizing the difference in the pace of work in your organization compared to their disaster work.

Cynicism. During disaster work, responders often see the worst in individuals and systems, and it is easy to become cynical. These feelings are expected, and they typically diminish over time. Try to help your team members regain perspective by reviewing the successes and positive results from their assignment.

Dissatisfaction with routine work. Saving lives and protecting our fellow citizens' health and safety can be rewarding and energizing, but most work does not provide such dramatic and immediate reinforcement. As a result, some returning team members may perceive their daily work routine as lacking in meaning and satisfaction. Ask about the positive things your employees learned and experienced during the disaster response, and find ways to incorporate these things into their work. For example, you may consider giving them a role in your company's emergency response planning.

Easily evoked emotions. Sometimes the combination of intense experiences, fatigue, and stress leaves disaster responders especially vulnerable to unexpected emotions. For example, they may cry easily, be quick to anger, or experience dramatic mood swings. These are fairly common reactions that typically subside over time. You can help responders cope with their emotions in the following ways:

- Provide support and education to all your staff members, and allow them to discuss their experiences with you in order to determine the best way to decrease these reactions in the workplace.

- Encourage returning employees to be aware of and monitor their reactions.

- If strong emotions become disruptive in the workplace, consider the following strategies:

  - Discuss the options of additional leave.

  - Help disaster responders locate a stress management or responder stress training course.

  - Encourage them to seek professional help. Some disaster responders are concerned about being stigmatized when seeking mental health or substance misuse support services, so it is important for you to create a "safe place" without judgment for employees to discuss accessing support services if needed.

Sharing experiences. Though returning employees may want to share their experiences with others, some may feel uncomfortable doing so. You can help ease team members' worries by taking the following actions:

- Consider facilitating group meetings that provide a structured opportunity for your employees to share experiences, especially coping skills, with others who have had similar experiences. Encourage returning employees to reflect on their experience in terms of the following:

  - How did they function in the stressful disaster environment?

  - What unrecognized skills or talents did they discover?

- Caution staff to take care when discussing disturbing scenes. Others may be upset by graphic descriptions of the disaster environment.

Difficulties with colleagues and supervisors. Returning employees may not experience a "welcome back" from their colleagues that meets their expectations. Some coworkers may resent the additional workload they had to carry as a result of employees' absence, or they may resent the recognition that the disaster responders receive upon their return. Consider taking steps to avert these difficulties:

- Be sure to show proper appreciation for the impact that everyone feels when one or more employees are on assignment and others are not.

- Remind staff that everyone is a part of the response effort, not only those directly deployed but also those who remain in their regular posts providing coverage for those in the field.

- Be aware that, if the returning staff were exposed to potentially contagious illnesses while on the disaster assignment (or coworkers believe this to be the case), returning staff may be isolated or stigmatized. Accurate information, delivered to the entire team by an unbiased source (such as a local medical expert), can help ease this type of situation.

Check Yourself: How Are You Feeling Now That Your Employees Have Returned?

You also need to be aware of your own reactions and adjustments as a result of your team's disaster assignment and return. Seeking support from other supervisors you work with (or friends in similar positions) can help you prepare for and adjust to the return of your team members. Planning for every possibility is important—consider taking the following actions:

- Be prepared with resources and referrals for staff members who may require help addressing severe or prolonged stress symptoms that are affecting their work.

- Know what types of interventions you can employ if you witness team members degrading others who are seeking help.

- Be sure to apply self-care recommendations to yourself, especially if you are starting to identify with returning staff members' descriptions of stress symptoms, such as sleep problems, stomach ailments, or irritability.

When to Suggest That Your Staff Seek Help

Stress is an anticipated reaction to situations such as disasters and other traumatic events, and many signs of stress typically diminish over time. Returning employees may need more support, however, if they exhibit one or more of the following symptoms:

- Disorientation (e.g., appearing dazed, experiencing memory loss, being unable to give the date or time or recall recent events)

- Depression (e.g., feeling continuing sadness, withdrawing from others)

- Anxiety (e.g., feeling constantly on edge or restless)

- Acute psychiatric symptoms (e.g., hearing voices, experiencing delusional thinking)

- Inability to care for self (e.g., not eating, bathing, or handling day-to-day life tasks)

- Suicidal or homicidal thoughts or plans; feelings of hopelessness or despair

- Problematic use of alcohol, illicit drugs, or prescription medication

- Evidence of domestic violence, child abuse, or elder abuse

Section 64.4

Families of Returning Disaster Responders and Depression

This section includes text excerpted from "Adjusting to Life at Home," Substance Abuse and Mental Health Services Administration (SAMHSA), 2014. Reviewed October 2019.

Increasing attention is being paid to the challenges that emergency and disaster responders face as they perform their work and then return to their loved ones and normal routine. As the family member of a response worker, you have faced your own challenges in keeping your household functioning while your loved one was away.

Returning Home

Reunions following disaster assignments away from home are usually eagerly anticipated by all. While they can sometimes be harder than we expect, they can be effectively managed. When welcoming a loved one who is returning from disaster response work, keep the following in mind:

- Homecoming is more than an event; it is a process of reconnection for you and all those connected to your loved one.

- Even though coming home represents a return to safety, security, and "normality" for your loved one, the routines and pace at home are markedly different than life in a disaster zone.

- In your loved one's absence, you and other household members have likely assumed many roles and functions that may now need to change. Be patient during this period and recognize that many routines may not return—at least immediately—to what they were like previously.

- It may be helpful to take time to reconnect with your returning loved one before inviting your larger social circle to visit. Take the time you need first.

Adjusting to Life at Home

Some other things to keep in mind while adjusting to the return of a loved one include the following:

- Celebrating a homecoming is important and should reflect your own style, preferences, and traditions.

- Asking your returning loved one to refrain from discussing graphic, gruesome, and highly distressing details will help to avoid upsetting or traumatizing others. This is especially important when discussing the experience with, or in the presence of, children. Consider sharing the more positive aspects of your experience.

- Talking about disaster experiences is a personal and delicate subject for both you and your loved one. Many people prefer to limit sharing such experiences with only a coworker or close friend. Often the need or desire to talk about the disaster experience will vary over time. Let your returning loved one take the lead. Listening rather than asking questions is the guiding rule. You might feel abandonment or anger about your loved one having been away, which might make it hard for you to listen actively and with empathy. These feelings are natural and will likely go away over time.

- Keeping your social calendar fairly free and flexible for the first few weeks after the homecoming is important. Respect the need for time alone and time with significant others, especially children. Explain to those who may feel slighted that this is a strong recommendation for returning disaster responders.

- Allowing your loved one an adjustment period will help her or him to adapt physically to the local time zone as well as to environmental changes, such as temperature, continuous noise, or interruptions.

- Engaging in activities you enjoyed doing together, such as playing games, shopping for food, sharing favorite meals, and other activities can help you reconnect.

- Knowing that your children's reactions may not be what you or your returning loved one may have expected or desired is important. Very often children will act shy at first. They may withdraw or act angry as a response to their parent's absence. Be patient and understanding concerning these reactions and give children time to get reacquainted.

- Being flexible with your homecoming expectations will allow you to share time without placing too much pressure on anyone.

It is normal to experience some disappointment or letdown when the homecoming is not what you had hoped. The reality of homecomings and reunions seldom matches one's ideas or desires.

Signs of Stress in Disaster Responders

These are normal reactions to working in stressful situations, but if they persist for more than two weeks or worsen, professional help may be needed. Contact your primary care physician or seek assistance from a trusted mental-health professional. Below is a list of some of the common signs of stress to look for in your returning loved one:

- Anxiety, restlessness, fear
- Insomnia or other sleep problems
- Fatigue
- Recurring dreams or nightmares or intrusive thoughts
- Stomach or gastrointestinal upset/appetite change
- Heart palpitations/fluttering
- Preoccupation with the disaster events or people they helped
- Sadness and crying easily, hopelessness, or despair
- Hyper-vigilance; easily startled
- Irritability, anger, resentment, increased conflicts with friends/ family
- Overly critical and blaming others or self
- Grief, guilt, self-doubt
- Increased use of alcohol or other drugs, misuse of prescription medication
- Isolation or social withdrawal
- Morbid humor
- Decision-making difficulties
- Confusion between trivial and major issues
- Concentration problems or distractibility
- Job- or school-related problems

- Decreased libido/sexual interest

- Decreased immune response (e.g., frequent colds, coughs, other illnesses)

Multiple Disaster Response Assignments

Responders may be called to another disaster assignment after only a short time home. This can be challenging and stressful for everybody. It is natural to feel sad, even to cry. You have reconnected once again and begun to establish routines. Try to understand if your loved one distances her or himself physically or emotionally in preparation for leaving. At the time of departure, it is important that you let your loved one know how proud you are of her or his sacrifice and commitment. Expressing pride while saying goodbye is positive and can help strengthen everyone.

Chapter 65

Grief, Bereavement, and Coping with Loss

What Is Grief?

"Grief" and "grieving" are used to describe the feelings a person has after a death or other loss. You also may feel grief after a really hard experience (sometimes called a "trauma") such as being attacked or your home getting destroyed. That is because the experience has caused you to lose important parts of the way your life used to be.

Feeling grief is normal. Every person has her own reactions to loss. Here are some reactions you might have if you are grieving:

- Strong emotions, such as sadness, anger, worry, or guilt

- Few or no feelings, like you, are emotionally numb

- Crying spells or feeling like there is a lump in your throat

- Physical reactions, such as having stomach aches or not sleeping

- Spiritual reactions, such as feeling disappointed in your religion or feeling even more connected to it

This chapter contains text excerpted from the following sources: Text under the heading "What Is Grief?" is excerpted from "Dealing with Loss and Grief," girlshealth.gov, Office on Women's Health (OWH), March 12, 2015. Reviewed October 2019; Text beginning with the heading "Life after Loss" is excerpted from "Coping with Grief," *NIH News in Health*, National Institutes of Health (NIH), October 2017.

Grief can go on for many months, but it should lessen over time. Everyone is different, but you should expect to feel at least a little better after a couple of months. If your grief does not get better over time, you may need the help of a therapist. Also, you should reach out for help without waiting if you have signs of depression. These include feeling worthless, having trouble functioning in your life, or thinking about hurting yourself.

Life after Loss

Losing someone you love can change your world. You miss the person who died and want them back. You may feel sad, alone, or even angry. You might have trouble concentrating or sleeping. If you were a busy caregiver, you might feel lost when you are suddenly faced with lots of unscheduled time. These feelings are normal. There is no right or wrong way to mourn. Scientists have been studying how we process grief and are learning more about healthy ways to cope with loss.

The death of a loved one can affect how you feel, how you act, and what you think. Together, these reactions are called "grief." It is a natural response to loss. Grieving does not mean that you have to feel certain emotions. People can grieve in very different ways.

Cultural beliefs and traditions can influence how someone expresses grief and mourns. For example, in some cultures, grief is expressed quietly and privately. In others, it can be loud and out in the open. Culture also shapes how long family members are expected to grieve.

"People often believe they should feel a certain way," says Dr. Wendy Lichtenthal, a psychologist at Memorial Sloan-Kettering Cancer Center (MSKCC). "But such 'shoulds' can lead to feeling badly about feeling badly. It is hugely important to give yourself permission to grieve and allow yourself to feel whatever you are feeling. People can be quite hard on themselves and critical of what they are feeling. Be compassionate and kind to yourself."

Adapting to Loss

Experts say you should let yourself grieve in your own way and time. People have unique ways of expressing emotions. For example, some might express their feelings by doing things rather than talking about them. They may feel better going on a walk or swimming, or by doing something creative such as writing or painting. For others, it may be more helpful to talk with family and friends about the person who is gone, or with a counselor.

"Though people don't often associate them with grief, laughing and smiling are also healthy responses to loss and can be protective," explains Dr. George Bonanno, who studies how people cope with loss and trauma at Columbia University. He has found that people who express flexibility in their emotions often cope well with loss and are healthier over time.

"It's not about whether you should express or suppress emotions, but that you can do this when the situation calls for it," he says. For instance, a person with emotional flexibility can show positive feelings, such as joy, when sharing a happy memory of the person they lost and then switch to expressing sadness or anger when recalling more negative memories, such as an argument with that person.

Grief is a process of letting go and learning to accept and live with loss. The amount of time it takes to do this varies with each person. "Usually people experience a strong acute grief reaction when someone dies and at the same time they begin the gradual process of adapting to the loss," explains psychiatrist Dr. M. Katherine Shear at Columbia University. "To adapt to a loss, a person needs to accept its finality and understand what it means to them. They also have to find a way to reenvision their life with possibilities for happiness and for honoring their enduring connection to the person who died."

Researchers like Lichtenthal have found that finding meaning in life after loss can help you adapt. Connecting to those things that are most important, including the relationship with the person who died, can help you coexist with the pain of grief.

Types of Grief

About 10 percent of bereaved people experience complicated grief, a condition that makes it harder for some people to adapt to the loss of a loved one. People with this prolonged, intense grief tend to get caught up in certain kinds of thinking, says Shear, who studies complicated grief. They may think the death did not have to happen or happened in the way that it did. They also might judge their grief—questioning if it is too little or too much—and focus on avoiding reminders of the loss.

"It can be very discouraging to experience complicated grief, but it's important not to be judgmental about your grief and not to let other people judge you," Shear explains.

Shear and her research team created and tested a specialized therapy for complicated grief in three National Institutes of Health (NIH)-funded studies. The therapy aimed to help people identify the thoughts, feelings, and actions that can get in the way of adapting to the loss. They also focused on strengthening one's natural process of adapting to the loss. The studies showed that 70 percent of people taking part in the therapy reported improved symptoms. In comparison, only 30 percent of people who received the standard treatment for depression had improved symptoms.

You may begin to feel the loss of your loved one even before their death. This is called "anticipatory grief." It is common among people who are long-term caregivers. You might feel sad about the changes you are going through and the losses you are going to have. Some studies have found that when patients, doctors, and family members directly address the prospect of death before the loss happens, it helps survivors cope after death.

Life beyond Loss

National Institutes of Health (NIH)-funded scientists continue to study different aspects of the grieving process. They hope their findings will suggest ways to help people cope with the loss of a loved one.

Although the death of a loved one can feel overwhelming, many people make it through the grieving process with the support of family and friends. Take care of yourself, accept offers of help from those around you, and be sure to get counseling if you need it.

"We believe grief is a form of love and it needs to find a place in your life after you lose someone close," Shear says. "If you are having trouble moving forward in your own life, you may need professional help. Please don't lose hope. We have some good ways to help you."

Chapter 66

Coping with the Holiday Blues

Spend Time with People You Care About

Sometimes staying at home is the more appealing option. But spending time with those you care about can help you feel connected to others. Reach out to the people with whom you can be yourself for one-on-one or small group gatherings. If the people you love do not live nearby, schedule a time for a video call. Just seeing a loved one's smiling face can make a big difference in your mood.

Give Back

If you are feeling isolated or lonely, try volunteering in your community. Stock shelves at the local food bank, help out at a nursing home or spend time at a nearby animal shelter. It feels good to help others, and you might find you have a skill that your community really needs. Plus, volunteering is a great way to surround yourself with other people and take your mind off of your worries for a while.

This chapter includes text excerpted from "Beat the Holiday Blues," Office on Women's Health (OWH), U.S. Department of Health and Human Services (HHS), December 10, 2015. Reviewed October 2019.

Do Not Compare Yourself to Others

An article on social media encouraged people to avoid looking during the holidays. Pictures can be misleading and make it look like people are having a lot more fun than they actually are. Social media allows people to share their best moments, which are not always an accurate representation of everyday life. Try to remember that your friend with the "perfect" life has bad times, too—they just do not share those pictures.

Sweat It Out

You probably see exercise as a must-do on every health-related list you ever read. It is there for a reason. Exercise has a long list of benefits, including helping you deal with stress and anxiety. If it is too cold in your area to enjoy a walk or run, now is a good time to see what workout DVDs are available at your local library. There are smartphone apps that can also guide you through a workout.

Get Some Sun

For some people, the winter season means seasonal affective disorder (SAD) brought on by lack of sunlight. People with SAD experience many of the same symptoms as people with depression. If you find that you have these kinds of symptoms every year or for months at a time over the winter season, talk to your doctor. People with light to moderate SAD may find relief by spending extra hours outdoors, while people with moderate to severe SAD often benefit from light therapy and/or antidepressants.

Have Fun without Overdoing It

Enjoying good food and drink is part of what the holidays are all about, but set limits for yourself, especially with alcohol. At the moment, it may seem like a stress reliever, but alcohol is only putting any feelings of stress or anxiety on hold. It does not solve any problems, and it can make things worse.

Be Honest about How You Are Feeling

Sometimes the hardest part of this season is thinking you should feel a certain way, even when you do not. Do not force it. When friends or family ask how you are doing, be honest. You never know who else might be feeling the same way.

Ask for Help

If there is something your friends and family can do to make the holidays more enjoyable for you, tell them. No one but you knows what you need. But if you feel like you have tried everything and you still feel down, consider getting help from a professional. Talking to a therapist, even for a few weeks, might be just the boost you need to get over your holiday blues and feel yourself again.

Chapter 67

Social Inclusion and Peer Support

Social Inclusion

Social inclusion of people experiencing homelessness through peer support and consumer involvement or social connections is a key component of recovery.

People experiencing homelessness have lost the protection of a home and their community. They are often marginalized and isolated within the larger society. Also, people with mental and/or substance use disorders frequently face challenges in building and maintaining social connections. They may fail to seek out treatment for fear of discrimination or feel unworthy of help. Helping people experiencing homelessness overcome these beliefs and participate in treatment is a key step in recovery.

Social inclusion offers opportunities to reengage with the community and form positive relationships. Consumer involvement is the practice of integrating people with lived experience of homelessness

This chapter contains text excerpted from the following sources: Text under the heading "Social Inclusion" is excerpted from "Social Inclusion," Substance Abuse and Mental Health Services Administration (SAMHSA), August 12, 2019; Text beginning with the heading "What Is Peer Support?" is excerpted from "Value of Peers, 2017," Substance Abuse and Mental Health Services Administration (SAMHSA), November 17, 2017.

into staff and leadership roles at homeless service agencies. Consumers may provide peer support as role models and resources for other services. Peer support creates a sense of belonging for both the individual providing the service and those receiving the support.

What Is Peer Support?

Peer support encompasses a range of activities and interactions between people who have shared similar experiences of being diagnosed with mental-health conditions. This mutuality—often called "peerness"—between a peer worker and person using services promotes connection and inspires hope.

Peer support offers a level of acceptance, understanding, and validation not found in many other professional relationships. "I am an expert at not being an expert, and that takes a lot of expertise," said one (anonymous) peer worker, highlighting the supportive rather than directive nature of the peer relationship. By sharing their own lived experience and practical guidance, peer workers help people to develop their own goals, create strategies for self-empowerment, and take concrete steps towards building fulfilling, self-determined lives for themselves.

What Does Peer Support Specialist Do?
Support the Recovery of Individuals

Peer workers offer encouragement, practical assistance, guidance, and understanding to support recovery. Peer support workers walk alongside people in recovery, offering individualized supports and demonstrating that recovery is possible. They share their own lived experience of moving from hopelessness to hope. They share tools that can complement or replace clinical supports by providing strategies for self-empowerment and achieving a self-determined life. They support people in recovery to connect with their own inner strength, motivation, and desire to move forward in life, even when experiencing challenges. Peer workers offer different types of support, including:

- Emotional (empathy and camaraderie)

- Informational (connections to information and referrals to community resources that support health and wellness)

- Instrumental (concrete supports such as housing or employment)

- Affiliamonal support (connections to community supports, activities, and events)

Improve Mental-Health Systems

Peer support is valuable not only for the person receiving services but also for behavioral health professionals and the systems in which they work. Peer workers educate their colleagues and advance the field by sharing their perspectives and experience in order to increase understanding of how practices and policies may be improved to promote wellness and resiliency. This is particularly important in mental-health systems, where historical oppression, violence, and discrimination present significant barriers to recovery for many people. Peer workers play vital roles in moving behavioral health professionals and systems towards recovery orientation.

Is Peer Recovery Support Effective for People with Mental-Health Conditions?

The research on peer support in mental-health systems is still emerging, but findings are promising. The research to date suggests that peer recovery support may result in:

- Increased empowerment and hope
- Increased social functioning
- Increased engagement and activation in treatment
- Increased community engagement
- Increased quality of life and life satisfaction
- Reduced use of inpatient services
- Decreased self-stigma
- Decreased costs to the mental-health system
- Decreased hospitalization

Chapter 68

Helping a Family Member or Friend with Depression

Does Depression Look the Same in Everyone?

No. Depression affects different people in different ways. For example:

Women have depression more often than men. Biological, life cycle, and hormonal factors that are unique to women may be linked to their higher depression rate. Women with depression typically have symptoms of sadness, worthlessness, and guilt.

Men with depression are more likely to be very tired, irritable, and sometimes angry. They may lose interest in work or activities they once enjoyed, have sleep problems, and behave recklessly, including the misuse of drugs or alcohol. Many men do not recognize their depression and fail to seek help.

This chapter contains text excerpted from the following sources: Text beginning with the heading "Does Depression Look the Same in Everyone?" is excerpted from "Depression Basics," National Institute of Mental Health (NIMH), 2016. Reviewed October 2019; Text beginning with the heading "How Can I Communicate Better?" is excerpted from "Helping a Family Member Who Has PTSD," National Center for Posttraumatic Stress Disorder (NCPTSD), U.S. Department of Veterans Affairs (VA), January 30, 2019.

Older adults with depression may have less obvious symptoms, or they may be less likely to admit to feelings of sadness or grief. They are also more likely to have medical conditions, such as heart disease, which may cause or contribute to depression.

Younger children with depression may pretend to be sick, refuse to go to school, cling to a parent, or worry that a parent may die.

Older children and teens with depression may get into trouble at school, sulk, and be irritable. Teens with depression may have symptoms of other disorders, such as anxiety, eating disorders, or substance abuse.

How Can I Help a Loved One Who Is Depressed?

If you know someone who has depression, first help her or him see a healthcare provider or mental-health professional. You can also:

- Offer support, understanding, patience, and encouragement
- Never ignore comments about suicide, and report them to your loved one's healthcare provider or therapist
- Invite her or him out for walks, outings, and other activities
- Help her or him adhere to the treatment plan, such as setting reminders to take prescribed medications
- Help her or him by ensuring that she or he has transportation to therapy appointments
- Remind her or him that, with time and treatment, the depression will lift

Where Can I Go for Help?

If you are unsure where to go for help, ask your health provider or check out the National Institute of Mental Health (NIMH) Help for Mental Illnesses webpage at www.nimh.nih.gov/findhelp. Another federal health agency, the Substance Abuse and Mental Health Services Administration (SAMHSA), maintains an online Behavioral Health Treatment Services Locator at (findtreatment.samhsa.gov). You can also check online for mental-health professionals; contact your community health center, local mental-health association, or insurance plan to find a mental-health professional. Hospital doctors can help in an emergency.

If You or Someone You Know Is in crisis, Get Help Quickly

- Call your or your loved one's health professional.

- Call 911 for emergency services.

- Go to the nearest hospital emergency room.

- Call the toll-free, 24-hour hotline of the National Suicide Prevention Lifeline at 800-273-TALK (800-273-8255); TYY: 800-799-4TTY (4889).

If You or Someone You Know Is in Crisis, Get Help Quickly

- Call your or your loved one's health professional.

- Call 911 for emergency services.

- Go to the nearest hospital emergency room.

- Call the toll-free, 24-hour hotline of the National Suicide Prevention Lifeline at 800-273-TALK (800-273-8255); toll-free TYY: 800-799-4TTY (800-799-4889).

How Can I Communicate Better?

You and your family may have trouble talking about feelings, worries, and everyday problems. Here are some ways to communicate better:

- Be clear and to the point.

- Be positive. Blame and negative talk will not help the situation.

- Be a good listener. Do not argue or interrupt. Repeat what you hear to make sure you understand, and ask questions if you need to know more.

- Put your feelings into words. Your loved one may not know you are sad or frustrated unless you are clear about your feelings.

- Help your family members put feelings into words. Ask, "Are you feeling angry? Sad? Worried?"

- Ask how you can help.

- Do not give advice unless you are asked.

If your family is having a lot of trouble talking things over, consider trying family therapy. Family therapy is a type of counseling that includes your whole family. A therapist helps you and your family communicate, maintain good relationships, and cope with tough emotions.

During therapy, each person can talk about how a problem is affecting the family. Family therapy can help family members understand and cope with depression.

Your health professional or a religious or social services organization can help you find a family therapist who specializes in mental health.

How Can I Take Care of Myself?

You may have your own feelings of fear and anger about the trauma. You may feel guilty because you wish your family member would just forget all the problems and get on with life. You may feel confused or frustrated because your loved one has changed, and you may worry that your family life will never get back to normal. All of this can drain you. It can affect your health and make it hard for you to help your loved one. If you are not careful, you may get sick yourself, become depressed, or burn out and stop helping your loved one. To help yourself, you need to take care of yourself and have other people help you.

Tips to Care for Yourself

- Do not feel guilty or feel that you should know it all. Remind yourself that nobody has all the answers. It is normal to feel helpless at times.

- Do not feel bad if things change slowly. You cannot change anyone. People must change themselves.

- Take care of your physical and mental health. If you feel yourself getting sick or often feel sad and hopeless, see your doctor.

- Do not give up your outside life. Make time for activities and hobbies you enjoy. Continue to see your friends.

- Take time to be by yourself. Find a quiet place to gather your thoughts and "recharge."

- Get regular exercise, even just a few minutes a day. Exercise is a healthy way to deal with stress.

- Eat healthy foods. When you are busy, it may seem easier to eat fast food than to prepare healthy meals. But, healthy foods will give you more energy to carry you through the day.

- Remember the good things. It is easy to get weighed down by worry and stress. But, do not forget to see and celebrate the good things that happen to you and your family.

Get Help

During difficult times, it is important to have people in your life who you can depend on. These people are your support network. They can help you with everyday jobs, or by giving you love and understanding.

You may get support from:

- Family members

- Friends, coworkers, and neighbors

- Members of your religious or spiritual group

- Support groups

- Doctors and other health professionals

Part Eight

Suicide

Chapter 69

Understanding Suicide

What Is Suicide?

Suicide is when people direct violence at themselves with the intent to end their lives, and they die as a result of their actions. Suicide is a leading cause of death in the United States.

A suicide attempt is when people harm themselves with the intent to end their lives, but they do not die as a result of their actions. Many more people survive suicide attempts than die, but they often have serious injuries. However, a suicide attempt does not always result in a physical injury.

Why Is Suicide a Public-Health Problem?

Suicide is a significant problem in the United States:

• Around 41,149 people killed themselves in 2013.

• Over 494,169 people with self-inflicted injuries were treated in U.S. emergency departments in 2013.

• Suicides result in an estimated $44.6 billion in combined medical and work loss costs.

These numbers underestimate this problem. Many people who have suicidal thoughts or make suicide attempts never seek services.

This chapter includes text excerpted from "Understanding Suicide," Centers for Disease Control and Prevention (CDC), June 15, 2015. Reviewed October 2019.

How Does Suicide Affect Health?

Suicide, by definition, is fatal and is a problem throughout the life span. In 2013, suicide was the second leading cause of death among persons aged 15 to 24 years, the second among persons aged 25 to 34 years, the fourth among person aged 35 to 54 years, the eighth among persons aged 55 to 64 years, the seventeenth among persons 65 years and older, and the tenth leading cause of death across all ages.

People who attempt suicide and survive may experience serious injuries, such as broken bones, brain damage, or organ failure. These injuries may have long-term effects on their health. People who survive suicide attempts may also have depression and other mental-health problems.

Suicide also affects the health of others and the community. When people die by suicide, their family and friends often experience shock, anger, guilt, and depression. The medical costs and lost wages associated with suicide also take their toll on the community.

Who Is at Risk for Suicide?

There is no single cause of suicide. Several factors can increase a person's risk of attempting or dying by suicide. However, having these risk factors does not always mean that suicide will occur.

Risk factors for suicide include:

- Previous suicide attempt(s)

- History of depression or other mental illness

- Alcohol or drug abuse

- Family history of suicide or violence

- Physical illness

- Feeling alone

Suicide affects everyone, but some groups are at higher risk than others. Men are about four times more likely than women to die from suicide. However, women are more likely to express suicidal thoughts and to make nonfatal attempts than men. The prevalence of suicidal thoughts, suicide planning, and suicide attempts is significantly higher among young adults aged 18 to 29 years than it is among adults aged greater than or equal to 30 years. Other groups with higher rates of suicidal behavior include American Indian and Alaska Natives, rural populations, and active or retired military personnel.

How Can We Prevent Suicide?

Suicide is a significant public-health problem, and there is a lot to learn about how to prevent it. One strategy is to learn about the warning signs of suicide, which can include individuals talking about wanting to hurt themselves, increasing substance use, and having changes in their mood, diet, or sleeping patterns. When these warning signs appear, quickly connecting the person to support services is critical. Promoting opportunities and settings that strengthen connections among people, families, and communities is another suicide prevention goal.

Chapter 70

Suicide in the United States

Suicide Rates from 1999 through 2017 for Both Males and Females, with Greater Annual Percentage Increases Occurring after 2006

- From 1999 through 2017, the age-adjusted suicide rate increased 33 percent from 10.5 per 100,000 standard population to 14.0 (Figure 70.1). The rate increased on average by about one percent per year from 1999 through 2006 and by two percent per year from 2006 through 2017.

- For males, the rate increased by 26 percent from 17.8 in 1999 to 22.4 in 2017. The rate did not significantly change from 1999 to 2006, then increased on average by about 2 percent per year from 2006 through 2017.

- For females, the rate increased by 53 percent from 4.0 in 1999 to 6.1 in 2017. The rate increased on average by two percent per year from 1999 through 2007 and by 3 percent per year from 2007 through 2017.

This chapter contains text excerpted from the following sources: Text beginning with the heading "Suicide Rates from 1999 through 2017, Suicide Rates Increased for Both Males and Females, with Greater Annual Percentage Increases Occurring after 2006" is excerpted from "Suicide Mortality in the United States, 1999–2017," Centers for Disease Control and Prevention (CDC), October 3, 2018; Text under the heading "Suicide, a Leading Cause of Death in the United States" is excerpted from "Suicide," National Institute of Mental Health (NIMH), April 2019.

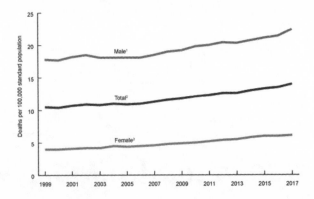

Figure 70.1. *Age-Adjusted Suicide Rates, by Sex: United States, 1999–2017.* (Source: National Center for Health Statistics (NCHS), National Vital Statistics System, Mortality.)

Suicide Rates for Females Aged 10 to 74

- Suicide rates for females were highest for those aged 45 to 64 in both 1999 (6.0 per 100,000) and 2017 (9.7) (Figure 70.2).

- Suicide rates were significantly higher in 2017 compared with 1999 among females aged 10 to 14 (1.7 and 0.5, respectively), 15 to 24 (5.8 and 3.0), 25 to 44 (7.8 and 5.5), 45 to 64 (9.7 and 6.0), and 65 to 74 (6.2 and 4.1).

- The suicide rate in 2017 for females aged 75 and over (4.0) was significantly lower than the rate in 1999 (4.5).

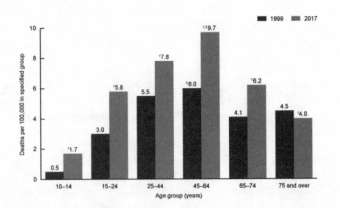

Figure 70.2. *Suicide Rates for Females, by Age Group: United States, 1999 and 2017.* (Source: National Center for Health Statistics (NCHS), National Vital Statistics System, Mortality.)

Suicide Rates for Males Aged 10 to 74

- Suicide rates for males were highest for those aged 75 and over in both 1999 (42.4 per 100,000) and 2017 (39.7) (Figure 70.3)

- Suicide rates were significantly higher in 2017 compared with 1999 among males aged 10 to 14 (3.3 and 1.9, respectively), 15 to 24 (22.7 and 16.8), 25 to 44 (27.5 and 21.6), 45 to 64 (30.1 and 20.8), and 65 to 74 (26.2 and 24.7).

- The suicide rate in 2017 for males aged 75 and over (39.7) was significantly lower than the rate in 1999 (42.4).

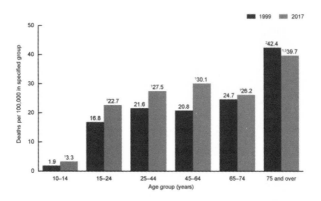

Figure 70.3. *Suicide Rates for Males, by Age Group: United States, 1999 and 2017.* (Source: National Center for Health Statistics (NCHS), National Vital Statistics System, Mortality.)

Suicide, a Leading Cause of Death in the United States

- According to the Centers for Disease Control and Prevention (CDC) WISQARS Leading Causes of Death Reports, in 2017:

  - Suicide was the tenth leading cause of death overall in the United States, claiming the lives of over 47,000 people.

  - Suicide was the second leading cause of death among individuals between the ages of 10 and 34, and the fourth leading cause of death among individuals between the ages of 35 and 54.

  - There were more than twice as many suicides (47,173) in the United States as there were homicides (19,510).

Table 70.1. Leading Cause of Death in the United States (2017)

Rank	Select Age Groups						
	10–14	15–24	25–34	35–44	45–54	55–64	All Ages
1	Unintentional Injury 860	Unintentional Injury 13,441	Unintentional Injury 25,669	Unintentional Injury 22,828	Malignant Neoplasms 39,266	Malignant Neoplasms 114,810	Heart Disease 647,457
2	Suicide 517	Suicide 6,252	Suicide 7,948	Malignant Neoplasms 10,900	Heart Disease 32,658	Heart Disease 80,102	Malignant Neoplasms 599,108
3	Malignant Neoplasms 437	Homicide 4,905	Homicide 5,488	Heart Disease 10,401	Unintentional Injury 24,461	Unintentional Injury 23,408	Unintentional Injury 169,936
4	Congenital Abnormalities 191	Malignant Neoplasms 1,374	Heart Disease 3,681	Suicide 7,335	Suicide 8,561	CLRD 18,667	CLRD 160,201
5	Homicide 178	Heart Disease 913	Malignant Neoplasms 3,616	Homicide 3,351	Liver Disease 8,312	Diabetes Mellitus 14,904	Cerebro-vascular 146,383
6	Heart Disease 104	Congenital Anomalies 355	Liver Disease 918	Liver Disease 3,000	Diabetes Mellitus 6,409	Liver Disease 13,737	Alzheimer's Disease 121,404
7	CLRD 75	Diabetes Mellitus 248	Diabetes Mellitus 823	Diabetes Mellitus 2,118	Cerebro-vascular 5,198	Cerebro-vascular 12,708	Diabetes Mellitus 83,564

Table 70.1. continued

	Select Age Groups						
Rank	10–14	15–24	25–34	35–44	45–54	55–64	All Ages
8	Cerebro-vascular 56	Influenza & Pneumonia 190	Cerebro-vascular 593	Cerebro-vascular 1,811	CLRD 3,975	Suicide 7,982	Influenza & Pneumonia 55,672
9	Influenza & Pneumonia 51	CLRD 188	HIV 513	Septicemia 854	Septicemia 2,441	Septicemia 5,838	Nephritis 50,633
10	Benign Neoplasms 31	Complicated Pregnancy 168	Complicated Pregnancy 512	HIV 831	Homicide 2,275	Nephritis 5,671	Suicide 47,173

(CLRD: Chronic Lower Respiratory Disease)

Table 70.1 shows the 10 leading causes of death in the United States and the number of deaths attributed to each cause. Data are shown for all ages and select age groups where suicide was one of the leading ten causes of death in 2017. The data are based on death certificate information compiled by the CDC.

Chapter 71

Suicidal Behavior, Risk, and Protective Factors

Warning Signs of Suicide

If someone you know is showing one or more of the following behaviors, she or he may be thinking about suicide. Do not ignore these warning signs. Get help immediately.

- Talking about wanting to die or to kill oneself
- Looking for a way to kill oneself
- Talking about feeling hopeless or having no reason to live
- Talking about feeling trapped or in unbearable pain
- Talking about being a burden to others
- Increasing the use of alcohol or drugs
- Acting anxious or agitated; behaving recklessly
- Sleeping too little or too much

This chapter contains text excerpted from the following sources: Text under the heading "Warning Signs of Suicide" is excerpted from "Suicidal Behavior," MentalHealth.gov, U.S. Department of Health and Human Services (HHS), February 26, 2018; Text beginning with the heading "Risk Factors for Suicide" is excerpted from "Risk and Protective Factors," Centers for Disease Control and Prevention (CDC), September 3, 2019.

- Withdrawing or feeling isolated
- Showing rage or talking about seeking revenge
- Displaying extreme mood swings

Risk Factors of Suicide

A combination of individual, relationship, community, and societal factors contribute to the risk of suicide. Risk factors are those characteristics associated with suicide—they might not be direct causes.

- Family history of suicide
- Family history of child maltreatment
- Previous suicide attempt(s)
- History of mental disorders, particularly clinical depression
- History of alcohol and substance abuse
- Feelings of hopelessness
- Impulsive or aggressive tendencies
- Cultural and religious beliefs (e.g., belief that suicide is a noble resolution of a personal dilemma)
- Local epidemics of suicide
- Isolation, a feeling of being cut off from other people
- Barriers to accessing mental-health treatment
- Loss (relational, social, work, or financial)
- Physical illness
- Easy access to lethal methods
- Unwillingness to seek help because of the stigma attached to mental health and substance abuse disorders or to suicidal thoughts

Protective Factors of Suicide

Protective factors buffer individuals from suicidal thoughts and behavior. To date, protective factors have not been studied as extensively or rigorously as risk factors. Identifying and understanding protective factors are, however, equally as important as researching risk factors.

- Effective clinical care for mental, physical, and substance abuse disorders
- Easy access to a variety of clinical interventions and support for help-seeking
- Family and community support (connectedness)
- Support from ongoing medical and mental-healthcare relationships
- Skills in problem-solving, conflict resolution, and nonviolent ways of handling disputes
- Cultural and religious beliefs that discourage suicide and support instincts for self-preservation

Chapter 72

Relationship between Posttraumatic Stress Disorder and Suicide

How Common Is Suicide?

It is challenging to determine the exact number of suicides. Many times, suicides are not reported and it can be very difficult to determine whether or not a particular individual's death was intentional. For suicide to be recognized, examiners must be able to say that the deceased meant to die. Data from the National Vital Statistics System (NVSR), a collaboration between the National Center for Health Statistics (NCHS) of the U.S. Department of Health and Human Services (HHS) and each U.S. state, provides the best estimate of suicides. Overall, men have significantly higher rates of suicide than women. From 1999 to 2010, the suicide rate in the U.S. population among males was 19.4 per 100,000, compared to 4.9 per 100,000 in females.

Does Trauma Increase an Individual's Suicide Risk?

A body of research indicates that there is a correlation between many types of trauma and suicidal behaviors. For example, there is

This chapter includes text excerpted from "The Relationship between PTSD and Suicide," National Center for Posttraumatic Stress Disorder (NCPTSD), U.S. Department of Veterans Affairs (VA), October 30, 2018.

evidence that traumatic events such as childhood abuse may increase a person's suicide risk. A history of military sexual trauma (MST) also increases the risk for suicide and intentional self-harm, suggesting a need to screen for suicide risk in this population.

Does PTSD Increase an Individual's Suicide Risk?

It is shown that posttraumatic stress disorder (PTSD) alone out of six anxiety diagnoses was significantly associated with suicidal ideation or attempts. An association between suicidal behaviors and both mood disorders and antisocial personality disorder points to a robust relationship between PTSD and suicide. High levels of intrusive memories can predict the relative risk of suicide with PTSD. Anger and impulsivity have also been shown to predict suicide risk in those with PTSD. Further, some cognitive styles of coping such as using suppression to deal with stress may be additionally predictive of suicide risk in individuals with PTSD.

Can PTSD Treatment Help?

Individuals with PTSD who present with intermittent but manageable suicidal thoughts may benefit from trauma-focused therapy. Two effective treatments for PTSD, cognitive processing therapy (CPT) and prolonged exposure (PE) have been shown to reduce suicidal ideation. The effect of PTSD treatment on suicidal ideation was greater for women who completed CPT.

Trauma from exposure to suicide can contribute to PTSD. In particular, adults and adolescents are more likely to develop PTSD as a result of exposure to suicide if one or more of the following conditions are true:

- If they witness the suicide

- If they are very connected with the person who died

- If they have a history of psychiatric illness

Traumatic grief is more likely to arise after exposure to a traumatic death such as suicide. Traumatic grief refers to a syndrome in which individuals experience functional impairment, a decline in physical health, and suicidal ideation. These symptoms occur independently of other conditions such as depression and anxiety.

Chapter 73

Suicide among Teens and Young Adults

Chapter Contents

Section 73.1

Teen Suicide

This section includes text excerpted from "NIMH Answers Questions about Suicide," National Institute of Mental Health (NIMH), September 2016. Reviewed October 2019.

What Are Some of the Risk Factors for Suicide?

Risk factors vary with age, gender, or ethnic group and may change over time. Some factors that increase an individual's risk for suicidal thoughts and behaviors are:

- Depression, anxiety, and other mental disorders

- Substance abuse disorder

- Chronic pain

- Prior suicide attempt

- Family history of suicide

- Family violence, including physical or sexual abuse

- Firearms in the home

- Having recently been released from jail or prison

- Exposure to the suicidal behavior of others, such as family members or peers

It is important to note that many people who have these risk factors are not suicidal.

How Common Is Suicide in Children and Teens

In 2014, suicide was the second leading cause of death for young people ages 10 to 24. Although these numbers may make suicide seem common, it is still a rare event.

Suicidal thoughts or behaviors are more common than suicide deaths and are signs of extreme distress. Suicidal thoughts and behaviors are not harmless bids for attention and should not be ignored.

What Are the Warning Signs?

The following are some of the signs you might notice in yourself or a friend that may be a reason for concern:

- Talking about wanting to die or wanting to kill oneself
- Making a plan or looking for a way to kill oneself, such as searching online
- Buying a gun, or stockpiling pills
- Feeling empty, hopeless, or feeling like there is no reason to live
- Feeling trapped or in unbearable pain
- Talking about being a burden to others
- Increasing the use of alcohol or drugs
- Acting anxious or agitated; behaving recklessly
- Sleeping too little or too much
- Withdrawing from family or friends or feeling isolated
- Showing rage or talking about seeking revenge
- Displaying extreme mood swings
- Saying good-bye to loved ones, putting affairs in order

Seeking help is a sign of strength; if you are concerned, go with your instincts and seek professional help. Reaching out to a friend you are concerned about is also a sign of strength.

What Can I Do for Myself or Someone Else?

Immediate action is very important. Here are a few resources:

- National Suicide Prevention Lifeline: 800-273-TALK (800-273-8255), confidential help 24-hours-a-day.
- Veterans Crisis Line: 800-273-8255, press 1
- Crisis Text Line: text CONNECT to 741-741
- Treatment referral routing service: 800-662-HELP (800-662-4357), funded by the Substance Abuse and Mental Health Services Administration (SAMHSA)

What If Someone Seems Suicidal on Social Media?

Many social media outlets, including Facebook, Twitter, YouTube, Tumblr, and Google+, have ways to report suicidal content and get help for the content creator. Each social media site has a different procedure, so search the website's help page for assistance.

Section 73.2

Suicide among Young Adults

This section includes text excerpted from "Suicide Prevention,"
Youth.gov, September 10, 2014. Reviewed October 2019.

Developmentally, the years between childhood and adulthood represent a critical period of transition and significant cognitive, mental, emotional, and social change. While adolescence is a time of tremendous growth and potential, navigating new milestones in preparation for adult roles involving education, employment, relationships, and living circumstances can be difficult. These transitions can lead to various mental-health challenges that can be associated with an increased risk of suicide.

Suicide is the second leading cause of death among youth age 15 to 24. Approximately one out of every 15 high school students reports attempting suicide each year. One out of every 53 high school students reports having made a suicide attempt that was serious enough to be treated by a doctor or a nurse. For each suicide death among young people, there may be as many as 100 to 200 suicide attempts. For some groups of youth—including those who are involved in the child welfare and juvenile justice systems; lesbian, gay, bisexual and transgender (LGBT); American Indian/Alaska Native; and military service members—the incidence of suicidal behavior is even higher.

Despite how common suicidal thoughts and attempts (as well as mental-health disorders which can be associated with increased risk for suicide) are among youth, there is a great deal known about prevention as well as caring for youth and communities after an attempt or death. Parents, guardians, family members, friends, teachers, school administrators, coaches and extracurricular activity leaders, mentors, service providers, and many others can play a role in preventing suicide and supporting youth.

Preventing Youth Suicide

Suicide is a serious public health problem that can have lasting, significant effects on youth, families, peers, and communities. The causes of suicide among youth are complex and involve many factors. Reducing risk factors and increasing protective factors and resilience is critical.

Knowing the warning signs is also critical. Warning signs for those at risk of suicide include: talking about wanting to die, feeling hopeless, having no reason to live, feeling trapped or in unbearable pain, seeking revenge, and being a burden on others; looking for methods and making plans such as searching online or buying a gun; increasing use of alcohol or drugs; acting anxious or agitated; behaving recklessly; sleeping too little or too much; withdrawal or isolation; and displaying rage and extreme mood swings. The risk of suicide is greater if a behavior is new or has increased and if it seems related to a painful event, loss, or change. Paying attention to warning signs for mental-health challenges that can be associated with increased risk for suicide is also important.

No one person (parent, teacher, counselor, administrator, mentor, etc.) can implement suicide prevention efforts on their own. The participation, support, and active involvement of families, schools, and communities are essential. Youth-focused suicide prevention strategies are available. Promotion and prevention services are also available to address mental-health issues. Schools, where youth spend the majority of their time, are a natural setting to support mental health.

Chapter 74

Older Adults: Depression and Suicide Facts

How Common Is Suicide among Older Adults?

Older Americans are disproportionately likely to die by suicide.

- Although they comprise only 12 percent of the U.S. population, people age 65 and older accounted for 16 percent of suicide deaths in 2004.

- 14.3 of every 100,000 people age 65 and older died by suicide in 2004, higher than the rate of about 11 per 100,000 in the general population.

- Non-Hispanic White men age 85 and older were most likely to die by suicide. They had a rate of 49.8 suicide deaths per 100,000 persons in that age group.

What Role Does Depression Play?

Depression, one of the conditions most commonly associated with suicide in older adults, is a widely under-recognized and undertreated medical illness. Studies show that many older adults who die by

This chapter includes text excerpted from "Older Adults: Depression and Suicide Facts," National Institute of Mental Health (NIMH), April 20, 2007. Reviewed October 2019.

suicide—up to 75 percent—visited a physician within a month before death. These findings point to the urgency of improving detection and treatment of depression to reduce suicide risk among older adults.

- The risk of depression in the elderly increases with other illnesses and when ability to function becomes limited. Estimates of major depression in older people living in the community range from less than 1 percent to about 5 percent, but rises to 13.5 percent in those who require home healthcare and to 11.5 percent in elderly hospital patients.

- An estimated 5 million have subsyndromal depression, symptoms that fall short of meeting the full diagnostic criteria for a disorder.

- Subsyndromal depression is especially common among older persons and is associated with an increased risk of developing major depression.

Is Not Depression Just Part of Aging?

Depressive disorder is not a normal part of aging. Emotional experiences of sadness, grief, response to loss, and temporary "blue" moods are normal. Persistent depression that interferes significantly with ability to function is not.

Health professionals may mistakenly think that persistent depression is an acceptable response to other serious illnesses and the social and financial hardships that often accompany aging—an attitude often shared by older people themselves. This contributes to low rates of diagnosis and treatment in older adults.

Depression can and should be treated when it occurs at the same time as other medical illnesses. Untreated depression can delay recovery or worsen the outcome of these other illnesses.

What Are the Treatments for Depression in Older Adults?

Antidepressant medications or psychotherapy, or a combination of the two, can be effective treatments for late-life depression.

Medications

Antidepressant medications affect brain chemicals called "neurotransmitters." For example, medications called "selective serotonin reuptake inhibitors" (SSRIs) affect the neurotransmitter serotonin. Different medications may affect different neurotransmitters.

Some older adults may find that newer antidepressant medications, including SSRIs, have fewer side effects than older medications, which include tricyclic antidepressants and monoamine oxidase inhibitors (MAOIs). However, others may find that these older medications work well for them.

It is important to be aware that there are several medications for depression, that different medications work for different people, and that it takes four to eight weeks for the medications to work. If one medication does not help, research shows that a different antidepressant might.

Also, older adults experiencing depression for the first time should talk to their doctors about continuing medication even if their symptoms have disappeared with treatment. Studies showed that patients age 70 and older who became symptom-free and continued to take their medication for two more years were 60 percent less likely to relapse than those who discontinued their medications.

Psychotherapy

In psychotherapy, people interact with a specially trained health professional to deal with depression, thoughts of suicide, and other problems. Research shows that certain types of psychotherapy are effective treatments for late-life depression.

For many older adults, especially those who are in good physical health, combining psychotherapy with antidepressant medication appears to provide the most benefit. A study showed that about 80 percent of older adults with depression recovered with this kind of combined treatment and had lower recurrence rates than with psychotherapy or medication alone.

Another study of depressed older adults with physical illnesses and problems with memory and thinking showed that combined treatment was no more effective than medication alone. Research can help further determine which older adults appear to be most likely to benefit from a combination of medication and psychotherapy or from either treatment alone.

Are Some Ethnic/Racial Groups at Higher Risk of Suicide?

For every 100,000 people age 65 and older in each of the ethnic/racial groups below, the following number died by suicide in 2004:

- Non-Hispanic Whites—15.8 per 100,000

- Asian and Pacific Islanders—10.6 per 100,000

- Hispanics—7.9 per 100,000

- Non-Hispanic Blacks—5.0 per 100,000

What Research Is Being Done?

National Institute of Mental Health (NIMH)-funded researchers designed a program for healthcare clinics, to improve recognition and treatment of depression and suicidal symptoms in elderly patients. A study of the program showed that it reduced thoughts of suicide and that major depression improved.

Examples of other ongoing completed NIMH-funded studies on topics related to depression and suicide in older adults include:

- Overcoming barriers to treatment for depression

- Improving adherence to treatment

- The relationship between other medical illnesses and depression

- Physical function and depression

- Depression treatment for depressed older adults in homecare

- Treatment services for depression

- Death rates of depressed older adults, compared to others

- Depression treatment for low-income older adults

- Depression treatment for caregivers of older adults

Chapter 75

Warning Signs of Suicide and How to Deal with It

Chapter Contents

Section 75.1

Warning Signs of Suicide

This section includes text excerpted from documents published by
three public domain sources. Text under the headings marked 1 are
excerpted from "How You Can Play a Role in Preventing Suicide,"
U.S. Department of Health and Human Services (HHS), September
10, 2012. Reviewed October 2019; Text under the heading marked 2
is excerpted from "Suicide Prevention," U.S. Department of Veterans
Affairs (VA), April 22, 2019; Text under the heading marked 3 is
excerpted from "Suicide Prevention," Office on Women's Health
(OWH), U.S. Department of Health and Human Services
(HHS), August 28, 2018.

Facts about Suicide[1]

The effects of suicide are not limited to those who die. Suicide is a
serious public health problem that has shattered the lives of millions of
people, families, and communities nationwide. We can all take action
to reduce its toll. A variety of strategies are available for individuals
and organizations across the United States to help prevent suicide.

- Suicide is the 10th leading cause of death in the United States,
  claiming more than twice as many lives each year as homicides.

- On average, more than 33,000 Americans died each year
  between 2001 and 2009 as a result of suicide—more than 1
  person every 15 minutes.

- More than 8 million adults reported having serious suicidal
  thoughts in the past year, 2.5 million people reported making a
  suicide plan in the past year, and 1.1 million reported a suicide
  attempt in the past year.

- Nearly 16 percent of students in grades 9 to 12 report having
  seriously considered suicide, and 7.8 percent report having
  attempted suicide once or more in the past 12 months.

Although suicide can affect anyone, the following populations are
known to have an increased risk for suicidal behaviors:

- Individuals with mental and/or substance use disorders;

- Individuals bereaved by suicide;

- Individuals in justice and child welfare settings;

- Individuals who engage in nonsuicidal self-injury;

- Individuals who have attempted suicide;

- Individuals with medical conditions;

- Individuals who are lesbian, gay, bisexual, or transgender (LGBT);

- American Indians/Alaska Natives;

- Members of the Armed Forces and veterans;

- Men in midlife; and

- Older men

Suicide Is Preventable[2]

Suicide is a national health concern that affects all Americans. Everyone has a role to play in preventing suicide. That is why we need to work with community partners across the country including faith communities, employers, schools, and healthcare organizations to prevent suicide.

Know the Warning Signs[3]

People who consider suicide often feel like there is no hope. They may often feel sad, lonely, trapped, or alone. Some people who have survived suicide attempts have said that these feelings go away and do not last forever.

The main warning signs of suicide include:

- Thinking or talking about suicide

- Misusing substances like drugs or alcohol

- Feeling no sense of purpose or belonging

- Anger

- Feeling trapped (feeling like there is no way out)

- Hopelessness (feeling there is nothing to live for)

- Withdrawal (from family, friends, work, school, activities, or hobbies)

- Anxiety (restlessness, irritability, or agitation)

- Recklessness (high risk-taking behavior)

- Severe mood swings or highs and lows

Other warning signs of suicide include:

- Looking for ways to die (e.g., internet searches for how to commit suicide; looking for guns or pills)

- Talking about hopelessness, helplessness, or worthlessness

- Thinking about death a lot

- Suddenly acting happier or calmer after showing other suicide warning signs

- Loss of interest in things they used to care about (e.g., hobbies, relationships, work, school)

- Visiting or calling loved ones and saying goodbye, especially after a long absence

- Making arrangements or putting their affairs in order

- Giving things away, such as prized possessions

A suicidal person needs to see a doctor or mental-health professional right away.

What You Can Do[1]

If you believe someone is at risk of suicide:

- Ask them if they are thinking about killing themselves. (This will not put the idea into their heads, or make it more likely that they will attempt suicide.);

- Call the U.S. National Suicide Prevention Lifeline at 800-273-TALK (800-273-8255).

- Take the person to an emergency room or seek help from a medical or mental-health professional.

- Remove any objects that could be used in a suicide attempt; and

- If possible, do not leave the person alone.

Section 75.2

Preventing Suicide

This section includes text excerpted from "Preventing Suicide: A
Technical Package of Policy, Programs, and Practices," Centers for
Disease Control and Prevention (CDC), February 23, 2017.

Preventing Suicide Is a Priority

Suicide, as defined by the Centers for Disease Control and Prevention (CDC), is part of a broader class of behavior called "self-directed violence." Self-directed violence refers to behavior directed at oneself that deliberately results in injury or the potential for injury. Self-directed violence may be suicidal or nonsuicidal in nature.

Suicide is a death caused by self-directed injurious behavior with any intent to die as a result of the behavior.

Suicide attempt is defined as a nonfatal self-directed and potentially injurious behavior with any intent to die as a result of the behavior. A suicide attempt may or may not result in injury.

Suicide Is Highly Prevalent

Suicide presents a major challenge to public health in the United States and worldwide. It contributes to premature death, morbidity, lost productivity, and healthcare costs. In 2015, suicide was responsible for 44,193 deaths in the United States, which is approximately one suicide every 12 minutes. In 2015, suicide ranked as the 10th leading cause of death and has been among the top 12 leading causes of death since 1975 in the U.S. Overall suicide rates increased 28 percent from 2000 to 2015. Suicide is a problem throughout the life span; it is the third leading cause of death for youth 10 to 14 years of age, the second leading cause of death among people 15 to 24 and 25 to 34 years of age; the fourth leading cause among people 35 to 44 years of age, the fifth leading cause among people ages 45 to 54 and eighth leading cause among people 55 to 64 years of age.

Suicide rates vary by race/ethnicity, age, and other population characteristics, with the highest rates across the life span occurring among non-Hispanic American Indian/Alaska Native (AI/AN) and non-Hispanic White population groups. In 2015, the rates for these groups were 19.9 and 16.9 per 100,000 population, respectively. Other population groups disproportionately impacted by suicide include middle-aged adults (whose rates increased 35 percent from 2000 to 2015, with steep increases seen among both males (29%) and females (53%) aged 35 to 64 years; Veterans and other military personnel (whose suicide rate nearly doubled from 2003 to 2008, surpassing the rate of suicide among civilians for the first time in decades); workers in certain occupational groups, and sexual minority youth, who experience increased suicidal ideation and behavior compared to their nonsexual minority peers.

Suicides reflect only a portion of the problem. Substantially, more people are hospitalized as a result of nonfatal suicidal behavior (i.e., suicide attempts) than are fatally injured, and an even greater number are either treated in ambulatory settings (e.g., emergency departments) or not treated at all. For example, during 2014, among adults aged 18 years and older, for every one suicide there were 9 adults treated in hospital emergency departments for self-harm injuries, 27 who reported making a suicide attempt, and over 227 who reported seriously considering suicide.

Suicide Is Associated with Several Risk and Protective Factors

Suicide, like other human behaviors, has no single determining cause. Instead, suicide occurs in response to multiple biological, psychological, interpersonal, environmental and societal influences that interact with one another, often over time. The social-ecological model—encompassing multiple levels of focus from the individual, relationship, community, and societal—is a useful framework for viewing and understanding suicide risk and protective factors identified in the literature. Risk and protective factors for suicide exist at each level. For example, risk factors include:

- **Individual level:** History of depression and other mental illnesses, hopelessness, substance abuse, certain health conditions, previous suicide attempt, violence victimization and perpetration, and genetic and biological determinants

- **Relationship level:** High conflict or violent relationships, sense of isolation and lack of social support, family/loved one's history of suicide, financial and work stress

- **Community level:** Inadequate community connectedness, barriers to healthcare (e.g., lack of access to providers and medications)

- **Societal level:** Availability of lethal means of suicide, unsafe media portrayals of suicide, stigma associated with help-seeking and mental illness.

It is important to recognize that the vast majority of individuals who are depressed, attempt suicide, or have other risk factors do not die by suicide. Furthermore, the relevance of each risk factor can vary by age, race, gender, sexual orientation, residential geography, and sociocultural and economic status.

Protective factors, or those influences that buffer against the risk for suicide, can also be found across the different levels of the social-ecological model. Protective factors identified in the literature include:

- Effective coping and problem-solving skills

- Moral objections to suicide

- Strong and supportive relationships with partners, friends, and family

- Connectedness to school, community, and other social institutions

- Availability of quality and ongoing physical and mental-healthcare

- Reduced access to lethal means

These protective factors can either counter a specific risk factor or buffer against a number of risks associated with suicide.

Suicide Is Connected to Other Forms of Violence

Exposure to violence (e.g., child abuse and neglect, bullying, peer violence, dating violence, sexual violence, and intimate partner violence) is associated with increased risk of depression, posttraumatic stress disorder (PTSD), anxiety, suicide, and suicide attempts. Women exposed to partner violence are nearly 5 times more likely to attempt suicide as women not exposed to partner violence.

Exposure to adverse experiences in childhood, such as physical, sexual, emotional abuse and neglect, and living in homes with violence, mental health, substance abuse problems, and other instability, is also associated with increased risk for suicide and suicide attempts. The psychosocial effects of violence in childhood and adolescence can be observed decades later, including severe problems with finances, family, jobs, and stress—factors that can increase the risk of suicide. Suicide and other forms of violence often share the same individual, relationship, community, and societal risk factors suggesting that efforts to prevent interpersonal violence may also prove beneficial in preventing suicide. The CDC has developed technical packages for the different forms of interpersonal violence to help communities identify additional strategies and approaches. Further, just as risk factors may be shared across suicide and interpersonal violence, so too may protective factors overlap. For example, connectedness to one's community, school, family, caring adults, and pro-social peers can enhance resilience and help reduce risk for suicide and other forms of violence.

Suicide Can Be Prevented

Like most public health problems, suicide is preventable. While progress will continue to be made into the future, evidence for numerous programs, practices, and policies currently exists, and many programs are ready to be implemented now. Just as suicide is not caused by a single factor, research suggests that reductions in suicide will not be prevented by any single strategy or approach. Rather, suicide prevention is best achieved by a focus across the individual, relationship, family, community, and societal-levels and across all sectors, private and public.

Table 75.1. Preventing Suicide

Strategy	Approach
Strengthen economic supports	• Strengthen household financial security • Housing stabilization policies
Strengthen access and delivery of suicide care	• Coverage of mental-health conditions in health insurance policies • Reduce provider shortages in underserved areas • Safer suicide care through systems change
Create protective environments	• Reduce access to lethal means among persons at risk of suicide • Organizational policies and culture • Community-based policies to reduce excessive alcohol use
Promote connectedness	• Peer norm programs • Community engagement activities

Table 75.1. Continued

Strategy	Approach
Teach coping and problem-solving skills	• Social-emotional learning programs • Parenting skill and family relationship programs
Identify and support people at risk	• Gatekeeper training • Crisis intervention • Treatment for people at risk of suicide • Treatment to prevent re-attempts
Lessen harms and prevent future risk	• Postvention • Safe reporting and messaging about suicide

Section 75.3

Treating People with Suicidal Thoughts

This section includes text excerpted from "Suicide Prevention," National Institute of Mental Health (NIMH), July 15, 2019.

Treatments and Therapies
Brief Interventions

Safety planning: Personalized safety planning has been shown to help reduce suicidal thoughts and actions. Patients work with a caregiver to develop a plan that describes ways to limit access to lethal means such as firearms, pills, or poisons. The plan also lists coping strategies and people and resources that can help in a crisis.

Follow-up phone calls: Research has shown that when at-risk patients receive further screening, a Safety Plan intervention, and a series of supportive phone calls, their risk of suicide goes down.

Psychotherapies

Multiple types of psychosocial interventions have been found to help individuals who have attempted suicide. These types of interventions may prevent someone from making another attempt.

- **Cognitive-behavioral therapy (CBT)** can help people learn new ways of dealing with stressful experiences through training. CBT helps individuals recognize their thought patterns and consider alternative actions when thoughts of suicide arise.

- **Dialectical behavior therapy (DBT)** has been shown to reduce suicidal behavior in adolescents. DBT has also been shown to reduce the rate of suicide in adults with a borderline personality disorder, a mental illness characterized by an ongoing pattern of varying moods, self-image, and behavior that often results in impulsive actions and problems in relationships. A therapist trained in DBT helps a person recognize when her or his feelings or actions are disruptive or unhealthy, and teaches the skills needed to deal better with upsetting situations.

Medication

Some individuals at risk for suicide might benefit from medication. Doctors and patients can work together to find the best medication or medication combination, as well as the right dose. Because many individuals at risk for suicide often have a mental illness and substance use problems, individuals might benefit from medication along with psychosocial intervention.

Clozapine is an antipsychotic medication used primarily to treat individuals with schizophrenia. To date, it is the only medication with a specific U.S. Food and Drug Administration (FDA) indication for reducing the risk of recurrent suicidal behavior in patients with schizophrenia or schizoaffective disorder.

If you are prescribed a medication, be sure you:

- Talk with your doctor or a pharmacist to make sure you understand the risks and benefits of the medications you are taking.

- Do not stop taking a medication without talking to your doctor first. Suddenly stopping a medication may lead to "rebound" or worsening of symptoms. Other uncomfortable or potentially dangerous withdrawal effects also are possible.

- Report any concerns about side effects to your doctor right away. You may need a change in the dose or a different medication.

- Report serious side effects to the FDA MedWatch Adverse Event Reporting program online or by phone at 800-332-1088. You or your doctor may send a report.

Other medications have been used to treat suicidal thoughts and behaviors, but more research is needed to show the benefit of these options.

Collaborative Care

Collaborative Care has been shown to be an effective way to treat depression and reduce suicidal thoughts. A team-based Collaborative Care program adds two types of services to usual primary care: behavioral healthcare management and consultations with a mental-health specialist.

The behavioral healthcare manager becomes part of the patient's treatment team and helps the primary care provider evaluate the patient's mental health. If the patient receives a diagnosis of a mental-health disorder and wants treatment, the care manager, primary care provider, and patient work together to develop a treatment plan. This plan may include medication, psychotherapy, or other appropriate options.

Later, the care manager reaches out to see if the patient likes the plan, is following the plan, and if the plan is working or if changes are needed to improve the management of the patient's disorders. The care manager and the primary care provider also regularly review the patient's status and care plan with a mental-health specialist, such as a psychiatrist or psychiatric nurse, to be sure the patient is getting the best treatment options and improving.

Chapter 76

Recovering from a Suicide Attempt

How Did It Get to This Point?

The time right after your suicide attempt can be the most confusing and emotional part of your entire life. In some ways, it may be even more difficult than the time preceding your attempt. Not only are you still facing the thoughts and feelings that led you to consider suicide, but now you may be struggling to figure out what to do since you survived.

It is likely that your decision to try to kill yourself did not come out of the blue. It probably developed over time, perhaps from overwhelming feelings that seemed too much to bear. Experiencing these emotions might have been especially difficult if you had to deal with them alone. A variety of stressful situations can lead to suicidal feelings, including the loss of a loved one, relationship issues, financial difficulties, health problems, trauma, depression, or other mental health concerns. It is possible that you were experiencing some of these problems when you started to think about suicide.

While the events that lead to a suicide attempt can vary from person to person, a common theme that many suicide attempt survivors report is the need to feel relief. At desperate moments, when it feels

This chapter includes text excerpted from "A Journey toward Health and Hope," Substance Abuse and Mental Health Services Administration (SAMHSA), 2015. Reviewed October 2019.

like nothing else is working, suicide may seem like the only way to get relief from unbearable emotional pain.

Just as it took time for the pain that led to your suicide attempt to become unbearable, it may also take some time for it to subside. That is okay. The important thing is that you are still here; you are alive, which means you have time to find healthier and more effective ways to cope with your pain.

What Am I Feeling Right Now?

Right now, you are probably experiencing many conflicting emotions. You may be thinking:

- "Why am I still here? I wish I were dead. I could not even do this right."

- "I do not know if I can get through this. I do not even have the energy to try."

- "I cannot do this alone."

- "How do I tell anyone about this? What do I say to them? What will they think of me?"

- "Maybe someone will pay attention to me now; maybe someone will help me."

- "Maybe there is a reason I survived. How do I figure out what that reason is?"

Right after a suicide attempt, many survivors have said that the pain that led them to harm themselves was still present. Some felt angry that they survived their attempts. Others felt embarrassed, ashamed, or guilty that they put their family and friends through a difficult situation. Most felt alone and said they had no idea how to go on living. They did not know what to expect and even questioned whether they had the strength to stay alive. Still, others felt that if they survived their attempt, there must be some reason they were still alive, and they wanted to discover why.

You are probably experiencing some of the same feelings and may be wondering how others have faced these challenges.

Am I the Only One Who Feels This Way?

Knowing how others made it through can help you learn ways to recover from your own suicide attempt.

It is estimated that more than one million people attempt suicide each year in the United States, from all parts of society. In other words, you are not alone. However, it can be hard to know how other survivors recovered because suicide is a personal topic that often is not discussed openly and honestly. This can leave those affected feeling like they do not know where to turn.

Shame, dreading the reaction of others, or fear of being hospitalized are some of the reasons that prevent people from talking about suicide. This is unfortunate because direct and open communication about suicide can help prevent people from acting on suicidal thoughts.

It is okay if you feel conflicting emotions right now. Other suicide attempt survivors know that what you are experiencing is normal. They understand that your concerns are real. Going on will not be easy, and finding a way to ease your emotional pain may be challenging, but this can be a time to start down a new path toward a better life—to start your journey toward help and hope.

Those who have recovered from a suicide attempt want you to know that:

You are not alone. You matter. Life can get better. It may be difficult, but the effort you invest in your recovery will be worth it.

Right now, moving forward may seem impossible. And while it probably will not be easy, many other survivors will tell you that they are glad they held on and worked for a better life. By taking a few steps now, and then a few more when you are ready, you can regain your strength.

Sometimes it can be helpful just to take a few steps forward, even when you do not feel like it. In fact, you might start to remember that others care about you. You might discover that suicide is not the only way to relieve your pain. You may find that your feelings will change, either on your own or by working with a counselor.

Taking the First Steps

Making big changes right now might be out of the question for you. You may not even know where to begin. That is okay. Recovery is a process, and it is important that you move at your own pace. There are a few things you might want to do to ease your transition back to everyday life.

First, it might be less stressful to decide in advance how to deal with others' questions about your suicide attempt. The people around you may be surprised by your suicide attempt and have questions or comments about what happened. Thinking about what you might say in advance can help you prepare for their reactions.

Second, reestablishing connections may help you feel better. Often, the stress or depression that leads to a suicide attempt can cause people to disconnect from others who care about them or the things they used to enjoy doing. Reconnecting with the people and things you love or loved can help instill hope.

Third, because suicidal thoughts might return, you will want to be prepared with a plan to stay safe. A safety plan is a tool that can help you identify triggers (such as events or experiences) that lead to suicidal thoughts and can help you cope if the pain that led to your suicide attempt returns.

Fourth, finding and working with a counselor can help you start to recover. Unlike friends or family, a counselor is an unbiased listener who will not be personally affected by your suicide attempt. The counselor's role is to help you sort through your feelings and find ways to feel better. You may find it helpful to use this booklet with your counselor to begin discussing your experiences and feelings about your suicide attempt. A counselor can be a peer supporter, psychiatrist, social worker, psychologist, or other skilled people. If counseling is not possible, there are also ways you can help yourself, but please remember that you do not have to go through this alone.

Talking with Others about Your Attempt

One of the most difficult tasks you might face will be responding to the questions people ask about your suicide attempt. The shame, guilt, confusion, and other emotions that might follow an attempt can make it tough to speak about it with others, especially if people respond in a way that does not feel supportive.

Often, those closest to you may be feeling lots of emotions about your attempt. They may be scared, confused, or angry about what happened, causing them to focus on their own feelings, rather than being as supportive as you need them to be. Their reactions might hurt you, whether they mean to or not.

To make it easier, here are some suggestions that can be helpful:

It Is Your Story to Tell, or Not

The details of your experience are personal, and it is up to you to determine what you want to share and with whom. Sharing what happened with your doctors, nurses, counselors, or peer supporters can help them give you the right kind of support. In most cases, they are required to keep the details of what you share confidential.

You may want to share some of the details and your feelings about what happened with other people you trust, such as family or friends. How much you share, or the details you decide to give, are up to you and what you feel comfortable with.

People Do Not Always Say the Right Things

It is difficult to predict how people will respond when they learn that you tried to kill yourself. Some people might change the subject or avoid the topic altogether because of their fear of death or suicide. Others who are close to you may be confused, hurt, or angry about what has happened. They may judge or blame you. They may feel betrayed or be wondering what they could have done to prevent you from attempting suicide.

Often, those who care the most about you have the strongest reactions to your suicide attempt because they cannot imagine life without you. It is helpful to remember that a strong reaction may reflect your family's or friends' depth of concern about you.

Sometimes you may feel that they are being overly controlling. It may seem like they are watching everything you do or will not leave you alone because they are afraid you may attempt suicide again. This can be very frustrating when you are trying to recover from an attempt.

It can take time to repair the trust in your relationships. If you can show that you are committed to safety, it might allow those close to you to feel more comfortable giving you the space you need.

Learning more about suicide can help the people who care about you be more supportive. If they better understand what led to your suicide attempt, they might be better able to give you what you need, especially if you communicate your needs in a clear and direct way.

Direct Communication May Help You Get What You Need

While it may be hard for you to talk about what happened, it is also important for you to try your best to be direct in communicating what you need. It may seem obvious to you, but others may not understand or know the best way to support you. This period can be challenging because you might want to ask people for help, but you do not want to scare anyone if you are still struggling. This is especially true if you are concerned that people might overreact and insist on care in a hospital when you believe you just need more support and understanding.

A system for monitoring the intensity of your suicidal thoughts, should you have them, can help you notice if things are getting better or worse. It can also help you communicate how much assistance you need from those supporting you. Using a scale from 1 to 5 (with 1 being minimal distress or no thoughts of suicide and 5 being extreme distress and thoughts of imminent suicide) can make it easier to express how you are feeling. The tips on this page provide additional ideas on asking for help.

Take note of not only what is going on around you and through your mind when you are at a "4" or a "5," but also when you are at a "1" or a "2." These may be situations, people, or strengths that will help you get through the hard days.

Support Can Make Things Easier

It might be hard at first, but having someone you feel comfortable talking to after your attempt is very important. You may face some challenges as you move forward; knowing there is at least one person you can turn to will make the road to recovery less daunting. Being alone with suicidal thoughts can be dangerous. Having supportive people around you and educating them on how to help you can be a crucial part of staying safe.

Ask Yourself, "What Do I Need from a Support Person?"

Different people need different things after a suicide attempt, so make sure the person you choose meets your unique needs. Maybe you need someone who will listen to you without judgment, or maybe you need someone who will come and be with you when you are feeling alone. Perhaps it would be helpful to have someone close to you who can go with you to appointments, or perhaps you want to schedule regular phone calls with a trusted friend. No matter what kind of assistance you need, it is helpful to have at least one person with whom you can share your thoughts of suicide—someone who will stay calm and help you when you need support. Once you know what you need, it may be easier to find someone to help. And remember, because you might not get everything you need from one person, it can be helpful to have a variety of people available to support you, if possible.

Reestablishing Connections

It is likely that the overwhelming life events, stress, and depression that led to your suicide attempt affected your ability to enjoy life.

Struggling with suicidal thoughts can be exhausting and leave you with little energy to do the things you once loved. It also can put stress on your relationships with friends and family. The irony of depression and suicidal thinking is that they may cause you to give up the things in life that help you feel better, just when you need them the most.

Even up until the moment of their attempts, many suicide attempt survivors report that there was an internal struggle going on inside them. One side argued that suicide was the best way to end the pain they were experiencing. The other side struggled to find another way to feel better. To put it another way, most people with suicidal thoughts had reasons for dying AND reasons for living.

Before your suicide attempt, you might have lost connections to your reasons for living, but it is important to reestablish those connections because they can help instill hope. They can remind you about the things you love in life. The exercise on the previous page will help you consider reasons for living. Personalizing this can help remind you of where you were before you started to feel suicidal and where you would like to be again.

Planning to Stay Safe

You might still have thoughts of suicide after your attempt, even if you have decided that you want to stay alive. Perhaps the pain that led to your suicide attempt is still there. It is okay to have suicidal thoughts. Everyone needs to feel relief from unbearable pain, and suicidal thoughts may be one of the ways you have learned to cope. What is important is that you do not act on those thoughts and that you try to find other, safer ways to ease your pain. A safety plan can help you do this.

Moving toward a Hopeful Future

After you have taken your first steps back into daily life, it might be time to consider taking on a few more challenges. You have already made it through the toughest part. Now it is time to think about doing some things that can give you a greater sense of wellbeing and happiness.

Chapter 77

Coping with Trauma after Someone Attempts Suicide

Suicidal thoughts and actions generate conflicting feelings in family members who love the person who wishes to take her or his own life. Some important points on how to take care of yourself and your family member following a suicide attempt are provided to help you move forward.

What Happens in the Emergency Department
Goal

The goal of an emergency department visit is to get the best outcome for the person at a time of crisis—resolving the crisis, stabilizing the patient medically and emotionally, and making recommendations and referrals for followup care or treatment. There are several steps in the process, and they all take time. When someone is admitted to an emergency department for a suicide attempt, a doctor will evaluate the person's physical and mental health. Emergency department staff should look for underlying physical problems that may have contributed to the suicidal behavior, such as side effects from medications, untreated medical conditions, or the presence of street drugs that can cause emotional distress. While emergency department staff prefer to

---

This chapter includes text excerpted from "After an Attempt," Substance Abuse and Mental Health Services Administration (SAMHSA), 2018.

assess people who are sober, they should not dismiss things people say or do when intoxicated, especially comments about how they might harm themselves or others.

Assessment

After the emergency department staff evaluate your family member's physical health, a mental-health assessment should be performed, and the physician doing the exam should put your relative's suicidal behavior into context. The assessment will generally focus on three areas:

1. What psychiatric or medical conditions are present? Are they being or have they been treated? Are the suicidal thoughts and behavior a result of a recent change, or are they a longstanding condition?

2. What did the person do to harm herself or himself? Have there been previous attempts? Why did the person act, and why now? What current stressors, including financial or relationship losses, may have contributed to this decision? Does the person regret surviving the suicide attempt? Is the person angry with someone? Is the person trying to reunite with someone who has died? What is the person's perspective on death?

3. What support systems are there? Who is providing treatment? What treatment programs are a good match for the person? What do the individual and the family feel comfortable with?

Finally, a doctor may assess in more detail the actual suicide attempt that brought your relative into the emergency department. Information that the treatment team should look for includes the presence of a suicide note, the seriousness of the attempt, or a history of previous suicide attempts.

What the Emergency Department Needs to Know: How You Can Help

Inform the emergency department personnel if your relative has:

*   Access to a gun, lethal doses of medications, or other means of suicide

*   Stopped taking prescribed medicines

*   Stopped seeing a mental-health provider or physician

- Written a suicide note or will

- Given possessions away

- Been in or is currently in an abusive relationship

- An upcoming anniversary of a loss

- Started abusing alcohol or drugs

- Recovered well from a previous suicidal crisis following a certain type of intervention

Confidentiality and Information Sharing

- Family members are a source of history and are often key to the discharge plan. Provide as much information as possible to the emergency department staff. Even if confidentiality laws prevent the medical staff from giving you information about your relative, you can always give them information. Find out who is doing the evaluation and talk with that person. You can offer information that may influence the decisions made for your relative. If you ever again have to accompany your relative to the emergency department after an attempt, remember to bring all medications, suspected causes of overdose, and any names and phone numbers of providers who may have information. Emergency department personnel should try to contact the medical professionals who know the situation best before making decisions. Other important information about your relative's history to share with the emergency department staff include:

- A family history of actual suicide—mental-health professionals are taught to pay attention to this because there is an increased risk in families with a history of suicide.

- Details about your relative's treatment team—a recent change in medication, the therapist is on vacation, etc. This information is relevant for emergency department staff because if they do not feel hospitalization is best, they need to discharge your family member to a professional's care.

- If the person has an advance directive, review this with the emergency department treatment team. If you have a guardianship, let them know that as well.

You may want to get permission from the staff and your relative to sit in on your relative's evaluation in the emergency department to listen and add information as needed. Your role is to balance the emergency department staff's training and the interview of the patient with your perspective. The best emergency department decisions are made with all the relevant information.

If your relative has a hearing impairment or does not speak English, she or he may have to wait for someone who knows American Sign Language or an interpreter. It is generally not a good idea to use a family member to interpret in a medical situation.

Next Steps after the Emergency Department

After your relative's physical and mental health are thoroughly examined, the emergency department personnel will decide if your relative needs to be hospitalized—either voluntarily or by a commitment. If hospitalization is necessary, you can begin to work with the receiving hospital to offer information and support and to develop a plan for the next steps in your relative's care. If involuntary hospitalization is necessary, the hospital staff should explain this legal procedure to your relative and you so that you both have a clear understanding of what will take place over the next 3 to 10 days, while a court decides on the next steps for treatment. If the emergency department's treatment team, the patient, and you do not feel hospitalization is necessary, then you should all be a part of developing a followup treatment plan. In developing a plan, consider the following questions. Questions Family and Friends Should Ask about the Followup Treatment Plan:

Ask your family member:

- Do you feel safe to leave the hospital and are you comfortable with the discharge plan?

- How is your relationship with your doctor, and when is your next appointment?

- What has changed since your suicidal feelings or actions began?

- What else can I/we do to help you after you leave the emergency department?

- Will you agree to talk with me/us if your suicidal feelings return? If not, is there someone else you can talk to?

Ask the treatment team:

- Do you believe professionally that my family member is ready to leave the hospital?

- Why did you make the decision(s) that you did about my family member's care or treatment?

- Is there a follow-up appointment scheduled? Can it be moved to an earlier date?

- What is my role as a family member in the safety plan?

- What should we look for and when should we seek more help, such as returning to the emergency department or contacting other local resources and providers?

Remember: It is critical for the patient to schedule a followup appointment as soon as possible after discharge from the emergency department

What You Need to Know

Make safety a priority for your relative recovering from a suicide attempt. Research has shown that a person who has attempted to end her or his life has a much higher risk of later dying by suicide. Safety is ultimately an individual's responsibility, but often a person who feels suicidal has a difficult time making good choices. As a family member, you can help your loved one make a better choice while reducing the risk.

Reduce the Risk at Home

To help reduce the risk of self-harm or suicide at home, here are some things to consider:

- Guns are high risk and the leading means of death for suicidal people—they should be taken out of the home and secured.

- Overdoses are common and can be lethal—if it is necessary to keep pain relievers such as aspirin, Advil, and Tylenol in the home, only keep small quantities or consider keeping medications in a locked container. Remove unused or expired medicine from the home.

- Alcohol use or abuse can decrease inhibitions and cause people to act more freely on their feelings. As with pain relievers, keep only small quantities of alcohol in the home, or none at all.

Create a Safety Plan

Following a suicide attempt, a safety plan should be created to help prevent another attempt. The plan should be a joint effort between your relative and her or his doctor, therapist, or the emergency department staff, and you. As a family member, you should know your relative's safety plan and understand your role in it, including:

- Knowing your family member's "triggers," such as an anniversary of a loss, alcohol, or stress from relationships.

- Building supports for your family member with mental-health professionals, family, friends, and community resources.

- Working with your family member's strengths to promote her or his safety.

- Promoting communication and honesty in your relationship with your family member.

Remember that safety cannot be guaranteed by anyone—the goal is to reduce the risks and build supports for everyone in the family. However, it is important for you to believe that the safety plan can help keep your relative safe. If you do not feel that it can, let the emergency department staff know before you leave.

Maintain Hope and Self-Care

Families commonly provide a safety net and a vision of hope for their suicidal relative, and that can be emotionally exhausting. Never try to handle this situation alone—get support from friends, relatives, and organizations such as the National Alliance on Mental Illness (NAMI), and get professional input whenever possible. Use the resources on the Internet, family, and friends to help you create a support network. You do not have to travel this road alone.

Moving Forward

Emergency department care is by nature short-term and crisis-oriented, but some longer-term interventions have been shown to help reduce suicidal behavior and thoughts. You and your relative can talk to the doctor about various treatments for mental illnesses that may help to reduce the risk of suicide for people diagnosed with illnesses such as schizophrenia, bipolar disorder, or depression. Often, these illnesses require multiple types of interventions, and your relative may benefit from a second opinion from a specialist.

If your relative abuses alcohol or other drugs, it is also important to seek help for this problem along with the suicidal behavior. Seek out a substance abuse specialist.

Ultimately, please reach out for help in supporting your family member and yourself through this crisis. Remember that the emergency department is open 24 hours a day, 365 days a year to treat your family member, if the problem continues and if your family member's medical team is unavailable to provide the needed care.

Part Nine

Additional Help and Information

Chapter 78

Glossary of Terms Related to Depression

agitation: A condition in which a person is unable to relax and be still. The person may be very tense and irritable, and become easily annoyed by small things.

anticonvulsant: A drug or other substance used to prevent or stop seizures or convulsions. Also called "antiepileptic."

antidepressant: Medication used to treat depression and other mood and anxiety disorders.

antipsychotic: Medication used to treat psychosis.

anxiety: An abnormal sense of fear, nervousness, and apprehension about something that might happen in the future.

anxiety disorder: Any of a group of illnesses that fill people's lives with overwhelming anxieties and fears that are chronic and unremitting. Anxiety disorders include panic disorder, obsessive-compulsive disorder, posttraumatic stress disorder, phobias, and generalized anxiety disorder.

avoidance: One of the symptoms of posttraumatic stress disorder (PTSD). Those with PTSD avoid situations and reminders of their trauma.

This glossary contains terms excerpted from documents produced by several sources deemed reliable.

behavioral therapy: Behavioral therapy focuses on a person's actions and aims to change unhealthy behavior patterns.

benzodiazepine: A type of central nervous system (CNS) depressant prescribed to relieve anxiety and sleep problems. Valium and Xanax are among the most widely prescribed medications.

bipolar disorder: A depressive disorder in which a person alternates between episodes of major depression and mania (periods of abnormally and persistently elevated mood). Also referred to as manic depression.

cerebellum: A part of the brain that helps regulate posture, balance, and coordination. It is also involved in the processes of emotion, motivation, memory, and thought.

cerebral cortex: The gray matter that covers the surface of the cerebral hemispheres, whose functions include sensory processing and motor control along with language, reasoning, decision-making, and judgment.

cognition: Conscious mental activities (such as thinking, communicating, understanding, solving problems, processing information and remembering) that are associated with gaining knowledge and understanding.

cognitive behavioral therapy (CBT): Cognitive behavioral therapy helps people focus on how to solve their current problems. The therapist helps the patient learn how to identify distorted or unhelpful thinking patterns, recognize and change inaccurate beliefs, relate to others in more positive ways, and change behaviors accordingly.

comorbidity: The existence of two or more illnesses in the same person. These illnesses can be physical or mental.

delusions: Beliefs that have no basis in reality.

dementia: Loss of brain function that occurs with certain diseases. It affects memory, thinking, language, judgment and behavior.

depression: A mental condition marked by ongoing feelings of sadness, despair, loss of energy, and difficulty dealing with normal daily life. Other symptoms of depression include feelings of worthlessness and hopelessness, loss of pleasure in activities, changes in eating or sleeping habits, and thoughts of death or suicide.

dysthymia: A depressive disorder that is less severe than major depressive disorder but is more persistent.

early intervention: Diagnosing and treating a mental illness when it first develops.

eating disorder: Eating disorders, such as anorexia nervosa, bulimia nervosa, and binge-eating disorder, involve serious problems with eating. This could include an extreme decrease of food or severe overeating, as well as feelings of distress and concern about body shape or weight.

hallucinations: Hearing, seeing, touching, smelling or tasting things that are not real.

hypertension: Also called "high blood pressure," it is having blood pressure greater than 0 over 90 mmHg (millimeters of mercury). Long-term high blood pressure can damage blood vessels and organs, including the heart, kidneys, eyes, and brain.

insomnia: Not being able to sleep

interpersonal therapy (IPT): This therapy is based on the idea that improving communication patterns and the ways people relate to others will effectively treat depression. IPT helps identify how a person interacts with other people. When a behavior is causing problems, IPT guides the person to change the behavior.

ischemia: Lack of blood supply to a part of the body. Ischemia may cause tissue damage due to the lack of oxygen and nutrients.

light therapy: Light therapy is used to treat seasonal affective disorder (SAD), a form of depression that usually occurs during the autumn and winter months, when the amount of natural sunlight decreases. During light therapy, a person sits in front of a "light box" for periods of time, usually in the morning. The box emits a full spectrum light, and sitting in front of it appears to help reset the body's daily rhythms.

major depressive disorder: Also called "major depression," this is a combination of symptoms that interfere with a person's ability to work, sleep, study, eat, and enjoy once-pleasurable activities.

mania: Feelings of intense mental and physical hyperactivity, elevated mood, and agitation.

meditation: Meditation is a mind and body practice. There are many types of meditation, most of which originated in ancient religious and spiritual traditions. Some forms of meditation instruct the practitioner to become mindful of thoughts, feelings, and sensations and to observe them in a nonjudgmental way.

mental health: A state of successful performance of mental function, resulting in productive activities, fulfilling relationships with other people, and the ability to adapt to change and to cope with adversity. Mental health is indispensable to personal well-being, family and interpersonal relationships, and contribution to community or society

mental illness: A health condition that changes a person's thinking, feelings, or behavior (or all three) and that causes the person distress and difficulty in functioning.

migraine: Headaches that are usually pulsing or throbbing and occur on one or both sides of the head. They are moderate to severe in intensity, associated with nausea, vomiting, sensitivity to light and noise, and worsen with routine physical activity.

mood disorders: Mental disorders primarily affecting a person's mood.

obsessive-compulsive disorder (OCD): An anxiety disorder in which a person suffers from obsessive thoughts and compulsive actions, such as cleaning, checking, counting, or hoarding. The person becomes trapped in a pattern of repetitive thoughts and behaviors that are senseless and distressing but very hard to stop.

panic disorder: An anxiety disorder in which a person suffers from sudden attacks of fear and panic. The attacks may occur without a known reason, but many times they are triggered by events or thoughts that produce fear in the person, such as taking an elevator or driving.

phobia: An anxiety disorder in which a person suffers from an unusual amount of fear of a certain activity or situation.

physical therapy: Therapy aimed to restore movement, balance, and coordination.

postpartum depression: Postpartum depression is when a new mother has a major depressive episode within one month after delivery.

posttraumatic stress disorder (PTSD): An anxiety disorder that can occur after you have been through a traumatic event.

premenstrual dysphoric disorder (PMDD): A severe form of premenstrual syndrome, which causes feelings of sadness or despair, or even thoughts of suicide, feelings of tension or anxiety, panic attacks, mood swings or frequent crying, and other severe symptoms.

psychiatrist: A doctor who treats mental illness. Psychiatrists must receive additional training and serve a supervised residency in their specialty. They can prescribe medications.

psychoeducation: Learning about mental illness and ways to communicate, solve problems and cope.

psychosis: The word psychosis is used to describe conditions that affect the mind, where there has been some loss of contact with reality. When someone becomes ill in this way it is called a "psychotic episode."

psychotherapy: A treatment method for mental illness in which a mental health professional (psychiatrist, psychologist, counselor) and a patient discuss problems and feelings to find solutions. Psychotherapy can help individuals change their thought or behavior patterns or understand how past experiences affect current behaviors.

puberty: Time when the body is changing from the body of a child to the body of an adult. This process begins earlier in girls than in boys, usually between ages 8 and 13, and lasts 2 to 4 years.

resilience: Resilience refers to the ability to successfully adapt to stressors, maintaining psychological well-being in the face of adversity. It's the ability to "bounce back" from difficult experiences.

schizoaffective disorder: A mental condition that causes both a loss of contact with reality (psychosis) and mood problems (depression or mania).

schizophrenia: A severe mental disorder that appears in late adolescence or early adulthood. People with schizophrenia may have hallucinations, delusions, loss of personality, confusion, agitation, social withdrawal, psychosis, and/or extremely odd behavior.

seasonal affective disorder (SAD): A depression during the winter months, when there is less natural sunlight.

serotonin syndrome: Serotonin syndrome usually occurs when older antidepressants are combined with selective serotonin reuptake inhibitors. A person with serotonin syndrome may be agitated, have hallucinations (see or hear things that are not real), have a high temperature, or have unusual blood pressure changes.

social phobia: Social phobia is a strong fear of being judged by others and of being embarrassed. This fear can be so strong that it gets in the way of going to work or school or doing other everyday things.

St. John's wort: St. John's wort is a plant with yellow flowers that has been used for centuries for health purposes, including depression and anxiety.

stimulants: A class of drugs that enhances the activity of monamines (such as dopamine) in the brain, increasing arousal, heart rate, blood pressure, and respiration, and decreasing appetite; includes some medications used to treat attention-deficit hyperactivity disorder (e.g., methylphenidate and amphetamines), as well as cocaine and methamphetamine.

suicide: Death caused by self-directed injurious behavior with any intent to die as a result of the behavior.

tolerance: A condition in which higher doses of a drug are required to produce the same effect achieved during initial use; often associated with physical dependence.

trauma: A life-threatening event, such as military combat, natural disasters, terrorist incidents, serious accidents, or physical or sexual assault in adult or childhood.

yoga: An ancient system of practices used to balance the mind and body through exercise, meditation (focusing thoughts), and control of breathing and emotions.

Chapter 79

Directory of Organizations That Help People with Depression and Suicidal Thoughts

Government Agencies That Provide Information about Depression

Agency for Healthcare Research and Quality (AHRQ)
Office of Communications
5600 Fishers Ln.
Seventh Fl.
Rockville, MD 20857
Phone: 301-427-1104
Website: www.ahrq.gov

Centers for Disease Control and Prevention (CDC)
1600 Clifton Rd.
Atlanta, GA 30329-4027
Toll-Free: 800-CDC-INFO
(800-232-4636)
Toll-Free TTY: 888-232-6348
Website: www.cdc.gov

Resources in this chapter were compiled from several sources deemed reliable; all contact information was verified and updated in September 2019.

*Child Welfare Information
Gateway*
Children's Bureau/ACYF
330 C St., S.W.
Washington, DC 20201
Toll-Free: 800-394-3366
Website: www.childwelfare.gov
E-mail: info@childwelfare.gov

girlshealth.gov
Office on Women's Health
(OWH)
200 Independence Ave., S.W.
Rm. 712E
Washington, DC 20201
Toll-Free: 800-994-9662
Website: www.girlshealth.gov

Globalchange.gov
U.S. Global Change Research
Program (USGCRP)
1800 G St., N.W.
Ste 9100
Washington, DC 20006
Phone: 202-223-6262
Fax: 202-223-3065
Website: www.globalchange.gov

HealthCare.gov
Centers for Medicare &
Medicaid Services (CMS)
Toll-Free: 800-318-2596
Toll-Free TTY: 855-889-4325
Website: www.healthcare.gov

healthfinder.gov
National Health Information
Center (NHIC)
1101 Wootton Pkwy
Rockville, MD 20852
Website: www.healthfinder.gov
E-mail: healthfinder@hhs.gov

*Health Resources and
Services Administration
(HRSA)*
5600 Fishers Ln.
Rockville, MD 20857
Toll-Free: 877-464-4772
Toll-Free TTY: 877-897-9910
Website: www.hrsa.gov

*National Cancer Institute
(NCI)*
9609 Medical Center Dr.
BG 9609, MSC 9760
Bethesda, MD 20892-9760
Toll-Free: 800-4-CANCER
(800-422-6237)
Website: www.cancer.gov
E-mail: NCIinfo@nih.gov

*National Center for
Complementary and
Integrative Health (NCCIH)*
National Institutes of Health
(NIH)
9000 Rockville Pike
Bethesda, MD 20892
Toll-Free: 888-644-6226
Toll-Free TTY: 866-464-3615
Website: www.nccih.nih.gov
E-mail: info@nccih.nih.gov

*National Center for Health
Statistics (NCHS)*
Toll-Free: 866-441-6247
Phone: 301-458-4000
Website: www.cdc.gov/nchs/
index.htm
E-mail: nchsquery@cdc.gov

National Center for Posttraumatic Stress Disorder (NCPTSD)
U.S. Department of Veterans Affairs (VA)
810 Vermont Ave., N.W.
Washington, DC 20420
Toll-Free: 800-273-8255
Phone: 802-296-6300
Website: www.va.gov
E-mail: ncptsd@va.gov

National Institute of Mental Health (NIMH)
6001 Executive Blvd.
Rm. 6200, MSC 9663
Bethesda, MD 20892-9663
Toll-Free: 866-615-6464
Phone: 301-443-4513
TTY: 301-443-8431
Toll-Free TTY: 866-415-8051
Fax: 301-443-4279
Website: www.nimh.nih.gov
E-mail: nimhinfo@nih.gov

National Institute on Aging (NIA)
Bldg. 31, Rm. 5C27
31 Ctr Dr., MSC 2292
Bethesda, MD 20892
Toll-Free: 800-222-2225
Toll-Free TTY: 800-222-4225
Website: www.nia.nih.gov
E-mail: niaic@nia.nih.gov

National Institutes of Health (NIH)
9000 Rockville Pike
Bethesda, MD 20892
Phone: 301-496-4000
TTY: 301-402-9612
Website: www.nih.gov
E-mail: NIHinfo@od.nih.gov

National Women's Health Information Center (NWHIC)
Office on Women's Health (OWH)
200 Independence Ave., S.W.
Rm. 712E
Washington, DC 20201
Toll-Free: 800-994-9662
Phone: 202-690-7650
Toll-Free TDD: 888-220-5446
Fax: 202-205-2631
Website: www.womenshealth.gov

Office of Disability Employment Policy (ODEP)
U.S. Department of Labor (DOL)
200 Constitution Ave., N.W.
Washington, DC 20210
Toll-Free: 866-ODEP-DOL (866-633-7365)
202-693-7880
Website: www.dol.gov/odep
E-mail: odep@dol.gov

Office of Minority Health (OMH) Resource Center

1101 Wootton Pkwy, Tower
Oaks Bldg.
Ste. 600
Rockville, MD 20852
Toll-Free: 800-444-6472
TDD: 301-251-1432
Fax: 301-251-2160
Website: minorityhealth.hhs.gov
E-mail: info@minorityhealth.
hhs.gov

Public Health Emergency (PHE)

U.S. Department of Health and
Human Services (HHS), Office
of the Assistant Secretary for
Preparedness and Response
(ASPR)
200 Independence Ave., S.W.
Rm. 638G
Washington, DC 20201
Website: www.phe.gov

Substance Abuse and Mental Health Services Administration (SAMHSA)

5600 Fishers Ln.
Rockville, MD 20857
Toll-Free: 877-SAMHSA-7
(877-726-4727)
Toll-Free TTY: 800-487-4889
Fax: 301-480-8491
Website: www.samhsa.gov
E-mail: SAMHSAInfo@samhsa.
hhs.gov

U.S. Department of Education (ED)

400 Maryland Ave., S.W.
Washington, DC 20202
Toll-Free: 800-USA-LEARN
(800-872-5327)
Phone: 202-401-2000
Toll-Free TTY: 800-437-0833
Website: www.ed.gov
E-mail: edpubs@edpubs.ed.gov

U.S. Department of Health and Human Services (HHS)

200 Independence Ave., S.W.
Washington, DC 20201
Toll-Free: 877-696-6775
Website: www.hhs.gov

U.S. Food and Drug Administration (FDA)

10903 New Hampshire Ave.
Silver Spring, MD 20993-0002
Toll-Free: 888-INFO-FDA
(888-463-6332)
Phone: 301-796-8240
Toll-Free TTY: 866-300-4374
Website: www.fda.gov

U.S. National Library of Medicine (NLM)

8600 Rockville Pike
Bethesda, MD 20894
Toll-Free: 888-FIND-NLM
(888-346-3656)
Phone: 301-594-5983
Website: www.nlm.nih.gov

Private Agencies That Provide Information about Depression

AIDS InfoNet
International Association of
Providers of AIDS Care (IAPAC)
2200 Pennsylvania Ave., N.W.
Fourth Fl. E.
Washington, DC 20037
Website: www.aidsinfonet.org

Alzheimer's Association
225 N. Michigan Ave.
17th Fl.
Chicago, IL 60601
Toll-Free: 800-272-3900
Website: www.alz.org

American Academy of Child and Adolescent Psychiatry (AACAP)
3615 Wisconsin Ave., N.W.
Washington, DC 20016-3007
Phone: 202-966-7300
Fax: 202-464-0131
Website: www.aacap.org

American Academy of Family Physicians (AAFP)
11400 Tomahawk Creek Pkwy
Leawood, KS 66211-2680
Toll-Free: 800-274-2237
Phone: 913-906-6000
Fax: 913-906-6075
Website: www.aafp.org
E-mail: aafp@aafp.org

American Academy of Pediatrics (AAP)
National Headquarters
345 Park Blvd.
Itasca, IL 60143
Toll-Free: 800-433-9016
Phone: 847-434-4000
Fax: 847-434-8000
Website: www.aap.org
E-mail: csc@aap.org

American Art Therapy Association (AATA)
4875 Eisenhower Ave.
Ste. 240
Alexandria, VA 22304
Toll-Free: 888-290-0878
Phone: 703-548-5860
Fax: 703-783-8468
Website: www.arttherapy.org
E-mail: info@arttherapy.org

American Association for Geriatric Psychiatry (AAGP)
6728 Old McLean Village Dr.
McLean, VA 22101
Phone: 703-556-9222
Fax: 703-556-8729
Website: www.aagponline.org
E-mail: main@aagponline.org

American Association for Marriage and Family Therapy (AAMFT)
112 S. Alfred St.
Alexandria, VA 22314-3061
Phone: 703-838-9808
Fax: 703-838-9805
Website: www.aamft.org
E-mail: central@aamft.org

American Association of Suicidology (AAS)
5221 Wisconsin Ave., N.W.
Second Fl.
Washington, DC 20015
Phone: 202-237-2280
Fax: 202-237-2282
Website: www.suicidology.org
E-mail: info@suicidology.org

American College Health Association (ACHA)
8455 Colesville Rd.
Ste 740
Silver Spring, MD 20910
Phone: 410-859-1500
Fax: 410-859-1510
Website: www.acha.org
E-mail: contact@acha.org

American Counseling Association (ACA)
6101 Stevenson Ave.
Ste. 600
Alexandria, VA 22304
Toll-Free: 800-347-6647
Phone: 703-823-9800
TDD: 703-823-6862
Fax: 703-823-0252
Toll-Free Fax: 800-473-2329
Website: www.counseling.org

American Foundation for Suicide Prevention (AFSP)
199 Water St.
11th Fl.
New York, NY 10038
Toll-Free: 888-333-AFSP
(888-333-2377)
Phone: 212-363-3500
Fax: 212-363-6237
Website: www.afsp.org
E-mail: info@afsp.org

American Medical Association (AMA)
AMA Plaza, 330 N. Wabash Ave.
Ste. 39300
Chicago, IL 60611-5885
Toll-Free: 800-621-8335
Phone: 312-464-4782
Website: www.ama-assn.org

American Psychiatric Association (APA)
800 Maine Ave., S.W.
Ste. 900
Washington, DC 20024
Toll-Free: 888-35-PSYCH
(888-357-7924)
Phone: 202-559-3900
Website: www.psychiatry.org
E-mail: apa@psych.org

American Psychological Association (APA)
750 First St., N.E.
Washington, DC 20002-4242
Toll-Free: 800-374-2721
Phone: 202-336-5500
TDD/TTY: 202-336-6123
Website: www.apa.org

American Psychotherapy Association
2750 E. Sunshine St.
Springfield, MO 65804
Toll-Free: 800-205-9165
Phone: 417-823-0173
Fax: 417-823-9959
Website: www.
americanpsychotherapy.com
E-mail: cao@
americanpsychotherapy.com

Anxiety and Depression Association of America (ADAA)
8701 Georgia Ave.
Ste. 412
Silver Spring, MD 20910
Phone: 240-485-1001
Fax: 240-485-1035
Website: www.adaa.org
E-mail: information@adaa.org

Arthritis Foundation
1355 Peachtree St., N.E.
Ste. 600
Atlanta, GA 30309
Toll-Free: 844-571-4357
Phone: 404-872-7100
Website: www.arthritis.org

Association for Behavioral and Cognitive Therapies (ABCT)
305 Seventh Ave.
16th Fl.
New York, NY 10001
Phone: 212-647-1890
Fax: 212-647-1865
Website: www.abct.org
E-mail: clinical.dir@abct.org

Beacon Tree Foundation
9201 Arboretum Pkwy.
Ste. 140,
North Chesterfield, VA 23236
Toll-Free: 800-414-6427
Website: www.beacontree.org
E-mail: info@beacontree.org

Brain and Behavior Research Foundation
747 Third Ave.
33rd Fl.
New York, NY 10017
Toll-Free: 800-829-8289
Phone: 646-681-4888
Website: www.bbrfoundation.org
E-mail: info@bbrfoundation.org

Brain Injury Association of America (BIAA)
1608 Spring Hill Rd.
Ste. 110
Vienna, VA 22182
Toll-Free: 800-444-6443
Phone: 703-761-0750
Fax: 703-761-0755
Website: www.biausa.org
E-mail: info@biausa.org

Canadian Mental Health Association (CMHA)
250 Dundas St., W.
Ste. 500
Toronto, ON M5T 2Z5
Canada
Phone: 416-646-5557
Website: www.cmha.ca
E-mail: info@cmha.ca

Canadian Psychological Association (CPA)
141 Laurier Ave., W.
Ste. 702
Ottawa, ON K1P 5J3
Canada
Toll-Free: 888-472-0657
Phone: 613-237-2144
Fax: 613-237-1674
Website: www.cpa.ca
E-mail: cpa@cpa.ca

Caring.com
2600 S. El Camino Real
Ste. 300
San Mateo, CA 94403
Toll-Free: 800-973-1540
Phone: 650-312-7100
Website: www.caring.com

Center for Anxiety™
200 W. 57th St.
Ste 404
New York, NY 10019
Toll-Free: 888-837-7473
Phone: 646-837-7473
Fax: 646-837-5495
Website: www.centerforanxiety.org
E-mail: info@centerforanxiety.org

Cleveland Clinic
9500 Euclid Ave.
Cleveland, OH 44195
Toll-Free: 800-223-2273
Phone: 216-444-2200
TTY: 216-444-0261
Website: my.clevelandclinic.org

The Dana Foundation
505 Fifth Ave.
Sixth Fl.
New York, NY 10017
Phone: 212-223-4040
Fax: 212-317-8721
Website: www.dana.org
E-mail: danainfo@dana.org

Depressed Anonymous (DA)
P.O. Box 17414
Louisville, KY 40214
Phone: 502-569-1989
Website: www.depressedanon.com
E-mail: depanon@netpenny.net

Depression and Bipolar Support Alliance (DBSA)
55 E. Jackson Blvd.
Ste. 490
Chicago, IL 60604
Toll-Free: 800-826-3632
Fax: 312-642-7243
Website: www.dbsalliance.org

Eating Disorder Referral and Information Center
Website: www.edreferral.com

Family Caregiver Alliance (FCA)
101 Montgomery St.
Ste. 2150
San Francisco, CA 94104
Toll-Free: 800-445-8106
Phone: 415-434-3388
Website: www.caregiver.org
E-mail: info@caregiver.org

Geriatric Mental Health Foundation (GMHF)
American Association for Geriatric Psychiatry (AAGP)
6728 Old McLean Village Dr.
McLean, VA 22101
Phone: 703-556-9222
Fax: 703-556-8729
Website: www.gmhfonline.org
E-mail: main@aagponline.org

International Foundation for Research and Education on Depression (iFred)
P.O. Box 17598
Baltimore, MD 21297
Fax: 443-782-0739
Website: www.ifred.org
E-mail: info@ifred.org

International OCD Foundation (IOCDF)
P.O. Box 961029
Boston, MA 02196
Phone: 617-973-5801
Fax: 617-973-5803
Website: www.iocdf.org
E-mail: info@iocdf.org

Kristin Brooks Hope Center (KBHC)
IMALIVE
Website: www.imalive.org/about-kbhc

Mental Health America (MHA)
500 Montgomery St.
Ste. 820
Alexandria, VA 22314
Toll-Free: 800-969-6642
Phone: 703-684-7722
Fax: 703-684-5968
Website: www.
mentalhealthamerica.net

Multiple Sclerosis Association of America (MSAA)
National Headquarters
375 Kings Hwy N.
Cherry Hill, NJ 08034
Toll-Free: 800-532-7667
Fax: 856-661-9797
Website: www.mymsaa.org
E-mail: msaa@mymsaa.org

National Alliance on Mental Illness (NAMI)
3803 N. Fairfax Dr.
Ste. 100
Arlington, VA 22203
Toll-Free: 800-950-NAMI
(800-950-6264)
Phone: 703-524-7600
Website: www.nami.org
E-mail: donorservices@nami.org

National Association of Anorexia Nervosa and Associated Disorders (ANAD)
220 N. Green St.
Ste. 127
Chicago, IL 60607
Phone: 630-577-1333
Website: www.anad.org
E-mail: hello@anad.org

National Association of School Psychologists (NASP)
4340 East-West Hwy
Ste. 402
Bethesda, MD 20814
Toll-Free: 866-331-NASP
(866-331-6277)
Phone: 301-657-0270
Fax: 301-657-0275
Website: www.nasponline.org

National Eating Disorders Association (NEDA)
1500 Bdwy.
Ste. 1101
New York, NY 10036
Toll-Free: 800-931-2237
Phone: 212-575-6200
Fax: 212-575-1650
Website: www.
nationaleatingdisorders.org
E-mail: info@
NationalEatingDisorders.org

National Federation of Families for Children's Mental Health (NFFCMH)
15800 Crabbs Branch Way,
Ste. 300
Rockville, MD 20855
Phone: 240-403-1901
Website: www.ffcmh.org
E-mail: ffcmh@ffcmh.org

National Suicide Prevention Lifeline
Toll-Free: 800-273-8255
Website:
suicidepreventionlifeline.org

The Nemours Foundation
10140 Centurion Pkwy, N.
Jacksonville, FL 32256
Website: www.nemours.org

Parkinson's Disease Foundation (PDF)
1359 Bdwy.
Ste. 1509
New York, NY 10018
Toll-Free: 800-4PD-INFO
(800-473-4636)
Website: www.pdf.org
E-mail: info@pdf.org

Postpartum Support International (PSI)
6706 S.W. 54th Ave.
Portland, OR 97219
Toll-Free: 800-944-4PPD
(800-944-4773)
Phone: 503-894-9453
Fax: 503-894-9452
Website: www.postpartum.net
E-mail: support@postpartum.net

Psych Central
55 Pleasant St.
Ste. 207
Newburyport, MA 01950
Website: www.psychcentral.com
E-mail: talkback@psychcentral.
com

Suicide Awareness Voices of Education (SAVE)

7900 Xerxes Ave., S.
Ste. 810
Bloomington, MN 55431
Toll-Free: 800-273-8255
Phone: 952-946-7998
Website: www.save.org

Suicide Prevention Resource Center (SPRC)

43 Foundry Ave.
Waltham, MA 02453-8313
Toll-Free: 800-273-TALK
(800-273-8255)
TTY: 617-964-5448
Website: www.sprc.org

Index

Index

T

talk therapy *see* psychotherapy
TCA *see* tricyclic antidepressant
temporomandibular joint dysfunction (TMJ), fibromyalgia 264
"Teen Depression" (NIMH) 114n
"Teens Who Recover from Hard-to-Treat Depression Are Still at Risk for Relapse" (Omnigraphics) 392n
tetracyclics, major depression 49
thalamus, depicted *13*
therapists
  cancer 282
  depression among teens 116
  depression in elders 348
  types, overview 398–401
thought disorder, schizophrenia 91
thyroid hormones, postpartum depression 163
"Tips for Disaster Responders— Understanding Compassion Fatigue" (SAMHSA) 459n
TMS *see* transcranial magnetic stimulation
tobacco
  mental disorders 218
  mental-health medications 349
tolerance
  alcohol use 225
  defined 554
  disruptive mood dysregulation disorder (DMDD) 74
  persistent depressive disorder (PDD) 55
transcranial magnetic stimulation (TMS), brain stimulation therapies 355
transition
  disaster response and depression 463
  perimenopausal depression 110
  premenstrual syndrome (PMS) 76
  suicide among young adults 512
trauma
  brain injury 269
  compassion fatigue 460
  defined 554
  described 451

trauma, *continued*
  heart disease 293
  major depression 47
  suicide 507
traumatic brain injury (TBI), depression 269
"Traumatic Brain Injury and Depression" (AHRQ) 269n
traumatic grief, posttraumatic stress disorder (PTSD) 508
treatment-resistant depression, overview 390–2
tricyclic antidepressants
  depression in older adults 517
  mental-health medications 339
  Parkinson disease (PD) 307
  persistent depressive disorder (PDD) 55
tricyclics
  antidepressants 384
  anxiety disorders 234
  major depression 49
triggers, overview 421–7
Tylenol, coping with trauma 543
"Types of Therapist" (NCPTSD) 398n

U

"Understanding Suicide" (CDC) 493n
underweight, body image 447
unemployment, overview 211–5
"Unemployment and Depression Among Emerging Adults in 12 States, Behavioral Risk Factor Surveillance System, 2010" (CDC) 211n
U.S. Department of Education (ED)
  contact 558
  publication
    evaluating acceptance and commitment therapy 330n
U.S. Department of Health and Human Services (HHS)
  contact 558
  publications
    handling depression 317n
    health insurance and mental-health services 404n
    HIV and AIDS 297n

597